Z2M!

Z2M! Publishing: P.O. Box 335, Powhatan, VA 23139

ZOE TO THE MAX

ENJOYING YOUR LIFE AS MUCH AS GOD WANTS YOU TO

DR. E. TRACY SPAUR

ZOE TO THE MAX!

©2006 E. Tracy Spaur

Library of Congress Control Number:
2006933782

ISBN-13: 978-0-9788107-0-2
ISBN-10: 0-9788107-0-8

Design: Mickey Moore Design Associates
www.mickeymoore.com

Inside Illustrations: Stephanie Spaur

The Holy Bible: New International Version. 1973, 1978, 1984.
by International Bible Society.
Grand Rapids: Zondervan Publishing House.
Any emphases (bold, underline or parenthetical comments) within
scripture are the author's.

Z2M! Publishing: P.O. Box 335, Powhatan, VA 23139

DEDICATION

This book is dedicated to my mother and father who gave me a strong Christian foundation. I also stand on the shoulders of the many teachers, preachers, and authors who have brought me to the understanding I have today.

Special thanks to my wife Valerie who is not only my biggest fan but corrected my many grammatical errors and supported me in this eighteen month project. I am grateful to my artistic daughter Stephanie for drawing the forty-five illustrations that spice-up the layout of the book. Special thanks to my good friend Michael D. Moore for his exceptionally talented work in the cover design and layout of this book—he is a true man of God and poured in his passion for excellence. Most of all, I praise my Lord and Savior Jesus Christ who taught me to live *Zoe* to the Max and challenged me to write this book.

Contents

Dedication 5

Contents. 6

Introduction: Got Happy? 9

Section 1: *What is Zoe?*

Chapter 1: What is *Zoe*? 18
Chapter 2: The 4-1-1 on *Zoe*. 23
Chapter 3: *Zoe* to the Maximum! 28
Chapter 4: Pictures of *Zoe*—*Zoe* Water 37
Chapter 5: Pictures of *Zoe*—Bread of *Zoe* 45
Chapter 6: Pictures of *Zoe*—*Zoe* is Light 51
Chapter 7: Pictures of *Zoe*—Tree of *Zoe*. 57
Chapter 8: Pictures of *Zoe*—The Crown of *Zoe* 59
Chapter 9: The Book of *Zoe* 61

Section 2: *The Zoe Zone*

Chapter 10: The *Zoe* Zone 64
Chapter 11: Part 1: Enjoying the Presence of God. 66
Chapter 12: Part 2: *Zoe* Word. 95
Chapter 13: Part 3: Rejoice to Re-juice 115
Chapter 14: Part 4: Peace-Ruled Heart 127
Chapter 15: Part 5: Emotionally Healthy 133
Chapter 16: Part 5: The Paths to Emotional Health 153
Chapter 17: Part 6: Inside the Wall of Contentment 197
Chapter 18: Part 7: Holiness 222
Chapter 19: Part 8: Authentic Relationships 230

Contents

Chapter 20: Part 9: Physically Rested 245
Chapter 21: Part 10: Sweet Spot Ministry 259
Chapter 22: Step Into the Zone 270

Section 3: Living in the Zoe Zone

Chapter 23: Living in the Zone 274
Chapter 24: Made Fresh Daily 280
Chapter 25: Coffee 286
Chapter 26: *Zoe* Party 290
Chapter 27: Failure 294
Chapter 28: *Zoe*—Zapping Thoughts 300
Chapter 29: Grace 305
Chapter 30: Worry 313
Chapter 31: The Pace of Life 316
Chapter 32: The Power of Imagination 321
Chapter 33: *Zoe* Strategies 323

Section 4: Staying in the Zoe Zone

Chapter 34: The University of Adversity 332
Chapter 35: "The Perfect Storm" 342
Chapter 36: Entering the Fog Zone 345
Chapter 37: Tsunami of Hope 347

Endnotes 355

Appendix A 365

About the Author 368

Introduction: Got Happy?

re you as happy as you can possibly be right now? Are you really enjoying the life you're living? Right now? As you read this sentence? I can honestly say, "Yes!" Right now, I am enjoying my life every—every day! I am convinced God meant for you and I to really enjoy our life to the maximum extent. I want to show you how you can enjoy your life "to the max!"

As I look around at most of the people I know, I don't see many people fully enjoying their lives—do you? I want to show you how you can significantly increase your level of happiness in the midst of your current life situation. I truly believe God wants to teach you and me how to enjoy our lives in a supernatural way and to an increasingly greater and greater extent. Even if you are already enjoying high levels of happiness, this book will encourage and enhance your enjoyment.

I know all that sounds pretty "over the top." Advertisers constantly bombard us with claims and products that over promise and under deliver (we've all been duped) but the ideas and insights I will share with you are real-life solutions that work for me every day.

The idea for this book came to me after I spoke in May of 2004 at my church, Southside Nazarene Church, in Richmond, Virginia. Our church is larger than most churches so it was quite a scary thought for me to stand before 1,500 people as a lay speaker. We were in the middle of a sermon series that our Pastor Jerome Hancock was preaching entitled "Your Life on DVD." The premise for the series was the way we live our lives each day is becoming a story that is being recorded by God and others. My part of the series was entitled "Play." In other words, how should we live our lives today? The message God gave me over several months of preparation was from John 10:10 where Jesus declares His mission is to bring us a life that can be lived to the fullest extent possible! It was entitled "*Zoe* to the Max!" which I will explain in this book. For several months I was inundated by the overwhelming response to that message. Some told me I should preach the message everywhere! One of my friends, Russ Randall, told me he felt I should develop a seminar based on the concept of "*Zoe* to the Max!" and share it with groups and churches. All this was a little overwhelming for me to take in at the time. I ended up sharing the same message at other churches later that year with a similar positive response. In March of 2005, I was driving down the road listening to a teaching tape of Dr. John Townsend. The subject was about how to accomplish big tasks by breaking them down into little steps each day. He told of a successful author who wrote a huge novel by simply writing for 15 minutes each morning. As I was listening to this, God's Spirit spoke to my spirit, "Why don't you write a book about *Zoe* to the Max!" When that happened, I was suspicious as to whether the prompting was really from God, because it was so "out of no where." Over the following weeks I asked my wife and small-group Bible study to pray with me about this "wild" idea to see if it was really God or not. I became convinced the prompting really WAS from God, because I had a peace in my heart and, instead of being afraid of the possibility, I became excited about it!

This book began with that original "*Zoe* to the Max!" sermon, and over the next three months I carried small notebooks in my pocket so I could write down every thought the Spirit brought to me. Those thoughts filled four notebooks. The scope of the book kept expanding to become a compilation of all the lessons I have learned in life about how to live a victorious, happy life. I am not a professional writer: I don't know how to write a book, but I have a passion to share what I know will positively impact your life. This book will inspire you to move to a new level of enjoyment. Simply put, it will show you how I have learned to really enjoy my life "to the max!"

"Less-than" Lives

I have observed over my 50 years most people have settled for a "less-than-they-could-have" happiness level. They've settled for what they have. They are dependent on events or circumstances to bring them happy feelings. They experience their happiness vicariously through other people on TV or through the movies or a novel. Some "zone out" on the treadmill of their busy schedules. They live for the weekends and vacations. For many, happiness is an occasional event.

Others medicate themselves with alcohol or other chemicals in order to feel a little numb. Their lives are "less-than" lives. Some of you reading this book may be at wit's end and looking for some answers. I am here to say God desires for us to live a happier life.

Where am I coming from?

Let me tell you a little about myself so you will know where I am coming from. I'm not trying to become a famous writer or a millionaire. I believe God wants me to write this book for YOU. I know God is our Creator and that He has a purpose for our lives. All the beauty and complexity of nature, especially that of man, cannot be explained by billions of accidental gene mutations and big explosions. I believe God is the Creator of all. Although I was taught the evolutionary theories in my core scientific training at the Medical College of Virginia, I reject it as man's attempt to interpret scientific evidence apart from God. Evidence is simply factual information. I have no problem studying scientific evidence. In fact, I have always loved science, majoring in biology in my undergraduate studies with a minor in chemistry. The truth is, scientific evidence can be interpreted in various ways depending on whether you believe in God or not. Scientists who support the theory of creation or "intelligent design" look at the same scientific evidence, but conclude the evidence is the thumbprint of God.

There are many books that go into all the debate over the interpretation of the evidence. One of the most recent books I recommend is *The Case for A Creator* by Lee Strobel. There are also great websites like www.CreationResearch.org and www.AnswersInGenesis.org which give plenty of information on the creationist's perspective. The bottom line for me is if you really believe all of this physical "stuff" came from an explosion and the complexity and brilliant function of the human body can be explained by random mutations, then *Zoe to the Max!* is impossible for you to ever experience. Without acknowledging God as Creator, you are left as one of six billion "mutational accidents" spinning purposelessly on this leftover chunk of "explosion debris" we call Earth. If we are "accidents," then we have no designed purpose other than survival, and I have no answers to help you live a happier life other than to challenge you to explore God, because He wants to reconcile with you.

I thank God I have found a purpose more noble than mere survival, and my chances of enjoying life are not dependent on luck! I live everyday in a dynamic, personal relationship with God.

God is my continual source of joy and real enjoyment in life! That may sound crazy to some or seem presumptuous, but it is a daily, moment-by-moment reality in my life. The same is true for millions of other believers living over the past 2,000 years. If you haven't yet experienced this kind of relationship with God, then this is where you should start. Doesn't it make sense that the "creation" (you and me) should look to our "Creator" to learn purpose and optimal function? The enjoyable life that God plans for you BEGINS when you let Him into the "control center" of your life.

Funeral Church Services

I know plenty of people who have "been to church" a lot of times, but the churches they have attended are really not very "alive" with any enthusiasm about God. The services are not much different than people attending a funeral. All churches are not created equal. Some are very formal and filled with ritual and tradition and may have lost the enthusiasm and passion that Christ meant for churches to experience. I'm not advocating any particular denomination as there are many awesome churches and great denominations. In contrast, there are many that are lifeless and cold. They give information without transformation. Other denominations go to the opposite extremes of wild emotionalism or ultra-conservative legalism. If your church experience has been limited to one of these churches, then maybe your church experience has given you the wrong impression about God.

Manageable Religion

I'm not talking about having a religion, but about having a relationship with God. If religion is all you are familiar with—there's LOTS more for you to experience. It's easier to maintain religion than to maintain a vital relationship with God, because intimacy with Christ is all about inner life and motives that are all-encompassing. Religion is segmented. We do "this" and do "that" and schedule it in. The rest of our time is free for us to control. We relegate religion to its role and we do what we wish with the rest. Having a relationship with God is messier: It involves your loving God with your whole life. I'm talking about swimming in His love rather than just showing up for a religion class. God doesn't want to be on our 'To Do' list!

Check the Owner's Manual

Your parents also had much to do with your understanding of God. Think about it. Your parents laid the foundation for your concept of God, or lack of concept. As you grew up, you were exposed to other people and their principles for living. You discovered lots of different ways to live life by watching TV, reading books and going to school. You learned different philosophies and principles on which to build your life. You selected the principles which made the most sense to you based on your observations and experiences. But let me ask you this: How do you know you made the right choices? How do you know you have the best perspective of life and an accurate view of God? It's worth looking into this area.

Let's look to some principles that have stood the test of time throughout the ages. As you look through all of the writings in the history of mankind, one book stands out as unique. It stands head and shoulders above the rest. One book claims to be the Owner's Manual and has the credentials to back it up. That one book has been the "best seller" every year since the printing press was invented. I'm talking about the Holy Bible. If you have not seriously examined this book and what it claims, then you are ignoring what most historians agree is the greatest book in the history of mankind!

The Bible answers all the important questions of life. It tells us the origin of life and how evil came into this world. It tells us how God interacted with man through early history. He gave a promise to Abraham to bless the world through his descendant. Abraham's family became known by his grandson's name, Israel. Over the generations, the children of Israel eventually strayed from a close relationship with God. During that time, God revealed many prophecies about the coming of a Messiah that would deliver man from sin. In 5/6 BC God sent His son, Jesus, as the Messiah to be born and show mankind the way to really live. Many historians agree Jesus was the greatest man who ever lived. He changed the entire course of history. You should not ignore Him or ignore what He said and did.

Jesus showed us the love of God and taught us about a revolutionary way to enjoy life. The religious leaders hated Him because he exposed their hypocrisy and claimed that he committed blasphemy in declaring that he was from God. For this he was condemned and put to death by Roman execution. After his death he was buried in a Roman-guarded tomb to prevent his body from being stolen by his followers. Three days later, God miraculously raised Him from the dead! No other person who has ever claimed to be the Messiah has risen from the dead! More than 500 people witnessed him as alive from the dead over a forty-day period of time.

Having conquered sin and death, Jesus ascended to God with a promise that His Holy Spirit would come and indwell every believer. Ten days later the Holy Spirit came and filled 120 of Jesus's followers with a supernatural power to live a different kind of life. They came out of that experience with a supernatural joy and power that caused 3,000 people to want this same experience that very day! Over the next days and weeks, Jerusalem was "turned upside down" by the power of these changed lives.

This different kind of life was far beyond normal "existing." Jesus taught about a different kind of living that is supernaturally powered. It comes from believing Jesus is the Messiah and His death on the cross paid the penalty for the sins of all who put their faith in Him. Through Jesus we can have a new-birth experience with God that causes a transformation into a new kind of enjoyable, eternal life called *Zoe*.

Zoe is Supernatural

Zoe is a Greek word for a new kind of supernatural life that Jesus came to bring. Jesus came to show us how to receive this supernatural *Zoe* and experience it to the maximum level now and throughout all of eternity. Sounds like good news—that's why it is called "The Gospel."

Jesus has the corner on the market when it comes to the Gospel of eternal *Zoe*! He is its one and only supplier. Jesus said *"I am the way, the truth and the life (Zoe). No man can come to the Father except through Me"* (John 14:6 New International Version, parentheses added). If you don't have a close and personal relationship with God through Jesus, then you have NO POSSIBILITY of experiencing this kind of enjoyable life—this kind of *Zoe*. The Bible says apart from this relationship you are *"... separated from the life (Zoe) of God ..."* (Ephesians 4:18, parentheses added). The good news is that you can change that. You can experience this life—this *Zoe*—right now. It is available to you because of what Jesus did for you

2,000 years ago. You don't have to meet with the pope or call a preacher or a rabbi. God's Spirit is with you right now as you are reading this sentence. He desires that you invite Him into your life. He loves you and even inspired me to write this book so you would be reading this sentence right now. You have the opportunity to open up your spirit and begin this relationship with God.

Answer that Door!

Jesus is knocking at the "door" of your life. The Bibles teaches Christ comes and knocks at the "door" of our heart. He said, *"Here I am! I stand at the door and knock. If anyone hears my voice and opens the door, I will come in …"* (Revelations 3:20). That means He initiates this relationship. He is the one who offers to come in long before we know Him. That's awesome! He knocks. He is trying to get our attention.

Do you hear Him knocking? Knocking is a physical sound that is made on a door to gain the occupant's attention. Jesus is trying to get your attention. There may be some circumstances in your life that indicate Jesus is knocking at your door. I know when I am knocking on a door and no one answers, I knock again a little more firmly. Transfer that idea now to God. How loudly does He have to knock to get your attention?

The voice of God is usually not audible. God is spirit and He speaks to us deep within our spirit. Often our world is so loud and busy we don't hear His voice. Right now He is calling out your name. If you will just take a moment right now and listen, you will hear Him speak your name inside your spirit. The Greek word for "voice" is the word *phone*.[1] That makes me think of how many times people have tried to call me on my cell phone but I didn't hear my phone ring because I had the ringer volume on low or vibrate. Think about it... God has been phoning you, but you have been living so loudly you haven't been able to listen. He is knocking and calling out to you, but possibly you have your phone on silent. Turn your phone on! Stop ignoring the knocking and listen for His call, and you will hear it. The next step is to simply open the door of your life to Him. You can do this through a simple but sincere prayer. A simple "save me God" request from your heart is the essence. It can be a simple prayer that invites God to come into your life and forgive you of your sins through Jesus' death on the cross. Here are some words you can pray if you like, but they must be from your own sincere heart.

"God, I want you in my life. Please forgive me for my sinfulness. I believe Jesus was the Savior sent from You to pay the penalty for all my sins. Come into my life and transform me. I want to have a close relationship with you and experience the *Zoe* you have promised."

Once you pray for this, the supernatural part is up to God. You will begin to feel the changes He makes deep down inside your life. You will be like a little baby that is beginning to grow from the inside out. Your new spiritual life needs to be nurtured and fed. That's where your responsibility comes in. I suggest you start learning from the Bible with the story of Jesus found in the book named John. Next read the book of Philippians and then the remainder of the New Testament. Find a church that will teach you and inspire you to grow in this relationship. Each church has a little different style in its music and teaching and personality. Keep on attending different churches until you find the one that helps you grow spiritually. Get connected to a small-group Bible study at that church so you can ask questions and grow in your faith. Then get involved as a volunteer and help the church reach out to others.

SECTION ONE

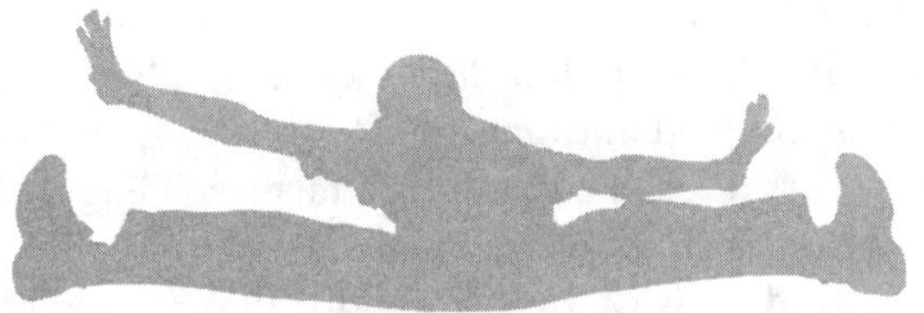

What is Zoe?

What's in Your Backyard?

I heard about a Texas farmer who lived his whole life on a cattle farm. It was one hundred acres of sagebrush out in the middle of nowhere and wasn't good for much other than grazing cattle. He struggled financially from year to year, barely getting by. After his death, a group of oil prospectors found a huge reservoir of crude oil right under his farm. So the struggling farmer was actually a multi-millionaire all along, but didn't know it. His riches were available—but undiscovered and untapped!

I think we are a lot like that Texas farmer. We're living on top of a huge reserve of God's power available to us to really enjoy life in a supernatural kind of way. Even though these resources are right in the backyard of our lives, we either don't know about them, or we haven't yet learned how to drill an oil well. I want to teach you how to drill for that oil! First I want to show you how big that reserve is. Then I want show you how to drill down and tap into it. And then I want to teach you how to pump the oil out and keep it flowing for the rest of your life!

Greek Geek Drills in John 10:10

I found oil in John 10:10 when I studied the original Greek words. Since the New Testament was originally written in the Greek language, it must be translated into English for us to be able to understand it. I often find a lot of rich meaning in studying the original Greek words, because every Greek word does not necessarily have an equivalent English word that conveys all its meaning. Therefore, every translation of a Greek word is an important decision because the translators chose English words that best convey the meaning. Since every word of scripture was breathed out of the heart of God and was selected to deliver a meaning God intended, it is important to understand the complete meaning. *"All Scripture is God-breathed and is useful for teaching, rebuking, correcting and training in right-*

eousness, *so that the man of God may be thoroughly equipped for every good work"* (2 Timothy 3:16-17).

There are several Greek words that I will be referring to in this book. Obviously, the title word "Zoe" shows that. Thankfully you don't have to take a course in Greek to be able to study the language! There are many great language aides which have been developed by Greek language scholars that can help average people like you and me to understand it better. I don't claim to be a language scholar and everything I have learned about Greek has been self-taught. I guess you could say we need to become somewhat of a Greek Geek. The Greek language uses words that are rich in meaning and it often takes two or three English words to express what one Greek word means. Also, the word order and the grammar influence the meaning of the sentence much more in Greek than in English. In addition, there are some Greek verb tenses that have no English counterparts. That's one reason for the many different English translations of the same Bible. The other reason is the complication of trying to understand a book that was written almost 2,000 years ago! When I was a kid, there were only three or four translations of the Bible, and most everyone used the King James Version. It was more simplistic in those days: As they say, "ignorance is bliss." Other versions were looked on with some suspicion that perhaps liberal theologians were trying to "alter the Word of God." I once even read a book which accused all other translations but the King James Version of theological heresy.

Let me explain how different translations of the Bible developed. The original writings of the Bible are called manuscripts. These manuscripts had to be copied multiple times by hand.

It's amazing and really supernatural that all the copies of these ancient manuscripts are in almost complete agreement with one another

It's amazing and really supernatural that all the copies of these ancient manuscripts are in almost complete agreement with one another (with the variations being mostly spelling differences and a few minor word additions or deletions among some of the copies). These copies were eventually translated into English and other languages. Printing was first done on a wide scale after the year 1611 when the King James Version (KJV) was completed. At the time, it was the only translation of the Bible available in English. Four hundred years have passed since then and the meanings of a number of words in the English language have gradually changed. Language is in a constant state of change as words change meaning over time. For example, in my lifetime, the meaning of "bad" has evolved and can now mean good, and "wicked" can now mean even better than "bad." "Grass" and "weed" are now smoked. Words like "eight-track" and "record player" are almost archaic. There are also many new words like "CD," "MP3", "laptop," "rap," "microwave," "Internet," etc. Because languages are continuously changing, the Bible requires new translations so the original meaning is understood in our current language.

Creating new translations of the original Bible is more complex than translating one Greek word into one English word. On the other hand, if you tried to include the full meaning of each word each time it is used, it would make the sentences really long and difficult to read. The Philips Translation of the Bible attempts to do that. If you want to get a broader perspective of what a particular verse means, you can read that same verse in several translations. What I like to do is start with the New International Version and then, if one particular verse interests me, I'll go to my Bible software and study it. It's really not as hard as it sounds. There are many good Bible software programs available now. I use *Logos Bible Software: Libronix Digital Library.* Before that, I used *Strong's Exhaustive Concordance* which assigns each word in the Bible a number. These numbers are called Strong's numbers and make it possible for anyone to look up the meaning and usage of the original language words. Once you find the Strong's number of a particular word, you can turn to the back of Strong's and look up the meaning in the lexicon. Strong's numbers are also used in other resources. With *The Englishman's Concordance* you can find every occurrence of a particular Strong-numbered word in the Bible.

Zoe Defined

Studying the original Greek words is how I discovered the word "Zoe." *Zoe* is the Greek word translated in most modern English versions as "life." However, I found that is inadequate, as you will see. As I studied the meaning of *Zoe*, I saw Strong's Concordance showed three synonyms for *Zoe* which are each translated as "life" in most versions of the New Testament—*zoe, bios and psyche*. But then I asked myself, "Why did God use three different Greek words?" There must be a difference in their meanings or God would have used the same word. So I researched the differences, and I found each word means something different.

Bios is only used 11 times in the New Testament, and it refers to "the course of this life" or "the duration of life." It's more of a philosophical word. Jesus used bios in Luke 8:14 when he was teaching the Parable of the Sower: *"The seed that fell among thorns stands for those who hear, but as they go on their way they are choked by life's (bios) worries, riches and pleasures, and they do not mature"* (parentheses added). *Bios* refers to life as the sequence of events we experience.

Psyche is used 105 times in the New Testament, and it refers to "the breath of life; our natural, physical life existence." Jesus used *psyche* in John 10:11 when He said, *"I am the good shepherd. The good shepherd lays down his life* (psyche) *for the sheep"* (parentheses added). *Psyche* is our physical life. If you are not dead, then you have *psyche*. The meaning of the word *psyche* has evolved over time to mean the human soul, mind or spirit but originally *psyche* meant existing—breathing in oxygen and exhaling carbon dioxide.

Zoe is used the most: 134 times. *Zoe* refers to the kind of life God gives us when we are spiritually transformed. Strong's Lexicon defines *Zoe* as:

"... the state of one who is possessed of vitality or is animate ... of the absolute fullness of life ... life real and genuine, a life active and vigorous, devoted to God, blessed ..." [1]

Zoe is the best life that God can give now and "In the Christian sense of eternal life, i.e., that life of bliss and glory in the kingdom of God which awaits the true disciples of Christ after the resurrection." [2] *Zoe* is living that genuine vital and enjoyable life that is full and meaningful. It is living while you're still living!

Zoe versus *Psyche* & *Bios*

Psyche and *bios* refer to our physical existence during the course of this life. *Zoe* is the divine ability that is granted to believers to really enjoy life! It is to love, appreciate and enjoy the events of our bios and the breath of our *psyche*. Jesus used both words, *psyche* and *Zoe*, in the same sentence to show the contrast in meaning, whereas most translations do not differentiate. *"The man who loves his (psyche) life will lose it, while the man who hates his (psyche) life in this world will keep it for eternal (Zoe) life"* (John 12:25, parentheses added). Jesus teaches if you focus your attention and affection on your mere physical existence in this world, you will miss the opportunity He offers to experience the eternal, enjoyable life.

John contrasts *Zoe* and *bios* in his later epistle. First he used *bios* declaring, *"For everything in the world—the cravings of sinful man, the lust of his eyes and the boasting of [bios] life what he has and does—comes not from the Father but from the world"* (1 John 2:16, parentheses added). Then in 1John 5:11-13, he changes to using *Zoe* when referring to the kind of life Jesus brings us: *"And this is the testimony: God has given us eternal [Zoe] life, and this [Zoe] life is in his Son. He who has the Son has [Zoe] life; he who does not have the Son of God does not have [Zoe] life. I write these things to you who believe in the name of the Son of God so that you may know that you have eternal [Zoe] life"* (parentheses added). *Zoe* is not just existing: It is enjoying life, **really** enjoying life! It is genuinely living the full life that God intended—an active and vigorous life that is blessed by God and lived in God.

How is *Zoe* Used in the New Testament?

Zoe (or any other Greek word) is defined by both lexicon (dictionary) definition, and by how it is used in other places in the New Testament and in other secular literature written during the time of the New Testament. When I studied the way God uses *Zoe*, I uncovered a great deal of meaning. The next chapters show what I learned from those explorations of *Zoe* as it is used in various passages.

Chapter 2: The 4-1-1 on *Zoe*

*Z*oe is the exciting, vital, deep and enjoyable life God experiences all the time. Listen to this: *"For as the Father has (Zoe) life in Himself, so He has granted the Son to have (Zoe) life in Himself"* (John 5:26, parentheses added). The Father has *Zoe* in Himself. He is full of vitality and joy and pure love—it is His very being and nature. If you think that God is some lazy Santa Claus sitting on a throne all day or some grumpy tyrant, you are wrong. God is full of *Zoe*! He enjoys Himself and His creation. He is the author and originator of *Zoe* and because He is love, He wants to share His *Zoe* with us.

I think many of us have developed the wrong impression of God: We have gotten the impression He is stoic ... and serious ... and maybe He even has a frown on His face. I agree with Dallas Willard when he writes, "God is the most joyous being in the universe." What is your image of God? Do you see Him as full of *Zoe* and wanting to share that with you? Or do you see Him as wanting to help you learn how to enjoy your *Zoe* to the Max?

Zoe Is God's Eternal Will for Us

God wants us to share in His character and in His very being. He wants us to enjoy His *Zoe* to the Max! *"<u>For my Father's will</u> is that everyone who looks to the Son and believes in Him shall have eternal (Zoe) life, and I will raise him up at the last day"* (John 6:40, parentheses and emphasis added). God wants you and me to experience *Zoe* now, and for all of eternity. *Zoe* is God's eternal will for you and me! This is awesome!

History is truly His-story. It's actually a five-act play:

Act I: God's eternal plan for you and me was *Zoe* to the Max with Him in the Garden of Eden.

Act II: Enter temptation, and mess up occurs in the Garden of Eden. Man becomes separated from *Zoe*.

Act III: Enter Jesus—God's remedy and rescue plan. The most famous and well-known verse in the Bible is, no doubt, John 3:16, *"For God so loved the world that He gave His one and only Son, that whoever believes in Him shall not perish but have eternal life (Zoe)"* (parentheses added). Jesus brought redemption to all who put their faith in Him, and *Zoe* is restored. *"In Him* (Jesus) *was life (Zoe) ..."* (John 1:4, parentheses added). Jesus brought *Zoe* into the world 2,000 years ago so that we could experience it. That was His stated mission, *"I have come that you may have (Zoe) life and have it to the fullest"* (John 10:10, parentheses added). I want you to take this in: Jesus came ... with a purpose ... He said, *"I have come ... that ... YOU* (yes, you ... the one reading this book!) *... may have Zoe ... ."*

Act IV: Second chance. Jesus offers us an opportunity to be reconciled with God and experience *Zoe* to the Max NOW! Let me ask you a question, are you taking up the offer? Are you experiencing all the *Zoe* that Jesus meant to bring you? Are you experiencing it to the maximum level that is possible for you to experience right now? When I asked myself that question, I had to answer, "No," but I made a promise to myself that I would begin to pursue *Zoe* to the Max for the rest of my life! Will you join me? I want to experience the maximum level of *Zoe* to which Jesus can lead me!

Act V: Eternity. Continuing the experience of *Zoe* directly from The Source of *Zoe* for all of eternity is God's desire! When we are in heaven and fully experiencing *Zoe* to the Max 24/7, I don't want to hear Jesus say to me, "Tracy, you could have had a lot more of this before. Why didn't you believe what I said? Why did you live so far below where you could have?" God's plan is for us to share *Zoe* with Him to the maximum level now and forevermore.

Jesus Is the Way to *Zoe*

Jesus said, *"I am the way and the truth and the (Zoe) life. No one comes to the Father except through me"* (John 14:6, parentheses added). Jesus is THE *Zoe*. It is in a personal relationship with Him we experience *Zoe*, because He is it! Jesus is even called *"The Prince of Zoe"* in Acts 3:15. There is no other way to *Zoe* because HE IS ZOE! *"And this is the testimony: God has given us eternal (Zoe) life, and this (Zoe) life is in His Son. He who has the Son has (Zoe) life; he who does not have the Son of God does not have (Zoe) life"* (1 John 5:11-12, parentheses added). God is the giver of eternal *Zoe*, but it is not dumped out of the sky. It comes to us in the person and presence of Jesus. If we have Jesus, we can have *Zoe*. The only question is, how much *Zoe* do we experience? My goal is for you and me to experience it "to the max!"

I have a sunroom on the back of my house where I enjoy sitting and having a good time with God. One morning I was feeling down and depressed with no feelings of energy or optimism. I felt no sense of God's presence, and I didn't know why. Was I messed up physically, emotionally or spiritually? I went to my journal to try to figure it out. Here's my entry from that morning, "Why am I feeling this way? Then the Holy Spirit broke through with this message ... THIS THING IS REAL, TRACY! Wow. God was just showing me how I would feel without His power in my life. How would my life be without Zoe to the Max? Now I'm just lying here with the biggest smile on my face. I can't stop smiling. Thank you, Daddy." Jesus is the only way to Zoe! It's not a state of mind; it is a state of relationship connection with Jesus.

The Spirit Gives *Zoe*. The Words of Jesus are *Zoe*.

Two important truths about *Zoe* are in one verse, *"The Spirit gives (Zoe) life; the flesh counts for nothing. The words I have spoken to you are spirit and they are (Zoe) life"* (John 6:63, parentheses added). *Zoe* comes as the Spirit of Jesus lives in us. It cannot be generated by the flesh. Man-made philosophies, yoga, etc., may bring a sense of temporary peace, but they cannot bring *Zoe*. The Holy Spirit of God gives *Zoe*. It is supernatural.

The words of Jesus are *Zoe*-giving. His words are like Popeye gobbling down a can of spinach. His words generate *Zoe*! That is why *Zoe* and the scriptures are inseparable. Everyday I seek God for a "*Zoe* word" that I can feast on throughout the day. It strengthens me and invigorates me as I am infused with *Zoe* from God. Today, as I am writing this, I was feasting on the phrase from Acts 3:15: *"Jesus is the Prince of Zoe."* He is the Prince ... a man who is pre-eminent in the sphere of *Zoe*! He knows all about it. He can deliver the *Zoe* I need. As I pondered on that from time to time throughout the day, it gave me new *Zoe*. It helped me enjoy the routine things. Like every field, dentistry has its boring moments. It's amazing to me how the *Zoe* flows when I close my eyes and soak in the words of Jesus and enjoy the moment. His words are life-giving: they *"are Spirit and they are (Zoe) life"* (parentheses added). I'll show you more about this later when I share with you how to experience the *Zoe* Zone.

Zoe Is a Gift—Part of Our Inheritance

Zoe is not earned: It does not take some kind of spiritual achievement. *Zoe* is received, not achieved. It is part of our inheritance in God. If you are God's child, you have access to the inheritance of His *Zoe*. *"And everyone who has left houses or brothers or sisters or father or mother or children or fields for My sake will receive a hundred times as much and will inherit eternal (Zoe) life"* (Matthew 19:29, parentheses added). Zoe is God's inheritance to you and me, *"For the wages of sin is death, but the gift of God is eternal (Zoe) life in Christ Jesus our Lord"* (Romans 6:23, parentheses added).

The Essence of *Zoe* Is Jesus

When you condense all the scriptures about *Zoe* down to the essence of what it is, *Zoe* comes from the presence of Jesus being fully manifested and experienced in our lives because *Zoe* is Jesus. Notice *Zoe* in this passage, *"That which was from the beginning, which we have heard, which we have seen with our eyes, which we have looked at and our hands have touched—this we proclaim concerning the Word of (Zoe) life. The (Zoe) life appeared; we have seen it and testify to it, and we proclaim to you the eternal (Zoe) life, which was with the Father and has appeared to us"* (1 John 1:1-2, parentheses added). The apostle John testifies that *Zoe* *"...appeared; we have seen it ... ."* Jesus IS *Zoe*. He is the source and manifestation and essence of the very *Zoe* of God.

Like John, I want to *"testify to Zoe and proclaim to you,"* that the enjoyable, vital and exciting life that God has sent us in Jesus is available for you and me to experience ... now! The Spirit of Jesus wants to show you and me how to experience that maximum level of *Zoe* that is ours as heirs of God!

Zoe is Available Now!

Zoe begins NOW. You don't have to wait for heaven. God wants you and me to enjoy our life with Him now and continue the rest of our lives and for all of eternity! *" ... Godliness has value for all things, holding promise for both the present (Zoe) life and the (Zoe) life to come"* (1 Timothy 4:8, parentheses added). *Zoe* is promised to us BOTH now AND in the life to come.

That is a sampling of the 4-1-1 on *Zoe*, but a complete listing of every *Zoe*-containing scripture is in Appendix A for your further study. Now I want to go back to the passage in John 10:10 I referred to in the first chapter and drill some more "oil" for you.

Chapter 3: *Zoe* to the Maximum!

Zoe is God's awesome plan for us. But it's more than that—He has promised us *Zoe* to the MAXIMUM! Jesus said He came that you and I *"might have Zoe* (life) *and have it to the fullest"* (John 10:10, parentheses added).

What does God mean when He says "to the fullest"? The Greek word for the phrase "to the fullest" is *perissos* [per·is·sos]: 1. exceeding some number or measure or rank or need; 1a. over and above, more than is necessary, superadded; 1a1. exceeding abundantly, supremely; 1a2. something further, more, much more than all, more plainly; 1b. superior, extraordinary, surpassing, uncommon; 1b1. pre-eminence, superiority, advantage, more eminent, more remarkable, more excellent.[1]

You could say Jesus wanted us to have *Zoe* that is "over and above, exceeding abundantly, and much more." I simply say, *Zoe* to the Max! So when I say "*Zoe* to the Max!" I am quoting Jesus' desire and purpose for us from John 10:10: *"I have come that you may have Zoe ...."* That's a purpose statement, and His purpose is for us to experience *Zoe* to the maximum. That is so awesome to consider. My God and Savior desires for me—purposes for me—to experience a vital, dynamic and enjoyable life to the maximum level! What an awesome God!

"Now wait a minute!"

I know this is radical stuff I'm teaching here, and I know some of you may be thinking I have "my head in the clouds." So I want to pause here for a moment to address two concerns some may have.

<u>1. "Isn't happiness worldly?"</u> I have heard it preached, and I was also caught up in the erroneous concept God doesn't promise us happiness, but He promises us joy. I no longer make this distinction, because I have found it is not biblically supported. *Zoe* to the Max includes ALL the positive emotions of happiness, joy, blessings,

rejoicing and cheerfulness. I think the proper distinction is happiness is a feeling usually based on external circumstances, which can be felt by believers and non-believers alike. Joy is different in that it can only be experienced by believers because joy is a fruit of the Spirit of God living in us (Galatians 5:22). In that way, joy is much deeper than happiness because it does not depend on circumstances. But having joy does not EXCLUDE feeling happiness. Both were created by God to be enjoyed by His children! I can be happy, AND I can be joyful. Joy is an inner sense of cheerfulness that is generated from our relationship with the Spirit of God.

Let's look at all the Greek words that imply happiness.

The Greek word for joy is *chara* [khar·ah] (used 59 times): "joy, gladness." The root is *chairo* [khah·ee·ro] (used 74 times): 1. to rejoice, be glad; 2. to rejoice exceedingly; 3. to be well, thrive.[2] When we experience all that, happiness is not very far away!

The Greek word for blessed is *makarios* [mak·ar·ee·os] (used 50 times): "blessed, happy."[3] Several of the translations simply use the word "happy" instead of "blessed." The Greek word for rejoice is *agalliao* [ag·al·lee·ah·o] (used 11 times): "to exult, rejoice exceedingly, be exceeding glad."[4]

All these words sound pretty happy to me! You see, there is no biblical reason to say believers are not to be the happiest people on planet Earth! It is God's plan and possibility for us. We just need to learn how to live the way God wants us to live so we can tap into all these positive emotions.

2. "How can we experience happiness when there is suffering, pain and evil?"

Suffering in this life is a fact. I know there are bad times and Satan is the enemy of our souls. There is evil in this world as well as poverty and disease. Jesus promised us in this world, we would have times of trouble. All of this is true, and many authors have written about the grace God gives to endure the bad things in life with joy in our hearts and praise on our lips.

I know there are times when we will not be happy. I'm a dentist. I know about unhappiness! There are times when our circumstances are bad and we can experience pain, suffering, sickness, death or persecution. During the worst of times, when we can't feel happy or glad, we can still have the deep sense of joy and a peace that passes all understanding. No one enjoys pain. But even during those painful times, Christ's promise of John 10:10 is not suspended. He can still give us *Zoe* DURING THAT TIME. We are to live in eternal *Zoe* beginning now, and continuing on through whatever we face in life, then throughout all eternity! Paul said it this way, *"But even if I am being poured out like a drink offering on the sacrifice and service coming from your faith, I am glad and rejoice with all of you. So you too should be glad and rejoice with me"* (Philippians 2:17-18).

Some people think we should go around crying bitter tears with a long face because we live in a fallen world of suffering. That kind of world was exactly the one that Jesus entered 2,000 years ago in Bethlehem! Into that dark time, the excited angel announced to the shepherds, *"Do not be afraid. I bring you good news of great joy that will be for all the people. Today in the town of David a Savior has been born to you; He is Christ the Lord"* (Luke 2:10-11). It was good news of great joy! Christ came to bring "Zoe to the Max!"

When we are seeking *Zoe* to the Max we learn to *"Do everything without complaining or arguing, so that you may become blameless and pure, children of God without fault in a crooked and depraved generation, in which you shine like stars in the universe as you hold out the word of (Zoe) life"* (Philippians 2:14-16, parentheses added). We are not to be filled with the negativity of complaining and arguing; instead we are to be full of *Zoe* to the Max! We are to be holding out *"the word of Zoe"* to this *"crooked"* world—the word that shows God's plan for *Zoe*. This causes us to shine like stars because of the *Zoe* that we are experiencing!

What I'm saying is the Bible is full of positive, happy emotions that were all created by God FOR US TO ENJOY. I will not concede any of that enjoyment

> **Believers have access to both joy AND happiness.**

as property of Satan or "worldly sensuality." I refuse the notion that happiness is only found "out there" in the bars and nightclubs and with sinful activities and worldly recreation. Believers have access to both joy AND happiness. Lost people can only experience periods of happiness based on lust or sensuality or positive circumstances. We are not restricted like that! The Bible says, *"When times are good, be happy; but when times are bad, consider: God has made the one as well as the other"* (Ecclesiastes 7:14). *"But may the righteous be glad and rejoice before God; may they be happy and joyful. Sing to God, sing praise to his name, extol him who rides on the clouds—his name is the Lord—and rejoice before him"* (Psalm 68:3-4). *"We are filled with an inexpressible and glorious joy"* (1 Peter 1:8).

We experience happiness because we reap the blessings of a life lived to please God and serve others. The Bible teaches us how to live a happier life because we can have better relationships and be better parents and have better marriages and be better employers and employees. We sow the "good" seeds and reap the "good" benefits. The Word says, *"The one who sows to please his sinful nature, from that nature will reap destruction; the one who sows to please the Spirit, from the Spirit will reap eternal (Zoe) life"* (Galatians 6:8, parentheses added). This eternal *Zoe* includes both the happiness and joyfulness that come from living life God's way!

Worldly happiness versus Godly happiness

Happiness can come from either an inside source or an outside source. People who don't have *Zoe* must look to external sources to feel happiness. They are dependent on something outside themselves to come to them and make them feel happy. They wait for the weekend or a holiday or a vacation. They look to recreation or music to lift them up. They are dependent on the weather to make them feel good or bad. I'll just call this external-only happiness—worldly happiness.

Worldly happiness only comes from external stimulation. Godly happiness, on the other hand, is an "inside job." The *Zoe* God gives is an internal source of happiness that is not dependent on outside circumstances. Jesus said *Zoe* comes from within us. John 7:37-39: *"Whoever believes in me, as the Scripture has said, streams of (Zoe) living water will flow from within him"* (parentheses added). God puts the *Zoe* source within us so it is not dependent on external circumstances. *Zoe* is available right now, regardless of your external circumstances.

Worldly happiness is a response to good or bad things. If things are bad, people are unhappy. If things are good, they are happy. When an unbeliever asks, "Why are you happy?" they are really curious about your external source of happiness. They want to know what external circumstance is going well for you right now to make you feel happy. Often what they are seeing is the internal *Zoe*. There may be no external circumstance that is making us happy. Rather, it is our internal response to God.

Christ-followers also don't have to be sad in response to the external bad things—we can set the tone of happiness inwardly. We choose to enjoy all the good as much as possible, and we also can choose to NOT allow the bad to take away our happiness. It is a control issue. We are internally controlled, not externally.

When I was a teenager, I remember a man was visiting my grandfather from Washington, DC. I distinctly remember him opening the trunk to his car and as he was rearranging something, he just blurted out "Praise the Lord!" He was just praising God for life! He was optimistic and rejoicing in the Lord for no particular reason, and that was the first time I had ever seen *Zoe* to the Max like that. I had never seen anyone so full of the Spirit they were just praising God for no particular reason! I thought to myself, "I want to be like that! I want to be that happy and that joyful and that positive!"

There's *Zoe* "in them-thar' hills."

I have found most Christians live under the notion *Zoe* is received from positive external sources like church services, revivals, sermons, concerts, etc. When they want to be inspired, they think of going to church or to a Christian concert. God uses these means as one way to provide *Zoe* experiences for us, but when we only look to those external means to experience *Zoe*, we are only going to experience limited amounts of *Zoe*. They experience "*Zoe* to the Minimum" not "*Zoe* to the Maximum." To experience *Zoe* to the Maximum we need to learn how to tap into it. We must learn to drill wells into the internal source of *Zoe* made possible by the indwelling Holy Spirit. The Holy Spirit is our teacher. He wants to teach us how to drill into and pump *Zoe* out of our internal source and experience it at any time, at any place to the maximum level.

> Look to external sources = *Zoe* to the Mini
> Look to internal sources = *Zoe* to the Max!

God has placed THE source of *Zoe* within us. He said, *"I will come to you"* and *"The Comforter is with you and will be IN you."* *"In you"* is internal, right? Revelation 3:20 says Jesus wants to *"come in and dine with him and he with me."* I'll talk about this verse in depth later, but suffice it to say Jesus wants to enter our internal "dining room" where we sit down together and have an evening meal. It is this refreshing internal connection that renews us and fills us with all joy and peace and hope through the power of the Holy Spirit. The result is we emerge from our dining room experience with an internal happiness.

Now, where were we?

When Jesus says He came to bring us *"Zoe* to the Max!" He infers *Zoe* has degrees of vitality and enjoyment. The desire of Jesus is we experience increasing degrees of *Zoe* as we reach to the maximum level. So what I am asking myself is this:

"How maximum is maximum?"

Is that "maximum" as measured by God, or by me? What is the maximum level of *Zoe* that can be experienced by man? I think God has a level of *Zoe* for you and me to experience that is far beyond anything that we could possibly reach! I think of Ephesians 3:20: *"Now to him who is able to do* __immeasurably more__ (there is the Greek word for "maximum" *perissos* [per·is·so]) *than all* __we ask or imagine__*, according to his power that is at work within us"* (parentheses and emphasis added).

What makes you and me think we are living at the highest level of *Zoe* that is possible? Why do we stop seeking to raise the level of our experience? Do we think we have "rung the bell" and reached the maximum level of *Zoe* to which Jesus can lead us? I THINK NOT! I am currently on a journey to explore just how maximum "maximum" is! I want to pursue *Zoe* to the maximum, maximum, maximum! How about you?!!!

Are you experiencing the absolute maximum level of *Zoe* God wants you to experience? That's why He had me write this book—to challenge you and show you how to maximize the *Zoe* that Jesus came to give you. I am constantly realizing how short I fall of experiencing the maximum enjoyment of life God means for me to enjoy. I believe you and I can live with more hope and more joy and more peace than we are having now. *Zoe* to the Max is available to us, but we need to learn how to tap into it. Or should I say how to tap into "Him"?

Claim Your Promise!

Zoe is promised to us in Christ, through the Holy Spirit: *"Paul, an apostle of Christ Jesus by the will of God, according to the promise of Zoe (life) that is in Christ Jesus"* (2 Timothy 1:1, parentheses added). We are not to ask God for more *Zoe* as though it were some vitamin: We are to ask God for more of Jesus, and to experience Him more results in experiencing *Zoe* more! *Zoe* is part of our inheritance we can experience in Christ. *"So that, having been justified by his grace, we might become heirs having the hope of eternal Zoe (life)"* (Titus 3:7, parentheses added).

Feeling *Zoe* to the Max is a result of experiencing God in ever-increasing degrees and living His principles in a way He can bless us and we can enjoy those blessings.

Let me ask you an important question:

**If there were no heaven or no eternity,
would you want to live in Christ?**

If there were no heaven or hell or afterlife, would you still be a Christ-follower? Many folks were "scared" into salvation out of fear of missing heaven and many of them continue to serve God by this fear. Others view this life as a time to endure in preparation for heaven. Is that all this life is about? I think not! God has *Zoe* to the Max for us to experience NOW and forever. And that alone is worth everything! Woo who!

I can answer the question above without a moment's hesitation, "Yes! A thousand times, yes!" I would still be a Christ-follower even if there were no eternity. I would still be a Christ-follower even if there were no heaven. Heaven is an awesome benefit that awaits me, but I would still live in Christ because living in *Zoe* to the Max is the most awesome way to live! Jesus is my constant friend and companion. Living with Him by my side is the happiest way to live! It helps me in every way. I swim in love and float on peace and walk on top of my problems! I have great relationships and a great church family and a meaningful calling, and I'm happy with myself every day as I walk with God moment by moment—I am living *Zoe* to the Max! Woo who!

Heaven is my eternal "icing on the cake" and I'm looking forward to it. But I'm not living for "pie in the sky, by and by." I'm eating my *Zoe* pie now! I'll get an even bigger piece in heaven! So if you are "hanging on by a thread" until you make it to heaven you are missing out on the "sweet now and now."

Move from Momentary *Zoe* to Sustained *Zoe*

Most Christians are happy with their faith. They wouldn't want to give it up. They would love to see others transformed by the power of God, but I don't see many who are really enjoying their lives as much as they could. Not many are living in the overflowing joy of that relationship. They break into joy a couple of times a week, mostly at church singing as they sense a breakthrough of worship, or maybe during a private worship time. What I'm saying to you is more *Zoe* is available to you everyday. Most of us know times of momentary *Zoe* when we "get blessed" or times of revival. I believe God wants you and me to experience high levels of *Zoe* every day. He wants to teach you how to experience maximum amounts of *Zoe*, of maximum duration and quality. Could it be God has a "*Zoe* Zone" that is possible for you to live in, but you have settled for something less? I have discovered *Zoe* to the maximum level is there for me to experience every day IF I CHOOSE TO PURSUE IT!

> *I have discovered Zoe to the maximum level is there for me to experience every day IF I CHOOSE TO PURSUE IT!*

My friend Nancy called recently to ask me a question (which I will not embarrass her by telling!). After we had talked for a few minutes, she asked me if I was enjoying my Memorial Day holiday, and I said, "Yes I am. I was just sitting here enjoying myself thoroughly and writing my book—did I tell you I was writing a book?" She said excitedly, "NO! You're kidding me! What's it about?" I answered, "It's about that *Zoe* to the Max sermon I preached last year." Nancy shouted, "That's great. I was just telling my sister about that the other day and how I remembered your message about *Zoe* last year at church. I am so excited you are doing it because people need to hear that. They are so caught up on the treadmill of life they don't realize God wants us to enjoy life more."

I want every Christian to get off the "treadmill of the average" and learn how to experience "*Zoe* to the Max!" My challenge to you is to take advantage of the will of God so you will experience *Zoe* to the maximum level possible. I have discovered there is a whole lot more *Zoe* available to me than I had ever imagined! NO ONE HAD EVER MODELED LIVING ZOE TO THE MAX FOR ME! NO ONE HAD EVER TOLD ME THIS IS POSSIBLE! I'm here to tell you IT IS! The old hymn says, "A higher plain than I have found, Lord, plant my feet on higher ground." Enjoy life more! Take bigger bites of *Zoe*!

Zoe to the Max!
Experiencing joy to the max!
Experiencing peace to the max!
Experiencing love to the max!
Experiencing patience to the max!
Experiencing God to the max!

This is our birthright as children of the Father of *Zoe*! It is an open door that stands before you and me. The Holy Spirit is there to teach you everyday. He is there to guide you as you explore the vast territory of *Zoe* Land. Will you join me?

Chapter 4: Pictures of *Zoe*—*Zoe* Water

When Jesus was describing this *Zoe* kind of life, He used various analogies to illustrate what *Zoe* looks like. As I studied *Zoe*, I found Jesus used the most basic elements, like water, bread, light and trees, to teach us what *Zoe* is. I'd like for us to look at each one of these elements beginning with water. Water is an essential element for our lives. Without water we would die: Our bodies are made up mostly of water. It is no accident that Jesus described *Zoe* as water. He was teaching us two things:

1. We need Zoe
2. We thirst for Zoe.

Without *Zoe* we cannot experience really living! We have an innate thirst for *Zoe* just like we thirst for water, and only *Zoe* can satisfy that thirst.

I just got off the phone with Sherry. She is a new Christian and is learning how to walk with Christ out of her old life and into her new life in Christ. She's a delightful young, single mom who is learning the new joys of drinking this *Zoe* water. *Zoe* was what she had been thirsting for all her life and didn't realize it. She tried other things, but they had not quenched that inner thirst to really live. Only *Zoe* water has quenched that thirst, and it is so refreshing to hear her rejoicing in her newfound *Zoe*.

Jesus called it *Zoe* water in a story recorded in John 4:4-14. He begins talking to a lady at a well about *Zoe* water in John 4:10. Notice how he talks about thirst and water and *Zoe*: *"Jesus answered her, 'If you knew the gift of God and who it is that asks you for a drink, you would have asked Him and He would have given you living (Zao–the root word for Zoe) water'"*(parentheses added). He calls *Zoe* water a gift from God that can be requested. Here again we see our God is a giving God. He wants to give us *Zoe* water if we will ask Him.

Thirsty—But Not for Long

The woman doesn't "get it." Neither do we. She started talking about Jacob's well. In John 4:13, Jesus answered, *"Everyone who drinks this water* (from Jacob's well) *will be thirsty again, but whoever drinks the water I give him will never thirst."* The *Zoe* water Jesus is offering here is a thirst-quenching life that causes us to "never thirst." Does that mean we never want more *Zoe?* No, it means when we get thirsty for really living, we have immediate access to a fresh drink of *Zoe* water so we never need to live thirsty. We will always have *Zoe* water available to us to drink any time we want.

Think about our need for physical water. We get thirsty on a regular basis throughout the day, right? I think Jesus was also teaching us we need His *Zoe* water on a regular basis throughout the day. I need *Zoe* every few hours to keep my spiritual enthusiasm to an optimum. I thirst and immediately drink of God's *Zoe* water!

An Implanted Spring of *Zoe* Water

The remainder of verse 14 is really an eye-opener. Listen from where the *Zoe* water will come: *"Indeed, the water I give him will become in him a spring of water welling up to eternal (Zoe) life"* (John 4:14, parentheses added). *Zoe* water is a source of ongoing satisfaction because Jesus implants within us AN INTERNAL SPRING of *Zoe!* Jesus uses the Greek word *pege* which means "a spring, or a well that is fed by a natural source of water"[1] In other words, *Zoe* water comes from an internal spring of *Zoe*. A *pege* is a natural spring, that is, a continual source that comes from the depths of the earth. Jesus was saying that the *Zoe* He gives will come up out of us like a spring, "welling up." The Greek word for "welling up" is *hallomai*, which means "to leap up, jump up, bubble up or to spring up, gush up."[2]

I'm loving this picture! Can you see it? The *Zoe* water that can satisfy our continuous thirst is coming from an internal source—a spring—that is continuously bubbling up with more and more *Zoe*. That *Zoe* is "leaping up, jumping up, bubbling up and gushing up"! This means it's more than you can drink. It's so much *Zoe* you have extra gushing out of you. We are like an open fire hydrant, or a geyser walking around gushing *Zoe* all over! Why? Because we have an internal *Zoe* spring that is jumping out—full of life! We are "really living," and it splashes out on everyone around us!

I want to learn how to tap into God's *Zoe* so that not only is my thirst satisfied with *Zoe* to the Max, but it is overflowing onto others throughout the day with that exciting, vital, enthusiasm for life! What's jumping out of you onto others? Do you have a reputation for being a *Zoe* geyser? Or is your *Zoe* spring stopped up? Look back at what Jesus said again: *"Indeed, the water I give him WILL BECOME in him A SPRING of water WELLING UP to eternal (Zoe) life."* (John 4:14, parentheses and emphasis added). Remember Jesus is talking about you and me. His words mean what they say. Is your spring gushing out *Zoe* like that? Could it be your spring is clogged up so only a squirt or dribble is coming out? Stop and ask God right now—*right now*—to unclog your *Zoe* spring and teach you how to tap into Him so that your *Zoe* spring starts gushing!

Say this prayer: "Jesus, I want you to unclog my *Zoe* spring. I know your Word is true, so make this spring of *Zoe* water leap up out of me. Unclog me, Lord! Show me what stops up my *Zoe* spring and help me remove whatever it is. I want to overflow with *Zoe* to the Max and gush out on others. Teach me how to tap into you better so I can be what you said I could, and should, be."

Heavenly Springs

This idea of a spring (*pege*) of *Zoe* is used two other times in the New Testament: Revelation 7 and Revelation 21. It's so important to see how all this is linked together. First, look at Revelation 7:17: *"For the Lamb at the center of the throne will be their shepherd; He will lead them to <u>**springs of living (Zoe) water**</u>. And God will wipe away every tear from their eyes"* (parentheses and emphasis added).

Wow! Can you envision that? The spring of *Zoe* water God implants within us at our new birth apparently originates in heaven. The Great Shepherd will one day guide us to this original source. It's the same Greek phrase that Jesus used in John 4:14 when He said, *"pege of Zoe water."* We have that available to us now! Praise God! You've heard about people looking for the mythical "fountain of youth," but we have found the real "fountain of *Zoe*"! And also notice that it says "their shepherd" will lead them to the springs. This again shows how Jesus WANTS US to experience *Zoe* to the Max! What a Shepherd! What a Savior!

There is a third passage containing the phrase "spring of *Zoe* water" is Revelation 21:6. Here we see again the concept of thirsty people and *Zoe* springs: *"To him who is thirsty, I will give to drink …"* (Revelation 21:6a). The thirst for *Zoe* is the longing for an enjoyable life, an exciting life, and a meaningful life. So many TV commercials play to this longing. They appeal to the longing of so many for "the life you've always wanted to live." God knows we all want that, and God wants to satisfy that thirst. We need *Zoe*. We are needy people, and He is a giving God! So He offers to give us a drink of *Zoe* water from the spring which flows, a never-ending source of satisfaction! So what will that cost me? It must be really expensive, right? Come on, what's the bottom line??

"…To him who is thirsty I will give to drink…WITHOUT COST from the spring of the water of life (Zoe)" (Revelation 21:6b, emphasis added).

Without cost? Come on, what's the catch? You would think it is very expensive, and it was! It was a great cost—to Jesus, because it cost Him His (*psyche*) life, but He offers it to us "without cost." The costly offered, without cost.

What It Costs Me

To hear some people talk, you would think it cost them greatly to follow Christ. They make it sound like it was SO much. So much maybe it was almost an even trade? I don't think so! I give my rather inconsequential life to Him, and He gives me *Zoe* to the Max now and forever in heaven!! That's not an even trade! That's called the best deal that you or I could ever make!

This caused me to stop and think about what I give up to follow Christ. I kept on writing and writing and writing. The following is the "rant" I went on, like the rant of a Southern gospel preacher with the intermittent "amens" after each sentence.

What I Give Up to Follow Christ

I give up my relentless pursuit for happiness and meaning in life for *Zoe* to the Max!

I give up my weariness to receive His rest.

I give up my guilt to live free and forgiven.

I surrender my self-centered attitude to be transformed into a source of life-giving service.

I give up being "stuck in the muck" of revenge and bitterness in order to swim in love for all eternity.

I leave parties that end up destroying me to join the party that ends up blessing me now and forever.

I give up the uncertainty of making the wrong decisions to receive the certainty that God is guiding my life in the best way possible.

So can somebody please tell me what this is costing me?

I give up the worries of not knowing what is going to happen to receive the peace of knowing my Father is going to make it happen.

I give up the revenge that eats at my soul.

I give up the hate that grows like a cancer.

I give up the fear of the future, and I give up the guilt of the past.

I give up my need to achieve and prove I have value to receive the honor of being a child of God.

I give up a life of eternal isolation to live in an eternal community in the presence of pure Love.

I give up the rat race of trying to impress others in exchange for true appreciation from God and others.

I give up the temporary thrill of "being the best" in exchange for the continuing eternal thrill of being honored and loved BY THE VERY BEST in the universe, no matter how I perform!

So can somebody please tell me what this is costing me?

I give up my futile attempt at being "the god of my universe," and I recognize ahead of time who is truly the God of the universe.

I give up my need to get the approval of others in exchange for the approval of God.

I give up death for life.

I give up hell for heaven.

I give up hate for love.

Can someone please tell me what this is costing me?

I give up merely existing in exchange for really living!

I give up cheap thrills followed by guilt for the joy that lasts forever, followed by goodness and mercy.

I give up shaking my fist at God in exchange for letting God shake my hand.

I give up dulled senses for a resurrected awareness of the glory of God in everything.

I give up "the school of hard knocks" for the personal mentoring of the Holy Spirit.

I give up guessing what to do in exchange for the wisdom of God.

Can someone please tell me what this is costing me?

I give up my "everything" in exchange for His everything.
I give up what I cannot keep to get what I cannot lose!
What a deal!
I give up!
What an offer!
I give up!
What a "trade"!
I give up!

I give up nothing! God is offering me **the free gift** of an internally installed spring of *Zoe* that gushes up, jumps up and bubbles up *Zoe* forever! It's a free gift—free to us—but paid for by Christ Jesus our Lord and Savior. We couldn't earn it if we had to.

To top it all off, in Revelation 22 we see God calling out to us! *"Whoever is thirsty, let him come; and whoever wishes, let him take the free gift of the water of (Zoe) life"* (Revelation 22:17, parentheses added). Free *Zoe* water! Come and get it!

Rivers of *Zoe* Water

I think of the TV commercials that say "But wait! That's not all!" then they go on to tell you about another benefit. This whole concept of *Zoe* water and internal springs of *Zoe* water and the heavenly springs of *Zoe* water blow my mind—but that's not all! There is also a RIVER of *Zoe* water! We are talking about an increased volume of *Zoe* water. A river is a source that is of much greater volume than a spring. The Greek word for river is *potamos* [pot·am·os], which can also be translated as "torrent" or "flood."[3] It's the normal word for a river, like the River Jordan, but it is also used in Matthew 7:27 when Jesus taught the parable of the man who built his house on the sand: *"The rain came down, the streams rose, and the winds blew and beat against that house, and it fell with a great crash."* The word translated as "streams" is the same word *potamos*. It means so much rain came, the rivers overflowed and engulfed the house! That's a lot of water.

The River of *Zoe* is the Central Feature of Heaven

The implication is that *potamos* is a huge volume of water, so when you read the following passage in Revelation 22, I want you to keep that in mind: *"Then the angel showed me the <u>river (potamos) of the water of (Zoe) life</u>, as clear as crystal, flowing from the throne of God and of the Lamb"* (Revelation 22:1, parentheses and emphasis added).

The river (*potamos*) of *Zoe* water is "as clear as crystal." You would expect that, wouldn't you? God's *Zoe* is clear and pure. I suppose you could theologize about that more, but I'll let you contemplate on that. What I want to theologize about is the second part of the verse. It shows us THE source of the river of *Zoe*. Get this: The river flows FROM the throne of God and from the Lamb! The throne of God is the original source of *Zoe* water! **God is the ultimate and original source of Zoe!** *Zoe* literally FLOWS in huge volume from His throne! So when you and I are seeking *Zoe* to the Max we are not getting sidetracked from the central purpose of God—we are seeking the throne of God. And what's gushing out of the throne of God is so much *Zoe*, that it is a river of *Zoe*!

Zoe flows FROM the throne, *"DOWN THE MIDDLE OF the great street of the city."* *Zoe* to the Max is the central feature of heaven. God is full of *Zoe*, and it flows out of His throne and then it runs "right smack dab" down the middle of the main street of New Jerusalem!

The reason I am focusing on *Zoe* so much is because it was the mission of Jesus (John 10:10) and it is at the center of heaven originating from the throne of God!!! It could be a river of love or a river of grace or a river of holiness or a river of power, but it isn't any of those things. It is a river of *Zoe*! SEEKING ZOE IS SEEKING WHAT

GOD IS ALL ABOUT! *Zoe* is not a "side-show." It is at the very center of the activity of heaven.

Let's Put This All Together

Where does all the *Zoe* come from? It starts from the throne of God, located in the Holy City of New Jerusalem. Then it flows as a river from the Great Throne, down through the middle of the great street of that great city. I believe from there it feeds the heavenly springs of Revelation 7:7 which then feed down to every believer's internal spring of *Zoe* and from there it gushes out to the world! So when we seek to experience *Zoe* to the Max we are experiencing the central feature of heaven and showing a thirsty world how satisfying God is. Our soul and life should never be thirsty, because we are always satisfied by the *Zoe* that comes from the throne of God!

Chapter 5: Pictures of *Zoe*—Bread of *Zoe*

Jesus also described *Zoe* as bread. Bread and water, then, are the two essential elements for survival: something to eat and something to drink. Today we think of bread as only the carbohydrate portion of the food pyramid, but in biblical times the word "bread" had a broader meaning synonymous with "food." Bread is symbolic of our need for food to survive and thrive.

We not only eat food to survive, but we also ENJOY eating our food as one of the great pleasures in life. So when Jesus compared *Zoe* with bread, He was stating *Zoe* both sustains our spiritual lives and gives us pleasure. We are satisfied and sustained by *Zoe* bread and *Zoe* water. *Zoe* is really at the essence of our spiritual lives.

Jesus brought up the subject in response to the crowds asking for a miraculous sign like Moses giving manna from heaven. Jesus corrected them, explaining in John 6:32-35: "*'I tell you the truth, it is not Moses who has given you the bread from heaven, but it is my Father who gives you the true bread from heaven. For the bread of God is He who comes down from heaven and gives (Zoe) life to the world.' 'Sir,' they said, 'from now on give us this bread.' Then Jesus declared, 'I am the bread of (Zoe) life. He who comes to me will never go hungry, and he who believes in me will never be thirsty'*" (parentheses added).

Never go hungry and never be thirsty! That means *Zoe* is the great satisfier. We hunger for *Zoe* bread, and we thirst for *Zoe* water on a daily basis.

Manna and *Zoe* Bread

Jesus further teaches He is the true bread from heaven—the *Zoe* bread. John 6:47-51: "*I tell you the truth, he who believes has everlasting (Zoe) life. I am the bread of (Zoe) life. Your forefathers ate the manna in the desert, yet they died. But here is the bread that comes down from heaven, which a man may eat and not die. I am the (Zoe) living bread that came down from heaven. If anyone eats of this bread, he will (Zoe) live forever. This bread is my flesh, which I will give for the (Zoe) life of the world"* (parentheses added).

Jesus was comparing His *Zoe* bread to the manna the Jews were given in the desert. Let's see what that meant:

__1. Zoe sustains our spiritual life.__ Just like manna was needed to sustain life in the desert, so *Zoe* bread is needed to sustain spiritual life in the desert of this world.

__2. Zoe is needed daily.__ Manna was needed every day. Our spiritual lives have the same need. We need *Zoe* bread everyday. That's why Jesus taught us to pray: *"Give us this day our daily bread"* (Matthew 6:11). The Greek word for daily bread is the same word that Jesus used when He said, *"I am the bread of Zoe."* I have always thought this "daily bread" prayer was only directed to our physical and financial needs, but it just occurred to me that if Jesus said He was *"The Bread of Zoe,"* it would include our daily need for spiritual "bread" as well. We must feed ourselves daily from God's Word and connect with the presence of the Spirit of Jesus. I'll talk about this in depth later, but we have a daily need for *Zoe* bread to stay healthy.

When I was a kid, my Grandpa Amick and my dad were newspapermen. They had paper routes and later supervised paper route delivery people so I became very familiar with the newspaper business. The subscription options were: daily, daily & Sundays, or Sundays only. I think many Christians are on the "Sundays only" subscription plan. They only get *Zoe* bread once a week. No wonder their spiritual lives are so weak and *Zoe*-less when they only eat once a week. I agree with the saying on a church marquee which said, "Eating only once a week makes one weak." Jesus was teaching us the DAILY need for spiritual nourishment, which leads to the next point.

__3. Zoe doesn't store well; it must be picked fresh daily.__ The children of Israel would receive supernatural bread from God called "manna" every day as they traveled through the wilderness. That daily manna could not be stored, or it would spoil. Why do you think God did that? He could have just as easily made a manna that would last for weeks, or one that came only weekly. I believe He was setting the stage for the spiritual comparison that manna represents. Jesus is our spiritual manna, and we MUST have some fresh Jesus every day!

We cannot live off yesterday's spiritual food. What we get on Sundays doesn't last past Monday, much less all week! God designed for us to pick fresh *Zoe* bread every day. He doesn't want a "Sundays only" relationship with us. He wants "daily and Sundays." God said, *"The people are to go out each day and gather enough for that day. In this way I will test them and see whether they will follow my instructions"* (Exodus 16:4). The instructions are the same today. "Take *Zoe* bread daily." It even had to be gathered in the morning because it would spoil in the heat of the day. I'm not sure if that has a spiritual application, but I do think it is important to have a time with God to get our *Zoe* bread in the morning before the heat of the day conflicts and problems arise.

Just as day-old manna began to spoil and stink and develop maggots, so it is true with our spiritual bread. Yesterday's spiritual bread is spoiling, and too many Christians are trying to live off old spiritual food. No wonder some have such bad attitudes and grumpy dispositions—they are trying to make it all week on spoiled food!

<u>**4. Zoe is eternal.**</u> Manna sustained their physical life, but *Zoe* bread sustains our spiritual life both now and for all of eternity!

<u>**5. Zoe is Jesus.**</u> Manna was a physical substance from God. Jesus came in the form of man but became our spiritual *Zoe*. This is why Jesus continued teaching in John 6 that He was the Bread of *Zoe* and that "this bread is my flesh."

Cannibals?

What Jesus said next has been very controversial and misunderstood. It must be understood in the context of a further application of this comparison between manna and Himself as the Bread of *Zoe*. Naturally, if He is the Bread of *Zoe*, we must eat of the Bread to receive its *Zoe*-giving qualities. With that in mind, the next teaching is not so strange:

John 6:53-58: *"Jesus said to them, 'I tell you the truth, unless you eat the flesh of the Son of Man and drink his blood, you have no (Zoe) life in you. Whoever eats my flesh and drinks my blood has eternal (Zoe) life, and I will raise him up at the last day. For my flesh is real food and my blood is real drink. Whoever eats my flesh and drinks my blood remains in me, and I in him. Just as the (Zoe) living Father sent me and I (Zoe) live because of the Father, so the one who feeds on me will (Zoe) live because of me. This is the bread that came down from heaven. Your forefathers ate manna and died, but he who feeds on this bread will (Zoe) live forever'"* (parentheses added).

This passage was so shocking to His disciples they said, *"This is a hard teaching. Who can accept it?"* Aware his disciples were grumbling about this, Jesus said to them, *"Does this offend you?"* The answer, of course, was "Yes." Was Jesus advocating cannibalism? Because of these statements, *"Many of his disciples turned back and no longer followed him"* (John 6:66). Also because of these statements, the Romans persecuted the early Christians because they believed Christians were cannibals.

Here's what I believe Jesus was saying: He is the path to *Zoe*. He is the Bread of *Zoe*. From this bread, we can experience life-changing eternal *Zoe* and daily spiritual nourishment. So in order to experience this *Zoe*-giving power, we must take the bread and eat it. Bread must be eaten in order for it to nourish us or satisfy our hunger. Jesus IS the Bread of *Zoe*, so we must internalize Him—eat Him, if you will—so the Spirit of Jesus can nourish our entire being. Compare it to our digestive system where bread is ingested, absorbed into our blood system, and transported to every cell of our body. Every cell is impacted by the ingestion of that bread.

Holistic Salvation

The born-again experience is the ingestion of Jesus to every cell of our being. Eating and drinking of Jesus is a spiritual way of showing how this transformation occurs. Jesus becomes absorbed into our system as we eat and drink of Him; every cell is impacted. Salvation is, therefore, holistic and meant to impact our whole being with His *Zoe*. I'll talk about this in greater detail later, but this passage illustrates clearly how salvation is holistic:

Physical: He wants to bring *Zoe* to our physical bodies by motivating us to take care of our bodies as the temple of the Holy Spirit and by healing our diseases.

Spiritual: He wants to bring *Zoe* to our spiritual lives by creating a new self—in the image of God—and transforming our character and actions.

Emotional: He wants to bring *Zoe* to our emotional self as He heals the hurts of the past and present and teaches us how to relate to ourselves and to others in emotionally healthy ways.

Mental: He wants to bring *Zoe* to our minds as He renews our minds and teaches us to control our thoughts and love God with our minds.

That's why the first and greatest commandment is to love the Lord with ALL your heart, soul, mind and strength. God cares about us as a whole being. Salvation is more than a spiritual experience. Modern Christianity has tended to limit salvation to involve only our spiritual selves and has ignored God's interest in the other aspects of our lives.

Some of the disciples in the following passage were only interested in their physical need for food. They saw the miracle of the multiplication of bread as a potential for a new bread factory. Jesus saw through this narrow view and proclaimed in John 6:63, *"The Spirit gives (Zoe) life; the flesh counts for nothing. The words I have spoken to you are spirit and they are (Zoe) life"* (parentheses added). Jesus was saying the Spirit gives *Zoe*. Our flesh cannot save us. Only the Spirit of God can do that—so the words of Jesus are *Zoe*-giving.

Communion

Therefore, the sacrament of communion is a celebration and remembrance of the sacrifice of Jesus, and, at the same time, it is a symbolic ingestion of Jesus. It is the symbolic eating and drinking of Jesus into our whole being. As we eat the bread and drink the wine, we are ingesting, or internalizing, the *Zoe* of Jesus—His body and blood. When we take communion, we are sending the bread and the wine to touch each cell in our body. It literally goes into our digestive system and is then absorbed into our blood and touches every cell in our body. Jesus is the Bread of *Zoe* so when He talks about the eating of Him, it is to ingest *Zoe*! This is so *Zoe* may touch every cell of our being. In that context, John 6:55 makes more sense, *"For my flesh is real food and my blood is real drink."* The next time you receive communion, think about how Jesus is the Bread of *Zoe* and receive it into every cell of your body.

Digestive Disorders

Some people have a digestive disorder called Whipple's Disease. It inhibits their ability to absorb nutrients. They are starving even though they are eating. Some of us have a spiritual form of Whipple's Disease. We come to church and listen to the preacher, but it is not being absorbed properly. It is not impacting the rest of our being, rather it is "passing through."

The Bread of *Zoe* is meant to be ingested, digested, and absorbed into every part of our lives. He wants every "cell" in our being to be nourished by *Zoe*. Jesus talked about *Zoe* bread and *Zoe* water—these are NOT accidental analogies. *Zoe* is just as necessary to our spiritual vitality as bread and water are to our bodies. We must continuously be absorbing Him. I want to take of Jesus and nourish every part of my being with His *Zoe*—to the Max! And as often as possible! *Zoe* to the Max!

Chapter 6: Pictures of *Zoe*—*Zoe* Is Light

The analogy of water shows *Zoe* satisfies the thirst in our soul. The analogy of bread shows *Zoe* nourishes and sustains our very being. God also wants us to understand *Zoe* shines out to others and guides our path, so He uses the concept of light. *Zoe* referred to as "light" is found twice in the New Testament: in John 1 and again in John 8.

First, in John 1:4-5: *"In him was (Zoe) life, and that (Zoe) life was the light of men. The light shines in the darkness, but the darkness has not understood it"* (parentheses added). In Jesus was *Zoe*. God could have said "In Jesus was love" or "In Jesus was power," but He said, *"In Him was Zoe"*!! Jesus really knew how to live! He enjoyed His life and had vitality and a joy that shined out of Him. He was full of *Zoe*, and the way He lived His life shined out like a light that drew people to him. People want to be around someone who is full of life, and people want to learn how to really live. The apostle Peter told Him, *"Lord, to whom shall we go? You have the words of eternal Zoe (life)"* (John 6:68, parentheses added).

The Absence of *Zoe* is Darkness

To understand the analogy of *Zoe* and light, you have to understand what light is and what it does. Darkness and light are contrasted: In order to understand the meaning of light, you need to compare it to darkness. We know the definition of darkness is "the absence of light." Therefore, darkness is the absence of *Zoe*. Light is electromagnetic radiation—*Zoe* is the presence of a positive energy that comes from an energy-emitting source. So when the scripture says *"In Him was Zoe,"* it identifies the emitting source AS Jesus. When it says *"And that Zoe was the light of men,"* it shows *Zoe* as the energy that comes OUT OF Jesus. When Jesus indwells us and we learn to live life His way, we experience the positive energy of *Zoe* as it begins to emanate from our lives. *Zoe* is an energy that others can see.

Darkness Does Not Understand *Zoe*

The passage continues in John 1:5: *"The light shines in the darkness, but the darkness has not understood it."* The *Zoe*-less darkness does not understand the light of *Zoe* because it does not possess it. It is impossible for lost people to understand *Zoe* by simply observing it in our lives. The old-timers used to say, "It's better felt than telt." *Zoe* is the positive and joyful energy that shines out of our lives, and those who do not have *Zoe* cannot understand where it comes from. They do not enjoy their life as much as the *Zoe*-possessors do. They cannot understand how someone could be so happy over "nothing."

Yesterday, one of my patients was unusually happy. I have known him for several years, but had never seen him this happy. One of his teeth needed a filling, so after my hygienist was finished with his cleaning, he came into my operatory. After a few minutes of conversation, he turned to me with a giddy look and asked, "Do you want to see the new love of my life?" and he pulled out his cell phone and showed me the image on the screen—a picture of a boat! He was happy because he had a new boat. Nothing wrong with a boat, of course, but it was a "thing" that was making him happy. And what happens when that "thing" gets old, or he loses it? He loses his happiness. Thank God our source of happiness is eternal.

But the darkness does not understand the light. People cannot understand how someone can have joy and peace in the midst of turbulence. They cannot understand how so much love and patience can shine out of a person's life unless he has won the lottery or fallen in love. They don't understand the *Zoe* of contentment without possessing some thing. The darkness does not understand the light.

Zoe Gives Direction

"Zoe is the light of men." Jesus repeats this in John 8:12: *"Jesus spoke again to the people, he said, 'I am the light of the world. Whoever follows me will never walk in darkness, but will have the light of (Zoe) life'"* (parentheses added). When we are tapping into the light of *Zoe*, our direction becomes clearer. When I am experiencing *Zoe* to the Max it sheds the light of understanding on many situations. On the other hand, when I am not experiencing *Zoe* to the Max I feel depressed, I get more confused. *Zoe* is a light that illuminates our path.

Jesus said when we follow Him, we will not walk in darkness. So if I find myself in a *Zoe*-less, "dark" situation, I may not be following His direction at that moment. I need to get out my compass and figure out where He is leading so I can follow. Instead of continuing on without *Zoe*, I need to stop and get my bearings. Jesus promises if I follow Him, I *"will not walk in darkness."*

I remember once when I was driving down a dark country road on a moonless night, and my headlights suddenly went out! I stopped the car as quickly as possible because I lost sight of the road! In the same way, then, when my *Zoe* lights go out, I need to stop as quickly as possible and get my lights back on before I run off life's path.

Immediate Direction

The headlights on a car illuminate the road immediately in front of us. They don't shine miles down the road, but only as far as we need to know for the present. God wants us to enjoy life now, even if we are facing a difficult decision. Being filled with *Zoe* helps me understand what I should do right now. Our immediate action is *Zoe*.

> *The Bible tells us not to worry about tomorrow, but we have Zoe to show us how to enjoy the way for today.*

When you are in the *Zoe* Zone (I talk about this later), you will have the right perspective and can think better. That's why God tells us not to worry about tomorrow, because He hasn't illuminated tomorrow for us yet. Each day has its own light. The Bible tells us not to worry about tomorrow, but we have *Zoe* to show us how to enjoy the way for today.

I was talking with a couple of my employees recently about worry. They were worrying about a problem that might happen if another employee who had recently been unreliable did not come to work on Monday. I told them not to worry about it because I was going to put it in God's hands. One of the girls said, "I don't know how you do that. It makes me 'a nervous wreck' thinking about it." I told her, "God knows the future, and I don't. He will take care of Monday, and I wouldn't waste time and energy worrying about problems that haven't happened yet. And God doesn't want you worrying about it." The other girl shook her head and said, "I worry about everything 24/7." How sad to spend today's happiness on tomorrow's problems.

Zoe is a Witness to the World

Light not only guides us, but it also guides others to our source of light. When you and I are living with *Zoe* to the Max we are like bright lights shining out to others. The brighter our *Zoe*, the brighter our light and the more it contrasts with the darkness. *Zoe* to the Max is a witness to darkness and a challenge to those who need to "crank it up a notch."

I think one of my most powerful witnessing tools is my *Zoe*. When people see and feel my *Zoe* to the Max it shines into their world and causes them to wonder why someone is so full of optimism and cheerfulness. The common greeting we Americans use, "How are you doing?" is a question we expect to be answered with "fine" or "good." When I am asked that question and *Zoe* is gushing out of me, I have to honestly answer "Fantastic!" or "Terrific" or "Great!" or "It's good to be alive!" That often opens up an opportunity for me to witness to the *Zoe* life that God has given me.

That's why Jesus said, *"You are the light of the world. A city on a hill cannot be hidden"* (Matthew 5:14). If you and I are in the *Zoe* Zone, WE CANNOT HIDE IT! *Zoe* to the Max cannot be hidden! It was not meant to be hidden! That's why Jesus also said, *"Neither do people light a lamp and put it under a bowl. Instead they put it on its stand, and it gives light to everyone in the house."* Our *Zoe* was meant to be *"put out there"* where others can see it. Sometimes my *Zoe* gushes out in my singing or humming or whistling. It is good PR for *Zoe*!

Have you ever heard someone whistling in a store, and when you heard it you wondered, "Who's whistling?" Didn't it make you want to find out where the sound was coming from to see who was whistling? It is in this way God wants our *Zoe* to be "put on its stand." A lamp should be put up on a stand so it can shine to everyone in the house. We are NOT TO HIDE our *Zoe*. We are to let it shine! *"In the same way, let your light shine before men, that they may see your good deeds and praise your Father in heaven"* (Matthew 5:14-16). Shine your *Zoe* to the world! When you shine, it shows others how dark their lives are. It gives them the opportunity to realize they are in darkness because they see the light shining. It may even remind and challenge other *Zoe*-possessors to turn up their *Zoe* lights.

Shine Like a Star!

The Bible says we are stars that shine to the world and point them to Christ. Just like the star of Bethlehem, we are to shine our *Zoe* light so the "wise men" will follow that light and find Christ. This is demonstrated in a passage in Philippians 2:14-16 and I would like for us to study it from the end of the verse and work our way back to the beginning. It ends with saying we are to "hold out the word of (*Zoe*) life ..." (parentheses added). The Word of *Zoe* is another way of describing the Word of God. The *Zoe*-giving words of Jesus are to be held out to the world, as Jesus said in John 6:63, *"The words I have spoken to you are spirit and they are (Zoe) life"* (parentheses added). The words of Jesus are *Zoe*, and we are to "hold out" the word of *Zoe*. This means our focus is on the Word of *Zoe*, our actions are driven by the Word of *Zoe*, and our speech is ready to proclaim the Word of *Zoe*.

As you do this, you *"shine like stars in the universe as you hold out the word of (Zoe) life ..."* (parentheses added). The light of *Zoe* shines so brightly in the darkness of this world, you shine as brightly as a star shines. Our society manufactures so much hype over movie "stars," and yet we, as followers of Christ, are the real stars. God doesn't call Hollywood celebrities "stars." He calls us *"stars in the universe"!* We are shining brightly in a dark sky, a sky dark as *"a crooked and depraved generation, in which you shine like stars in the universe as you hold out the word of (Zoe) life ..."* (parentheses added).

This world is characterized as *"crooked and depraved,"*, and we are the *Zoe* lights shining as bright as a star in the universe. You may be the only star in your universe. You may be the only star in your family or the only star at your job, but God has you there to shine out the *Zoe* brightly.

Next we ask, "How can we shine our *Zoe* to the 'star-level' of brightness?" "Star-level" *Zoe* brightness comes from those who are *"blameless and pure, children of God without fault."* Wow, that sounds like a high calling—and it is! Holiness is the key to increasing the brightness of *Zoe* to the "star-level." Holiness, just like *Zoe*, only comes from God. He alone can purify His children as He sanctifies their flaws.

Holy *Zoe*!

Different theologians interpret "holiness" differently, and debate whether it is obtainable. While I will cover this more thoroughly later, those who believe in "positional holiness" would say when God looks at us, He only sees the holiness of Jesus and not our actual behavior. The opposite view is that believers allow Jesus to create actual holiness within them by allowing the Holy Spirit to sanctify their character and behavior to the point they possess the degree of holiness Jesus has created in them. This view makes more sense to me when trying to understand the phrase *"blameless and pure, children of God without fault."* God wants to develop actual pureness in His children. That kind of holiness shines as brightly as any star! That should be our goal: To shine a *Zoe* light that is brightened to "star-level" by holiness.

The following phrase completes the picture: *"Do everything without complaining or arguing, SO THAT YOU MAY BECOME blameless and pure, children of God without fault in a crooked and depraved generation, in which you shine like stars in the universe as you hold out the word of (Zoe) life ..."* (Philippians 2:14-16, parentheses and emphasis added). We see an attitude of complaining and arguing blocks the holy work God wishes to accomplish in our lives. An attitude of complaining and arguing is an impurity and a fault that diminishes our *Zoe* light. God wants His work of holiness to continue purifying us until we can *"Do everything without complaining or arguing."* My personal prayer is for God to purify the complaining and arguing attitudes right out of my life so I may become *"blameless and pure, children of God without fault in a crooked and depraved generation, in which you shine like stars in the universe as you hold out the word of (Zoe) life ..."* (parentheses added).

Chapter 7: Pictures of *Zoe*—Tree of *Zoe*

Another great picture of *Zoe* is found in Revelation 22:2. I've already talked about the river of *Zoe*, but do you know what's on each side of the river of *Zoe*? *"On each side of the river stood the tree of (Zoe) life, bearing twelve crops of fruit, yielding its fruit every month. And the leaves of the tree are for the healing of the nations"* (parentheses added). It is the Tree of *Zoe*! Sometimes an analogy of a tree indicates strength, but in this case, the tree of *Zoe* is not just any tree, it is a fruit tree! Using the analogy of a fruit tree draws attention to the concepts of productivity in bearing the fruit and the enjoyment of consuming the fruit since fruit is usually tasty as well as nutritious.

Zoe Fruit

Trees bear fruit according to the type of tree they are. For example, peach trees bear peaches, while apples trees bear apples. So *Zoe* trees bear what kind of fruit? *Zoe* fruit! The *Zoe* tree yields a new crop of *Zoe* fruit every month! Fresh fruit! Fruit is for eating, right? One day we will get to eat some of that *Zoe* fruit! Revelation 2:7: *"He who has an ear, let him hear what the Spirit says to the churches. To him who overcomes, I will give the right to eat from the tree of (Zoe) life, which is in the paradise of God"* (parentheses added). Wow! To eat *Zoe* fruit from the tree of *Zoe* is a reward given to the over comers! It is mentioned again in Revelation 22:14: *"Blessed are those who wash their robes, that they may have the right to the tree of (Zoe) life and may go through the gates into the city"* (parentheses added).

Eating *Zoe* fruit is a right that will be granted to us. However, for those who try to change God's Word, Revelation 22:19 warns, *"And if anyone takes words away from this book of prophecy, God will take away from him his share in the tree of (Zoe) life and in the holy city, which are described in this book"* (parentheses added). Notice the phrase *"his share"* in the tree of *Zoe*. God has a share of the *Zoe* fruit in mind for you and me. It will be our right as children of God to eat *Zoe* fruit throughout all of eternity. Why not start eating some *Zoe* fruit right now? Jesus makes *Zoe* fruit available to us now! John 10:10 says He came that we might have *Zoe*, and have it to the max! *Zoe* is what God is all about! *Zoe* is everywhere! *Zoe* bread, *Zoe* water, *Zoe* light. Then add to that the reward of *Zoe* fruit for us to taste and enjoy forever! The joy of fruit is its taste. I wonder what *Zoe* fruit tastes like? We'll find out soon, won't we! Ha! Woo who!

The Tree of *Zoe* also reminds me about the first sighting of the tree of life in Genesis 2:9-10: *"And the Lord God made all kinds of trees grow out of the ground—trees that were pleasing to the eye and good for food. In the middle of the garden were the tree of life and the tree of the knowledge of good and evil. A river watering the garden flowed from Eden."*

Notice the similarity between the Garden of Eden and the New Jerusalem. They both have the tree of life in a central location. They both have a river. I wonder if the tree of life in the Garden of Eden was transplanted to the New Jerusalem? God has always been about *Zoe*! He wants us to eat of the tree of *Zoe* forever! What a plan! What a God!

Zoe Serves and Heals.

Also notice the tree of *Zoe* has leaves that are *"for the healing of the nations."* The Greek word for "healing" is the *therapeia* [ther·ap·i·ah] from which we get the English word "therapy." This particular word is only used four times in the New Testament and, oddly enough, it can be translated as either: 1. service rendered by one to another; 2. specifically medical service: curing, healing; 3. household service; a body of attendants, servants, domestics.[1]

No doubt the leaves do bring healing to the nations, but what diseases will be there in heaven? Maybe the meaning of healing is broader than physical healing. Perhaps a better interpretation is the leaves of the tree of *Zoe* will "serve to meet the needs" of the nations. The point is that the nations will go to the *Zoe* tree to receive benefits of every kind because the *Zoe* of God heals every hurt and serves every need.

When you have *Zoe*, you have the energizing power of God in your life, and He wants you to taste of the good fruit of *Zoe* and partake of the leaves of *Zoe* as they meet your every need. Taste *Zoe*; taste His kind of life! It's good. It will "cure what ails ya."

Chapter 8: Pictures of *Zoe*—The Crown of *Zoe*

The Greek word for "crown" is *stephanos* [stef·an·os]. It literally means "a crown as a mark of royal or (in general) exalted rank; 1a. the wreath or garland which was given as a prize to victors in public games; 1c. that which is an ornament and honor to one.[1] *Stephanos* is used eighteen times in the New Testament:

• Six times as a crown of authority or honor as worn by various heavenly beings. The word "diadem" is sometimes translated as "crown" and is used three times in the same way.[2]

• Four times as a crown of thorns that Jesus wore.

• Two times used metaphorically by Paul in honoring those He loved as his "crown of rejoicing" and "you are my joy and crown."

I'd like for us to look a little closer at the remaining six times *stephanos* is used because they indicate our crown of eternal reward and honor!

• 1 Corinthians 9:25: *"Everyone who competes in the games goes into strict training. They do it to get a crown that will not last; but we do it to get **a crown that will last forever**"* (emphasis added).

• Revelation 3:11: *"I am coming soon. Hold on to what you have, so that no one will take **your crown**"* (emphasis added).

• 2 Timothy 4:8: *"Now there is in store for me **the crown of righteousness**, which the Lord, the righteous Judge, will award to me on that day—and not only to me, but also to all who have longed for his appearing"* (emphasis added).

• 1 Peter 5:4: *"And when the Chief Shepherd appears, you will receive **the crown of glory** that will never fade away"* (emphasis added).

The final two times it is called "the crown of *Zoe*."

• James 1:12: *"Blessed is the man who perseveres under trial, because when he has stood the test, he will receive **the crown of (Zoe) life** that God has promised to those who love him"* (parentheses and emphasis added).

• Revelation 2:10: *"Do not be afraid of what you are about to suffer. I tell you, the devil will put some of you in prison to test you, and you will suffer persecution for ten days. Be faithful, even to the point of death, and I will give you* **the crown of** (**Zoe**) *life"* (parentheses and emphasis added).

The crown of *Zoe* shows *Zoe* is considered a type of eternal reward similar to the reward of eating from the tree of *Zoe*. The eternal reward of the crown of *Zoe* will be awesome, but what I want you to understand is *Zoe* can be enjoyed BEGINNING NOW! You don't have to wait until you get to heaven and receive your crown of *Zoe*. You can experience that *Zoe* right now. I mean right now! As you are holding this book! You can pray, "Father, I thank you for the crown of *Zoe* you are going to give me, but I would like to start enjoying *Zoe* now. Teach me how to experience now all the *Zoe* you have available for me."

Chapter 9: The Book of *Zoe*

The Book of *Zoe* is an actual book that contains the names of those who have been granted *Zoe* through their new birth/adoption into God's family. *Zoe* is the identifying feature of the children of God. It could have been called "The Book of Love" or "The Book of Holiness" or "The Book of Grace," but it was called "The Book of *Zoe*"! Do you see how central *Zoe* is to the being of God!

Philippians 4:3 is the first time the phrase "book of *Zoe*" is used. Here Paul is addressing his fellow believers: *"Yes, and I ask you, loyal yokefellow, help these women who have contended at my side in the cause of the gospel, along with Clement and the rest of my fellow workers, whose names are in the book of (Zoe) life"* (parentheses added).

The Book of *Zoe* is located in heaven and will be opened at the final judgment and used to judge the world. Revelation 20:11-15: *"Then I saw a great white throne and Him who was seated on it. Earth and sky fled from His presence, and there was no place for them. And I saw the dead, great and small, standing before the throne, and books were opened. Another book was opened, which is **the book of** (Zoe) **life**. The dead were judged according to what they had done as recorded in the books. The sea gave up the dead that were in it, and death and Hades gave up the dead that were in them, and each person was judged according to what he had done. Then death and Hades were thrown into the lake of fire. The lake of fire is the second death. If anyone's name was not found written in **the book of** (Zoe) **life**, he was thrown into the lake of fire"* (parentheses and emphasis added).

Also, final entry into the New Jerusalem will only be allowed to those whose name is in the Lamb's Book of *Zoe*. Revelation 21:27: *"Nothing impure will ever enter it, nor will anyone who does what is shameful or deceitful, but only those whose names are written in the Lamb's book of (Zoe) life"* (parentheses added).

When anyone is born again, the *Zoe* of God enters into him, and his name is recorded in heaven in the Book of *Zoe*. Revelation 3:5: *"He who overcomes will, like them, be dressed in white. I will never blot out his name from the book of (Zoe) life, but will acknowledge his name before my Father and His angels"* (parentheses added). Our names are recorded in the Lamb's Book of *Zoe* because we belong to "The Lamb." Revelation 13:8: *"All inhabitants of the earth will worship the beast—all whose names have not been written in the book of (Zoe) life belonging to the Lamb that was slain from the creation of the world"* (parentheses added).

The fact our name is written in the Lamb's Book of *Zoe* should be cause for great celebration on our part! Jesus, The Lamb, said in Luke 10:20, *"Do not rejoice that the spirits submit to you, but REJOICE that your names are written in heaven"* (emphasis added). Our joy now is to rejoice in the fact OUR NAME is written in the book of *Zoe*! REJOICE! It doesn't matter what circumstances or pain you may be going through now. The fact remains that YOUR name— YOUR NAME—right now—your name—is written in the Lamb's Book of *Zoe*! Hallelujah! And woo who!

SECTION TWO

The Zoe Zone

Chapter 10: The *Zoe* Zone

We see making *Zoe* to the Max available to every believer is significant in the heart of God and in the mission of Jesus. We have also seen *Zoe* has a prominent place in heaven and is our eternal reward. The question I want us to address in this section is: How do I experience *Zoe* to the Max!?

We have seen *Zoe* is available for all believers to experience because Christ is *Zoe*, and Christ dwells in us. He is the source of *Zoe*, and His desire is to teach us how to experience *Zoe* to the MAXIMUM level. But how do we get a handle on that?

My wife's family uses directional words like north, south, east and west to describe the location of things in their house. For example, instead of talking about the front or back of the house, they say the "north end" or "south end" of the house. Each room also has directional sides: the east wall, the west door, etc. My family is not accustomed to using those kinds of directional words, so this past Christmas, my daughter Rebekah was confused when her grandmother told her to place a plate of chicken salad sandwiches on the "north side of the table." Entering the dining room with a somewhat glazed-over look on her face, Rebekah whispered to grandpa, "Where is the north side of the table?"

Locating *Zoe* to the Max can be just as confusing if you aren't accustomed to the terms. It is truly a lifelong experience of discovery which requires learning new attitudes and being open to new thoughts and methods. The reason I am writing this book is to show you the accumulated lessons of more than forty years of following Christ. I have learned new lessons in just the last year that have brought *Zoe* to a higher level in my life. I believe the reason many Christians do not experience *Zoe* to the Max on a consistent basis is it requires simultaneous mastery in a number of areas. I have identified ten of these important areas which affect our relationship with

God, ourselves and others. When all ten of these areas are lived in God's way, *Zoe* is experienced to the highest level. I call it "living in the *Zoe* Zone." The *Zoe* Zone is achieved when you are functioning God's way in all ten of these areas.

Mastery in all ten of the areas will yield *Zoe* to the Max! It was fun to note Jesus declared his desire for us to have *Zoe* to the Max in John 10:10. I thought about calling this section "The 10:10 Zone." That has a cool sound to it, but I settled on the name "*Zoe* Zone" as a more descriptive term. In this section of the book, I'm going to break down each area of the *Zoe* Zone and show you how each one contributes to putting us in the *Zoe* Zone.

Chapter 11: *Zoe* Zone Part 1
Enjoying the Presence of God

The first and most important area to master in living in the *Zoe* Zone is to learn how to fully enjoy the presence of God in your life. As we have learned, God is full of *Zoe*, and He wants us to enjoy His *Zoe*. *Zoe*, however, is not a product He wraps up and sends down to us. *Zoe* is experiencing the very presence of God on a moment by moment basis. *Zoe* is enjoying God. Then we are able to enjoy ourselves and enjoy the events of life and enjoy our relationships with others as we live this life. But in order for us to fully enjoy the presence of God, we need to first examine our image of God for possible distortions.

Our Image of God

Our image of God affects our enjoyment of our relationship with Him. If we have the wrong image of God, we will be reluctant to seek the kind of closeness He desires. Our image of God has probably been skewed slightly because it was taught to us by flawed human beings. If our parents' image of God was slightly out of focus, or our church's image slightly skewed, then our teachers delivered that distortion to us. I believe most of us grew up with some misconceptions about what God is really like. We need to look for and correct these images of God in our minds because they affect how we think of Him, how we relate to Him, and what we ask of Him.

I once spoke with a new believer, and she told me she didn't think God would forgive her because she had an abortion a number of years earlier. Her image of God limited her ability to receive the forgiveness God was ready to give her. Another young believer told me of a sense of shame because she could not conceive how God could forgive her for the many affairs she had been involved in and the marriages she had hurt. Her image of God was a god who weighed her goodness against her badness and since there was much more badness, she felt she could never be forgiven. Let me ask you:

Do you know God for who He really is?

What is your notion of what God is like? Think about it. Does your image of God match who He really is? I came to the realization years ago my image of God was slightly "off." I began to evaluate my image of Him and found my image was of a "grace-poor" God. Our image of God came mostly from what others have taught us. How do you know they gave you the right image? Could it be "off" slightly from who He really is?

For example, dentistry has a general reputation for causing pain. Many people have a negative perception of me based on that reputation. When someone comes into my office and meets me for the first time, they may already have **a preconceived notion of what a dentist is like,** and transfer that notion to believing they know **ME.** It makes them fearful of me, even though they have never met me. How would that make you feel if you realized people assumed you were going to hurt them!

When parents have had a bad experience with a dentist, they tend to pass that fear on to their children. I get irritated with parents who say to their children, "The dentist isn't going to hurt you." Think about it from the child's perspective. If your parent told you that someone was not going to hurt you, you might start thinking to yourself, "Hurt? Why are they talking about hurt? Ohhh ... that means that the dentist **might hurt me!** I had better prepare myself for the possibility of being hurt. I had better watch out! Oh, no! Here he comes!"

God also has a PR problem. People have a preconceived notion of what He is like, and it is often not exactly accurate. People may be fearful of Him before they even meet Him. People project their images of God onto others. When you approach God, you come to Him with an attitude that is shaped by your preconceived notions. That attitude affects what you ask for, and how you ask for it, and what you think His response is going to be.

My Grandpa was the king of the family. To me, he was bigger than life, and was honored by everyone in our family. I remember we would go to visit him in his big house near Washington, DC. He would come in after work and sit back on his recliner with his shoes kicked off and huge feet projecting out. My job was to then take his socks off and rub them between his toes with back and forth, see-saw strokes! Gross! I can't believe now I did that or that he asked me to do that! But he was "king" in my eyes and whatever task he asked me to do was an honor.

I grew up with the following notions about God:

—God is one to be feared, respected and reverenced.

—We must not disobey Him because if we do, He will punish us.

—He is high and holy and expects us to live holy lives.

—We will one day stand before Him.

—He will judge us according to His laws so we had better prepare ourselves for that.

—He is just and righteous and will do the right thing.

While all of that is correct, it is incomplete. I was missing the whole grace and mercy and *Zoe* part, and I thought of God as more stoic and stern rather than the *Zoe*-filled God that He is. I did not know the God who is rich in grace and rich in mercy. Because of this, I had difficulty feeling intimate with God. Why would I want to get close to a God who is stern and demanding? Could I really enjoy hanging around someone who is looking for my imperfections and is ready to expose my faults? God had some "bad PR" in my mind, and I think in many others as well. He wants us to get it right and know who He really is.

God is a Good God

God really does have our best interest in mind. He loves to bless us with good things. Do you believe that about God? Do you think of Him as sitting there thinking of good things to bless you with, or looking for something to hit you with? I believe most of us think of God as a stern disciplinarian, rather than a happy father.

I was named after my dad's favorite brother, Tracy. My dad was the youngest of twelve children so his father didn't spend much time with him. His older brother, Tracy, ended up being a strong influence in his life. When I was a young kid, we would drive the six hours over the Appalachian Mountains to Clarksburg, West Virginia, where Uncle Tracy owned a tire shop. I vividly remember parking on a side street and Uncle Tracy coming out of his tire shop and giving my brother and me each a dollar! Wow! That was such an awesome thing! When we would see Uncle Tracy, he would often give us a dollar. That had such an impact on me as I child, I have developed the same characteristic. Often when I see kids at church or sometimes kids out in public, I will often give them a dollar. I have given away hundreds of dollars that way—one at a time. Giving a dollar to a child helps them to know they are special. I want them to feel they are valuable and loved.

I think God is a lot like my Uncle Tracy—He is a giving God. He loves to give with a smile for no particular reason except to let us know He loves us. Revelation 21:6: *"To him who is thirsty* **I will give** *to drink without cost from the spring of the water of life (Zoe)"* (parentheses and emphasis added). God is a giving God. He wants to give us *Zoe* water to quench our thirst for an enjoyable life. He wants to give it to us "without cost." The free gift of *Zoe*—the ability to enjoy a supernatural life to the fullest—is what He wants to give us. Our God is a giving God. He wants to give us an eternal inheritance and be our God. And we are going to be His children. He is a giving God!

Jesus said, *"Come to me, all you who are weary and burdened, and* **I will give you rest***"* (Matthew 11:28, (emphasis added). He wants to GIVE us rest. He doesn't like to see us struggle. He wants to teach us a better way of handling situations so the difficult ones don't wear us out. He wants to GIVE us rest. God is a giving God.

My Last Four Bucks

Each December we pack up our bags, put them in our RV and make the 21-hour drive to Oskaloosa, Iowa, for Christmas. It's a great time to see Valerie's side of the family and kick back for a week. During this time my dental practice is closed, and my income is reduced to whatever insurance payments and accounts receivable payments come in the mail. Having closed the office like this every year for more than twenty years, I learned to expect a predictable amount of income.

This "predictable" pattern changed dramatically one particular Christmas several years ago. Suddenly and inexplicably, my income dropped by 90% of what it normally had been every year previously. What was going on? God knows one sure way of getting my attention is to shut off my finances. Because of past lessons from God, I knew exactly what was going on. God was getting my attention for a serious conversation. Sadly, I had been neglecting my time with Him in my busyness. He reminded me the busy things I was doing "for Him" were actually excluding me "from Him". Nothing in my life was to ever marginalize Him. He got my attention. Message received. Lesson learned. From that time on, I have kept my focus on being with God, not just being busy for God.

My financial situation still remained bleak. God had managed to deplete all my money down to my last few dollars in both personal and business accounts. I suppose I could have asked my in-laws for a loan, but I reasoned it would have made them feel bad to know we were in such a predicament for having taken time off to travel out there to see them. Besides, all I needed to do was get home on my gasoline credit cards and get back to work.

We left for home and after borrowing the few remaining dollars my children had so I could to buy meals, I was down to my last four bucks. And when I say *last*, I mean LAST FOUR BUCKS! I knew West Virginia's toll road required $2, so that left me with $2 for a cup of coffee at the Beckley Starbucks! Praise God! The Starbucks exit was thirty miles away, and I could just taste that coffee. But then I realized that there was a second $2 toll! Oh no! What a bummer. There goes my Starbucks! Oh well, at least I had exactly what I needed for the tolls. "God knows exactly what I need," I thought to myself. He knows how to shut my money down to the EXACT four bucks needed to pay my tolls.

THEN IT HAPPENED! As I came to the second toll booth, I waited in line behind an SUV and then I handed my last $2 to the toll attendant, he said, **"Go ahead. They already paid your toll."** "What?!" I said. "He paid your toll!" the worker said impatiently as he flagged me forward. I wanted to ask why they paid it and if they said anything else to him, but he wasn't interested in having a conversation and wanted to hurry me through. I was not sure what had just happened, but what I knew was GOD HAD PAID MY TOLL! At the exact time and in the exact amount, He had arranged for someone to be right in front of me, on an open interstate, to get in the same toll lane, and pay my toll. And why would someone pay the toll for an RV? I wouldn't. Just think about it. Of all the cars on the interstate going here and there, God put a certain person right in front of me to be at the same toll booth, at the same time, and to go through the same lane, and have them pay the toll of the RV behind them!!!! God was showing me He knew EXACTLY where I was and exactly when I would be there. He was in ABSOLUTE control of my finances and knew EXACTLY what I needed to pay my tolls. AND, best of all, God knew I wanted that cup of Starbucks coffee! God knows how much I enjoy coffee, and He wanted me to know in a miraculous, yet simple, way He was there. God loves me, and He knows I love Him, and that I love Starbucks coffee!

I rejoiced going down the road as Valerie and I tried to wave at the SUV, but they easily sped ahead of a slow RV. Then as I pulled into Starbucks several miles down the road, I looked to see if I could find the vehicle in the parking lot, and, sure enough, there it was. The same window stickers I had noticed and the North Carolina tags Valerie had observed. After getting my coffee, I put a note on the window thanking them for being God's messenger of love for me. I may never meet them on this earth, but I hope to meet them in heaven and thank them personally.

Is your image of God an image of a God who is that good? That is who He is! When I talk about enjoying the presence of God, I'm talking about enjoying the One who is good and giving, not one who is harsh and demanding. To hear some people talk about their time with God, you would think they were donating blood or paying taxes. Their image of God is someone who demands their lives and demands their praise, so they had better obey or God will "get them." God is not like that; He wants to be good to us and wants us to enjoy being with Him.

God is a Loving God

God IS love. It is who He is. It is how He defines His character. 1 John 4:7-8: *"Dear friends, let us LOVE one another, for LOVE COMES FROM GOD. Everyone who LOVES has been born of God and knows God. Whoever does not LOVE does not know God, because GOD IS LOVE "* (parentheses added).

Do you think of God as love? When you think about going to Him, do you think about approaching love? He is love! When we go to Him, we are going before the very essence of love because the passage above says "love comes from God." When I talk about enjoying the presence of God, I'm talking about enjoying love. Having the correct image of God is very important.

God is Merciful and Gracious

Grace and mercy are aspects of God's character many folks don't get right because they are beyond our human understanding. Many feel God is harsh or judgmental or critical of them. This keeps them from being able to be intimate with Him just like they can't see themselves wanting to hug a Supreme Court Justice either! Often this is coupled with feeling unworthy before a holy God because of their sin and feelings of shame. This misunderstanding of who God is causes many to salute God from a distance instead of embracing Him up close. God wants to change that! He wants to have an "up close and personal" relationship with us.

The fact is, sin does separate us from the holiness of God and distances us from intimacy with Him, but God has made provision for overcoming this in Christ. The passage in Ephesians 2 lays out the problem and the solution. As I take us through the passage, I will insert my comments in parentheses:

"All of us also lived among them at one time (that is, we lived among, and were ourselves, sinners), gratifying the cravings of our sinful nature and following its desires and thoughts. Like the rest, we were by nature objects of wrath (we lived in rebellion against God's will and were judged as guilty, awaiting the sentence of the wrath of God against sin.). But because of his great love for us (Great love for whom? For us!), God, who is RICH IN MERCY (when you are rich in something, it means you have a whole lot of it—right?), made us alive with Christ even when we were dead in transgressions—it is by GRACE you have been saved. (Grace is when God gives us the good things that we don't deserve, out of His benevolent heart.) And God raised us up with Christ and seated us with him in the heavenly realms in Christ Jesus (He not only saved us but raised us and seated us with Christ.), in order that in the coming ages he might show the INCOMPARABLE RICHES OF HIS GRACE, expressed in his KINDNESS TO US in Christ Jesus. For it is by GRACE you have been saved, through faith—and this not from yourselves, it is the GIFT of God—not by works, so that no one can boast." (Ephesians 2:3-9, (parentheses added)

God is rich in two things:

    1. Mercy and

    2. Grace

Notice it doesn't say He is rich in anger or rich in judgment. Neither did it say that he is rich in justice or revenge. God's great heart of love is rich in mercy. This means He loves us so much He is willing and wanting to find a way to be merciful to us. That's why He sent Christ to make us alive from the dead. This was not done because we deserved it or earned it, but because by the grace of God we are saved. Now this concept of grace is hard for us to wrap our minds around. The best understanding of grace and mercy is this:

—When we DON'T get the bad things we deserve—that's mercy.

—When we get the good things we DON'T deserve—that's grace.

God is rich in both. He is rich in NOT giving us the bad things that we really do deserve. He is also rich in giving us the good things we really DON'T deserve.

If you feel you don't deserve all the good things God has given you—you are right—that's grace! If you feel you should be punished for all the sinful things you did—you're right But you won't get the punishment—that's mercy! The punishment you deserve has

> **Now death is working backwards in us and we can be restored to Zoe!**

already been paid by Christ on the cross, and, therefore, you receive mercy instead of justice.

Another aspect of His grace is shown in His kindness in sending Christ to us. Christ established the reason why the justice of God can be satisfied. Justice demanded that sin be atoned for. This demand was satisfied in Christ. I can't help but think of the great allegory, *The Chronicles of Narnia: The Lion, The Witch and The Wardrobe*. I recommend you see the movie because it will help you understand redemption better. Jesus is represented by Aslan, the Lion of Judah. He gave his life as a substitute for Edmond, the traitor, who represents you and me. Aslan referred to the ancient prophecy stating if a willing victim who had committed no treachery were to be killed in the traitor's place, the Table would crack and death itself would start working backwards and restore the life of the innocent victim.

Christ offered Himself in the traitor's place—my place and your place. Now death is working backwards in us and we can be restored to *Zoe*! All this is the gift of God. A gift is not earned—it can only be received or rejected. Our salvation is a gift to be received.

My need for grace did not stop at salvation. For most of my adult life, I thought of grace as being something I needed only at the time of my salvation, but after that, doing right was more or less up to me. How wrong I was! Grace is needed on a continuing basis because grace includes ALL the good things God wants to keep giving me—none of which I deserve. God is gracious and merciful to us because we continue to need His forgiveness and mercy for the times we fail. We fail at our attempts to walk perfectly with Christ. We don't love broadly enough, nor are we patient enough. I realize now that I need the grace of God daily to teach me during the times I fall short of God's best responses to daily situations. My inadequacies need the mercy of God, and I enjoy the grace of the good things I don't deserve every day.

A passage in Hebrews paints a beautiful picture of God's attitude toward our neediness: *"For we do not have a high priest who is unable to sympathize with our weaknesses, but we have one who has been tempted in every way, just as we are—yet was without sin. Let us then approach the throne of grace with confidence, so that we may receive mercy and find grace to help us in our time of need"* (Hebrews 4:15-16).

Look at God's response to our failures: Our weaknesses are embraced by our sympathetic priest, Jesus. He has been where we are, and he has been tested just like us. He then goes with us to the throne of God, which is called ... ? What is His throne called? His throne is called GRACE! Just think of that! What do you think we might receive from the throne of grace? You got it—grace! That is why we can go in confidence because we know the throne of grace is not going to dispense justice, but rather mercy and grace. Instead of receiving a well-deserved "yelling session," we will receive mercy and find grace to help us in our time of need. Wow, what a gracious and merciful God.

God is a Blessing God!

Our God is not only loving and gracious and merciful, but He wants to bless us. God has wanted to bless all of His people from Adam and Eve to Noah and then to Abraham. In Genesis 12:1-3 and 18:18, God promised to bless Abraham and ALL his descendants. This blessing was a special blessing that contained the prophecy of the coming of Christ who would be the blessing of God to live among us and set us free. God sealed His blessing with a covenant, or promise, which became known as "The Covenant." This covenant was broken by the children of Israel and they lost the blessing God intended. But God still kept His promise of Christ, and made a New Covenant with all believers—including you and me! This New Covenant is a better covenant built on better promises to all the descendants of Christ: *"'This is the covenant I will make with the house of Israel after that time,' declares the Lord. 'I will put my laws in their minds and write them on their hearts. I will be their God, and they will be my people'"* (Hebrews 8:10).

This New Covenant, or blessing of God, was to be internalized within the believers. The internalizing is done by the power of the Holy Spirit, who, since Pentecost, now indwells every believer. God says, *"I will put my laws IN their minds and write them ON their hearts"* (parentheses added). That's the internalizing that happens through salvation. God wants to move in and "set up camp." He wants to take His blessing right into the middle of every believer. What a blessing God!

God Wants To Come To Us

This "blessing God" is good and giving and loving and gracious, and He wants to bring His blessing to us and share Himself with us! Is this the image of God that you have? When you come to Him, do you feel you are coming to a God that wants to bless you? I challenge you to ask God to correct any distortions of His image in you.

John 14 teaches how much God wants to be with us. Jesus was teaching His disciples about what it would be like after He left them to return to the Father. He reassures them in John 14:18, *"I will not leave you as orphans; I will come to you."* The Greek word for orphan is *orphanos* [or·fan·os] which means "to be fatherless."[1]

Let's look at five lessons from John 14 that will show us how much God wants to spend time with us.

<u>**1. You are a child of God, not an orphan!**</u> God promises to come to you because you are His child. He will not leave you "fatherless." He has a family commitment to you. You have been adopted by God into His family. *"In love he predestined us **to be adopted as his sons** through Jesus Christ, in accordance with his pleasure and will"* (Ephesians 1:4-5 parentheses added). It was His PLEASURE and will to adopt you. Do you believe that? Do you know down deep inside

of your being that it was God's PLEASURE to adopt you? Do you act like you believe it when you approach Him?

This truth of adoption is paramount for you to get—to get way down in the core of your being. Many of us "say" we believe we are children of God, but then we live in worry or fear or insecurity. If you are a child of God, what do you have to worry about? Isn't your Father able to take care of you?

Orphans worry, children don't.

If you are a child of Almighty God, what is there to fear? Don't you trust your Father?

Orphans fear, children trust.

Do you act more like an orphan, or like an adopted child? You must believe you are a child of God deep down in the core of your being if you are going to enjoy God's presence and to experience *Zoe to the Max!* You need to believe God is your good Father, and that it is His pleasure for you to be His beloved, adopted child. You must know this in your "knower."

Your "knower" is located deep down inside of your innermost being. It is deeper than your intellect. It is in the core beliefs of your being—the beliefs you act upon. You may say you believe something, but do you really know it in your "knower"? We believe so many things in our heads, but not in our "knowers." We will stop acting like orphans once we know in our "knower" we are children of God.

2. "I will come to you." That is His promise to His disciples and to you and me as well. If you are His child, then He has promised He will come to you and be with you. He is not the God that is "way up there." He is Immanuel—God with us. We cannot go where He is, but He can come to where we are: *"I will come to you."* How can this be? Read the next verse, John 14:19: *"Before long, the world will not see me anymore, but you will see me. Because I live, you also will live. On that day you will realize that I am in my Father, and __you are in me, and I am in you__"* (emphasis added). So here's the situation: Jesus was about to leave His disciples so they would no longer see him, but because He has *Zoe*, and He is *Zoe*, they would also have

Zoe. He would return to them, and they would realize a new situation. It will be a weird unity thing, Jesus in the Father and us in Jesus and Jesus in us.

3. You will be "in me and I am in you." So the situation is going to change from a "Jesus around me" to a "me inside of Jesus and Jesus inside of me." That's a better deal! Jesus inside is better than Jesus alongside. A Jesus inside is always there.

Then Jesus goes on to explain to whom He will show Himself: John 14:21: *"Whoever has my commands and obeys them, he is the one who loves me. He who loves me will be loved by my Father, and I too will love him and __show myself to him__"* (emphasis added).

The news media is regularly reporting there are new sightings of Mother Mary. Last year, she "showed herself" as a concrete stain on the wall of an underpass on Chicago's Kennedy Expressway. Thanks to God we have a better deal than that. He said *"I will come and show myself to you."* He's not the God who's "way up there." He has come down and will show Himself to you and me. He wants to come to you and just hang out with you and experience *Zoe* to the Max with you and love you and show himself to you. Do you believe Jesus wants to show Himself to you? Do you know that in your "know-er"?

Now look at John 14:23: *"If anyone loves me, he will obey my teaching. My Father will love him, and we will __make our home with him__"* (emphasis added).

4. We will be roommates. Wow! "Make our home with him." I started to dig into what it means to "make His home" with me. I first thought it was another way of describing how He wanted to be with us—like building a house together. Then I thought it may be another way of talking about how our bodies as the temple of God. Perhaps He wants to build a temple in us? The translation for "home" in this context is the Greek word *mone* [mon·ay]. It's only used two times in the Bible—both here in John 14. The other passage is John 14:2: *"In my Father's house are many (mone) rooms"* (parentheses added). I know many of you are familiar with the translation using "mansion" for this verse. There have been hymns and songs about our "mansion just over the hilltop," but, unfortunately, the word "mansion" selected by the King James scholars has changed meaning over the past 400 years. Mansion now means "a huge, luxurious, costly house." *Mone* does not mean mansion. It is "a place of dwelling together, a place where people come together and stay together," but it is NOT the word for "house" or for "mansion."[3]

The root, *meno* [men·o], is translated as "remain or abide together."[4] That's the word used in John 15 when Jesus teaches us He is like the true vine, and we are the branches that need to (*meno*) remain in Him. *Mone* is a place where people room together, stay together and remain together. It not about a huge, mansion/house; it is a place where God wants to meet together with us.

So, let's put it all together. Jesus and the Father want to come to you, AND to make their room together, and to stay together—to make their *mone*, their home, WITH you. In other words, God wants be your roommate! Woo who! The Father and the Son want to come into you and me and set up a home together with us. They want us to live together—to stay together—to be roommates together! That is awesome, but there's more!

<u>5. We will be roommates in the Father's House forever!</u>

Back up in John 14:2-3: *"There are many rooms (mones) in my Father's house; I would not tell you this if it were not true. I am going there to prepare a place for you. 3 After I go and prepare a place for you, I will come back and take you to be with me so that you may be where I am"* (parentheses added).

Let me break this down for you. There are many *mones*—"room-mate locations"—in the Father's HOUSE. The Greek word for "house" is *oikia* [oy·kee·ah]: 1. a house; 1a. an inhabited edifice, a dwelling; 1b. the inmates of a house, the family; 1c. property, wealth, goods.[5]

So our Father does have a really big mansion/house (*oikia*), but it contains many *mones* where WE WILL ROOM! But notice Jesus goes on to say, "I go to prepare a place for you." The word "place" is the Greek word *topos* [top·os], which means a place; any portion or space marked off, as it were from surrounding space.[6] In other words, Jesus is preparing special places, "spaces marked off," for us to room in the Father's big house. I know my typically American independent mindset likes the thought of an individual, big "mansion" of my own that is separate from everyone else's—a place where I will have autonomy and privacy. But what Jesus is telling us is much better than that: We will all live INSIDE the Father's big house in specially "marked off" places just for us where we can room together with God and our other family members forever! It will be more like "The Waltons" house than the Trump mansion. We will be IN family forever! Or as Scott Marshall, my small-group pastor, says, "in community." God literally wants us to live in His house with His family forever! What a God! What a Father. That's "waaay mo' betta" than living in a mansion by myself!

Incredible Opportunity

This God, who is incredibly good, wants to spend time with us every day. He wants to bless us by adopting us in to His family and then He wants to come to us and show Himself to us and make his *mone* with us. He wants to be roommates with us every day and throughout all of eternity! Woo who!

It's awesome to think about our *mone* in the sky by and by, but I want to remind you that you are here in the "now and now," and God wants to make His *mone* with you NOW. He wants to room-up with you every day of your life and then, when your *bios* is over, take you to His house where you can room with Him forever! So the question is:

Why do we want to go to heaven to be with Him and yet neglect the opportunity that we have now to be with Him?

I want to challenge you to learn to enjoy the presence of God in your *mone* every day—NOW.

Secret Place

In Psalm 91, David calls his *mone* with God his "secret place:" *"He who dwells in the secret place of the Most High shall abide under the shadow of the Almighty"* (Psalm 91:1 New King James Version). The New International Version (NIV) uses the word "shelter" rather than "secret place." I prefer the translator's choice in the New King James Version of "secret place." The Hebrew word is *cether* [say·ther], which is translated: 1. covering, shelter, hiding place, secrecy; 2. protection."[7] However, when you study how it is used in other places in the Old Testament, you see it always describes a secret hiding place where a covert conversation can be held in safety. For example, when Jonathan warned David about his father Saul's evil intentions, he said, *"My father Saul is looking for a chance to kill you. Be on your guard tomorrow morning; go into (cether) hiding and stay there"* (1 Samuel 19:2, parentheses added).

In other places, *cether* is used as a secret message or secret action, such as Deuteronomy 27:15: *"Cursed is the man who carves an image or casts an idol—a thing detestable to the Lord, the work of the craftsman's hands—and sets it up in secret* (cether). *Then all the people shall say, 'Amen!'"* (parentheses added).

Our *mone* is this *cether*—a secret place of hiding and protection. We meet with our God in this secret place, and there we *"rest in the shadow of the Almighty."*

How to Have a Daily Mone with God?

My normal *mone* begins in the sunroom at the back of my house. There God and Jesus and I come together in intimate connection together as the vine and the branch reconnect and the sap begins to flow to me. What a great concept—God coming to be roommates with you and me every day!

I begin by seeking to be filled with the Spirit of God until I am fulfilled. Ephesians 5:18 tells us, *"Do not get drunk on wine, which leads to debauchery. Instead, be filled with the Spirit."* The analogy here compares being drunk with alcohol to being filled with the Spirit. We are not to get drunk on alcohol because it causes us to lose control of ourselves, which leads to debauchery. I spoke with a new Christian recently who shared that in her past she was so under the control of alcohol that many times she would find herself unable to remember anything that had happened, much less control herself when drunk on alcohol. That's what alcohol does. The more you drink it, the more it takes control of you. Instead of drinking wine and coming under the control of alcohol, we are admonished to drink of the Spirit of God until we "get drunk" on the Spirit. Not drinking "spirits" but drinking THE Spirit. That is what we are to do every day—get drunk on The Spirit!

That's my goal for my daily mone with God—to drink of Him until I am drunk WITH Him. I seek to get filled until I sense I am fulfilled. I don't start out that way. Each morning I am dragging around, and I don't feel joy or peace or excitement or *Zoe* to the Max! Sometimes I feel tired, depressed, or bored.

Each morning, I need a new drink of *Zoe* water—a fresh portion of *Zoe* Bread. Everything I need to live this supernatural *Zoe* to the Max life, I must receive FRESH FROM GOD, daily. Right now, as I am writing this section, it is the first morning of the first day of the year. I'm watching the sun rise. I desire the Son of God to rise in my heart as well. I begin with nothing, and seek to be filled with His everything. It's all about God and His love for us and His desire to have daily relationship with us. "Fill me Lord. Fill me Lord. That is the desire of my heart. Fill me with Your love and Your joy so I may experience your *Zoe* to the Max!" I begin with this kind of simple seeking. I am seeking God and expressing love for God along with prayers for a new in-filling of His Spirit—breathing in the Spirit.

Next we begin to exchange love. I express my love for Him and then I listen for Him to express His love back to me. Then I begin to thank Him for the many blessings He gives. I mix in praise for who He is: He is our awesome God, and we need to glorify Him. I love to look outside the glass doors of my sunroom as I have this *mone* so that I might take in some of the glory of His creation.

This exchange continues for the first five minutes or so until I begin to feel I am connecting with God. If I feel confused about how I am feeling after that, I may open my spiritual journal (I'll talk about the importance of journaling later) and begin to write my feelings and thoughts. I may ask the Holy Spirit to teach me whatever He wants to show me, or correct me if need be.

If my "blah-ness" continues, and I don't seem to be able to break through, I will just rest in His presence. God knows my heart, and He knows

> *It's like being with my wife: Sometimes we don't need to say anything; we just enjoy being together.*

all about my feelings. If I can't "break through" my feelings, I will then just wait in His presence. It's like being with my wife: Sometimes we don't need to say anything; we just enjoy being together. Dr. Larry Fine helped me with this concept. He showed me sometimes God wants us to just "be with Him." It's a relationship. God doesn't always want us to come seeking to receive a certain feeling. If we are only seeking a feeling, then are we really seeking God? Or are we seeking a good feeling from God? That is a piercing question. God knows we are trying to connect with Him, so whatever feeling we receive is less important that just "being with" God. Dr. Fine showed me I should be cautious of always seeking something FROM God, rather than seeking to be WITH God. He challenged me to stop coming to God with an agenda. My goal is to spend time with God, period.

Worship Idols

If I'm not careful, I find myself worshipping feelings rather than worshipping God. Feelings can become an idol. I also love to learn new concepts and ideas from God, but I must be aware that this also can become an idol for me. I can become obsessed with seeking the stimulation of learning something new from God instead of being focused on God himself. Do you see that? God wants you and me to just "be with Him." Whatever feeling we get from that should be secondary. Even if we get no feelings at all, we must not evaluate our time as bad. We must let God be God in our *mone* rather than our feelings or understanding being most important.

God does not want to be used as our heavenly vending machine—Put the prayer in the slot, pull the knob, and out comes the feelings. He is about relationship, a love relationship that is expressed in time and actions. If God wants me to just rest in His presence and not receive any change in my feelings, then I need to accept that. I love God beyond my feelings. God knows I am seeking to be with Him and that I need Him and need to be empowered by Him. He knows I love the good feelings of being loved and of joy and peace and *Zoe* to the Max! And He wants to give them to me—but He is not a vending machine.

Time for School

After this time of connection, it is time for my daily lesson from the Bible. The Holy Spirit is my teacher, and I am there to learn from Him every day. Jesus taught us this in John 14:26: *"But the Counselor, the Holy Spirit, whom the Father will send in my name, WILL TEACH YOU ALL THINGS and will remind you of everything I have said to you"* (emphasis added). The Teacher has daily lessons for you and me. Most Christians live as though they have already learned everything they need to know. They are living in

"Stupidville." They only go to school once a week when they go to church, and often they have to be force-fed there. The Teacher, however, is available to teach us every day! These daily lessons from the Word of God, which I'll teach about in the next chapter, are keys to experiencing *Zoe* to the Max!

J + P = H

During this time, I am breathing in the Holy Spirit and letting His love fill my soul. My goal is to be filled with hope and joy and peace. This is God's promise to us from Romans 15:13: *"May the God of hope fill you with all joy and peace as you trust in him, so that you may overflow with hope by the power of the Holy Spirit."* I ask the God of hope, the God who has hope and is the author of hope, to fill me will ALL joy and ALL peace so I may OVERFLOW with hope. I seek to be filled once again with the person of the Holy Spirit and with Him comes the evidential overflow of hope. That's the formula found in that verse: J+P=H. Joy plus Peace equals Hope. Joy—because the Spirit has come to make me smile. Peace—because I have given God all my problems and worries and dreaded events. As His peace fills my heart with calmness and pushes out all anxieties and whatever else is there, I am left with an overflowing, overwhelming sense of hope. That's when I have had a good time with God!!!!

This *mone* with God is often called "Time Alone with God" (TAWG), or quiet time or devotions. Those names don't seem to communicate the kind of mind-altering, mood-altering time I am talking about. Some people emerge from their "devotions" having missed meeting with God! How can you really meet with God and not be altered? I don't think it should be called devotions. I like something more like "good time with God."

A *Zoe* to the Max day begins with a "good time with God" in our *mone*. We drink of *Zoe* from the river of *Zoe* until our soul is satisfied. When I have an adequately good time with God, my day is off to a great start! Don't leave the gas station until you get your tank full!

Zoe to the Mini

A low level of relationship with God yields *Zoe* to the Mini. Minimum time spent in His Word. Minimum time spent in prayer. Minimum effort to connect with Him throughout the day—all of that adds up to what I call *Zoe* to the Mini. *Zoe* to the Mini is what many Christians settle for, but that is not what God wants for us! Jesus *"came that you might have Zoe and have it to the Max"* (John 10:10).

If you want a "good time with God," you've got to invest time in that relationship. I'm thinking of a NASCAR race and the desire of every driver to have the fastest pit stop possible. Twenty seconds, I think, is considered a good "pit stop" time. Every driver sees the pit stop as a "necessary evil." It is an interruption in the race of life.

Pit Stop Mentality

Zoe to the Mini comes from "pit stop" devotional times. If your time with God gets into the "pit stop" category, then the most you can expect to experience that day is *Zoe* to the Mini. God does not desire a "pit stop" relationship with you. Revelation 3:20: *"Behold, I stand at the door and knock; if anyone hears My voice and opens the door, I will come in to him and will dine with him, and he with Me."* We usually hear about this verse in relationship to a salvation invitation, but it teaches much more than that. It shows us the kind of ongoing relationship Jesus wants with us. He wants to sit down and have dinner with you. After He comes in, He wants to "dine with you," not "pit stop" with you. The Greek word for "dine" here is *deipneo* [dipe·neh·o].[8] Its root is *deipnon* [dipe·non], which means "supper, especially a formal meal usually held at the evening"[9] This is the word used to describe "The Last Supper." It was considered a dining experience, not a quick snack. The NIV translation, unfortunately, does a poor job of translating it as "eat with me." The Greek word for eating is *phago* [fag·o].[10] That word is used in John 4:31 as the disciples were urging Jesus to eat, *"Meanwhile his disciples urged him, "Rabbi, (phago) eat something."*

Our "good time with God" is to be the beginning of an evening meal, not a pit stop or bite to eat. Jesus wants to have an evening meal with us—a feast, a supper, together. During a dinner, there is time shared and conversation shared and food shared. Too many Christians want to have a snacking relationship with God. They want to use the "drive through window" and order a happy meal from God. Jesus has a let's-sit-down-and-share-dinner-together mentality.

I know some may be thinking, "But Tracy, I don't have that much time." I have found fifteen minutes a day is my minimum time for a good time with God. Anyone can do that. I'm not going to argue with anyone over being too busy for God. But it is usually an excuse. Mothers of babies and preschoolers have the hardest time of all. I have found, however, even most of them can find time to squeeze in their favorite television show or book. We're all busy with something, but if we are too busy for God, then something is out of order in our lives. If God is in control of our schedule, I think He can help us find time for Him. Don't you agree?

The "Sweetness" Level

Enjoying the presence of God is about love. Love takes time to express. And love takes time to kindle the intimacy to the level I call the "sweetness" level (for lack of a better term). "Sweetness" level is the level of intimacy when you become so close to God you get that "giggly" sense of His presence. It's when you know you are close to Him and that He can speak to your heart and you are listening. There your heart is: at rest and content. The "sweetness" level is hard to put in adequate terms, but I know when I have it, and I know when I don't. "Sweetness" is the level of intimacy that is built up over days and weeks of pursuing God with my whole heart. I think of the scriptures that talk about hungering and thirsting after God. It is a level of intimacy that has been kindled through consistent nurturing. It is a "with all your heart" kind of love.

God talks about this kind of love back in the beginning of the Bible. Deuteronomy 4:29: *"But if from there you seek the Lord your God, you will find him if you look for him with all your heart and with all your soul."* Seeking the Lord and finding Him is a "with all your heart" pursuit. It is at the center of what God wants most from our relationship with Him. It's also Commandment Number One: *"Love the Lord your God with all your heart and with all your soul and with all your strength"* (Deuteronomy 6:5). God's desire is to have this "with all your heart" kind of love with you and me. He loves us with a powerful "give you all" kind of love that compelled Him to leave heaven and become Immanuel (God with us). His love for us was an intense love that expressed itself best on Calvary. *"God so loved the world that He gave ..."* (John 3:16).

Currency Exchange Rate

God comes to us with this high quality kind of love and He ideally expects us to return "in-kind." This kind of love is expressed in the Greek word, *agape* [ag·ah·pay].[11] *Agape* is a with-all-your-heart kind of love. That's the kind of love God deals in. So if we want to really have relationship with Him the way He wants to have relationship with us, we must deal in the same currency. He deals in the currency of *agape.* When we seek the Lord with all our hearts and souls, then God responds because we are speaking His language—we are dealing in His currency—we are on His level of *agape.* When we connect with God on the *agape* level of love, we experience the "sweetness" level of relationship.

Therefore, when we slip from exchanging *agape* to some lower level of love because of some distraction, we lose that "sweetness" level of intimacy. I believe "sweetness" level can be entered into and maintained as long as we continue to exchange on the with-all-your-heart *agape* level. I've just realized that over the years, when I have neglected pursuing the "sweetness" for a period of time and have gotten distracted by projects or other "good" things, the "sweetness" level begins to diminish.

And by the way, we can't turn the "sweetness level" on and off like a light switch. When busyness and distractions divert our hearts from God for a period of time and then we decide we want the "sweetness" to revert to intimacy, I find it doesn't come back

> **When we get distracted from God, it seems to me He is "hurt" by our neglect of relationship with Him.**

instantly. When we get distracted from God, it seems to me He is "hurt" by our neglect of relationship with Him. I know that God is not a human, and I understand that it is not possible to explain God in human terms, but my experience has been that the relationship is "hurt" in some way by my neglect. I know He has not abandoned me; rather, I have demoted our relationship. He has promised to never leave me nor forsake me, but the "sweetness" level is not there. It loses that "giggly" feeling of intimacy that is so energizing.

It's like the old coal-fired steam engines—as long as the guy is scooping in shovels of coal, the fire stays hot and the steam rolls out. In the same way, when I start my days with a good shovelful of pursuing God until I hit the "sweetness" level, the steam of *Zoe* rolls!

And if I am flowing in the *Zoe* Zone and shoveling in other scoops, I continue the connection and love with my Jesus throughout the day. This is maintaining the "sweetness-level" edge! I love days like that! And day after day of that turns into week after week of "sweetness," which is *Zoe* to the Max!

Revival does not need to be an annual or special series of meetings followed by a back-to-normal-life season. God wants us to stay in a continuous state of intimacy and passionate love with Him. That is what "normal" Christianity is supposed to be. The "sweetness" level is God's plan for us every day if we will keep "scooping in" all of our heart's passion.

In the later parts of this book, I will show you how to rekindle the "sweetness" level. But for now, I want you to see a *Zoe* to the Max day begins with a good time with God when we dine with Him. We nourish our souls with His Word for the day. We exchange *agape* and renew the "sweetness" level of relationship. It is then we continue that "sweetness" level throughout the day.

Morning, Noon or Night?

I have heard the discussion of whether "devotions" or, as I call it, my "good time with God" should be held in the morning, or whenever you get a chance during the day, or at night before you go to bed. As you can conclude from the previous section, some kind of morning connection is essential. I know people are different. Some are "morning people" and some are "night owls." I am a night owl who gradually converted to a morning person. The reason I converted was because I saw the huge advantage it gave to my spiritual life with God throughout the day. It just makes sense if you get connected to God properly in the morning, the connection can continue on throughout the day. When I previously had my "devotions" at night, it was just that—devotions. I read my Bible with tired eyes and said a short prayer before I turned off the light, rolled over, and went to sleep.

The problem with that time of day is twofold. I was usually tired at the end of a long day so I would often nod off as I read or prayed. I remember my college roommate, Steve Hood. He was a devoted Christian brother who would pray on his knees before getting into bed at night. He would often fall asleep in this kneeling position beside his bed. I would come into the dorm sometimes and find him asleep on his knees. Of course, I couldn't let that opportunity go by without poking a little fun at him. "Have you prayed through yet, Steve?" Or sometimes I would shake him and startle him awake. He would usually mumble something like he was NOT asleep and then either get into bed or sometimes fall asleep on his knees again!

The second problem I had with having "devotions" at night was it was always AFTER the important events of the day. Doesn't it make sense to fill up your tank BEFORE you leave on a day-long trip? Otherwise, you will run out of gas. And that is exactly what kept happening to me. I was always playing catch up. My evening devotions ended up being post-game evaluations of how I had "played" that day. There were a lot of confessional times over failures and determinations to improve the next day.

I eventually negotiated a short five-minute morning-focus time. My morning prayer continued during my ride time and as I walked to class. I found as I called on God before the events of the day I had strength for those events. I also learned the power of scripture memorization, and I started to live with more *Zoe* in my life. Those short morning "snacks" I crammed into my schedule gradually grew as I hungered for more time with God and I eventually scheduled more time until I started experiencing "good times with God" in the mornings. That necessitated me going to bed a little earlier so I was not in a "morning coma."

Devotional Drudge

How stubborn I was for so many years of my Christian life! I was so busy, I didn't take time for really connecting with God on a daily basis. I would work or study, but I wasn't showing love to God. I did not appreciate or explore all the fun that exists in the area of intimacy. I had a working relationship with God, but failed to take advantage of the joy and *Zoe* that is found IN the intimacy area. I was a strong Christian, and highly committed to walking righteously and did everything most Christians do. My one area of glaring weakness was in this area of daily devotions.

The Holy Spirit tried to draw me in and show me I was neglecting spending time loving Him. I journaled many times about what the Spirit was saying to me. For example, on July 8, 1996, I wrote: *"Yesterday in the service for the 40 millionth time, the precious Spirit of God spoke to my heart concerning my lack of special time/romance time with Him. I opened my Bible to wherever it opened and it was Mark 9:14 19. The disciples couldn't cast a demon out of a little kid and Jesus was frustrated with them. It was not the demon or the people that frustrated him—it was His disciples....*

Today I make a new start to be consistent in my worship time. Not just "Tracy," the diligent harvester, who loves to work on messages and research, but "Tracy," child of God, is loved by His Father. It's like my daughters. I want them to be more affectionate with me. Jesus wants Me!!!!! Just think of that. He wants to spend time with me, and was chastising me for not spending more time loving Him!!! What a God I serve!"

I'm ashamed now of how many of those journal entries were about my struggles in the area that now gives me the most joy! How could I have been so stubborn and stupid for so long? I guess it goes to show that experiencing *Zoe* to the Max is not automatic—it's a lifelong learning experience as we get closer and closer to learning how to overcome self and how to live this life in Christ.

At first, I thought it was a self-discipline problem: that I didn't have enough self-control. Then I thought it was a priority problem with my preference for watching news over having my time with God. Then I thought it was workaholism with my preference for studying the Bible or working on some writing project or preparing for some church event. If I were on some Bible study project, I would have no problem digging into the Greek words or doing cross-reference studies, but to just spend time in His presence was not exciting enough for me. Then, sadly, I concluded it was A LOVE ISSUE. I just didn't love God enough to spend time with Him. Boy, it was a sad conclusion, but it was true. If I loved God more, I would want to spend more time with Him, right? You would think the discovery would have changed everything, but it didn't. It just identified the problem, but not the solution.

The Solution Emerges

The solution came when I began to pursue *Zoe* to the Max! I would like to say to those of you who are still struggling with your "quiet time" or "having devotions" or whatever you call it, that I, too, had trouble in this area. God was trying to teach me my time with Him was supposed to be MUTUALLY enjoyable. As long as I was there out of duty, or self-control, or even to worship or love God, it was not a two-way thing. I thought devotions were all about God, so it felt selfish when I started to seek enjoyment FROM God as part of my quiet time with Him. When I began to understand the mission of Jesus was about teaching me how to experience *Zoe* to the Max my devotion time took on a whole new meaning. I realized my reluctance to having devotions was that it was boring. I was there only to give God something, and not to receive. When I understood God wanted it to be a two-way exchange of love, I was onto something! A love relationship is an exchange of love. I wasn't just "serving God"—God wanted me to experience more *Zoe* in all areas of my life!

Go to Bed!

Because of my night-owl tendencies, one of my real-life struggles was to make myself go to bed early. I eventually learned to resist the temptation to start any new projects after 9 pm. I also started watching the news at 10 pm rather than at 11 pm. And I discovered the late news is always repeated the next morning anyway. It came down to making my morning time a priority and learning the self-discipline to shut myself down and go to bed.

Control the Distractions!

One of my other struggles was with watching too much morning news. I tend to be a news addict in general, and watching news would encroach on my time with God. I have learned it is better for me to watch the news first thing as I am waking myself up. While I am brewing my Starbucks and watching news, I monitor the time to make sure it does not go much longer than about 15 minutes. Otherwise I am more interested in hearing the news than in hearing God. As I look back over my journal writings, they are often filled with my frustrations over letting other things come in and steal my morning time with God.

My Work for God Was Hindering My Love of God

My most recent struggle has been over spending that morning time on church projects instead of seeking God. I would let my "work for God" take away from the "work of God" in me. I reasoned doing church work was God's work, so it was okay to focus on it. The Spirit taught me the error of that. Working FOR God is not the same as spending time WITH God. Those who are in full-time church ministry can testify to learning that. I need my time with God so my strength is renewed to do the work of God for that day.

Once I learned God wanted a two-way exchange and He wants me to experience His "sweetness" level every morning, it motivated me. Once my day starts right, I am set for whatever happens that day. Prayer became the maintaining of that "sweetness" level throughout the day.

Prayer Continuation

Prayer, then, is not a periodic call for help, but a continuation of the "sweetness" level that was begun in the morning. That is what I think "pray without ceasing" means: The passage teaches us in 1 Thessalonians 5:17-18 to *"pray continually; give thanks in all circumstances, for this is God's will for you in Christ Jesus."* I found that to "pray continually" naturally flows once I have begun my day with my "good time with God." Continual prayer is an extension of enjoying my "sweetness" of relationship with God. He offers me "free, anytime minutes." I can enjoy His presence throughout the day because God wants to interact with me throughout the day. Continual prayer is not meant to be a "show-stopping" event. It doesn't mean we have to pull out a prayer rug, kneel down or bow down. I talk with God in a continual conversation in my spirit. It's like tuning into a favorite radio station and keeping it there all day.

WZOE

Radio waves are invisible to the eye, but they are real nonetheless. If you turn a radio on right now, undoubtedly you would be able to pick up several stations. You could choose music from rock to country to classical. All of those radio waves are going through the air at the same time, but you cannot hear them unless you have a radio and tune it into a specific frequency. You CHOOSE to turn it on, and you CHOOSE to tune it in. Our communication with God is like that. We can choose to begin our days by tuning into God and then we can choose to continue listening all day long. It's like setting our radios to W-Z-O-E. WZOE is God's channel, and we need to tune into that frequency and keep it on that frequency all day.

The problem comes when other people or circumstances try to change the channel. I'm sure we have all had that disagreement with someone over changing radio stations. It is our job to retune our own internal radio receivers back to WZOE throughout the day. Turn it on and tune it in because God wants to share your whole day with you. He doesn't just want a morning "devotional" with you. He wants to live your life with you! He wants to share the events of the day together with you. Let me explain what I mean by that.

Acts 17:28

When I was in college, I attended Nashville First Church of the Nazarene, which happened to be the home church of the Christian author and speaker, Bob Benson, who is now deceased. He was the teacher for my Sunday School class! At the time, I did not comprehend I had a famous author and speaker as a teacher. He was a wonderful person, but to listen to him was difficult for an immature college student with A.D.D. I later understood he was teaching us the scriptures he would write about in his books. He was fleshing out the concepts with us as weekly Bible lessons. One of the passages he was excited about at the time has since become one of my favorite bible verses. Acts 17:28: *"For in him we live and move and have our being"*. He talked about what it means for us to "share in the very being of Christ." In fact, he titled his book <u>Come Share the Being</u>.

Bob planted that verse in my mind, and years later when I revisited it, I discovered what he was excited about back then. In Christ we *Zoe*! We experience *Zoe* by living our lives in, and through, Him. He wants to be an intricate part of our everyday life. In Him, we *Zoe*.

When I am thirsty—God is the water of *Zoe*.

When I am hungry–God is the bread of *Zoe*.

When I need guidance–God is the light of *Zoe*.

Christ in Our Mundane

Then Acts 17:28 goes on to say, *"In Him we Zoe and move ...."* This means we move through our everyday actions with Christ. We get in our cars, and we move in Christ. The Greek word for "move" is *kineo* [kin·eh·o], which is familiar to me from my science background. Kinetic energy is the energy of motion. *Kineo* means: "1a. to set in motion, to be moved, move; of that motion which is evident in life; 1b. to move from a place, to remove."[11] Christ moves with us. He moves in us, and He moves us. We don't meet Him at church and then leave Him there until next week. He wants to move with us everywhere we go and be involved with us in everything we do. That's why the Lord's Prayer contains the rather mundane request "give us this day our daily bread." Christ wants be involved in our DAILY needs and movements TODAY. *Zoe* to the Max is moving in Christ every day in our mundane movements.

Zoe to the Max is incorporating God into the details. There is a commonly used expression, "the devil is in the details," but I say God wants to be helping us in the details and experiencing us in the details. God wants us to be in Him as we "move" and "have our being." That's talking about our identity and our foundation and our purpose. God wants to be all about us, and He wants us to be all about Him. I often encounter people who are reluctant to pray about the mundane things. "They seem too small, too trivial for Him to worry with," they say. This is a misunderstanding of how intimate Christ wants to be with us. He wants to live our lives WITH US, in all its mundane activities. *Zoe* to the Max is about understanding this and allowing Christ to *Zoe* in us in all our mundane moments.

Knowing God Is Experiencing God

So enjoying the presence of God means incorporating Him into the everyday fabric of our lives and experiencing and knowing Him better each day. Eternal *Zoe* is experiencing God eternally. Jesus said this in His prayer in John 17:2-3, *"For you granted him authority over all people that he might give eternal life to all those you have given him. Now this is eternal (Zoe) life: that they may know you, the only true God, and Jesus Christ, whom you have sent."* Eternal *Zoe* is experienced as we "know" God and Jesus. The Greek word for "knowing" is *ginosko* [ghin·oce·ko]—to learn to know, come to know, get a knowledge of perceive, feel.[12] In comparing it to other Greek synonyms, it differs in that it is "a knowledge grounded in personal experience." This "knowing" is not just mental acknowledgement—it is personal, experiential knowledge. It is knowledge based on personal experience. So eternal *Zoe* is enjoying and experiencing God every day in every way.

Romancing God

This morning as I was journaling, it was evident I needed a personal renewing of the sweetness level. Last week I never really took time to break through to the sweetness level. I don't know why I allow it to happen, but I do. I let the busyness of my *bios* steal the max out of my *Zoe*! God is not a thing. He is not an item or a gasoline station. He is a person. You have a relationship with a person. When we "break through" to a level of intimacy, it is more like romancing than digging. But it is not like a romance with a spouse: it is a romance between a child and father. We were made to be His sons and daughters. We were made to be in intimate relationship with our Father God. We were not made to BE God, but to be His children. We were not made to be His slaves. When we neglect intimacy, we do not lose our position as His child, but the intensity and closeness of our relationship with Him is diminished. Romancing and seeking Him to restore the sweetness of our relationship takes time and heart.

Getting into the *Zoe* Zone requires we learn to really enjoy the presence of our Father on a moment-by-moment basis. We are happiest and function best when we are deeply loving our Father at the "sweetness level" each day, and enjoying Him and knowing Him and experiencing Him each day. Enjoying the presence of God is essential to living *Zoe* to the Max because *Zoe* comes from God and *Zoe* flows out of enjoying His presence.

Chapter 12: *Zoe* Zone Part 2—*Zoe* Word

To enter the *Zoe* Zone, first we must learn to really enjoy the presence of God on a day-by-day, moment-by-moment basis. Enjoying God's presence begins by correcting our distorted image of God and realizing how much He loves us and wants to spend time with us. Therefore, we begin each day with a "good time with God" and then keep tuning and retuning to WZOE throughout the day.

The second area of importance in entering and maintaining the *Zoe* Zone is to receive our daily *Zoe* Word. Each day, the Holy Spirit has a special word for you from God's Word that will help, instruct, encourage or guide you. God has a specific *Zoe* Word for you that will empower you daily. This *Zoe* Word is for your nourishment throughout the day. Your connection to the *Zoe* of God is fueled by continual communication with God (WZOE) and continual nourishment from His Word. It takes both prayer and a *Zoe* Word to have a complete connection with God. This allows us to experience *Zoe* to the Max! Having your *Zoe* Word fuels prayer throughout the day.

The phrase "*Zoe* Word" comes from Jesus in John 6:63: "*The Spirit gives (Zoe) life; the flesh counts for nothing. The words I have spoken to you are spirit and they are (Zoe) life*" (parentheses added). The words of Jesus are spirit and *Zoe*. The words of Jesus have *Zoe* power—not just random words from the Bible, but a specific Word that the Holy Spirit gives to you for that day or event. Thus the phrase "*Zoe* Word" means the specific Word of God given to you by the Holy Spirit for each day.

The Greek word for "word" in the above verse is *rhema* [hray·mah]: "that which is or has been uttered by the living voice; thing spoken; word."[1] The *rhema* is the spoken word. The spoken words of Jesus produce *Zoe*. These spoken words were then written down by the apostles and became the written Word of God. The written Word of God then contains the *Zoe* producing *rhema* of God. Hebrews 4:12: "*For the word of God is living and active. Sharper than any double-edged sword, it penetrates even to dividing soul and spirit, joints and marrow; it judges the thoughts and attitudes of the heart."* The Word of God is living, and that Greek word for "living" in this verse is the root for *Zoe*. The Word of God is *Zoe*! It is living because it contains the *Zoe* (life-giving) words of God. It is alive! *Zoe* alive!

Parakletos—Our Personal Mentor

So the Word of God is powerful and alive, but it is even more powerful when we have a personal mentor to teach us how to understand and apply the Word of God. Jesus told us about our personal mentor in John 14. Remember, this is the section (chapters 13 thru 17) where Jesus gives "going away" instructions to His disciples. He tells them the Father will send the Holy Spirit who will stay with them always and be their teacher, guide and helper. John 14:15-17: *"If you love me, you will obey what I command. And I will ask the Father, and he will give you another Counselor to be with you forever—the Spirit of truth. The world cannot accept him, because it neither sees him nor knows him. But you know him, for he lives with you and will be in you"* (parentheses added).

Parakletos [par·ak·lay·tos] is an interesting word in the Greek language that is translated in different ways by different translators. It is translated as "Comforter" in the King James Version and "Counselor" in the New International Version. Others use "Helper" or "Advocate."[2] *The Theological Dictionary of the New Testament* defines it as "one summoned, called to one's side, especially called to one's aid." The best English words seem to be Helper or Supporter or Assister.[3] Later John uses *Parakletos* to refer to Jesus in 1 John 2:1 when he says, *"My dear children, I write this to you so that you will not sin. But if anybody does sin, we have (Parakletos) one who speaks to the Father in our defense—Jesus Christ, the Righteous One"* (parentheses added). Here some translate it as "Advocate" expressing the help as being more as a lawyer or legal aide. That is probably why the NIV translators settled on the translation "Counselor" for use in John 14 and 16.

As our personal mentor, *Parakletos* is available to give us specific instruction and training to handle different situations and live *Zoe* to the Max! If I am facing an unclear decision, my personal mentor is there for me to call upon. He is my "Helper" and "Counselor" so

I call on Him for wisdom and guidance. What an awesome mentor we have! *Parakletos* is there to help us, but we must take advantage of His presence in our lives.

Parakletos—Our Personal Teacher

With this information as a background, let's see what Jesus said about this *Parakletos*. We've already seen He is "the Spirit of truth". Then in John 14:25-26: *"All this I have spoken while still with you. But the (Parakletos) Counselor, the Holy Spirit, whom the Father will send in my name, will teach you all things and will remind you of everything I have said to you"* (parentheses and emphasis added). *Parakletos*, then, is the third member of the Holy Trinity—The Holy Spirit. The Holy Spirit is our *Parakletos*—the one "called alongside to aid us." He is there to come beside us and be our personal teacher and mentor! Did you get that? God has sent you a personal teacher, a personal mentor and trainer!

This personal mentor is such a powerful thing to me because it has positive implications for so many areas in my life. I don't have to know what to do—*Parakletos* will show me. I don't have to understand everything—*Parakletos* will teach me. I don't have to wander around without direction—*Parakletos* will guide me. Even if I am called on to defend my faith in front of some sort of powerful person or institution or media person, *Parakletos* will give me the words to say. Jesus told us that in Luke 12:11-12: *"When you are brought before synagogues, rulers and authorities, do not worry about how you will defend yourselves or what you will say, for the* **Holy Spirit will teach you** *at that time what you should say"* (emphasis added). The Holy Spirit is our mentor! He is the *Parakletos* sent to be our personal teacher. He is "The Spirit of Truth," so naturally He will teach us truth.

In John 15, Jesus again refers to *Parakletos* as *"the Spirit of truth."* John 15:26: *"When the Counselor (Parakletos) comes, whom I will send to you from the Father, the Spirit of truth who goes out from the Father, he will testify about me"* (parentheses added). Here we see *Parakletos* will proclaim Jesus as the Son of God. In this verse you see all three persons of the Trinity working together.

In John 16, Jesus tells us more of the advantages of having *Parakletos*. John 16:7: *"But I tell you the truth: It is for your good that I am going away. Unless I go away, the Counselor (Parakletos) will not come to you; but if I go, I will send him to you"* (parentheses added). Jesus had to return to the Father in order for the *Parakletos* to be able to come. I don't really understand why that is so. I think it was because the transaction of salvation needed to be completed by His death, resurrection, and ascension back to the Father. I don't think we'll fully understand that kind of statement until Jesus can explain it to us face to face.

Jesus also uses the Greek word *sumphero* [soom·fer·o] which is translated in the NIV as "it is for your good" [that *Parakletos* is coming]. The word *sumphero* means "good, profitable, better, expedient, helpful or advantageous."[4,5] Most translations I have studied choose either "better" or "advantageous." I agree with those choices because when you study how the word *sumphero* is used elsewhere in the New Testament, the sentences seem to make more sense when substituting the word "better" or "advantageous" than simply "for your good." That distinction may not seem significant, but if the coming of the Holy Spirit is "for our good," that is positive. But if "it is better for you," that is more advantageous.

The advantage of having the Holy Spirit as our *Parakletos* is He can be with us everywhere, all the time, as compared to Jesus who (in His flesh) could only be one place at a time. Back in John 14:17, we saw this distinction: *"But you know him, for he lives **with** you and will **be in you**"* (emphasis added). Apparently prior to the death, burial, and resurrection of Jesus, and the day of Pentecost fifty days later, the Holy Spirit was WITH believers, but after Pentecost the Holy Spirit was IN the believers. That's better! We have a full-time, live-in, personal mentor and teacher!

Shucks, we have our own personal trainer 24/7!

I don't think we fully appreciate the presence of *Parakletos* in our lives. He is there to help us—to help us as a personal mentor and to do some personal training and teaching. Hiring a "personal trainer" is the "in" thing for the rich and famous. Shucks, we have our own personal trainer 24/7! He is there to mold our character and give us wisdom and specific guidance. I often call on His help for decisions about what I should do, and I listen for His voice to guide me. I also lean hard on Him for new lessons and insights into God's Word. The insights you see in this book are the product of my personal teacher—my *Parakletos*, and He is now teaching it to you as well! Praise God and woo who!

Holy Spirit's Ministry to the World

The Holy Spirit has this ministry to believers and also a ministry to the world: *"When he comes, he will convict the world of guilt in regard to sin and righteousness and judgment: in regard to sin, because men do not believe in me; in regard to righteousness, because I am going to the Father, where you can see me no longer; and in regard to judgment, because the prince of this world now stands condemned"* (John 16:8-11). The Holy Spirit will show the world their sinfulness so they can know they need God to forgive them. He will also convict the world of righteousness—showing them there is a right way of living and a wrong way. Finally, the Holy Spirit will convict the world of impending judgment.

Parakletos—Personal Guidance

In John 12, Jesus redirects His comments to the ministry of *Parakletos* to believers. John 16:12: *"I have much more to say to you, more than you can now bear."* Wow, there is a lot you can read between the lines. I wonder what He would have said? Jesus had much more He wanted to say to His disciples, but they were not able to understand it or take it in at that time. But in the next sentence, He gives us good news. John 16:13: *"But when he, the Spirit of truth, comes, he will guide you into all truth."* Praise God! The Spirit of truth (*Parakletos*) will teach us the things Jesus wanted to teach them. It began with the Spirit of truth reminding the apostles of what Jesus had said so they could accurately record the Gospels (John 14:26: *"He will remind you of everything I have said to you."*) The Spirit also gave new revelations to Paul and the other New Testament authors so they could record the additional teachings. Now He wants to teach us from what has been written, but I believe *Parakletos* is still guiding us to all truth today. The only truth we can know for certain is "The Truth" as written in the Bible. The Bible is our only reliable source of Truth; however, I also believe the Holy Spirit is still active in the world revealing additional Truth to us today. However, none of that Truth should EVER contradict or supercede the written

Word. But it can explain and broaden our understanding of the original written Word. Groups like the Mormons try to elevate their book to the level of the Holy Scriptures, and that is definite heresy. Revelation 22:18-19 clearly warns against adding to or taking away from the Word of God. Spiritual discernment is needed in reading books other than the Bible. I believe the Holy Spirit inspires writers today who are declaring truth about many subjects. These writers teach and inspire us to new levels of understanding. These books are clearly inspired by the Holy Spirit and give great insight into understanding the things of God and our understanding of ourselves and how to relate to others. At the same time, there are books that are off-base, misleading or deceptive.

I know some folks who spend too much time reading other Christian books and neglect God's Word. Nothing should take preeminence over the Word. Books should be a supplement, not a substitute.

Individual Lessons

The teaching ministry of *Parakletos* also includes individual instruction. This instruction, too, must be considered carefully, because we are susceptible to deceiving ourselves or being deceived by others. Whenever someone says to me, "God told me to tell you …" I listen with healthy suspicion. Humans are fallible; I am fallible. I hope I don't write something wrong in this book by I may! You and I may think God has told us something when it was really just indigestion from the pizza we ate last night!

I always examine and reexamine anything I think the Spirit is telling me. Of course, it must line up with the written Word, so that's why I feel most comfortable with anything that comes to me during the time I am reading or meditating on God's Word. If it comes to me outside of that time, I consider it very carefully. However, with all that being said, *Parakletos* teaches me regularly from a variety of sources, and I have become quite comfortable over the years with my ability to discern His voice. Jesus taught that His sheep recognize His voice in John 10:4-5: *"When he has brought out all his own, he goes on ahead of them, and his sheep follow him because they know his voice. But they will never follow a stranger; in fact, they will run away from him because they do not recognize a stranger's voice."*

You Have a Good Teacher, But Are You a Good Student?

Parakletos is your teacher, but are you learning? A teacher has a hard time teaching someone who isn't trying to learn. How eager are you to learn? What have you learned recently from your teacher? When asked, most Christians have trouble coming up with anything they have learned recently. Is it because the Holy Spirit is not teaching? No, I think it's because they haven't been good students. Good students are motivated to learn. Are you a motivated student? Ask God to help you be more motivated! Paul said the believers from Berea were motivated to learn. Acts 17:11: *"Now the Bereans were of more noble character than the Thessalonians, for they received the message with great eagerness and examined the Scriptures every day to see if what Paul said was true."* When I meet with God each day, I ask *Parakletos* to teach me from the Scriptures. That is the promise of Jesus: *"The Holy Spirit, whom the Father will send in my name,* ***will teach you all things ...***" (John 14:26, emphasis added). He is the one who is to be our teacher. That is His desire. He wants to teach us something every day. Do you want to learn something every day? Jesus said in Matthew 5:6, *"Blessed are those who hunger and thirst for righteousness, for they will be filled."* I think when we come to God and our hunger for Him, and to "know" Him better, and to learn from His Word, is stirred, we will be blessed by being satisfied.

Off the Bottle?

"Grow up and act like an adult!" I can't tell you how many times I have been told that in my life! I've been a fun-loving guy my whole life, and I am often given to comedy and attention-getting stunts and joking comments. This has drawn the criticism of some who wish me to be more serious. And just about every one of us has heard the phrase "Grow up and act your age!"

When it comes to spiritual maturity, the Bible says to "Grow up and act your age!" Often times I think God is frustrated with us because of our lack of maturity. He wants us to grow up and be a more adult, mature Christian. 1 Corinthians 3:1-3: *"Brothers, I could not address you as spiritual but as worldly—mere infants in Christ. I gave you milk, not solid food, for you were not yet ready for it. Indeed, you are still not ready. You are still worldly. For since there is jealousy and quarreling among you, are you not worldly? Are you not acting like mere men?"*

Paul differentiates here between Christians who are on two ends of the spectrum of spiritual development. On one end are the spiritual infants who are "on the bottle," and on the other end are those who are taking solid foods because they are fully mature spiritual adults. God's Word is spiritual food for us. It contains everything we need to grow up spiritually and become adults—mature believers. It contains the beginning, simple "milk" all the way to the complex "solid foods" that require thinking and chewing and digesting. If we are going to grow more mature, we need to learn how to feed ourselves the solid foods of the Bible.

I made a comedy video for church recently to illustrate our need for solid food. The video started with me warming up a bottle of milk for a lunch I was hosting for "a couple friends." I handed the bottle to my 9-month old friend Hudson Marshall who took it readily. Then the camera panned over to my other friend, 21-year-old Dave Janosik, who pretended to be a "big baby" and took the bottle too! Next I served baby food to Hudson who hadn't yet developed the motor skills to feed himself well. I spoon fed him while challenging him to feed himself. Then I did the same for Dave who, acting as a baby, also had trouble feeding himself, but then got the hang of it. Our next course was a huge red apple which Hudson did not seem to know how to handle. He could not manage to pick it up, nor did his newly erupted teeth allow him to really bite into it. Dave, on the other hand, bit in aggressively while showing off his adult teeth to Hudson. The main entrée was a Big Mac that seemed almost as big as Hudson's head. He didn't know how to handle such a huge burger so he pulled off the top bun. I helped him get a grip on the sides of the burger, but he ended up mashing it into one big pile of hamburger mush. In contrast, Dave devoured his Big Mac saying, "I'm lovin' it!"

...handle the Big Macs of God's Word.

All of us start out as baby Christians who need the "milk" of the Word to grow. But after being on milk for a while, we need to wean off it and begin to take on the skills to handle more solid foods until we can finally handle the Big Macs of God's Word. The bottom line is this: If you don't learn how to feed yourself, you'll end up a spiritual big baby. The Bible talks about this in Hebrews 5:11-6:1: *"We have much to say about this, but it is hard to explain because you are slow to learn. In fact, though by this time you ought to be teachers, you need someone to teach you the elementary truths of God's word all over again. YOU NEED MILK, NOT SOLID FOOD! Anyone who lives on milk, being still an infant, is not acquainted with the teaching about righteousness. But SOLID FOOD IS FOR THE MATURE, who by constant use have trained themselves to distinguish good from evil. Therefore let us leave the elementary teachings about Christ and GO ON TO MATURITY..."* (emphasis added).

Go on to maturity! Don't you want to be mature? Let's "grow up and act like an adult" and leave those "big baby" days behind! We don't want to look like Dave sucking on a bottle! We need to develop our motor skills and our eye-hand coordination and open wide and use our spiritual incisors to incise and our molars to mash and chew those Big Macs that are in God's Word and digest them. Then we can grow up and start acting like adults.

Getting a Grip on the Bible

The milk of the Word is found by simply listening to or reading the Bible. In order to get the solid foods, we need to learn to study the Bible. I learned a useful illustration about Bible study from a parachurch organization called The Navigators. They taught me "The Hand Illustration." The five fingers of our hand each represent a different way of getting a hold of God's Word.

<u>**Listening is the pinky finger.**</u> Listening is the beginning method of getting hold of God's Word. Listening can be done in person—like listening in church. It can be through someone teaching the Word in small group, or on the radio, through CD, or the television. Listening to God's Word is helpful, but if your only input method for the Word of God is listening, then you will have a hard time grasping God's Word and growing up. Most spiritual big babies only get "spoon fed" once a week at church. If you are going to "grow up and act like an adult" you're going to need a better grip on God's Word. You need to add that second finger.

<u>**Reading is the ring finger.**</u> The next level is reading—either a passage or chapter or entire books or the whole Bible. Some people read a chapter or two a day. That gives the "big picture" of the Bible, the

big concepts and themes. To me, reading is like scanning the Bible. If you never go deeper than reading the Bible, you are passing over a lot of solid food. I first scan a chapter or book looking for a passage the Holy Spirit wants me to study. Then I stop and begin to study, and this is the next finger of the Hand Illustration.

<u>**Studying is the middle finger.**</u> Study is where I get most of "the good stuff." Have you ever been to Niagara Falls? I could open a map and show you Niagara Falls is just north of Buffalo, New York. After seeing it on the map, have you really seen Niagara Falls? No. Reading is like looking at Niagara Falls on a map: You see the big picture and learn the facts, but to experience Niagara Falls you've got to get deeper than a map. You've got to get in a car and go there. Study is when we "go there."

The word "study" intimidates a lot of people. It sounds like something smart and boring theologians do. But you don't have to be smart to study God's Word. I know people who are very smart, but they don't know how to really study God's Word. I also know people who are very simple, yet they know how to study God's Word.

Let me simplify studying for you by showing you my seven-step plan of how to study God's Word.

Seven Steps to Studying the Bible

<u>**1. Ask for help.**</u> Whom are you going to ask? Ask your teacher. Teacher? We've already talked about the fact you have a personal teacher that is with you 24/7. He will show you where the solid food is and how it applies to you individually. He is your Teacher, and the Bible is your Textbook. The Teacher and the Book were meant to work together.

Do you need encouragement? That encouragement is the Teacher and the Book. Do you need hope? It's in the Book. It's the Teacher AND the Book, working together that encourages us and gives us hope: *"For everything that was written in the past was written to teach us, so that through endurance and the encouragement of the Scriptures we might have hope."* (Romans 15:4)

Begin by "asking for help" from your Teacher. Then as you scan God's Word by reading, your Teacher will show you where the solid food is. That's when a passage "jumps out at you." I don't know how to explain this well because it is a supernatural phenomenon, but as you are reading the Bible, a word or phrase will suddenly "come alive" to you as the Holy Spirit speaks to your heart. It's like a light bulb turns on in your spirit, and you know that "you've got mail" from God in that passage. That is when you should stop reading and begin to study that passage. To study, you need to learn to be a slow reader. Fast readers miss the good stuff. Slowly read and re-read the passage or verse, asking your Teacher to show you what it means. Your Teacher has a personalized lesson from God for you everyday— a lesson on your level.

Your Teacher can also use other resources that have been developed by other believers to help you understand the meaning of the verses better. There are many study aides such as study Bible notes, Bible software, Strong's Exhaustive Concordance, Englishman's Concordance, Bible dictionaries, commentaries, etc. But it's not essential for you have these resources to study. All you really need is the Teacher and the Book.

Whatever passage the Holy Spirit leads you to becomes the area of focus for your study. Study only one phrase at a time. My friend Adam Foldenauer came to me after I preached about this at Southside Nazarene Church and shared that somehow he had picked up the false notion reading a large volume of scripture was the proper way to study the Bible. I shared with him I often spend a week or two on one verse.

Ask for help from *Parakletos* as you slowly read the first phrase of the verse. Then stop and follow step two.

2. Question it. What does that phrase mean? Study is about taking time to ask questions. Ask yourself and ask your Teacher what the phrase means. Here are six techniques I use:

A. What's the opposite? I ask myself what the opposite meaning would be. For example, let's apply that to the first phrase of Romans 15:13: *"May the God of hope, fill you with all joy and peace ...."* I think of the opposite of "hope" as being "despair." He is not the God of despair! What if He were? No, He's the God of hope! Then I look at the words "fill you." The opposite would be "drain you". What if God wanted to drain you? Wouldn't that be awful? No, He is the God who wants to fill us! Hallelujah!

B. What is NOT being said? I ask myself, "Of all the things in the world that could be said here, why was this chosen?" Applying this to the phrase "God of hope," I would ask myself, "Why isn't He called the God of love or God of judgment or God of holiness? Why does He call Himself the God of hope?" It's because He wants to communicate to us that He is about optimism!

C. Read it backwards. This technique looks at the end of the phrase first, and then asks "where does this come from, and why?" Apply that to our *"May the God of hope fill you with all joy and peace ...."* Start with the last word "peace." Where does peace come from? Back up one word to "and." Peace and something else comes from where? Back up one more word to "joy." Peace and "joy" come from where? Back up one more word to "all." All joy? Peace and ALL joy come from where? Back up to "fill you." Now it's starting to give us some answers. Peace and all joy come from being filled! It is something that you are filled with! Back up one more word to "hope." Hope fills us with all joy and peace. Back up again to "God of hope." God is the one who can fill us with all joy and peace! What a God!

D. What are the verbs? Look for the verbs—words that ask you to do something or to be something. In the phrase "May the God of hope fill you with all joy and peace ..." you think about the word "fill." What does God want to do for us? He wants to fill us! How awesome is that! Fill: Fill means the peace and joy delivered to us from God are crammed into us.

E. Emphasize different words. This technique teaches you to emphasize a different word each time you re-read the phrase. For example:

"MAY the God of hope, fill you with all joy and peace ..."
"May THE God of hope, fill you with all joy and peace ..."
"May the GOD of hope, fill you with all joy and peace ..."
"May the God OF hope, fill you with all joy and peace ..."
"May the God of HOPE, fill you with all joy and peace ..."

Each time you read the sentence, you are thinking about what the emphasized word means, listening to the voice of the Holy Spirit as you do.

F. Look it up. This is the traditional idea of looking up the meaning of original language words. I start by looking up the meaning of a word in Strong's Concordance. Sometimes I do a cross-reference study of that word in other passages. The Bible computer software I have does this nicely, but, as I said earlier, you don't have to do all that. Ask your Teacher to show you what the phrase means to you. It's the Teacher AND the Book.

Then the next step is to turn that phrase into a prayer.

3. Pray it. "Father, you said __________ so I pray this will happen in my life." Or, "Help me to be like you and to become like this __________." Or turn a phrase into a prayer and pray it back to God. For example, the phrase "God of hope" could be turned into the prayer: "God, you said you are the God of hope, and right now I need hope in my life. God of hope, please fill me. I thank you that you are the God of hope!" You always know that you are praying in the will of God when you are praying the Word of God. I love to pray God's Word back to Him because I can pray with such conviction.

Next, take the phrase you are studying and pack it for your spiritual lunch. I call this ...

4. Find your Zoe Word. Remember Jesus said in John 6:63 *"The Spirit gives (Zoe) life; the flesh counts for nothing. The words I have spoken to you are spirit and they are (Zoe) life"* (parentheses added). The words of Jesus are *Zoe*. They have *Zoe* power—life -giving power to help you really live each day. A *Zoe* Word is a specific word from the Bible the Holy Spirit gives you for a particular day. So, what I do is look for a memorable or meaningful word in the phrase I just studied. Usually my *Zoe* Word is the whole phrase I have been looking at, but it is sometimes just one word. Next, I write that *Zoe* Word or phrase on something like a 3 X 5 card and put it in my pocket. Sometimes I'll put it on the marquee of my laptop screensaver or as a reminder on my electric calendar. Since I have been doing this for so long, I don't usually need a reminder unless I am starting a new study passage. That *Zoe* Word is now my spiritual lunch for the day, and I will recall it many times throughout the day. The next step is to ...

5. Apply it. You apply the *Zoe* Word to your life throughout the day depending on what it is. Apply the *Zoe* Word to everything that happens to you that day. Recently, I applied "God of Hope" to the problems of the day. Whatever problem I faced, I would say "God of hope!" or if I got discouraged I would pray "God of hope."

Whatever that card in my pocket says, is what I apply to my life. Today my *Zoe* Word was from the parable of the talents in Matthew 25. The Teacher led me to the phrase "He hid his Lord's money." The concept of money in this parable applies broadly to include our abilities and possessions of any kind. I was applying it today to my talents and was confessing all day that everything I had was "My Lord's money." It was very humbling to me to apply this truth all day to my life. My profession as a dentist is "My Lord's money." My ability to preach effectively is "My Lord's money." The compliments I receive from people are "My Lord's money." My ability to sing is "My Lord's money." This book is "My Lord's money."

As you apply your *Zoe* Word to your life each day, you will be blessed because you are fulfilling James 1:22-25: *"Do not merely listen to the word, and so deceive yourselves. Do what it says. Anyone who listens to the word but does not do what it says is like a man who looks at his face in a mirror and, after looking at himself, goes away and immediately forgets what he looks like. But the man who looks intently into the perfect law that gives freedom, and continues to do this, not forgetting what he has heard, but doing it—he will be blessed in what he does."*

As we apply God's Word to our lives we will be blessed! That sounds like *Zoe* doesn't it? When you apply God's Word to your everyday life you will experience *Zoe* to the Max because you are living by God's Word. This blessing of applying God's Word leads naturally to step six.

6. <u>Celebrate it.</u> As you apply, celebrate! Celebrate your *Zoe* Word for the rest of the day. Depending on what the word is, you can praise the nature of God or His character or what He promises to do in your life. This step helped me today because I opened the new Yellow Pages edition only to discover that for the second year in a row, I have been left out of the listing of dentists! Isn't that incredible? Somehow they goofed up last year and after several phone calls, I discovered how the error happened and was assured it was fixed for the next year's publication. Well, guess what? It wasn't! How outrageous is it to be in business for 25 years and then to suddenly be dropped, and then for it to happen a second time?! Fortunately, I was celebrating my *Zoe* Word for that day which was "My Lord's money." I was able to give it to the Lord because my dental practice belongs to Him and so, after the initial shock of the situation, I was able to continue my celebration even though the Yellow Pages folks had left out "My Lord's practice." He has blessed me with more business than I can handle anyway, so maybe it was a blessing in disguise! Celebrate! Celebrate your *Zoe* Word!

God wants us to rejoice in His Word. The Psalmist said in Psalm 119:14-16, *"I rejoice in following your statutes as one rejoices in great riches. I meditate on your precepts and consider your ways. I delight in your decrees; I will not neglect your word."* God's Word is great riches! We should celebrate it as such! I asked our congregation the following question: "Which would you get more excited about: The Publishers Clearing House folks knocking on your door with a $10,000 prize, or a *Zoe* Word given to you by God? God help us if we value the prize more! We need to learn to rejoice in the riches of knowing the Teacher and the Book and delight when He gives us a special *Zoe* Word!

Psalm 119:111-112: *"Your statutes are my heritage forever; they are the joy of my heart. My heart is set on keeping your decrees to the very end."* The greatest source of joy I find in my life is when my Teacher shows me MY *Zoe* Word. This past week after preaching a message about this, the Holy Spirit gave me my *Zoe* Word for Monday during my prayer just before looking at my Bible. He said "Well done!" I recognized that from Matthew 25 as the Master said to the productive servants, "Well done, good and faithful servant ... Come and share in the Master's happiness!" Wow! The Holy Spirit was giving me a word of commendation! Boy, did I celebrate that day! God Himself had told me "Well done!" I didn't really need any other compliments from anyone else because I heard from God! I can't tell you what joy I received from that for several days—and even now! God wants to have this type of relationship with you too! Come on in and discover the joy that is in receiving your personal *Zoe* Word from your Teacher each day! This leads naturally into step seven.

<u>**7. Snack on it.**</u> The Word of God is meant to feed our souls throughout the day, not just once. Our *Zoe* Word is our spiritual food to snack on throughout the day. Do you only eat once a day?

Why do you think you should only eat of God's Word once a day?! No wonder we lack *Zoe* and are so spiritually weak. The Word of God is meant to be our spiritual food throughout the day! The Bible contains the Bread of Life (*Zoe*). God wants us to snack on the Bread of *Zoe* throughout the day.

So when you are sitting at a stop light or waiting in line at a store or driving down the road, you can pull out your 3x5 index card with your *Zoe* Word on it and have a snack right then. That's why you need to write it down so you can remind yourself of what your Teacher is trying to teach you and remember to snack on it. This is also called meditation, and we will get to that shortly.

His Words are tasty and nourishing snacks. Jeremiah 15:16: *"Your words were found, and I did eat them; and Your word was unto me the joy and rejoicing of my heart: for I am called by Your name, O LORD God of hosts."* This is the way I can kick-start my *Zoe* any time during the day. I simply snack on my *Zoe* Word. I say it aloud, but I often say it in my mind when others are around. Sometimes I will accidentally speak my *Zoe* Word "under my breathe" as I am praying it or confessing it or celebrating it, and my dental assistant will think I am asking for an instrument or my patients will think I am saying something to them! I guess it would be a little disconcerting to have your dentist mumble "thank you, God" as they are working on your teeth!

Snacking helps me to *"'Love the Lord your God with all your heart and with all your soul and with all your mind.' This is the first and greatest commandment."* (Matthew 22:37-38) When you study God's Word, you are actively loving God with ALL YOUR MIND, because to study is to engage your mind throughout the day.

Repeat Daily!

Those are the seven steps I use to study a phrase from God's Word. Then the next day, I go right back to the same passage and look at the next phrase. I keep going back to the same passage until my Teacher is done teaching me there. I always stay in the same "green pasture" the Shepherd leads me to until He decides to lead me out. Doesn't that make sense? Why should we move on when the Teacher is not finished teaching us? That's like leaving class in the middle of a lecture. I study a phrase at a time until I have memorized it. Memorization is not really that hard if you study the verse well enough with this phrase-by-phrase method.

This brings me back to the hand illustration. Beginning with the pinky finger of LISTENING, to the ring finger of READING, to the middle finger of STUDYING we come to ...

<u>Memorizing is the pointer (or index) finger.</u> Really, we've already been doing that. Good phrase-by-phrase study makes memorizing a natural byproduct. Memorizing is very beneficial to you because the Holy Spirit, your *Parakletos*, your Teacher, has more to work with. There have been many times when I am facing various situations that *Parakletos* was able to remind me of a verse I have memorized. Although I formerly memorized verses because I was told memorization was a good spiritual discipline, I now memorize as a natural byproduct of my study. Memorization used to be a laborious ritual of flipping through my stack of cards to review and re-review. I felt good I was accomplishing a goal, but I didn't really enjoy it like I do now. I now think memorization should only be the beginning goal. The final goal should be the assimilation of that verse, or verses, into our spirit, mind and life. I know people who can quote the verse, but they don't "live" the verse. I think God is much more pleased when we are *"doers of the Word,"* not merely memorizers.

As you snack on your *Zoe* Word each day, you are actually meditating on God's Word and using the thumb in the hand illustration.

<u>Meditating is the thumb.</u> It's a slow and steady absorption of the nutrients from God's Word that will sustain you. When you celebrate God's Word and continually snack on God's Word, you are actually progressing beyond study to meditation. Meditation is really any thoughtful review of scripture. It doesn't have anything to do with a yoga-type meditation, one of which encourages you to empty yourself of everything. Christian meditation is when you fill yourself with God and His Word.

Meditation comes from the idea of ruminating. The word "ruminating" comes from the suborder in the animal kingdom *ruminanta*. It is a scientific classification based on the digestive system of any hoofed animal (like cattle or sheep) which digests its food in two steps, the second of which is called "ruminating."

The first part of their stomach is known as the forestomach and the second part is known as the reticulum. The forestomach is where the chewed grass goes initially. The process of fermentation begins

there as the microbes begin to digest the cellulose. When the animal is resting, the forestomach begins a reverse contraction and regurgitates the chewed grass back up the esophagus for a second chewing. This re-chewing then breaks the pre-digested food down more completely and sends it back down to the second part of the stomach which is called the reticulum. From there it goes on into the small intestines and the entire digestive system.

Meditating is chewing and re-chewing the Word of God. Pardon the comparison but we are literally regurgitating our *Zoe* Word throughout the day.

There's a disease of the digestive system called Rapid Gastric Emptying. It's when food moves too quickly out of the stomach. Some of us have a spiritual case of Rapid Gastric Emptying. We need to slow down and take time to properly digest God's Word.

Prosperity Guaranteed or Your Money Back!

Joshua 1:8 promises success to those who meditate on God's Word day and night. Psalm 1 guarantees those who delight in God's Word and meditate on it day and night will grow like a fruitful tree that is planted by the river. Biblical meditation day and night promises:

- sustained nourishment!
- seasonal fruitfulness!
- endurance during times of adversity!
- prosperity in all we do!

That sounds like *Zoe* to the Max! God's Word has the power to produce *Zoe* to the Max in our lives as we learn how to meditate on it and delight in it! *"Great peace have they who love your law, and nothing can make them stumble"* (Psalm 119:165).

Check Your Pulse

What if, by some magical power or technological marvel, the "*Zoe*" character my daughter Stephanie has been drawing in this book jumped out of this page right here and said!

"Hey! I'm glad you are reading this book! I'm taking a survey of

people who are reading it, and I want to ask you a question, "What new thing is God teaching you from His Word TODAY?"

What would you say? Would you be able to quickly tell what God is teaching you today? Or maybe from yesterday? You and I should be growing and learning from God's Word every day and be able to share the *Zoe* Word your Teacher is teaching you EACH DAY. You should not have to scratch your head, ponder for a while and then make up some vague spiritual-sounding answer. It should be on the "top of your mind" because it is as fresh as daily manna!

Journaling

A tool which has helped me in learning all this is a spiritual journal. I've been journaling since 1981. I started out using a small three ring binder, then larger binders and, for the last 10 years, my laptop. Whether on paper or computer, a journal is a prayer tool and a thinking tool and a tool for the recording of important spiritual events. Someday my daughters and grandchildren will be able to read how I grew in God. It's not a diary but I record my thoughts, prayers and questions about my spiritual relationship with God. I write the date, and then I write the prayers of my heart to God. Often I will then write about my questions or struggles and ask God for answers or help. As I write, I am also listening to my Teacher and asking Him questions. Then I will record what I am learning in the scriptures that day.

If you were to read my journal, you would see my struggles and questions and experience my joys and lessons. Occasionally, I will look back and read some old entries in my journal and see what God has taught me and praise Him. Tonight I was searching in our attic for something, and I found a box of keepsakes—there was my first journal! What a joy it was to read my entry on May 6, 1981, when through a friend at church, God gave me my first "job" as an associate in a local dental practice. It was truly a "God thing" because the doctors approached me to offer a job. I didn't go to them first. Working for them is how God originally positioned me to buy the practice I have had for 25 years. Then I read my entries just before graduation from dental school. On May 15, 1981, I wrote, "My last day before becoming a doctor. It seems strange to me to know that in roughly 24 hours that I will enter into a title that will change my life on earth. Up until now, I have been called by one title and now I will be another. This title, however, is not to be mentioned along side of the brilliance of being a child of God and brother of Jesus! Lord, don't let this doctor stuff go to my head. Help me to always know that You have given this to me." Wow, what a blessing to be able to read that and recall what I was dealing with then! I read on through the entries of my first two months in practice when I was the poorest I have ever been in my life. My wife had resigned from her job due to her sickness during her pregnancy with our first daughter Nena, and I was just starting to work and had very little income. I recorded times when I ran out of gas and overdrew our checking account and times when I doubted God and then how He helped me through those hard times and rebuilt my faith. Without that journal I would have lost the memory of those struggles. My journal also shows my spiritual "gaps" when I failed to journal because I was too busy. It helped me to learn consistency. Now I write in my journal as I feel the need, not as a legalistic task to accomplish. I recommend journaling for all these reasons.

Zoe to the Max is strongly linked to meditating on my *Zoe* Word. If I need my *Zoe* notched up, I look to my *Zoe* Word because His Word promises encouragement and hope. Romans 15:4: *"For everything that was written in the past was written to teach us, so that through endurance and the encouragement of the Scriptures we might have hope."*

Chapter 13: *Zoe* Zone Part 3
Rejoice to Re-juice!

The *Zoe* Zone begins by learning how to enjoy the presence of the Lord every day. It is enhanced by spending time with the Teacher and the Book until you get your *Zoe* Word. This gives a great start to the third important area in mastering *Zoe* to the Max and that is to learn how to rejoice in the Lord and in the day that He as made.

"This is the day the Lord has made;
let us rejoice and be glad in it."
Psalm 118:24

This is the day! THIS! This IS (present tense) the day! Not yesterday or tomorrow or next Sunday—today, right now as you are reading this sentence. This is THE day. Not tomorrow when your problem is gone. Not this weekend when you get off work. Not next week when you get paid. God is the God of now.

"The Lord has made ...." God is the Creator. He is the one who provided this day for you. You and I didn't decide we were going to live today—God did! If it weren't for Him, we wouldn't have a day to enjoy. If it weren't for God creating this day, you wouldn't have the opportunity to read right now! We don't live in OUR world; we live in GOD'S world. We don't live our life; we live the life God has given us to live.

"This is the day that the Lord has made ...." This day is *"brought to you by—God."* The Lord has made this day for you and me to live in and since He has given us this opportunity to live it, you and I ought to be grateful and rejoice!

God wants you to do two things today: 1. Rejoice! 2. Be glad! Rejoice today. Be glad today. Enjoy this day NOW. *Zoe* to the Max is for NOW! God's will is for us to enjoy each and every NOW. What are you supposed to be doing now? Rejoice and be glad! That is a command—to rejoice and be glad in it!

Rejoice: The word "rejoice" in Hebrew is *gil* [gheel]: to rejoice, exult, be glad. To be joyful, i.e., be in a state of an attitude or feeling of favorable circumstance. Note: This joy may be expressed in song, shouts, or even joyous shrieks and calls.[1] I guess that includes shouting woo who! To rejoice, then, is to be in a glad and joyful attitude over favorable circumstances. The favorable circumstances are that you and I are children of God and His presence is with us as we meditate on the *Zoe* Word our personal Teacher has given us which brings the prosperity of the Lord's blessings right now. To rejoice is to express this verbally through song and praise. That all sounds like *Zoe* to the Max to me!

The root of rejoice" is "to circle around," from which we get the idea "to circle in joy." It means vigorous, enthusiastic expressions of joy.[2] Got the idea? God wants us to learn how to enthusiastically rejoice in the *Zoe* He has for us every day.

Be Glad: The Hebrew word is *samach* [saw·makh]. The meaning is similar to rejoice, but with more emphasis on being happy.[3] Rejoice has a more spiritual meaning, whereas "be glad" has a more secular application. Either way, we have it covered! We can rejoice in God and His blessing, and we can be just plain happy. What a powerful combination. "Let us rejoice and be glad in it!"

Rejoice is a Choice!

Ready, get set, go! Start right now. "I will rejoice" is a statement of decision, intention, and conviction. Rejoice is a choice. It is not necessarily a feeling, but it is a decision to appreciate and celebrate and praise God. I choose to rejoice in, and enjoy every day. It is a conscious choice, not an automatic feeling.

I've talked about my sunroom and how I enjoy sitting in it. Right now it is a beautiful Saturday, and I am editing this chapter. The sky is clear blue, and the leaves are almost full-sized and spring green. What a wonderful day! And, yet, as I look up through the skylights, they are covered with tree pollen, sticks and dirt. I can't really enjoy the blue sky because the skylights are dirty. I bet I could enjoy my view better if I cleaned the skylight. I think I will go do that right now! ...Twenty minutes later ... Wow, what a difference! How bright and clear and pure! The leaves are greener; the sky is bluer and brighter! Now, let me ask you: What changed? Did the sky change?

No. Did the leaves change? No. Only one thing changed. My perspective changed. I decided to clean up my perspective of the world. This is what I mean by changing your attitude. I could have chosen to view the world as dirty and cloudy. Or I could have chosen to complain about the window being dirty or focus on looking at dirt on the window. All those were perspective choices. I chose that I would change my perspective. I didn't change reality, only my perspective of reality.

When I realize I am not enjoying a particular circumstance, I then choose to begin enjoying myself instead. I choose to "be glad in it." I will be glad in whatever I am doing. I remind myself throughout the day it is God's desire that I rejoice and be glad in this day. Rejoice is a choice. That's why it is right to pursue *Zoe* to the Max everyday. That is what Jesus came to give you and me, and that is what He wants us to experience. I have learned the importance of choosing to be glad during every event of every day. Rejoicing in everyday is a learning experience. *Zoe* to the Max is a learning experience. It is learning to be glad.

Be glad in the spite of it.

Be glad in the middle of it.

Be glad in the beginning of it and in the end of it.

Be glad IN it.

Rejoice is a choice. I'm as glad as I want to be. I'm as joyful as I want to be. That is the truth. The fact is I can be as glad as I choose to be, and I can rejoice as much as I want. That's not because I have control over making myself glad. It's because I have the choice of tapping, or not tapping, into God. I have the choice. God has already made the provision and possibility. He has made the day, and, through Jesus, He has made the *Zoe*. All that is left is for me to make the decision that says, "I WILL rejoice." It is a decision of the will, and of faith. "I will ...." Faith says "I'm going to enjoy myself today, and I'm going to experience *Zoe* to the Max today."

Rejoice in the drive.

Rejoice in the day.

Rejoice in the weather.

Rejoice in the process, not just the result.

Rejoicing in the Lord and in all He has made and all He has done rejuvenates and re-juices us!

Old Testament Rejoicing

When I did a study of the use of the word "rejoice," I found rejoicing is the general disposition God wants us to have. He first talked about rejoicing when describing the Feast of Tabernacles:

"On the first day you are to take choice fruit from the trees, and palm fronds, leafy branches and poplars, and rejoice before the Lord your God for seven days" (Leviticus 23:40).

Then in Deuteronomy 12:7, He wanted them to rejoice in the temple: *"There, in the presence of the Lord your God, you and your families shall eat and shall rejoice in everything you have put your hand to, because the Lord your God has blessed you."* And again in Deuteronomy 12:12: *"And there rejoice before the Lord your God, you, your sons and daughters, your menservants and maidservants ... "* And in Deuteronomy 12:18: *"... rejoice before the Lord your God in everything you put your hand to."* This continues as God tells them to rejoice in the various feasts and while giving offerings. The Hebrew word for rejoice, *samach* [saw·makh] is used 152 times, 52 of those in the book of Psalms.[4]

God wants us to rejoice as we seek Him. *"But may all who seek you rejoice and be glad in you; may those who love your salvation always say, "Let God be exalted!"* (Psalm 70:4). We should see all of creation as rejoicing in God. Get a pen right now and underline each time you see words like "rejoice" or "joy" or "glad" in the following passages: Psalm 96:11- 97:1 *"Let the heavens rejoice, let the earth be glad; let the sea resound, and all that is in it; let the fields be jubilant, and everything in them. Then all the trees of the forest will sing for joy; they will sing before the Lord, for he comes, he comes to judge the earth. He will judge the world in righteousness and the peoples in his truth. The Lord reigns, let the earth be glad; let the distant shores rejoice."*

Psalm 98:8-9, *"Let the rivers clap their hands, let the mountains sing together for joy; let them sing before the Lord, for he comes to judge the earth. He will judge the world in righteousness and the peoples with equity."*

New Testament Rejoicing

In The New Testament, the Greek word for rejoice is *chairo* [khah·ee·ro]: to rejoice, to be glad to delighted."[5] It's used 74 times, but I want to draw your attention to a couple of passages: Paul says in Philippians 4:4 *"Be rejoicing in the Lord always. Again I say, Be rejoicing."* He takes the rare step of repeating a command to show how important it is to constantly be rejoicing. The Message says it this way, *"Celebrate God all day, every day. I mean, revel in him!"* Again in 1 Thessalonians 5:16, Paul proclaims, *"Be joyful always."*

God's will is that we live in a constant state of rejoicing in the Lord! Rejoicing is meant to be a continuous habit. It's not a personality issue. It's not a location issue. It's not a money or position issue, IT IS A GOD ISSUE. Wherever God is, rejoicing can occur! I am embarrassed as I reflect back on my life how little I have practiced rejoicing compared to how much I do now. I've learned that rejoicing is like priming the pump of joy. God help us to learn to rejoice!

Some may say, "But I am suffering too much to rejoice." Paul addresses that in Romans 5:2-4: *"And we REJOICE in the hope of the glory of God. Not only so, but we also REJOICE in our sufferings, because we know that suffering produces perseverance; perseverance, character; and character, hope"* (emphasis added). You can rejoice in the hope your suffering will not endure. You can rejoice your sufferings are demonstrating and producing godly character. When I see a suffering Christian rejoicing in God, I see such a powerful demonstration of the glory of God. Anyone can rejoice in the good times, but only the mature and godly can rejoice in the midst of suffering. My friend Dan Foldenauer is a great example of this. He has been a marathon runner all his life and then was suddenly stricken with a paralyzing disease that put him in a wheel chair! Yet, in the midst of that mysterious condition, he chose to seek God's strength to help him rejoice in the middle of his suffering. What a witness he was to the nurses, doctors and physical therapists! Now he is out of the hospital, using a walker and expecting to make a full recovery. He used his suffering to develop character and that character gave him hope!

Rejoicing is Re-juicing!

When I sense I need re-juicing, I start rejoicing. I start praising God and thanking Him for who He is and for the day that He has made for us. I clean the skylights of my life. I rejoice as I refocus myself on the presence of God. I close my eyes and focus on inviting the power of the Holy Spirit to be manifested in my life and to bring me closer to Him. I envision the presence of God with me right there. I invite Him to come closer because I know what Psalm 16:11 says: *"You have made known to me the path of life; you will fill me with joy in your presence, with eternal pleasures at your right hand."* This is a key verse because it shows a direct correlation between the presence of God and being filled with joy and eternal pleasure.

To be in God's presence is to be in a joy-filling station. It's like going to a gas station and getting your tank filled with fuel. When you draw near to His presence, you have the opportunity to be filled with joy. The above verse says *"You will fill me with joy"*—that is a promise. Our part is to get into His presence. That takes more than just pausing to pray. God wants a relationship, not a business agreement. He won't let you treat Him like a vending machine. But the promise is when we invest in relationship with Him, we will be filled with joy. I often use joy as my gauge of connection. When I am filled with joy, I know I have connected well with God. If not, I continue seeking Him until the connection happens.

Look at the verse again. *"You have made known to me the path of life; YOU WILL FILL ME with joy in your presence, WITH ETERNAL PLEASURES at your right hand"* (emphasis added). See the promise of joy and eternal pleasures. The Hebrew word for pleasure is *na`iym* [naw·eem]: 1. pleasant, delightful, sweet, lovely, agreeable; 1a. delightful; 1b. lovely, beautiful (physical); 2. singing, sweetly sounding, musical.[6]

When we are in the presence of God, there are delightful pleasures that are sweet and lovely. So when we pause to rejoice in the presence of God and spend time drawing near to Him, it is a rejuvenating activity! Rejoicing is re-juicing!

An Attitude of Gratitude

Rejoicing in the Lord and enjoying *Zoe* to the Max are not events or circumstances—they are attitudes we choose to apply to our lives. God wants us to enjoy our lives as a habit, not a rarity. I try to remind myself of this by saying to myself what a rejoicing person would say right now:

"I'm enjoying this."

"This is fun."

"It's good to be alive right now."

"I like doing this."

"Thank you God for letting me do this."

"I'm enjoying myself right now."

Attitudes are choices we make by faith. You choose your attitudes. Nobody MAKES you have a certain attitude. We choose to set our minds on the things of God and begin to rejoice in the Lord. We move from mad to glad! We can be thankful instead of crank-ful. We can choose to agree with God's Word and say to ourselves the kinds of things that God wants us to say! I remind myself "God has given me this day and this moment and this activity. I'm going to appreciate what I am doing right now!" I am actually doing that right now as I am writing this. It's 9 pm and I've been working on this for about two hours now and am a little weary. I stopped a moment ago and realized I was not fully enjoying the writing process at this moment and so I began to rejoice in the Lord and thank Him for the privilege of writing this and being able to help others enjoy more *Zoe* in their lives. Now I can feel the influx of joy and peace as I sense the approval of God and the presence of the Holy Spirit! This stuff is real!

Zoe-Zap'n Trash Talk

Instead of speaking the Word of God and rejoicing in the Lord, most of us speak negative things that zap the *Zoe* out of us:

"I hate this."

"This is so stupid."

"Why do things like this always happen to me?"

"Can't anything go right today?"

"I can't stand this!"

These kinds of negative proclamations fly in the face of the positive directives from God's Word. No wonder we're not experiencing *Zoe* to the Max when we talk trash to ourselves. I'm reminded of the old computer phrase, "Garbage in, garbage out." I think applies here to our self-talk. "Trash in, trash out."

I know this may sound a bit trite, but I challenge you to an experiment. Try for one day saying to yourself what God wants you to say, and see if it doesn't impact you in a positive way. God responds to faith, and speaking the truth is an act of faith. Why not give thanks for the things you don't currently enjoy and watch your level of *Zoe* begin to rise? Or you can ignore what God says and speak to yourself with negative *Zoe*-Zapping statements. You choose. Or should I say, you already DO choose.

Enjoy Life!

Rejoice and be glad always includes enjoying God and enjoying life. :

"A man can do nothing better than to eat and drink and find satisfaction in his work. This too, I see, is from the hand of God, for without him, who can eat or find enjoyment? To the man who pleases him, God gives wisdom, knowledge and happiness, but to the sinner he gives the task of gathering and storing up wealth to hand it over to the one who pleases God. This too is meaningless, a chasing after the wind." (Ecclesiastes 2:24-26)

God wants us to enjoy ourselves in this life. *Zoe* is not the absence of negative feelings; it is the presence of a powerful, positive sense of God being with you. *Zoe* is positive. It is enjoying the day that the Lord has made and the things that the Lord has made for us.

I've got to tell you I am happier now than I have ever been. In my younger years I got the impression from all the people who are older than me that life would get worse and worse. "It's terrible to get old," is the quote I heard most often. I haven't found that to be true. The more I learn and grow and experience, the closer I get to God and the happier I am each year. The "good ole days" are now! I think each season of life is to be enjoyed to the maximum. I think that's the way that it should be and the way God designed it.

Enjoyment Dysfunctional

I realize also some people seem to be "enjoyment-dysfunctional" or "enjoyment-challenged" or "enjoyment-disadvantaged"—whatever the politically correct way of saying that would be. Some of them have trouble enjoying themselves very much of the time because they are controlled by their negative attitudes. Others seem to feel they do not have permission to enjoy life because they operate within the spiritually abusive teaching that makes holiness seem more like depression. Some have simply not seen good examples of Christians who are enjoying *Zoe* to the Max! They do not know they are supposed to enjoy life.

Others are hindered somewhat by their personality. Some personality types are more serious by nature, and they think more about the sobering problems of the world than others do. They have a melancholy-type personality, which tends to be more "enjoyment-dysfunctional." They are likely to see what is wrong with the world and what is "less than" it should be. The one "weed" in a field of flowers distracts them. These melancholy personalities get their feelings hurt more easily than others, and their perfectionistic standards often make them unhappy with their performance or the performance of others.

However, with all this understood, God's Word applies to every personality. For those with this melancholy personality, it takes more intentionality to enjoy life and focus on the positive. I encourage them to consider learning to enjoying life, even with its imperfections, is God's desire for the fully mature follower of Christ. They shouldn't feel guilty about enjoying life and enjoying the blessings of God. More fun-loving personalities also have to struggle with learning to enjoy life and enjoy God in the boring times and during the mundane activities of life. Goal-oriented personalities have difficulty enjoying life when their goals are not being met. Peace-loving personalities have difficulty enjoying life because of all the stressful things that are in life. Personalities do play a role in how we enjoy God, how we view life and how we express our enjoyment of God, but remember God made all the personalities so He can teach everyone how to enjoy *Zoe* to the Max regardless of personality.

Enjoy the Blessings!

Psalm 106:5: *"That I may enjoy the prosperity of your chosen ones, that I may share in the joy of your nation and join your inheritance in giving praise."* Look at that:

Enjoy the prosperity!

Share in the joy!

Join your inheritance!

Give praise!

God is a blessing God, and He wants His chosen ones to enjoy those blessings. Psalm 84:11: *"The Lord bestows favor and honor; **no good thing does he withhold** from those whose walk is blameless"* (emphasis added). He gives us everything we have for our enjoyment. He is a giving God, not a withholding God. That does not mean we will get everything we want or everything others have. Remember, He doesn't want to be viewed or treated as a vending machine. God is the giver, and He has a plan for dispensing His gifts. Sometimes sin, or self, or Satan thwarts that plan. But everything we have is from God, and we should rejoice in that. Rejoice in what you have, not what you don't have.

One of the comments I hear from those who have traveled on mission trips to third world areas is, "They have so little, and, yet, they have so much joy!" When you have God, you have *Zoe* no matter what possessions you have or don't have. Focus on being thankful for the positives, not preoccupied with the negatives.

God also has many spiritual blessings to give us. *"He has blessed us in the heavenly realms with every spiritual blessing in Christ"* (Ephesians 1:3). I want to tap into every spiritual blessing that God has for me, don't you? One of those blessings is to enjoy the joy He wants to bless us with. God has joy for us! It's one of the nine fruits of the Spirit listed in Galatians 5:22. Jesus said it like this: *"I have told you this so that my joy may be in you and that your joy may be complete"* (John 15:11). He wants you and me to have a complete joy. Enjoy the joy!

Enjoy all the Feelings

God wants us to enjoy all the feelings of life. Those feelings run the gamut. *Zoe* is not just dancing on tabletops all the time; *Zoe* is experiencing the kind of life God intended, and experiencing it the way that He intended. For example, God wants us to experience rest. When we are tired and need rest or sleep, God wants us to enjoy the *Zoe* of rest. *Zoe* might be to take a nap. Sometimes *Zoe* is to experience the sorrow of passionate prayer. It can be pouring our hearts out to the Lord for the lost. It may be weeping tears of sorrow, or tears of joy. Sometimes it is experiencing peace in the middle of adversity—the peace that comes as the grip of anxiety and worry and fear is loosened, one finger at a time. *Zoe* is experiencing life in all the fullness God designed to the maximum level. *Zoe* is to enjoy life the way God wants us to as taught by the Teacher day by day.

Of course, I would like to experience "inexpressible and glorious joy" all the time! But that is not the way God designed life to be. God gave us the capacity to experience a variety of feelings, and we must let God be God. Perhaps He has a different emotion for me to experience now. Sitting and listening to a friend pour out their sorrow is part of God's will for us. Sometimes love is silent. *Zoe to the Max* is appreciating each emotion as it occurs, then monitoring ourselves to make sure that we are rejoicing and being glad in the day that the Lord as made. *Zoe* is enjoying the life I am living right now—however that is unfolding and through whatever is happening. I can find rest or peace. I can find joy or faith. I can find contentment and appreciation. I can be thankful and rejoice. I must reassess each moment to see if I am experiencing life the way God intends for me NOW.

You may say, "But, Tracy, you don't know my specific situation." That is true. But I believe I do know God, and I know John 10:10 applies to us all—in all our situations. My friend Russ Randall questioned the authenticity of my claim that he could experience *Zoe* to the Max after losing his job since I had never experienced a job loss. I said, "Russ, it is your job to show us how a person who loses their job can experience *Zoe* to the Max!" I say the same to you, whatever your specific situation—personality, family, problems, circumstances—it is your opportunity and the glory of God to show the world how a follower of Christ can experience *Zoe* to the Max in the midst of your particular situation. None of us

> *None of us has equal situations. We can all find an excuse to hide behind.*

has equal situations. We can all find an excuse to hide behind. I think of Joni Eareckson Tada. Her diving accident in 1967 left her permanently paralyzed. She is showing us how a quadriplegic can experience *Zoe* to the Max! Her web site at www.joniandfriends.org shows a video introduction of one who is expressing *Zoe* to the Max! That encourages me, because I know if the same thing happened to me, I would still have God's *Zoe* overflowing in my life. Whatever your disadvantages or disabilities or circumstances are, it is an opportunity to show the world God can give *Zoe* to the Max no matter what the situation!

Zoe is the supernatural gift of really living life the way God intended and enjoying it to the maximum. It is not just a positive state of mind or a greater appreciation for the good things. Those good things can be achieved to a small degree through non-religious means such as the power of a positive attitude or through relaxation techniques or yoga, etc. But those self-generated good feelings dwarf in comparison to what having a personal, supernatural connection to the Son of God brings! We can experience both self-generated good feelings and supernaturally generated good feelings!

Juice Time!

So monitor your enjoyment level and monitor your energy level for dips. When you feel yourself dipping into your level of enjoyment, then you need to re-juice. One way to re-juice is to rejoice! God wants us to live in a state of rejoicing. Remember what God says, *"rejoice always and again I say rejoice!"* It is stated twice to show the significance of rejoicing. When we rejoice, it re-juices our emotions, and we enjoy a greater level of *Zoe*. God, give us this supernatural capacity to increase our enjoyment of life—all of life! Rejoice to re-juice!

Chapter 14: *Zoe* Zone Part 4
Peace-Ruled Heart

The *Zoe* Zone so far:
- 1 of 10—Learn to enjoy the presence of the Lord
- 2 of 10—Spend time with the Teacher and The Book
- 3 of 10—Rejoice to re-juice

Now we move from these three areas which involve more of the choices of our minds, to areas four through seven which involve the state of our hearts. Our hearts are the center of our stability. When our hearts are filled with negative emotions like worry, fear, anger, insecurity, withholding forgiveness, or discontentment, we cannot enjoy *Zoe* to the Max because our core is unsettled. In this section, I will start with area four, which is having a heart ruled by peace. Then in five and six, I will show you how the Holy Spirit wants to heal the emotionally unhealthy areas of our hearts and sanctify the carnality. Area seven will address how to protect our hearts from the assaults of discontentment.

Peace, Brother!

God made us to live with His peace in our hearts. We were not made to live with worry. We were not designed to live in anxiety and fear. God made us to live in the Garden of Eden, the place of delight. When we take on worry, anxiety, anger and fear, we are going against the Manufacturer's specifications. We are likely to blow a fuse or damage ourselves.

God meant for peace to rule in our hearts and reign as the norm. He doesn't want you to be ruled by worry, fear or anger. Our hearts are constantly to abide in peace, and when negative emotions try to take over, peace is there to cast them out. The *Zoe* Zone is a worry-free zone where peace rules!

The Word on Peace

God is the God of peace. He is referred to as the God of peace five times in the New Testament.

- Romans 15:33: *"The God of peace be with you all. Amen."*
- Romans 16:20: *"The God of peace will soon crush Satan under your feet."*
- Philippians 4:9: *"Whatever you have learned or received or heard from me, or seen in me—put it into practice. And the God of peace will be with you."*
- Hebrews 13:20: *"May the God of peace..."*
- 1 Thessalonians 5:23: *"May God himself, the God of peace, sanctify you through and through. May your whole spirit, soul and body be kept blameless at the coming of our Lord Jesus Christ."*

In the Old Testament, the Hebrew word for peace is *shālôm* [shaw·lome] and denotes a general sense of tranquility and in "its most common use it is a social rather than an individual term."[1] *Shālôm* is a blessing from God. Psalm 29:11: *"The Lord gives strength to his people; the Lord blesses his people with peace."* But the opposite is true for the wicked: *"'There is no peace,' says the Lord, 'for the wicked'"* (Isaiah 48:22).

In the Greek language New Testament, peace is *eirene* [i·ray·nay]. "The tranquil state of a soul assured of its salvation through Christ, and so fearing nothing from God and content with its earthly lot, of whatsoever sort that is."[2]

God is the God of peace both internal and external. When the angels announced the birth of Christ, they used the word "peace" in their proclamation. *"Glory to God in the highest, and on earth peace to men on whom his favor rests"* (Luke 2:14). Peace was proclaimed as the blessing upon those who received the favor of God. Grace and peace were the two blessings given in the greeting in 18 out of 22 epistles. This indicates how important it is we have peace in our hearts and lives.

Jesus used the phrase *"go in peace"* in Luke 7:50: *"Jesus said to the woman, 'Your faith has saved you; go in peace.'"* And another time he said, *"Daughter, your faith has healed you. Go in peace"* (Luke 8:48). I was not able to learn if the phrase "go in peace" was original with Jesus, or if it was a commonly used farewell phrase of the times. Either way, we can be sure Jesus used it intentionally and that He meant for them to be filled with peace as they left.

After His resurrection, Jesus entered the room saying, *"Peace be with you."* It wasn't a hippie-type peace with two fingers raised—

Jesus was coming to bring calmness and tranquility to their anxious hearts. *"On the evening of that first day of the week, when the disciples were together, with the doors locked for fear of the Jews, Jesus came and stood among them and said, 'Peace be with you!'* (John 20:19). *"Again Jesus said, 'Peace be with you! As the Father has sent me, I am sending you'"* (John 20:21). *"A week later his disciples were in the house again, and Thomas was with them. Though the doors were locked, Jesus came and stood among them and said, "Peace be with you!"* (John 20:26). Peace is what we need. Notice that He didn't say "Love be with you." Peace is what we need when we are in anxious situations. Jesus desires that peace for us.

As He ended His earthly ministry, His parting instructions in John 14-17 begin with peace: *"Peace I leave with you; my peace I give you. I do not give to you as the world gives. Do not let your hearts be troubled and do not be afraid"* (John 14:27). *"I have told you these things, so that in me you may have peace. In this world you will have trouble. But take heart! I have overcome the world"* (John 16:33). Here Jesus defined what He meant by peace. Peace is given as a gift, and it is not like the world's peace. Receiving this peace is a better choice than to let our hearts be troubled or fearful.

How to Let Peace Rule

<u>1. Trust in God.</u> Peace comes from trust. *"May the God of hope fill you with all joy and peace AS YOU TRUST IN HIM, so that you may overflow with hope by the power of the Holy Spirit"* (Romans 15:13, emphasis added). The filling of peace comes AS we trust in God, and THEN we will overflow with hope. When we don't have peace, we need to check our trust meter.

I'm a pretty healthy person—today was the first day in 25 years of dental practice I have stayed home sick and completely canceled a whole day. Self-employed people know that there are no paid sick days, so the thought of lost income immediately came to my mind, instantly followed by a confession of my trust in God, and peace ruled. I know I have a big God who knows what's going on in my life and is able to take care of me. That trust brought IMMEDIATE peace. My peace was not disturbed more than fifteen seconds! Peace is also controlled by our thoughts. That is why Isaiah said in 26:3-4, *"You will keep in perfect peace him whose mind is steadfast, because he trusts in you. Trust in the Lord forever, for the Lord, the Lord, is the Rock eternal."*

2. Keep your mind steadfast. Perfect peace comes from keeping your mind steadfastly focused on thoughts of trust. Our minds are powerful forces for peace or worry, and we must understand this power. Peace is partly an issue of the mind and partly an issue of the heart. It is essential that our mind be kept steadfast–redirected back to trust. Our mental focus is on trusting Him, and not on circumstances. Peace rules when our mind is steadfast on The Rock. But sometimes our problems are so overwhelming that our mind gets spinning, and we must ask the Spirit to control our minds, which is point three.

3. Let the Spirit take over. When we are so bombarded with fear and worry that we cannot keep our minds steadfast, then we need to call on the Spirit for back-up. Romans 8:6: *"The mind of sinful man is death, but the mind controlled by the Spirit is life and peace;"* The Spirit of God can help us control our thoughts when we cannot. During this time, your prayer can be "Spirit of God, take control of my thoughts and help me to trust you."

4. Let peace be the guard of your heart. Philippians 4:6-7: *"Do not be anxious about anything, but in everything, by prayer and petition, with thanksgiving, present your requests to God. And the peace of God, which transcends all understanding, will guard your hearts and your minds in Christ Jesus."* The word "guard" is the Greek word *phroureo* [froo·reh·o]: "to guard, protect by a military guard, either to prevent hostile invasion, or to keep the inhabitants of a besieged city from flight."[3]

Peace is like a guard that is stationed at your heart to keep worry and fear OUT and to keep trust in God and rest IN. Our hearts and minds need protection from the incoming assaults of worry and fear. Philippians 4:6 teaches us anxiousness is the enemy of our hearts and minds. We are not to let these enemies in. Instead we are to pray. PRAY ABOUT EVERYTHING YOU ARE ANXIOUS ABOUT. A lot of people don't pray about small things because they feel God doesn't want to be bothered with little things. Or they feel unworthy of taking up God's time with these small things. This verse teaches the opposite. Listen to this well:

If a thought makes you anxious—God says pray about it!

God says *"Do not be anxious about anything."* That covers it all. God does not want us to be anxious; instead, He wants us to pray about whatever makes us anxious. We are to make these prayers WITH thanksgiving.

<u>**5. Pray with "Thank You" notes attached.**</u> Normal prayer is "God, help me." "God, I need this or that." Praying with thanksgiving means to attach a "thank you" note to each request. "God, help me! And, God, I thank you for helping me. You always do." When we pray like that, He promises peace will guard over our hearts and minds, *"And the peace of God, which transcends all understanding, will guard your hearts and your minds in Christ Jesus."*

In order to experience *Zoe* to the Max we must learn the five principles above. God wants us to live each day with a peaceful heart - a heart and mind that are at peace because we are trusting in God. His peace rules our hearts. God doesn't want our hearts to be anxious, filled with that gnawing feeling. If there is any gnawing, then perfect peace is not yet perfect. Peace is the deep smile inside our trusting hearts. That peace guards us from anxiety and fear.

It's a Choice

Jesus said *"LET NOT your heart be troubled."* It is a choice. He didn't say, "I will not let your hearts be troubled." I hear people say, "I can't help it." They are wrong. Worry is a choice, and trust is a choice, and prayer is a choice. God wants His transcendent peace to rule our hearts, but it will not happen if we do not make the right choices. Trust in God, and peace will rule. You cannot trust in God and be troubled at the same time.

When you and I worry, it's because we are making the choice to allow anxious thoughts and fears to remain. Worry seems to be the most socially acceptable sin I see in the Christian community. Maybe some would say I am overstating this. A lot of Christians feel worry is an acceptable extension of concern. But worry is a biblically indefensible position. How can you worry and trust in God at the same time? God doesn't worry, and He tells us not to worry. When we allow ourselves to remain in a state of worry, we are stepping outside of God's will. George Mueller was a famous man of faith who said this, "The beginning of anxiety is the end of faith, and the beginning of true faith is the end of anxiety."[4] I wrote this quote from John Wesley in my Bible when I heard it: "I would no more worry than to curse or swear." If worry is not sin, it is its first cousin because it is certainly not faith and faith is what pleases God (Hebrews 11:6).

The peace of God ought to rule our hearts and minds. Our hearts should never be ruled by anxiety and fear. Keep your hearts and minds anxiety-free and fear-free by always choosing to trust in God as a habit. Choose to keep your minds focused on trust and when anxious thoughts and fears arrive, do not let them in the door! Let the peace of God answer the door! Let's review the five principles that make a peaceful heart and a peaceful mind a possibility:

1. Trust in God.
2. Keep your mind steadfast.
3. Let the Spirit take over.
4. Let peace be the guard of your heart.
5. Pray with "Thank You" notes attached.

Chapter 15: *Zoe* Zone Part 5
Emotionally Healthy

- 1 of 10—Learn to enjoy the presence of the Lord
- 2 of 10—Spend time with the Teacher and The Book
- 3 of 10—Rejoice to re-juice
- 4 of 10—Peace-ruled heart

As we move into this fifth area of the *Zoe* Zone, we will look at how our emotional health affects our *Zoe* experience. The subject of emotional health is addressed in the Bible in various ways, using terms like peace, faith, love and heart. It is also addressed in the field of psychology. Some people think psychology is an evil word. It is not. It is the study of why people act the way they do. Christianity and psychology both look at what motivates people to act in certain ways. It's important to look at what Christian psychologists and the scientific community, in general, have learned over the years as they have studied how human beings work. Since we know God is the Creator of man, the study of how man works and acts is really the study of the glory of God. Learning from this can help us understand how we can function better both emotionally, spiritually and physically. The Bible has much to say about how we should live, but it was not meant to include every detail of every subject of life. For example, the Bible doesn't teach us that eating too much sugar causes cavities in our teeth. But we have learned this through scientific study, and it is wise for us to use this knowledge to live responsibly. In the same way, there are many other truths about our emotional, mental, spiritual and physical makeup that are not addressed directly in the Bible. Yet, they are true. Of course, all of these discoveries <u>must not contradict the principles of the Bible.</u> Anything that contradicts God's Word must be rejected because the Bible is clearly superior TRUTH. I don't think that we, as Christians, need to be afraid of truth found in science or psychology. Truth is reality, and God is all about dealing with truth and reality. I believe Spirit-led Christians can pray for discernment as they learn from all fields of secular study. We should learn from the good and reject the bad.

Three Tanks

As we look at this area of emotional health, we first acknowledge humans are physical, emotional and spiritual beings. I will always be grateful to Pastor Bill Hybels for his teaching on this subject. He teaches there are three areas of our lives that need to be monitored and replenished regularly. These areas are physical, emotional and spiritual. It's as though we have three internal fuel tanks—a physical tank that holds our physical energy, an emotional tank that fuels our emotional strength and a spiritual tank that holds our spiritual reserves. All three sources of energy are important in being a healthy, balanced person, and, therefore, each tank must be monitored and replenished. Let's study each tank.

<u>A. Physical Tank:</u> We need physical energy to be mentally alert, feel good and function well.

<u>Monitored by:</u> When our physical fuel tank is low, we feel tired or sleepy. Obviously, when this tank is empty we cannot expect top performance, and we cannot expect ourselves to feel good when we are physically tired. Some people think they are spiritually weak when they are really just physically weary. For example, if you are married and try to work out a conflict late at night, you can't expect your best performance or best response because your physical reserves are gone. It doesn't mean you have a spiritual problem or character flaw when your response is less than best when you are physically tired.

<u>Replenished by:</u> Physical energy is renewed by physical rest, nutrition and sleep. Our physical fuel tanks are refilled with nutritional food, rest and sleep. Entire books have been written about this area so I won't try to duplicate what other authors have covered well. I will only mention the obvious. We must learn to respect our physical limitations and replenish our tank when it is low.

• <u>Adequate sleep</u> is important for us to feel good and function normally. No matter how spiritual you and I may be, we cannot function well without adequate sleep. Therefore, adequate sleep IS a spiritual activity. It is a stewardship issue. We are responsible to manage our physical resources and respect our physical limitations. Jesus Himself needed adequate R & R.

• <u>Good nutrition</u> is also important to physical health, but is often ignored. Your body is like a machine that needs the right kinds of fuel to operate as God designed. Without the right fuels, it will not work as designed. There are a lot of Christians who ignore their physical fuel tanks and wonder why they don't feel better. For example, if you fill your tank with too many processed carbohydrates, you feel slug-gish, and you are likely to gain weight.

• <u>A weekly day of rest</u> is an essential part of God's plan for long-term replenishment. He designed us to need one day of rest in seven in order for our bodies to be both physically and emotionally healthy. God set it up from the beginning of creation that man must have a weekly sabbath rest which will be discussed in detail later. Those who disregard this need will suffer negative consequences.

B. Emotional tank: Our emotional tank is the hardest tank to understand and easiest to overlook. We need our emotional energy to care about other people and love. When our emotional strength is gone, we want to "get away from it all."

<u>Monitored by:</u> When our emotional fuel tank gets low, our desire to care about others lessens. We might feel "tired of people" or "burned-out." We start to loose our passion for loving people or even being around people. The signs to monitor are subtle and mostly felt internally. Some people think when they feel this way, they are hav-ing a spiritual crisis or need a spiritual renewal when the reality is they are probably emotionally drained. Emotional energy is needed for us to have passion and empathy and to experience *Zoe* to the Max! It is part of feeling restored and ready to engage people again.

<u>Replenished by:</u> Emotional energy is renewed in different ways by different personalities. Some people are emotionally replenished by reading or walking. Others just need some "down time" alone with a book or movie. Some are replenished by recreational activities like golfing, fishing, shopping, hiking, yard work, sports or crafts. My wife loves to get a bottle of cherry Pepsi and watch old episodes of the Andy Griffith Show. I enjoy a fresh cup of Starbucks and read-ing the newest Christian book or sitting in my lounge chair in our sunroom and looking at God's creation. I am also replenished by kayaking or camping or hiking. Each of us need to learn the activi-ties that refill your emotional tank and then incorporate regular replenishing activities into your life. This is part of being a well-

rounded, emotionally healthy person. It is part of be a good manager of what God has given you. We need to learn that times of giving should be followed by times of replenishing. Our lives should have healthy cycles of serving, followed by replenishing. This may sound selfish to the workaholic-type personalities, but it is not. It is called good management. Serious, emotional burnout damage or emotional breakdown can occur when we neglect to regularly refill our emotional tanks. I believe emotional burnout contributes to Christians becoming vulnerable to temptation to "do something stupid" just because they disregarded their emotional tanks.

<u>C. Spiritual tank:</u> Our spiritual tank is what we have been talking about for most of this book. It needs to be monitored and topped off regularly to keep experiencing *Zoe* in our lives.

<u>Monitored by:</u> When our spiritual fuel tank starts to get low, we feel less desire for God and His Word and ministry. We need to take a regular look at this tank to make sure it is full of motivation and love for the Lord. I monitor my passion for each day's *Zoe* Word as a good indicator to me of my spiritual tank's level. Other monitors include how much passion we have for serving and loving God and others.

<u>Replenished by:</u> This entire book addresses the many ways in which we can replenish our spiritual fuel tanks! As we wrap ourselves around the Lord, we are renewed. I think of Isaiah 40:31: *"But those who hope in the Lord will renew their strength. They will soar on wings like eagles; they will run and not grow weary, they will walk and not be faint."* This verse teaches our spiritual energy is renewed by the Lord. Revival shouldn't be only once or twice a year. The *Zoe* Zone is living in a more or less continuous state of revival. Think of the word. Re-vive. "Vive" is to live (*Zoe*) and "re-" is to renew. So when we are seeking *Zoe* to the Max we are seeking continuous renewal of our life in Christ.

No Tank Switches Installed

God did not install fuel connectors between our tanks. There's no flip switch to go to another tank when one of them is empty. Friend, when you are out of gas, you are out. The only option is to refill. I don't care how "spiritual" you are—when your physical tank is empty, you need to stop and get some rest. No amount of prayer is going to change that. God has provided a means of refilling our physical tank—it's called sleep. God has provided a means of refilling our emotional tank—it's called sabbath rest. If one tank is full, it doesn't compensate for another being empty.

You've Got to Get this Concept!

Consider the following scenarios:

• Full physical tank + full emotional tank + EMPTY spiritual tank = a strong, good feeling person who is operating in the power of the flesh and needs a revival of passion for God and His Word

• Full physical tank + EMPTY emotional tank + full spiritual tank = a strong, but burned-out person who loves God but wants to "get away from it all" and needs some balance in the area of recreation

• EMPTY physical tank + full emotional tank + full spiritual tank = a tired person who wants to help others and loves God but feels weak and needs some rest

There are many other combinations possible, but I think you get the point. The *Zoe* Zone is when all three tanks are balanced and regularly replenished. This is called good fuel management. The focus of this chapter is on managing the emotional tank. That is the tank that is least well known and most abused. Let me show you how God led me to understand this whole area of emotional health.

Emotional Health?

Prior to 1993, I had no concept of emotional health. At that time, I put everything in life in one of two boxes: physical or spiritual. If someone had a problem, I would trace it to either their physical health or their spiritual health. So every problem could be solved by "really getting saved" or "getting entirely sanctified" or "giving it to God" or "praying more" or "having regular devotions" or "eating right and exercising" or "getting some sleep" or "going to the doctor." As I look back, I realize I may have done a disservice to some people who were hurting with quick-fix spiritual answers to their deep-seated emotional hurts. I regret that. If you were one of these people, I'm sorry. I didn't know any better and hadn't been taught any differently. I put the right medicine on the wrong wounds. I told a lot of weary people to "try harder," "set your priorities," and "be more disciplined." Good message—wrong application.

On March 11, 1993, I attended a church growth conference called "Age of Rage" sponsored by the Charles E. Fuller Institute. My pastor Jerome Hancock and several staff and lay leaders attended this as a part of our church's efforts to stay current with contemporary culture. The reason I remember the exact date of an event sixteen years ago is this conference LITERALLY changed my life. I would not be writing this book if it weren't for that conference.

I vividly remember the two presenters. One was Jeff Van Vonderen, a pastor of counseling at Church of the Open Door. The other was Ted Roberts, senior pastor of East Hill Foursquare Church. Both of them made the case for church leaders to understand the emotional hurt in our society and provide a recovery-minded, emotionally healthy approach to ministry. They taught us the connection between our spiritual health and our emotional health. They taught us sin causes emotional pain and man has become dysfunctional in relating to others because of it. They showed us how many of the problems people experience are not because they are spiritually weak, but because they are emotionally unhealthy. A spiritually healthy person can be an emotionally unhealthy person. I didn't know that was possible.

How does a person become emotionally unhealthy?

I learned children can get injured by emotionally unhealthy parents. For example, a child is promised a special trip. A date is set and the child anticipates as each day passes. On the morning of the trip, the parents change their minds and decide that they are "too tired" to go or they plan to do something else instead. The child is devastated. All of us have experienced a disappointment like that, but, if it happens often enough, the child gets wounded by the parents in the area of trust. If this occurs often enough the child learns that he or she can't trust the parents to do what they promise. The child fears that he or she might get let down at the last minute. To protect themselves emotionally from further harm, the child builds up "inner protective walls" that keep from further injury. This inner protective wall is constructed out of inner promises the child makes to him or herself. The child vows, "I can't trust people" or "I won't ask them for anything so I can't be disappointed again." or "Never trust anyone in authority. Look out for yourself because no one else will."

The problem with this protective wall is that it keeps out both the good and the bad. The love the child could experience is kept out by the protective wall and as the child grows up, he or she finds it difficult to have healthy trusting relationships with other adults because, inwardly, this hurt person is still hiding behind a wall so he or she won't get hurt anymore. These people become emotionally unhealthy with unwarranted suspicions and the inability to have intimate friendships. This unhealthiness also manifests itself in their relationship with God as well. "What if God lets me down?" is asked subconsciously. God isn't allowed behind the wall either.

Emotionally unhealthy people act and react in unhealthy ways. Psychologists have labeled this as dysfunctional. "Dysfunctional" means a person acts in ways which are either not helpful or are hurtful or irrational. He or she has trouble with relationships because he or she is somewhat suspicious or untrusting and therefore distant. There is also difficulty working through conflict because this person lacks the security to be open and vulnerable.

Dysfunctional people are not "bad people". They are wounded people who have learned unhealthy ways of relating to others because of the hurts they have experienced. Their emotional unhealthiness causes them to act in a dysfunctional manner. As these people grow up, they become dysfunctional parents who then, unknowingly, cause their children to be dysfunctional. On and on the cycle goes, affecting our entire society, including "good Christian families."

The question at this conference was then posed: "Do you know your emotional pains and dysfunctions? If not, then you may be blind to the hurts that are buried deep inside of your emotional memory." This was a totally new concept for me to learn. I learned these hurts drive us subconsciously.

Got Dysfunction?

I learned, because of the wide-spread nature of these emotional injuries, all families are probably dysfunctional to some extent. It is important to be able to identify what your family's dysfunction is/was. Once you understand your family dynamics, you can then begin to recover from the resulting unhealthiness. That's why the word "recovery" is used. The goal, then, is to recover from the hurts of the emotional damage and move toward emotional health.

As children, we all assume our family is "normal." We have no way of knowing any differently. We learn from our families how to live life and how to relate to others. If you were raised in a dysfunctional family, then, by definition, you must be somewhat dysfunctional yourself. You may not have the same type of dysfunction, but you had to act in a dysfunctional manner in order to cope with your environment. Dysfunction creates pain, and pain creates dysfunction. Perhaps you know the pain of having needs unmet by your family. The only question is: Have you identified your unhealthiness? If you ignore it and pretend it doesn't exist, it will still affect you on a subconscious level.

A few years ago, I accidentally cut my chin shaving, and then, before it could heal completely, I accidentally cut it again and then again a week later. The scab seemed to make it susceptible to getting cut. This pattern continued several times over the next months until I developed the habit of covering it up with my finger to keep myself from cutting it again. That looked a little silly, but who's watching? This seemed to work well, and eventually I stopped cutting it, but unfortunately the multiple incidents left a permanent mole-like bump. Every day I had to shave with one finger on my "bump" because I was fearful of cutting it again.

When we get "cut" emotionally over and over again, the hurt eventually becomes a scar that causes us to avoid certain activities. Many people find relationships difficult because they are protecting their "bumps" as the other person is protecting their "bumps," each trying to protect themselves from further injury.

Looking for Hurtful Memories

When I first heard this information at the "Age of Rage" conference, I was motivated to uncover any emotional unhealthiness inside me because I wanted to be the best I could be for God. If emotional unhealthiness was inside me and affecting me, I wanted to know about it and get it fixed. I started scanning my past, looking for any hurtful events that may have wounded me emotionally. It may be surprising to you to learn I had a difficult time remembering any hurtful memories because of the blessing of being raised in a good Christian home. My parents really did love God and did their best to raise me and my brother Doug and my sister Diane as well as they could. Along with having this good start, I invited God into my life at an early age and followed Him throughout my life.

My High School Wrestling Coach

After several more hours of teaching at this seminar and talking with my pastor between sessions, I finally remembered one bad experience with my wrestling coach in high school. I remembered one match in which I felt the referee had made a bad call and caused me to lose the match. In my immaturity, my anger boiled over, and I threw my head gear down as I walked to the bench. The referee then called a technical foal against our team causing us to lose a team point.

The next day at practice the coach decided to humiliate me in front of the guys for my "head gear throwing" incident. He called me out in front of the team and said "Okay, Spaur, why don't you show us how to throw your head gear down like you did last night." He made me throw it off a couple of times as "payback." After that I lost all respect for him and later quit the team. That was immature of me, but I guess it was a typical tenth grader's reaction. I hadn't thought of that incident in more than twenty years, but it was the only hurtful memory I could recall.

As we continued in the seminar, the presenters taught us inside of those hurtful memories are frozen emotions. These frozen hurts affect us every day in some subconscious way. When we are put in a situation that feels emotionally familiar, we instinctively move to protect our "bump." It becomes a "hot button" in our lives. If someone accidentally hits that "hot button", we overreact.

I did not know of any present affect this "wrestling coach incident" was having; however, I did not want anything to hinder me so I decided that I would do what they said and "process the hurtful memory."

Processing Hurtful Memories

In the case of my wrestling coach, there could be some anger toward the coach or feelings of shame that were "frozen" inside of me. The reason they got "frozen" was they were not properly processed at the time. Children and adolescents lack the maturity and may lack the support to properly process their hurt feelings. This is especially true if they are in a dysfunctional family or lack a strong self-image. They don't know what to do with their feelings, so they "stuff" them. These stuffed feelings become "frozen" over time in the subconscious.

The way to properly process these "frozen" feelings is to "unfreeze" them by re-feeling them. This requires spending time with our memory and imagination. This may sound weird to you as it did to me when I first heard it. I didn't know anything about "frozen" feelings, but since then I have learned psychologists and counselors call this "original pain work." I'm going to take the risk of sharing some private things with you about how I processed my memories in hopes that it will help you.

Original Pain—Prayer and Memory Therapy:

1. <u>Begin with a time of prayerful reflection.</u> Invite the Holy Spirit to come and assist you in remembering the hurtful event and heal your emotional hurts.

2. <u>Imagine yourself back to the age of the memory.</u> Try to imagine how you felt at the time, where you were, the environment or surroundings. In my case, I was a fourteen-year-old teenager.

3. <u>Imagine yourself re-living the event.</u> Try to put yourself there, and feel how you felt then. How do you feel toward the people in your memory? Draw the feelings out. Embrace the pain, shame, fear or anger.

4. <u>Defend yourself.</u> Say aloud what should have been said then. Now you are an adult, you know what should have been said to those who hurt you. Ask the questions which should have been asked. Tell everyone involved in the situation what should have been said.

This is what I said to the referee at that wrestling match, "You big, lazy ref, why couldn't you see that I clearly had the guy pinned!" I felt a wave of anger as I told that referee off! Then I went to my memory of wrestling practice the next day and pointed my finger at the coach and said, "Listen, Bud, how dare you humiliate me in front of all my team mates? You had no right to do that. You should have talked to me privately if you wanted to correct me. You humiliated me in front of all the guys, and that's wrong!" I was barking those words at him with the anger that was unfreezing after all those years. Finally, someone was telling him off! I was not a helpless teenager defenseless against the coach. I had a defender there!

5. <u>Say what should have been said to you.</u> I know this sounds weird, but say to yourself what you wish someone would have said

to you. It would have been right for someone to have been there to comfort you and protect you. You need to hear the words that should have been said. Here's what I experienced. I said to myself, "Tracy, you were treated unjustly. It's not right what happened to you!" Just then I started to feel tearful emotions welling up from deep within me. "I want you to know one day you will grow up and be successful and see

> *I could not believe the well of sadness, anger and deep emotions that rushed out of me at that moment.*

that this coach was just an immature, ego-maniac who got his thrills from controlling and humiliating teenagers. You're a good kid, and you don't deserve to be treated like this." I started crying more or less uncontrollably as I said these things to myself. I could not believe the well of sadness, anger and deep emotions that rushed out of me at that moment. No one had ever been my advocate like that before! No one had ever encouraged me like that before. I'm teary-eyed right now as I am writing this because that imaginary statement satisfied a deep unmet need I had.

6. <u>Invite Jesus into the memory and let him come and comfort everyone.</u> I imagined Jesus then coming into the picture. He spoke His words of encouragement to me, and I sensed His love and healing. I know this sounds weird but it was as if there were three of us there. My younger, hurt self, my present adult self, and Jesus. It was a healing time. I heard what I needed to hear and said what I needed to say and felt the healing presence of Jesus come and comfort me there. I think psychologists call this reintegration of the personality. They would say that part of me split off years ago, and now I was coming back together—I am told they call this "flooding."

It was all over in a few minutes. The volcano of emotion was gone, and I was just left in a state of shock after experiencing all those unfrozen feelings. How could that have been inside me all those years without me knowing about it? It really shocked me and even scared me to think those emotions had been deep inside me.

After this experience at the seminar, Jerome and I stayed up until late into the night talking about all this and his own hurtful memories. I clearly remember that talk while camping in the church parking lot in my RV. After the seminar was over, I felt a difference inside of me. I felt more open and more compassionate toward others, and more "free" inside. I knew there was truth in what I had discovered, and I wanted more!

My friend Becki was already into all this "emotional recovery" stuff that I had thought was just for the "other people." I realized it was for me too, so I asked her what I should do next. She suggested I read "Search for Significance" by Robert McGee and "Healing for Damaged Emotions" by David Seamonds. As I read these books, I became curious about what other memories might be hidden. I started spending time journaling and praying about this and asking the Holy Spirit to search my memory for other hurtful events.

Over the next few months I was able to remember other hurtful memories. It seems each processed memory would trigger another hurtful memory. They were linked like a chain. Each memory contained frozen pain of different sorts. One of my memories had to do with the shame I had about my appearance. Then I had to deal with some feelings of resentment I felt toward my dad and mom. Then I processed some resentment towards my grandparents and a guy I had a fight with in high school. I then dealt with my embarrassment over being suspended from school for three days for accidentally pulling the fire alarm while trying to show off to some girls. Then there was the memory of my junior high school principal telling me and my mother that I was not capable of handling algebra. Other memories are more private. Each memory had some pain to process using the six steps above. Frozen feelings of shame, anger, hurt, resentment, and regret found their way out of me. I kept track of each processed memory until I came up with a total of twelve memories! Think of that. I started out not being able to even remember one single hurtful memory, and all the time there were twelve in there! That makes me shake my head in wonder. How could twelve hurtful memories exist inside of me without my awareness of them?

After processing these painful memories and reading those books, I felt more real and more open and alive than ever before. I realize now through that series of events, God had healed my emotions. I could feel love better, and I could empathize with other people's pain better. It was like my "feeler" got fixed. I didn't know it needed fixed, but it did. After my emotional healing, I become a lot more patient with hurting people's struggles. I got rid of my simple "easy-fix" solutions. My advice became much wiser.

I became personally challenged to seek more healing, so I made an appointment with a Christian psychologist for further evaluation. He asked me if I had any "issues", and I told him about my experiences and I was there to get a "checkup from the neck up." I wanted to see if there were any other hidden issues that were hindering me in ways I was unaware. I could tell he was not very accustomed to requests like that. He gave me a couple of questionnaires to fill out and mail in. Those questionnaires asked me every question in the book. I wrote down answers and thoughts I had never told anyone else. I was a little nervous when I went to my next appointment because he knew ALL MY SECRETS. He concluded that I had two remaining issues.

Father Hurts

He said I had unmet emotional needs from my relationship with my father during my childhood years. My father taught me a strong faith in God. He is a true Christian and faithful worker in the church. He helps the poor and needy and strangers. He gives away bibles and gospel tracts wherever he goes. He is "the real deal" in his relationship with God. He taught me to fear and respect God. On the physical side, he was a hard worker—not a lazy bone in his body—and provided for the needs of our family. On the emotional side, he didn't do as well. He was not physically abusive, but emotionally distant. He was the youngest of twelve children and was emotionally neglected by his parents and verbally abused by his father. His father told him once, "Boy, you ain't worth the salt in your bread." I'm not exactly sure what that meant, but my wife tells me that when she makes bread that her recipe calls for one teaspoon of salt for every two loaves of bread. My dad got the message loud and clear. He's seventy-five years old now, and yet he clearly remembers the pain of those words spoken nearly sixty years ago. My dad didn't know how to be a nurturing father because he had never experienced it himself. He didn't know how to give what he didn't have. This caused him to harbor some unresolved anger that would come out occasionally and cause some friction in the family.

To assist me in healing this "father hurt," my counselor gave me a book called *Homecoming: Reclaiming and Championing Your Inner Child* by John Bradshaw. It helped me identify and grieve the losses I experienced even though it was a secular book and ignored the spiritual ramifications. The other book I discovered was *Making Peace with Your Father* by David Stoop. Dr. Stoop is a well-known Christian psychologist, and I would highly recommend that book for anyone dealing with father-related issues. *Father Hunger* is the other book which was also very helpful to me. I discovered I was injured because of what I did not receive. My dad did not know how to be emotionally connected with me because he was never emotionally connected with his father and absorbed in workaholic tendencies. I learned the "silent father" can still do a lot of damage to a child. I grieved the loss of not having a father that was emotionally connected with me, and I received the inner healing of My Heavenly Father. My oldest daughter, Nena, was twelve at the time of my emotional healing, so I was able to become a better nurturing father to her and to Stephanie, who was nine, and to Rebekah, who was five.

Friendship Dysfunction

The second area of need the counselor diagnosed was friendship dysfunction. By that he meant I did not have a friend that was just a friend. All of my relationships were connected with church ministry activities. We had ministry in common, but I had no one that I just hung out with because I liked them, and they liked me. The person I was the closest to was Rob Mills. He was our minister of music and then later our church administrator. He was also friendship dysfunctional as well as a workaholic, so we got along just fine! Seriously, we did some activities together outside of church with his wife Sue and my wife Valerie. I just liked him. He was funny, and we loved to crack jokes together and work on church projects together. My counselor advised me to have a "friend for friendship's sake." I learned a healthy friend is someone you just hang out with because you like being around them, not because you are working on a church project together.

I'm still working on this issue. During my childhood, my family never modeled this very well for me, although my mother disagrees. We were too much of a church-aholic family. We were always helping people, but these relationships were all one-way. My counselor said a healthy friendship is when two people are on equal footing. Not one being the giver and the other receiver. One is not less than the other. They equally want to be together.

I guess the two healthiest friendships I have now are Wynne Lankford and Russ Randall. Jerome Hancock is also a friend, but in a different way. He and I have an unusually close relationship. He confides in me about personal things, and we talk a lot. Most of our talk, however, is church related. My counselor would not count him as a "friend for friend's sake". Wynne is also on our church staff, but he and I just like each other for reasons other than church. We call and talk about real things, and he is genuinely interested in me as a person. Russ is also a friend. We have shared a lot over the years, and we are genuinely interested in each other. Our relationship has deepened over time. I hope to continue to learn what it means to be a friend and have a friend.

Independence, Dependence and Interdependence

I think part of my friendship dysfunction has something to do with the fact I was raised to be so independent I don't really know how to need other people. I was taught dependence was bad and independence was good. I was not really taught the healthy middle ground, which I've learned since is interdependence.

—Dependence means being needy - not a healthy position.

—Independence means not needing anyone - also, not a healthy position.

—Interdependence means that you are a healthy person who is self-sufficient, but knows when and how to ask for help in the areas where help is needed.

I am seeking to recover from my state of unhealthy independence to become a healthier, interdependent person. Part of that is learning how to be vulnerable and ask for help. One hindrance I have had with learning to be vulnerable is some people do not want me to be that honest. Some people want me to be their hero, and they don't like for their heroes to be imperfect. Others want to fix my vulnerabilities instead of just listening and empathizing.

Some people freak out when I truthfully answer the customary "How are you?" by saying, "Not too well right now." They look at me with this wide-eyed, mouth-opened, slap-their-cheeks look.

"What's wrong?" they exclaim. Then I have to stop and calm them down from the shock of hearing I am not on the top of the world right then. Sometimes it makes me wish I had just said the customary "Fine." But I am learning each time I explain to someone how I am really doing it is an opportunity to show them that I am an honest human being and that I do have needs.

Surprise Tears

So there you have my testimony of emotional healing which occurred over several years. I remember several years ago, when I was driving down the road with my family in our RV, Rebekah was sitting up front with me. Somehow we were talking about little league baseball and how I used to play on a team when I was young. Then Rebekah asked me a question that suddenly put me back in recovery mode. She asked, "Daddy, did you ever hit a home run?" As she asked that question, it hit me in an unexpected soft spot. I teared up as I answered in a somewhat broken voice, "No, honey, I was never able to do that, but I sure did want to and I tried as hard as I could, but I never could hit a home run." Somehow she had touched a spot that contained some hidden sadness. I was inwardly disappointed I had never been able to succeed in sports the way I wanted. I needed to grieve over that. Later that day, I spent some time going back to that feeling and really embracing it and grieving—grieving the fact I was never successful in sports. That's hard for a kid to embrace.

I've learned whenever I tear up, or have an unwarranted reaction to some event, it means there is a hurt that needs uncovering and healing. Then I go after that pain until I find the original source of hurt, and I grieve over the situation by embracing those feelings. Grieving is embracing the sadness of whatever the loss was. Some people run away from the pain and stuff it down. That leads to problems later on. I have found the healthier response is to:

Follow the pain to the hurt and then grieve the loss.

That is the formula for processing hurts. Embrace the grief; don't avoid it. If you avoid it, you will have a "beach ball eruption" later on. Let me explain.

Beach Ball Eruptions

Have you ever tried to hold a beach ball under water? How about trying to hold down two or more? It's hard to do, and it will wear you out. Stuffing emotional pain is like holding down those beach balls. You can hold it down for a time, but eventually it will wear you out. Holding in emotional pain takes a lot of energy.

I believe this explains why people have mid-life crises. They get to be thirty or forty years old, and they are emotionally weary but don't know why. Then they do something stupid. Sometimes they have an extramarital affair or change careers or move. They wear out from holding the beach balls down and are emotionally exhausted so the beach balls start to erupt! They explode! They lose it! They are suddenly fed up with their spouse and job and life in general. They are worn out and bored with life. They want to feel fresh and alive again so they start doing illogical things.

A much saner plan would be to seek emotional health before the beach balls erupt. It is better to find the beach balls underwater where they hide and poke holes in them, letting the air out slowly. The air is the emotional pain that needs to be processed before it erupts.

Depression

Sometimes frozen pain is experienced as depression. Depression can be anger turned inward. When you are angry with yourself at an early age, it can turn into a self-hatred that is subliminal and can manifest itself as depression. I have heard it said depression is frozen anger. I have seen many people freed from depression after they began to experience emotional healing.

Some kinds of depression are not emotional but physical. Some people's brains do not produce enough "feeling good" hormones. I'm told that when the neuro-chemical Serotonin is depleted that we feel depressed. Some families have a hereditary susceptibility to depression. If you suffer with depression, it may be due to either of these causes, but I would encourage you to seek emotional healing and see if that lessens your depression.

Leaning Trees

Last night I was meeting my daughter Stephanie at Panera Bread to help her balance her checkbook when I got a call from my wife

Valerie saying, "A tree just fell in the driveway!" A huge tree had fallen between my garage and the RV shed, completely covering my driveway. The tree covered an area as wide as five parked cars. It was a delayed reaction from Hurricane Isabel that had hit my property 21 months earlier. The particular tree that fell that night had been leaning at an angle after the storm, but I thought that since it hadn't fallen after all this time that it had perhaps reestablished itself as a "leaning tree." Well, my "leaning tree" is leaning no more.

How many "leaning trees" are in your life? The storms of your past may have done some damage that weakened a part of you. You may think you are "over it" and have cleaned up the mess long ago, but later on, at an unpredictable time, maybe years later, a "leaning tree" may crash down and create a huge problem.

A "leaning tree" may be something hurtful that was said to you during a stormy argument. At the time you felt you shrugged it off, but later it fell all over you. Or it may be something you did or said to someone else that hurt them, but they have not told you about it because they are holding it inside. One day something will trigger the "leaning tree", and it will come crashing down in a huge fall.

Some have said we need to bury the past and live in the present. I agree with that if we have first done a complete inventory, unpacked the baggage, processed the hurts and learned everything we can from it. Then we can bury it. Don't bury it while it is still alive! If you do, it will just lie inside you and kick the coffin.

Relationship Conflicts Uncover Needs

The quality of our relationships is also one of the greatest indicators of our emotional health. Emotionally unhealthy people have a lot of relationship problems. Their conflicts often reveal internal unhealthiness. For example, insecurities cause conflicts that would be unnecessary if the person were emotionally secure. Also, unhealthy fears make us overreact, and poor self-esteem causes us to be overly defensive and sensitive to criticism.

Do you have people in your life you have "cut off" or have unresolved conflict with or that you avoid? Most likely you need to examine yourself for your part in creating those conflicts. It's easy for us to blame everything on the other person. We can always justify our actions by pointing to something in the other person's life, but I have found our own emotional unhealthiness causes a lot of conflicts which are blamed on other things. We point to a flaw in the other person, but do not take responsibility for our own hyper-sensitivity or over-reaction to it.

Crisis Uncovers Need

Often it takes a falling-tree crisis like marital conflict, or problems with teenagers, or the loss of a job to reveal people's need for emotional healing. Crises lead people to seek counseling. Good counseling then reveals the need for emotional healing. Good Christian counseling is essential to helping people find emotional healing—not just biblical counseling but counseling that understands psychology also. Some "biblical" counselors are simply Bible teachers that try to answer every problem from a Bible-only perspective. Their counselees receive good spiritual advice but lack the emotional component that is needed. Most pastors are not good counselors. They are good spiritual advisors, but not necessarily good counselors. Hopefully they know their limits and refer people to Christian counselors.

To seek counseling does not mean you are weak. It means you are smart! People who are too proud or self-sufficient to seek help from others will suffer the consequences of remaining unhealthy. We can't always fix ourselves. We need those who have been trained and gifted by God to help us. About fifteen

> *To seek counseling does not mean you are weak.*

years ago my dental hygienist found a small cavity in my tooth. I checked it myself in a mirror, and, sure enough, she was right. It was a small cavity, one that I fix on others every day. I thought to myself, "I can fix that. I'll just gets some mirrors and fix my own tooth!" So I set up the necessary instruments and with the help of my dental assistant, I revved up my high speed drill and carefully started to drill on my tooth! It was very difficult and nerve racking to work backwards on myself. After a couple of attempts, I gave up. I couldn't bring myself to do it. What was so quick and simple for me to do on others was very difficult to do on myself. In the same way, we cannot counsel ourselves. We cannot see ourselves objectively. t doesn't mean we are not smart or we are unskilled, but it does mean we need someone else with a different perspective and professional training to guide us.

It doesn't have to take a crisis to reveal our need for emotional healing. Sometimes people discover it on their own spiritual journey like I did. You may be sensing a need right now as you are reading this chapter. That's a good beginning. It is better to discover the beach balls before they erupt, so that they can be slowly deflated. I encourage you to start your journey toward emotional healing. If you are still not convinced of your need, how about a little questionnaire?

<u>Emotional Health Quiz</u>

1. Yes or No? Are there any active or unresolved conflicts in your life?

2. Yes or No? Have you made a thorough inventory of your past hurts to unpack and discover how they have affected your life?

3. Yes or No? Do you have outbursts of anger that are not appropriate or proportional to the situation that triggered them?

4. Yes or No? Do you have at least one close friend, other than a spouse, that you hang out with?

5. Yes or No? Are any of your actions motivated by a need to gain the approval of other people or the fear of angering other people?

6. Yes or No? Have you analyzed the family you were raised in and figured out its dysfunctions?

7. Yes or No? When you perform, are you haunted by fears of failure and humiliation?

8. Yes or No? Do you have good relationships with all your close family members?

9. Yes or No? Are you wondering about what people think of you?

10. Yes or No? Do your children feel free to talk to you?

11. Yes or No? Have you been seriously accused of being a workaholic within the past year?

12. Yes or No? Do you often compare yourself with others?

KEY TO QUIZ

Unhealthy answers are "Yes" to any odd numbered question and "no" to any even numbered question.

Chapter 16: *Zoe* Zone Part 5 (cont.)
The Paths to Emotional Health

Maybe you thought emotional healing and counseling were only for those who were "really messed up." The truth is this whole world has been messed up by the sins and selfishness of man. We are all sinners, who were raised by sinners, who hurt or neglected each other, and all this produces dysfunction and emotional pain. Once you realize you need to be emotionally healthy, there are several paths to emotional health. First, ask the Holy Spirit to guide you as you find the best path for yourself. Don't be fooled into thinking emotional healing comes from some kind of miracle healing prayer or having some "super Christian" pray over you. Emotional health involves the work of self-examination and the work of applying truth and allowing that truth to renew your mind. It is a combination of your desire to be whole and the healing power of the Holy Spirit working together along with three elements: truth, grace, and time. Below is the formula for emotional healing.

TRUTH + Grace + Time = Emotional Healing

Truth

First, you need to learn and apply the truth to your life in every area of life. When I say truth, I mean The Truth as found in the Holy Scriptures ALONG WITH all that is true about ourselves and others. As I said earlier, all truth is ultimately from God. So emotional healing begins with a journey to uncover anything that is false in our lives. That's why it's work. It takes effort to do this kind of discovery. Once the falseness is uncovered, it needs to be replaced with the truth. Here are the areas you need to search thoroughly for false beliefs:

<u>1. Your past</u>—Work to discover any past hurts which have not been processed properly. The Original Pain Prayer and Memory Therapy mentioned in the last chapter is applying truth to

unprocessed hurts. This is hard work and sometimes painful but it is a good pain because it leads to freedom and emotional health.

2. Your beliefs—Work to discover any false beliefs you may have about yourself, God or others, replacing them with the truth.

3. Your motives—Work to discover your inner motives and why you do what you do. Uncover anything that is driving you and motivating you to prove something to others and replace that with the truth—God already approves of you.

4. Your emotions—Examine your feelings and how you react to others. Are they healthy reactions? Discover how you manage and process your emotions. How long do you hold on to hurts? How long does it take you to release them in forgiveness? Are you honest about your emotions?

5. Your actions—If "60 Minutes" did an investigation of your life, what inconsistencies would they report between your actions and your beliefs?

6. Your relationships—Examine your relationships for their health indexes. If you are married, is your spouse happy with your relationship? Is truth making it into your relationships? How about your relationships with your extended family members? Learn healthy ways to resolve conflict, handle stress, and have authentic relationships.

Learn the Truth. Live the Truth.

Believing the truth and operating in the truth in each of these six areas shows your emotional health. I challenge you to search for falseness in every area and then replace it with the truth. Enjoying life in the *Zoe* Zone is learning how to live in truth in all the areas above, and it requires a self-educational course of action. You are responsible to educate yourself in all six of these areas. Think of it as investing in yourself and your family. You and your family will reap tremendous benefits from this journey to emotional health and investment in learning how to live in truth. Our educational system does not cover these subjects, and neither do most churches, so it is your responsibility to educate yourself! I am fortunate to have a pastor who educates us about emotional health issues a couple of times a year as a part of his sermon topics. But if I had waited for my church to be my sole source of education, I wouldn't be writing this book now. You must get serious about educating yourself about every area of life.

One path to learning truth is reading. Fortunately, you have the advantage of learning from my educational experiences and learning by reading this book! I thank God for those who have taught me what I have learned thus far in this area and for the great Christian authors who are writing so many helpful books about emotional health. Twenty years ago there were only a handful of books available on this subject, mostly in the secular realm, but now it is an accepted part of Christian literature. Most Christian bookstores have a section entitled Christian Psychology or Christian Living.

One of the best foundational books on this subject is *Search for Significance* by Robert McGee. I also recommend you read books that address the specific issues of your life. Christian psychologists like David Stoop, Steve Arterburn, Frank Minirth, Paul Meier, John Townsend, and Henry Cloud, to name a few, are writing helpful books that can teach you truth in so many areas. If you are not a reader, many of these books are also available on CD or cassette.

Another path to learning truth is Christian counseling. Counseling used to be the "C" word around the church, but now it is more commonly accepted as part of the ministry of the Body of Christ. It is a branch of pastoral care for those who have a shepherd's heart or the gifts of mercy, wisdom and encouragement. It is truly another gift of ministry given by the Holy Spirit to the church. Some churches now have staff counselors. Our church has a Christian counseling center housed in the church facility that operates as a part of our overall ministry. Do not hesitate to seek Christian counseling! I respect anyone who does. I think it shows you are serious about being all God wants you to be. It will make you a better spouse, friend, parent and person. I admire anyone who is willing to admit he or she DOESN'T KNOW IT ALL.

What's Your Dysfunction?

Your goal in this self-education process is to learn what your dysfunctions are. That is the truth about you. Healthy people discover;

unhealthy people cover. When I was about twelve years old, my brother Doug and I would pretend to be secret agents. We had a name for our secret agent group. It was known as S.A.D.D.L.E. We spent a long time coming up with this acronym. It stood for Secret Agent Defense Department of Law Enforcement. Man, we were cool. We sent ourselves out on secret missions. Most of our missions had to do with hiding from the enemy, our Grandpa Amick. He thought of us as idle slaves who needed to be put to work after school each day. Our mission, after coming home from school, was to remain undetected from Grandpa's view from his house on the hill. We would run from a bush to the shed to the barn, all the while doing amazing acrobatic rolls and leaps that defied gravity that kept us from being detected by the enemy.

I believe EVERYONE has some area of hurt that remains beyond human detection. We subconsciously do flips and rolls, trying to remain undetected. That hidden hurt has created a "beach ball" that is hiding under the surface. I am a testimony of a person with a "more or less" ideal Christian upbringing and one who chose to live my whole life for God, and, yet, I had twelve hurtful memories like "beach balls" undetected under the surface. I had no idea they were affecting me in any way. As I shared with you, I was able to detect and deflate each one through prayer, my reading, and Christian counseling. I discovered and applied the truth to correct the wrong beliefs I had about God, myself and others. My questions to you are, "Do you know what your issues are?" and "Are you seeking to find emotional health?"

People who don't think they are dysfunctional and haven't sought the truth about their inner workings almost certainly have some undiscovered "beach balls" that are affecting them in ways in which they are not consciously aware. The only exceptions I have seen are the rare cases where people have been raised in ideally emotionally healthy homes and who have accepted Christ as young children and were raised in good churches. Even in these cases, I would be cautious about some possible hidden issues.

Hidden Issues

<u>1. Legalism.</u> Legalistic tendencies can develop in certain personalities who view Christianity more from a "what you do" angle rather than a "whose you are" angle. I'll talk more about this later.

Legalism creates an inner, overly critical perspective which makes them inwardly judgmental and harsh. Such people are inwardly unsympathetic and critical of others who fail and therefore can be harsh and demanding. They know the theological definition of grace but it doesn't make a practical difference in how they treat themselves or others. Formerly, I was this type of person, and, until I went through my emotional healing, I did not really understand grace.

2. Guilt-driven obedience. These folks are constantly motivated to do the right thing but they perform out of either fear or guilt. They are inwardly motivated by the fear of doing the wrong thing or what they "ought to" or "should do." They are sincere in their desire to obey, but it is for a slightly skewed reason. Obedience out of guilt is not healthy obedience. Healthy obedience is motivated by love for God, not fear of feeling guilty. God wants us to live freely. True love is not for obligation, but it is living out of the overflow of love.

3. Fear of self-exposure. These folks work hard at avoiding disclosure because they are afraid of what they might find. They work hard at deflection instead of detection. They are defensive about their family and beliefs. Instead of being open to examination and feedback, they avoid them out of fear. A healthy self is open to examination, not threatened by it. Blind spots require feedback from others in order to be seen, and health welcomes this assistance.

4. Spiritual pride. These folks are not very open to talking critically about their families or private feelings because of their pride. They have their theological beliefs figured out, and they defend the way they were brought up. They don't really want anyone messing with their world. They wouldn't call it pride, but it is certainly not humility either. Humility is the willingness to be open to examination of yourself, your past and your beliefs. If your beliefs are not open to examination, then you have to ask yourself, "Why?" Being an authentic person is being humble enough to admit you may not have it all figured out right. A humble person is open to the possibility some of their beliefs may be slightly off and willing to admit inconsistencies and seek change. The way you react when an error is publicly disclosed shows your degree of humility or pride. Spiritual pride is unwilling to be open but will find a way to rationalize or excuse their behavior.

5. Spiritual abuse. Some churches or families teach a type of perfectionistic Christianity. They teach if you are "really saved" or "really sanctified" or "baptized in the Holy Spirit," you will be able to live an ideal life. Every problem is viewed in spiritual terms. Prayer, bible reading and obedience are the answers to most every problem. Holiness of heart and life is valued higher than authenticity and openness. My denomination, the Church of the Nazarene, and other holiness denominations are susceptible to this type of spiritual abuse. Holiness is sometimes taught as the answer to EVERYTHING. Overzealous preachers and evangelists portray a holiness experience that purifies your life of every defect. Sin and weaknesses of all types are instantly cured by the sanctifying power of the Holy Spirit. This creates people who are not permitted to identify sin as sin. They call sin by other more religiously acceptable terms. They can't talk about weaknesses either because they open themselves up to becoming the targets of people "praying for them" that they will "get the victory." Openness, doubt, and authenticity are uncommon. Those who are open are viewed as weak or needy. Those who are honest with their doubts are viewed as people who need more spirituality and are lacking faith. Often family tension is hidden because in some religious circles, it is not acceptable to have problems. Spiritual abusers feel people who are "right with God" don't have those kinds of problems. So many people learn to keep quiet and not admit neediness so they won't be "looked down on" by other church people. Their issues are hidden behind a religious fear of being honest about neediness and consequently being seen as "less than" perfect.

Study Your Family

Part of the search for truth is to study the family in which you were raised. You are the product of a home and of a set of parents. Even if you were raised by people other than your birth parents, that was your home of origin. The adults who raised you influenced you greatly. If they were emotionally unhealthy, YOU ARE emotionally unhealthy by default. Some would counter this by pointing to the fact they are the opposite of their unhealthy parent(s), but often they go to the opposite extreme in order to cope with the unhealthy parent's behavior. This makes them also unhealthy, but in a different way.

For example, if your father was verbally abusive to you, his words are still in your memory right now, and they affect you negatively. You may have vowed to not be verbally abusive to your children like he was to you, and yet you may overcompensate in some way because you are trying too hard to NOT be like him. As my editor, Fiona, says, "The solution is to focus on HOW YOU WANT TO BE. To focus on the NOT, is like the moth being drawn to the flame." Because you are trying to prove them wrong, you are actually being controlled by them and not being truly who God meant you to be. I know people who are motivated because they are trying to prove someone wrong, not because they really want to do right. If you are trying hard to NOT be like one of your parents, then you are actually being controlled by them. Something may be driving you that is not healthy. You may be doing the right things, but for the wrong reasons. God doesn't want us to be "driven". He wants us to live a life of love and freedom and to enjoy serving others and experience *Zoe* to the Max as we do it all. This is why we need to study our family of origin to understand how it affected us, then and now.

Psychologists have studied dysfunctional family relationships and discovered some common traits. They have discovered if one person is dysfunctional, it generally causes everyone else to act in a dysfunctional manner in response to that person. One dysfunctional person can make the whole family unit dysfunctional. An example of a dysfunctional family could be one that has a mother with uncontrolled, angry outbursts, turning to alcohol to medicate her pain. Her children are afraid of her and are

> **One dysfunctional person can make the whole family unit dysfunctional.**

insecure because they never know what will upset her. They also never learn to handle stress in healthy ways so they too turn to medications for stress relief. They may turn to food or drugs or work or relationships or materialism or overachievement to cope with stress. The dysfunctional mother usually acts irresponsibly, which creates marital tension. The husband probably has to take up some of the "slack" and becomes OVERLY responsible, trying to keep peace in the family. So the husband does all sorts of things to compensate for the wife's problem. The children sense the marital tension. They get the message everyone should try to keep mother from being upset.

The children each try to do what they can to make the family more happy and peaceful. The oldest child may become an overachiever, taking on the unspoken assignment to be the hero that makes the family feel better because of his or her successes. Another child may take on the assignment of being the family clown. The job of this child is to crack jokes in order to distract the family from the sadness of the dysfunctional home. Another child may express the pain of the family by "acting out" at school. This child becomes the "black sheep" of the family because he or she doesn't know what else to do with the hurt. He or she acts "crazy" outside because he or she feels "crazy" inside. Other children may take on the role of the overly responsible one and become the family work-horse. This job is to make up

> *Everyone takes on an artificial role, instead of discovering who God made them to be.*

for all the tension by doing more than is expected. Another child may get lost in all the confusion, coping with the stress by hiding and becoming "invisible." The feeling is if he or she didn't exist, things would be better. The roles these children take on are all in RESPONSE TO the dysfunction in the home. Everyone takes on an artificial role, instead of discovering who God made them to be. They become inauthentic to whom they should be because of these unspoken roles.

In healthy families, each person takes responsibility for his or her behavior, and each person is allowed to develop into the person God wants them to be. The child's role is to discover and maximize his or her strengths and change or manage his or her weaknesses. The parents model a healthy marriage so the children observe healthy ways of conflict resolution and stress management. Conversations are open and honest. Each person is honored and is given permission to express how he or she feels. Each person is equally valued as an important part of the family. Love and grace are lived out in balance as each child is taught to take responsibility for his or her own attitudes, feelings and actions.

So much more could be said about the importance of studying your family of origin. We have all learned "unspoken principles" from the families in which we were raised. These principles need to be uncovered and examined to see if they line up with the truth. We all should understand from what mold we came. We all should know what our dysfunctional tendencies are and how and why we learned them. None of us is responsible for the dysfunctional home we came from, but we ARE ALL responsible to learn how it has affected us and take responsibility for getting healthy.

Distorted Images of God

Another area where we need truth detection is in our image of God. Do you see God for who He really is, or for who you have been taught He is? I referred to this earlier in the chapter about enjoying God's presence. I want to take a closer look at our image of God as it affects our emotional health SO POWERFULLY.

If our image of God is distorted, then our ability to relate to Him is also distorted. For instance, if we are looking at God through a distorted lens, we might be afraid of His reactions toward us. This affects how we feel about ourselves and others. Let me "push your envelope" and show you some examples of how a distorted image of God can affect us:

An Angry God

If we see God as angry, we will be fearful to bring him our doubts because of the fear of what He might do. We all have doubts from time to time. Can we bring our doubts to an angry God? An angry God might punish us. The truth is God wants us to bring Him all our doubts! He wants us to be honest with how we feel. Remember Doubting Thomas? He doubted Jesus had risen from the dead. The resurrected Jesus did not shun or ignore Thomas, but when He appeared to the disciples He addressed Thomas directly and ministered to his doubt. *"Jesus came and stood among them and said, 'Peace be with you!' Then he said to Thomas, 'Put your finger here; see my hands. Reach out your hand and put it into my side. Stop doubting and believe.' Thomas said to him, 'My Lord and my God!' Then Jesus told him, 'Because you have seen me, you have believed; blessed are those who have not seen and yet have believed'"* (John 20:26-29).

We are not told what tone of voice Jesus used when speaking to Thomas. As you read the passage above, you could envision Jesus as either angry or loving. I lean to the loving version because that is the general demeanor of Jesus and because he entered saying "Peace be with you." He came with peace and offered Thomas visual evidence of His resurrection and an opportunity to touch His pierced side. The point I want you to see is Jesus ministered to Thomas' doubts. He didn't rebuke him outright, but he encouraged him to stop doubting. When you bring Jesus your doubts, He will minister to your doubts too. He wants us to bring Him our honest doubts and let Him help us with them.

If we see God as harsh, then we will not go to Him for comfort. He wants to be our comforter. That's why God is called *"the God of all comfort"* in 2 Corinthians 1:3, *"the Father of compassion and the God of all comfort, who comforts us in all our troubles, so that we can comfort those in any trouble with the comfort we ourselves have received from God."*

If we feel He is unsympathetic with our failures, we will hide when we fail and be harsh with ourselves. God wants to comfort us, and He is sympathetic with our weaknesses. Hebrews 4:15 says Jesus is able *"… to sympathize with our weaknesses, but we have one who has been tempted in every way, just as we are—yet was without sin. Let us then approach the throne of grace with confidence, so that we may receive mercy and find grace to help us in our time of need."*

If we feel God is "fed up" with us, then we will be afraid to take Him our failures. When we fail again and again, we become ashamed of ourselves for our failures. At this point, we will push God away if we feel He is fed up with us too. The truth about God is the old meal time prayer "God is great and God is good." He is great enough to see our potential and not be fed-up with our temporary failures. And He is good enough to forgive our failures and absorb our shame. God is not fed up with us. The founding pastor of my church, Rev. Harold Mills, frequently began his prayers by expressing his gratefulness that our failures could never diminish the riches of God's grace. We are not bad enough to bankrupt Him. God knows our heart and He knows if we want to love Him. He understands our human weaknesses. He is willing to tolerate our failures until He can teach us how to be an overcomer. That is His goal— to change us, not exchange us.

> ## *We are not bad enough to bankrupt Him.*

God is not an angry God, but that is not to say He does not get angry. God is rightly angry over the evil in the world, and the Bible shows various times when He was angry and predicts His angry wrath will be demonstrated against the wicked in the last days. God can be angry but that is not his disposition toward HIS CHILDREN. He doesn't "lose his temper" with us. He is a good father to us. He disciplines us when necessary in order to change our behavior but never in anger, and never to simply punish us. His disciplinary actions towards His children are always corrective, not punitive. We are the children He loves, and He is the best father there could EVER be. Yes, you are to respect your Father, but don't be afraid of your Father.

Listen to what He says to us in 1 John 4:16-18 (emphasis added): *"And so we **know and rely on** the love God has for us. **God is love.** Whoever lives in love lives in God, and God in him. In this way, love is made complete among us so that we will have confidence on the day of judgment, because in this world we are like him. There is no fear in love. But perfect love drives out fear, because **fear has to do with punishment.** The one who fears is not made perfect in love."* *Love drives out the fear God is going to punish us. When we fear God in this sense, we are "not made perfect in love."* In other words, we lack the complete understanding of God in this area.

Possibly the phrase "fear of the Lord" in the Old Testament comes to mind at this time. The Hebrew word for that is *yir'ah* [yir·aw] which is translated as reverence or fear, i.e., a state of piety and respect toward a superior (Exodus 20:20; Proverbs 1:7).[1] *"The fear of the Lord is the beginning of knowledge, but fools despise wisdom and discipline"* (Proverbs 1:7). Reverence is to be our attitude toward God, not fear in the way we think of it. My point here is not to do an exhaustive study on the subject of "fear," but to get you to understand when Jesus died for us on the cross, He took the punishment for our sins. That changed everything! Hallelujah! Now we can have confidence in the work of Christ to free us from the fear of punishment. Now we are to reverence our Holy Father but not "fear" him in the negative sense because we are HIS CHILDREN and He loves us and wants to transform us into the ideal character of Christ. God is not angry with you. He wants to fill you with His perfect love and cast out the fear of punishment.

An Insecure God

Some people are afraid to express their true feelings and thoughts to God. Have you ever been angry with God and told Him so? I have. I have been so disappointed in and angry with God, I didn't want to pray or believe Him for anything else again! Have you ever been that disappointed in God? I think God wants to have an honest relationship with us. God is not insecure. Your anger or doubt will not cause Him to question Himself. If you think God is an insecure God you will be afraid to take Him your complaints. The truth is God wants us to bring Him our true feelings of anger or questions or doubts and tell Him exactly how we feel about Him. He can handle it. He is a VERY SECURE GOD! He knows who He is, and He is able to take your criticisms and not let it "get to him." He is full of so much grace. He is able to absorb our anger.

God wants an authentic relationship with you. He wants both your good and bad parts. If we withhold our true feelings, then we are not being authentic with God. God wants you to bring Him your anger because He wants an authentic relationship with you—anger and all. God wants an honest relationship with you. When you bring Him your honest criticisms, He can then show you His great love. When you bring Him your anger, He can show you His forgiveness. When you bring Him your doubts, He can show you His power. There are many people who are angry with God but never bring themselves to express it. They stay inwardly angry, and it creates an internal barrier with God. How can you have intimacy with God if you withhold your feelings toward Him? Take Him your anger and take Him your questions and take Him your criticisms. Then you will be closer because everything is out in the open. God can handle it.

Sometimes we project our own insecurities on God. If you are a person who does not receive criticism well, then you will likely project that on God. You will tend to think He reacts the same way you do. Criticism does not create a storm inside a secure person. They don't enjoy it, but they are not personally shaken by it. God is secure and loving, and He is able to listen to your criticism and be able to see beyond it. A secure God is more interested in having a close relationship with you than He is about being falsely criticized. He knows who He is, and He knows you love Him and He loves you.

God wants intimacy with you. Openness and honesty build intimacy. If your spouse were angry with you and never told you, it would create a barrier. Would you rather have him or her express that anger or repress it? How can you be close with someone who is secretly angry with you? It is better to get the anger out in the open and resolve it. God wants nothing between you and Him.

A Demanding God

How hard is it to please God? The answer to that question shows a lot about your image and theology of God. How understanding is God about your weaknesses? Do you see Him as understanding of your weaknesses and failures or as demanding better performance "or else"?

I see the answer in a scripture we have already studied, Hebrews 4:15. Jesus is said *"... to sympathize with our weaknesses."* He is sympathetic because He knows the struggle. He knows from personal experience. He's not saying, "Come on you, wimp! Don't give me that excuse." That's why salvation is by grace. That's why there is so much need for God's mercy in our failures. We need help! I'm so glad the passage ends by saying, *"Let us then approach the throne of grace with confidence, so that we may receive mercy and find grace to help us in our time of need"* (Hebrews 4:15). Grace, mercy, and help! We are offered all three. We don't serve a demanding God, but a gracious, merciful and helpful God. Yes, He has high standards to which we are called as we grow and develop the character of Christ, but He is our understanding Teacher and loving Father, not a demanding military drill sergeant.

Yes, God does expect holiness, but He also provides the means to obtain it. He empowers us to obey. He sets a goal for us and then becomes a merciful and encouraging coach who wants to help us achieve victory and success in living a holy life. I will go deeper into this subject in a later chapter.

Remember, the formula for emotional healing is truth + grace + time. The truth is God is not a demanding God, but He does have expectations. Does that make sense to you? He has demands and expectations, but He also has grace to forgive and the patience and forbearance to understand the process. He has both the grace to forgive and the time to allow the process to occur. Yes, He has demands, but that does not negate the reality of His grace and the time to help us meet His demands. Therefore, God should not be seen as a "demanding God."

A Serious God

If you view God as being a "serious" person, then you are missing a whole other side of His personality. God is the most fun-loving being in the universe! After all, who created fun and laughter and joy and excitement in the first place? You've got to see this. God wants you and me to experience His fun. He created us to enjoy life! That's what this book is all about. God wants you and me to experience *Zoe* to the Max! He wants us to have fun and enjoy this life He has provided for us. Yes, there are problems in this world. Sin and selfishness have tarnished everything. But the answer is stepping out of the darkness and into the light! We must learn to enjoy the light as *"... children of light"* (Ephesians 5:8). We are children of light who are shining in this world of darkness. We are to live the joy and have the fun that shows the world what it is like to walk in the light! If we are constantly burdened under the load of all the serious problems in the world, then how are we going to reflect to the world Jesus has the answers to those problems?

I have a patient who is a believer in Christ who is also a person of integrity and kindness. He is a leader in his church and was, for a time, the interim pastor. I have talked about spiritual things with him, and he knows I am a believer. What is most notable to me about him is he is such a sober person. I have rarely seen him smile or seem happy. I know a dentist's office is not known as a place to really exude joy, but over the past twenty years I have been his dentist, I wonder why I have not seen some kind of joy or happiness in his life. He serves the "serious God." This gentleman is not mean or cranky, but neither does he smile or show any kind of happiness or joy. If I were not a believer, and he were the only Christian I knew, I would not want whatever he has because it makes him sad. I would conclude Christians are really dull and depressed people.

If your image of God is the "serious God," then you will have trouble accepting this entire *Zoe* to the Max concept. I want to challenge you to see God for all He is. He has times of being serious, but He also has times of being joyful and exuberant. Listen, if you read the book of Revelation you will see God will eventually release His wrath on sin and Satan, but He will also lead His children into everlasting joy and *Zoe*. Why do you think joy will only happen when we get to Heaven? Why do you think *Zoe* is only "pie in the sky, by and by"? Is God weighed down with seriousness now, and then He will get happy after Judgment Day? I want you to reconsider your image of God as only being a "serious God".

A Moody God

If you were emotionally traumatized by an addictive personality-type parent, then you experienced a moody parent. This impression of your parent then naturally transfers over to your image of God. The children of a moody parent are uncertain of how their parent will respond. They become hyper -vigilant in detecting the moods of their unpredictable parent. They develop very sensitive "antennas" to perceive what the mood of the parent is at any particular time. When the moody parent enters the room, the child puts out an antenna to sense what kind of mood the parent is in. This creates an emotional insecurity.

If you have "a moody God" image, then you will frequently wonder if He is mad at you or not. If we feel like a failure, we think He probably feels the same way about us. If we are fed up with ourselves, we think He probably is too. On the contrary, God is predictable and consistent. He is steady and reliable. We don't have to be afraid He will "come home in one of those moods" and "go off" on us. His character is reliable. Moodiness is a trait God doesn't have and one from which He wants to deliver us.

A "Want-to-find-an-excuse-to-kick-us-out" God

Your theology of God affects your feelings toward God. If your theological understanding of God teaches God is looking for a reason to remove you, you will be constantly insecure in your relationship with Him.

"The Survivor" reality TV show entertains us with the fear of "who's going to get kicked off the island" each episode. "The Apprentice" show entertains us with the "who is going to get fired" each episode. "American Idol" eliminates contestants. Some have this kind of mentality of the Kingdom of God. Some think God is narrowing down or "pruning" or "refining" the church and kicking off the losers. They live with the fear God will find something wrong with them and "fire" them. They see God as a Donald Trump-type of

God, demanding top performance and looking for a reason to fire someone.

Examine your image of God in this regard. Does God want you in His family or not? Is God constantly doing a quality inspection of you to see if there are any defects which give Him a good excuse to "kick you off"? Instead, I challenge you to see God as your biggest cheerleader! Think of God's attitude towards us as being this:

NO ONE WANTS YOU IN HIS FAMILY MORE THAN GOD DOES.

God is not looking for reasons to kick you out. He is looking for reasons to bring you in! *"The Lord is not slow in keeping his promise, as some understand slowness. He is patient with you, NOT WANTING ANYONE TO PERISH, but everyone to come to repentance"* (2 Peter 3:9, emphasis added). God wants more and more people in His family.

God is your advocate, He is your Father, He is your Savior and friend. He wants to help you to learn how to be happy in His family and, yes, He will discipline you to correct character flaws that exist in your life—out of His love for you, not anger. Just as a loving father wants the best for His children, so your Heavenly Father wants you to possess the ideal character of Christ. Christ demonstrated to us what ideal character is. He set the example we are to emulate. God's family is not like "The Survivor". He is looking for ways to keep us on and improve us, not exclude us.

God is Full of Grace and Truth

We must discover and believe the truth about God. But truth alone is an incomplete way to experience God. We must also understand and experience grace. Otherwise, Christianity is just a set of unattainable rules. Knowing the truth is not enough—we need grace in dealing with ourselves and with others. God is the perfect blend of truth and grace, and He is willing to take the time to work His perfect work in our lives. Therefore God Himself embodies the healing formula of Truth + Grace + Time = Emotional Healing. God is all about truth, but He is also all about grace. Because He gave Himself for us through Christ, the demand for justice has been satisfied. The sinless Christ paid the penalty for all sin; therefore God can be gracious to us. God is the God of all grace. His throne is grace. Jesus was *"full of grace and truth"* (John 1:14). He was 100% truth and 100% grace. God has the grace to forgive our sins and the grace to forbear our weaknesses. When you and I see God, we need to see He is full of grace and truth. He is not angry with us. He loves us with a love that is incomprehensible to us. He knows the truth we need to know, but He has the grace to deal with any slowness we have to learn.

Your image of God then affects your image of yourself. You and I must see ourselves consistently with how He sees us. Once we see God for the truth of who He is then we can begin to see ourselves through His eyes of truth.

What Is the Truth about Ourselves?

The need for truth applies not only to our view of God but to our view of ourselves and others. We must learn how we view ourselves and then change to how we **should view ourselves.** After we accept the correct view, it is easier to learn the truth about how to treat others. How you view yourself affects how you relate to God and how you treat yourself and others.

Who You Are in Christ and Who You Are Apart from Christ

You and I must understand both the depravity of our lives apart from Christ and the exaltation of who we are in Christ. The truth of both is vital. First let's look at the truth about ourselves apart from Christ. Without Christ, we would be under the complete control of our sinful nature and would be capable of committing any or all of the following sins: *"The acts of the sinful nature are obvious: sexual immorality, impurity and debauchery; idolatry and witchcraft; hatred, discord, jealousy, fits of rage, selfish ambition, dissensions, factions and envy; drunkenness, orgies, and the like. I warn you, as I did before, that those who live like this will not inherit the kingdom of God"* (Galatians 5:19-21). You and I need never to look down on others in sin, because if it were not for Christ and His influence in our lives and families, we could be in the same fix. Do you believe that about yourself?

I want us to look at a passage in Ephesians 2:1-3 that gives the contrast once we are in Christ: *"As for you, you were dead in your transgressions and sins, in which you used to live when you followed the ways of this world and of the ruler of the kingdom of the air, the spirit who is now at work in those who are disobedient. All of us also lived among them at one time, gratifying the cravings of our sinful nature and following its desires and thoughts. Like the rest, we were by nature objects of wrath."*

I love the first word in the next verse because it made all the difference in the world for you and me. Ephesians 2:4: *"BUT because of his great love for us, God, who is rich in mercy, made us alive with Christ even when we were dead in transgressions—it is by grace you have been saved"* (emphasis added). This defines who made the change! It was God through Christ! It also explains why God did it. It was because of His great love and rich mercy! Notice it had nothing to do with how good or bad we were. He loved us first, and He extended this offer of mercy because He has a lot of it!

Then let's look at what position He has placed us in after this rescue took place. Ephesians 2:6: *"And God raised us up with Christ and seated us with him in the heavenly realms in Christ Jesus, in order that in the coming ages he might show the incomparable riches of his grace, expressed in his kindness to us in Christ Jesus."* So we see God "raised us up." I think of the song I love to sing, made famous by Josh Groban, "You Raise Me Up." He raised us up so we could stand on mountains of the heavenly realm! He raised us and seated us WITH CHRIST. We are not lowly slaves; we are kings! We are raised and seated with Christ! What exaltation! Don't ever put yourself down because Christ raised you up!

Exalted in Christ!

This exaltation was brought to us by the grace of God. Ephesians 2:8-9 is a familiar passage: *"For it is by grace you have been saved, through faith—and this not from yourselves, it is the gift of God—not by works, so that no one can boast."* So we are not to boast in ourselves or about how we deserved salvation. It was the gift of God, given to us by His grace out of His love and rich mercy.

Grace and mercy are different.

Mercy is when we DON'T get the BAD stuff
we deserve because of our sin and selfishness.

Grace is when we DO get the GOOD stuff
we don't deserve.

The good news is we get both mercy and grace! We don't get the bad stuff, but we do get the good stuff! Woo who!

God's Creation with an Assignment!

So we are exalted and re-created in Christ! Don't criticize yourself because you are God's creation! Ephesians 2:10: *"For we are God's workmanship, created in Christ Jesus to do good works, which God prepared in advance for us to do."* We are His creation, and you and I have been given assignments by God. We are to do the good works God has planned for us to do. He has plans for our lives. His plan is for us to do good works with the abilities and time and energy we have been given. Don't tell me you are "no good" or you are bored with your life. You have a divine assignment to accomplish for the Creator. That gives you value. That gives you purpose. How can you be bored with doing assignments pre-planned by God?

Let me ask you, What are the good works God has planned for you to do? Can you name them? If not, then you have discovery work to do in understanding what your gifts and abilities are and what God wants you to do with them. You have a purpose. It is not a purpose for "the Church," it is a purpose for YOU. You have value BECAUSE you have purpose. Who are you to put yourself down when God has raised you up to be seated with Christ and created a spirit in you which is created in Christ with a purpose to do good works and fulfill God's plan for your life?! This is the truth about you and your purpose. Woo who!

The Truth About Your Self-Image

Your image of yourself must reflect the truth about who made you, and why. You must view yourself and treat yourself like a creation of God! If I were to bring you a beautiful vase and tell you that this vase was made by God himself for you, how would you treat it? Wouldn't you treat it with value and respect? Wouldn't you admire it as a work of God? Wouldn't you just appreciate it so much as a gift from God and use it to honor Him?

YOU ARE THE VASE!

God formed each one of us like a potter forms a beautiful vase out of clay. And yet we are so quick to be critical of ourselves. We criticize our looks and our abilities. We compare ourselves to other vases. "Why couldn't God have made me like that one?" When we do such self-criticism, we are actually criticizing God Himself because we are criticizing His workmanship. Paul, quoting Isaiah, condemns our self-critical tendencies in Romans 9:20-21: *"But who are you, O man, to talk back to God? Shall what is formed say to him who formed it, 'Why did you make me like this?' Does not the potter have the right to make out of the same lump of clay some pottery for noble purposes and some for common use?"* God made us the way we are for a purpose. When we criticize that, we are "talking back" to God. God had the right to make us any way He wanted because He was the Creator. Our job is not to criticize, but to fully appreciate WHAT He made and then to discover what His purpose for us is. Whether we consider our purpose as "noble" or "common" is not for us to debate. God is the Creator, and we are the creation. Therefore, do not criticize yourself or put yourself down because the Creator created you! The Potter formed you with His own hands. So don't ask, "Why did you make me like this?" Ask "Since You made me like this, what do You want me to do?"

Your feelings about yourself should reflect, as much as possible, how God feels about you. You should not see yourself as less than God sees you, right? Your opinion of yourself should reflect God's opinion. He is the manufacturer and designer. Praise the Creator and rejoice in His creation for the good job He did on you! God doesn't make junk! You were made in His image. You were valuable enough for Jesus to die for you. You were valuable enough to be saved. You were valuable enough to be filled with the Holy Spirit. You were valuable enough to be given gifts and abilities. You are valuable enough to be given a purpose and assignment in this life. You are valuable enough God wants you to live with Him forever! So there! Don't tell me you are not valuable!

Below is a list of more scriptures about who we are in Christ. You could use these verses for a Bible study as you see God heal your self-deprecating tendencies. God didn't make junk, so don't trash yourself!

You Are Accepted by God

John 1:12 . . . . I am God's child.
John 15:15 . . . . I am Christ's friend.
Romans 5:1 . . . . I have been justified.
I Corinthians 6:17 . . . . I am united with the Lord, one spir-

it with Him.

I Corinthians 6:19-20 . . . . . I was bought with a price. I belong to God.

I Corinthians 12:27. . . . . . . I am a member of Christ's body.

Ephesians 1:1 . . . . I am a saint.

Ephesians 1:5 . . . . I have been adopted as God's child.

Ephesians 2:18 . . . . I have direct access to God by the Holy Spirit.

Colossians 1:14. . . . . I have been redeemed, forgiven of all my sins.

Colossians 2:10. . . . . I am complete in Christ.

You Are Established in Christ

Romans 8:1-2 . . . . I am free from condemnation.

Romans 8:28. . . . . I am assured God is working for my good.

Romans 8:33. . . . . I am free from condemning charges.

Romans 8:35 . . . . I am assured in the love of God.

2 Corinthians 1:21 . . . . I have been established and anointed by God.

Colossians 3:3 . . . . I am hidden with Christ in God.

Philippians 1:6. . . . . I know God's work in me will be completed.

Philippians 3:30. . . . . I am a citizen of heaven.

2 Timothy 1:7 . . . . I have not been given a spirit of fear, but one of power, love, and self-discipline.

Hebrews 4:16 . . . . I can find grace and mercy in time of need.

I John 5:18 . . . . I am born of God, protected from the evil one.

You Are Significant

Matthew 5:13-14 . . . . I am the salt and light of the earth.

John 15:1, 5 . . . . I am a branch of the true vine.

John 15:16 . . . . I have been chosen, appointed to bear fruit.

Acts 1:8. . . . . I am a personal witness for Christ.

I Corinthians 3:16 . . . . I am God's temple.

2 Corinthians 5:17 . . . . I am a minister of reconciliation for God.

2 Corinthians 6:1 . . . . I am God's co-worker.

Ephesians 2:6 . . . . I am seated with Christ in the heavenly realm.

Ephesians 2:10 . . . . I am God's workmanship.

Ephesians 3:12 . . . . I may approach God with freedom and confidence.

Philippians 4:13 . . . . I can do all things through Christ who strengthens me.[2]

Christian ID:

—I am a dearly loved child of God.

—I was chosen to be adopted into His family because of God's goodness, not my own.

—I was forgiven and made righteous by faith in Christ's sacrifice on the cross. Therefore, I do not focus on what I WAS but WHOSE I am.

You are CHOSEN

God chose you. You didn't find God; He found you. He chose you before you even knew Him. And He has appointed you for a mission. That gives you identity.

You are USEFUL

God has endowed you with usefulness. There's a way you can help others and support God's family. That gives you identity.

You are VALUABLE

You are valuable because you are the work of a Great Artist, you belong to a famous person, and Jesus paid for your freedom with His own life's blood. That makes you valuable.

The Falseness of the Performance Trap

The book *Search for Significance* is very helpful in this whole area of self-image. Robert McGee identifies four false beliefs which are commonly held about one's identity. My small group is currently studying this book, and I have studied it with several groups over the years because it is so effective. I want to briefly talk about three of these here and strongly encourage you to go through the book because McGee does an excellent job of developing the whole picture. Here is a snap shot:

The Performance Trap is the first false belief. When we place our self-worth on how well or how poorly we perform, we are building our identity on the false foundation of performance. The premise is if we perform well, then we are good. Or if we perform poorly, we are worthless. It is evident how widespread this belief is when so many people are willing to sacrifice so much to experience success and then build their significance on that foundation.

Last night David Blaine did what no other human being has ever done. He spent seven days submerged in a human aquarium and then tried to hold his breath for nine minutes while getting out of hand and feet cuffs. He came close to killing himself in order to get fame as a great performer. He is building his self-worth on performance. When he

> *We are God's children based on God's grace and mercy in forgiving us and making us righteous, regardless of our performance.*

is successful, he feels good about himself. But suppose he gets severely injured and can no longer do what he once did? His whole world will crumble because it is built on performance.

God does not want you and me to build our self-worth on the shifting foundation of performance. Instead, we are to build our self-worth on who we are in Christ. We are God's children based on God's grace and mercy in forgiving us and making us righteous, regardless of our performance. When I taught this concept to my small group, I illustrated it by giving each person a card with a random red number between 0 and 5,000,000. This number represented the number of sins for which they had been forgiven. I asked them how it felt to have committed that number of sins. There was a lot of joking going on as everyone laughed and poked fun at each other. I asked the person who had the 0 if she felt pretty good about herself having never sinned. She agreed it made her feel rather proud of herself. Then I asked the one who got the red 5,000,000 how she felt.

She felt really bad about having been such a sinner! Then I asked the group to tell me which person was more acceptable to God. Since I have such a smart group, they all said both were equally accepted by God because each one had been forgiven—they were both the same. It did, however, get them thinking about our human tendency to think higher of the person with the red 0 and lower of the person with the red 5,000,000.

Then I gave each one a blue card, again with a random number between 0 and 5,000,000. This number represented the number of good things they had done. I then asked them how they felt about themselves based on their blue number. Again, there was a lot of chatter and joking. When they settled down, I asked the person with the blue 0 to tell me how she felt about having done nothing good. She acknowledged she didn't feel too good about herself based on the fact others' blue numbers were higher than her blue number. Then I asked the one with the blue 5,000,000 how he felt about all his good works. Quite a bit of discussion followed as we explored how performance affects the way we feel about ourselves.

It is ironic even though the cards were distributed randomly, poor Michelle got both the red 5,000,000 AND the blue 0! She was both the worst of the sinners and did the least good works! Wow! That was a small chance in a group of twenty-five. I told Michelle not to take it too personally and God must really want her to learn that lesson!

The Falseness of People Pleasing

Another shaky foundation to build our self-worth on is the approval we seek from others. McGee calls this "approval addiction." It's when our value as a person is dictated by what other people say about us. We become people pleasers in order to gain their approval and feel valuable. People pleasers are very vulnerable to collapse based on criticism from key people. People pleasers become the puppets of others as they dance to try to gain and keep acceptance. God wants our self-worth to be based on His acceptance of us as adopted members of His family. Because of Christ, we are reconciled with God and accepted. If Christ is pleased with us as His children, then we need to value His opinion of us more highly than we do other people's opinion. If we value our adoption as much as we should, we can no longer be destroyed by criticism because we are standing on Christ.

People pleasers also compare themselves with others. They have a built-in radar when it comes to evaluating others. They rank their value by constantly comparing themselves with others.

Some seek to impress others by accumulating material possessions or prestige. Some move to prestigious communities or seek professional status, all to obtain the approval of others. I mentioned earlier about getting left out of the Yellow Pages. I lost my status as a dentist! I lost my identity! I was a "nobody."

The other week when I was teaching this concept, I spontaneously stood up on my chair and said, "I am standing on Christ's acceptance of me. I am secure." Then I stepped one foot over onto the edge of the chair next to me. I was doing the splits between two chairs. Then I asked, "If someone moves this chair, what is going to happen to me? That's what happens if my self-worth is partly based on other's approval and partly on Christ's approval." I then moved my leg back to just one chair and said, "What I need to do is not rely on someone else's approval but base my whole worth on Christ's approval of me." I need to stand fully on Christ's chair. If someone can kick the chair out from under me, then I must not have been standing fully on Christ's chair.

The Truth About Shame-Based Self-image

Shame is another false belief. A person with a shame-based image sees themselves as defective. Instead of the person experiencing a failure, they conclude he or she IS a failure. It is the internalization of failure. "I am a failure," is the conclusion. "I am defective. I am bad." These are the false beliefs some people reach when they are overly criticized and abused. Everyone experiences failures, but the shame-based person feels he or she, as a person, is a failure. As parents we must make sure we do not make our children feel they themselves are bad, but only their actions are bad.

The truth is God has made us a new creation. He has taken our old and made us new. The old person we were is gone and His new creation in Christ is what we are now. We are no longer "bad". God has re-made us so we are now "good." Shame can be removed and replaced with God's view of us as good.

The Truth About Healthy Boundaries

Another area where we need to learn truth is in how we interact with others. Are we interacting in emotionally healthy ways? One way in which we need to learn how to have healthy interactions with others is in the study of a subject called boundaries. A boundary is a way of describing where our personal responsibilities end and where another person's responsibilities begin. Inside this imaginary line or fence are all the things which belong to me and what I am responsible for, and beyond that imaginary boundary line there are the things for which others are responsible. For example, as an adult I am responsible to feed myself. That's inside my boundary. You are not responsible for feeding me. If you try to feed me, that would violate my boundary. Or if I expected you to feed me, that would be an unrealistic expectation of your boundaries and mine.

The study of healthy boundaries is the study of proper individual responsibilities. This knowledge plays an important role in our interactions with others. The two Christian psychologists Dr. John Townsend and Dr. Henry Cloud taught me this in their book *Boundaries: When to Say YES, When to Say NO to Take Control of Your Life*. I believe it is a must-read for everyone because it helps so much in understanding ourselves and in relating to others. Again, I won't try to completely cover this subject because it is done well by Townsend and Cloud in several books they have written. One is Boundaries in Dating, another being Boundaries with Kids. In their books they explore the ten laws of boundaries of healthy personal responsibilities and how to disengage from harmful or manipulative people.

If we don't understand this concept of boundaries, we will be in regular conflict with others, and we will also be in conflict with ourselves. We learned our sense of boundaries from our parents. If our parents had healthy boundaries, then they probably taught us healthy boundaries as a natural byproduct. But if they did not have healthy boundaries, then likely neither do we.

I was one who did not have a healthy sense of boundaries. My studies in this area have helped me tremendously, and I thank God for these books.

Let me give you a few examples of how healthy boundaries can help you. Drs. Cloud and Townsend talk about how boundaries are like an imaginary fence which goes around your yard. The fence identifies where your property begins and ends.

Inside Your Yard

There are four things inside your yard for which you are responsible.

1. Feelings. Your feelings are your responsibility. Others are not responsible for how you feel. Your feelings are yours and should neither be ignored nor placed in charge. It is irresponsible to blame others for how you feel because you choose how you will respond to the world. You choose what feelings you will hold on to, and you are responsible to process and get a handle on your own feelings. Whether you tend to be overly sensitive or not sensitive enough, your feelings are your responsibility. One day I walked into a restroom to wash my hands, and a urinal mysteriously flushed behind me! It startled me a little at first, until I realized its motion sensor was a little overly sensitive, even though I was more than ten feet away! Some people are like that. Their feelings are too easily offended, and they blame others for just walking by!

Healthy people take responsibility for their feelings. Irresponsible people blame others for the way they feel by playing the role of the victim. They throw their feelings over the fence and put them in other people's yards.

Overly responsible people TAKE THE BLAME for other people's feelings. They do one of two things. They are either overly helpful and climb over other people's fences and take responsibility for other people's feelings. Or they are complacent and allow other people to climb over their fence and leave feelings on their property. Overly responsible people are driven by a false sense of guilt which makes them feel guilty or "mean" if they don't continue to carry other people's feelings. The overly responsible person has developed a hypersensitive conscience that drives them with false guilt. This causes them to be become emotionally worn out because they are handling their own feelings plus the feelings of others.

2. Attitudes. Your attitudes are inside your yard and under your control. You are responsible for how you react to circumstances. You can choose your attitude toward things that happen inside or outside of your yard. No one gives you an attitude; you choose your attitude. Your attitudes come from your thoughts, and your thoughts are also inside your yard. Emotionally healthy people take responsibility for their own thoughts and attitudes.

3. Behaviors. You are responsible for your actions and inaction. They are inside your yard. You must take responsibility for your choices. You cannot change others, but you can choose our own actions and reactions. You can set limits on how much you will be around those who behave poorly or who violate your boundaries. You must learn to take responsibility for saying "no" to the bad and "yes" to the good.

4. Personality. We are responsible for understanding and managing our own personality and not blaming others. Some people are prone to be temperamental—90% temper and 10% mental! Seriously though, I would encourage you to study personality types to understand your own personality and those of others. It will help you understand and get along with others better. I like the books exploring personality written by Florence Littauer and by Tim LaHaye. There is no "right" personality—we are all different reflections of the personality of God. God loves diversity—that's why He made us all differently. Emotionally healthy people take responsibility to understand their own personality and accept the differences in other personalities.

Boundary Violators

There are so many problems which result from an unhealthy sense of boundaries. One problem is not listening to the "No" of others. "No" is a boundary identifying word. When someone says "No", he or she is stating where the boundary fence is. Boundary violators do not listen to the "No" of others. Instead, they try to move the fence or climb over it. When they hear "No", they think it means "try harder." Boundary violators basically disrespect the wishes of other people. Instead of honoring another's wishes, they try to change the other person's "No" into a "Yes." They may do this by using manipulation, guilt or control.

Weak Boundaries

The opposite of a boundary violator is one who has weak boundaries. They are not sure where their fences are, and they do not identify their boundaries when crossed by others. They never prosecute trespassers. They are the overly-compliant people—the people pleasers. They are outwardly "too nice" but inwardly resentful of others. People with weak boundaries have a hard time saying "No" and they say "Yes" even when they don't want to. They say "Yes" outwardly but inwardly they really want to say "No." There are many reasons why people have weak boundaries. One reason could be they don't feel valuable enough to have the right to identify their boundaries. They don't feel they deserve to have personal desires or personal limits. Their self-image is low. They need healing. Another reason could be they were raised by a boundary violator. Boundary-violating parents raise children with a weak sense of boundaries. A third reason for weak boundary definition is fear. They are afraid of rejection or anger if they say "No" to a request.

Spiritually Abusive Boundary Teaching

Sometimes people with weak boundaries have been spiritually abused by unhealthy Bible teaching in this area of boundaries. They have been taught a Christian should not have boundaries. A Christian should not have desires or wishes. A Christian should allow anyone to violate their boundaries as a demonstration of self-sacrifice. All of this is unbalanced and unhealthy application of what it means to be a Christian. There is a difference between "turning the other cheek" from a point of strength and allowing others to use you as a "doormat" from a point of weakness. Going the second mile should be a choice to give not a compulsion to surrender.

The truth is without healthy boundaries we cannot be a cheerful giver. I'm not talking about money—I am talking about giving of anything inside your boundaries, e.g., giving time, energy or actions. A cheerful giver is one who is giving out of "the overflow." They give because they want to give. However, if a person has weak boundaries they are often emotionally exhausted from carrying both their own and other people's responsibilities. This leaves them without a healthy sense of self and a depleted state of emotional energy. They are confused as to when they "want" to give and when they "ought" to give. They live in a world of "ought to's," and sometimes this is encouraged by manipulative or ignorant spiritual teachers. The preacher talks about what you "ought" to do without also teaching folks about healthy limits and healthy motivations.

True Giving Versus Being Robbed

When we give out of "ought to," then we are not voluntarily giving. We are responding to compulsion and duty. We are not really giving—we are giving up! True giving is because we "want to" not "have to." Robbery is being forced to give because we "have to."

Just because there is a need, doesn't mean you are the one God wants to use to meet it. God gives you a limited amount of resources of time, energy, talents and money. He gives enough resources to meet your needs and to have some extra to be able to give away to others. Most of what God gives you is FOR YOU. It is to feed, house, clothe, educate, entertain, etc., you and your family. If you give some of that away because you are being "robbed," then you will not have enough for your own needs. Of course, there are times when the Spirit will move you to give more than you should reasonably give in order to stretch your faith, but that is not what I'm referring to as the problem. I'm talking about routinely giving out of compulsion, guilt, or coercion because a preacher or person made you feel guilty or unspiritual if you wouldn't give.

You were created with God-given limits and God-given needs. Even Jesus had limits while He was in His earthly body. He had to take time to eat, and He got thirsty. He slept and took time to rest.

In Matthew 14:22-23: *"Immediately Jesus made the disciples get into the boat and go on ahead of him to the other side, while HE DISMISSED THE CROWD. After he had dismissed them, he went up on a mountainside BY HIMSELF to pray. When evening came, he was there alone"* (emphasis added). Why did Jesus dismiss the crowd? Wasn't there more He could have taught them? Why did He leave some needs unmet? Wasn't He being selfish by dismissing the crowd and being by Himself? Of course not! Jesus was living within his limits. He needed time alone to rest and pray.

You have limits also. For example, if God provides $30 to fill up your car with gasoline (old illustration!) so you can go to work and support your family, but some boundary-violating person walks up to you at the gasoline station and asks for the gas, what are you going to do? If God gave it to you to meet your needs and then you are persuaded by others to "give" that away, you are not being led by God— you are being manipulated by others. You are not giving, you are being robbed! And now YOU are going to suffer the consequences of not having enough gas to get to work and support your family.

Often boundary-violators are irresponsible people who get themselves into trouble, and then they manipulate, or should I say, "rob" others to get themselves out of trouble. Because you "can't" say "No," you suffer the consequences of being robbed. And the sad truth is the irresponsible person did not learn responsibility—they just learned crime pays!

Sadly, the story of the Good Samaritan is often misused to manipulate sensitive people into thinking every time they see a need, they are required to personally meet it. Scripture can be misrepresented to make people feel guilty about having any boundaries.

True Loving Versus Paying Extortion

Love is often expressed in giving. Giving should be out of the overflow of our hearts to others. It may be expressed through writing or phone calling or visiting or eating out together or any number of ways. God is love, and He wants us to be loving as well. God knows our inner motivations, so He knows when we are giving out of love or out of fear. Sometimes we are giving simply because we don't want to feel guilty. We are not giving out of love. It is more like paying extortion money. We are paying off our guilty conscience and are, therefore, loving ourselves! We are protecting ourselves from feeling guilty or from "looking bad". We are not acting out of love.

True Self-Nurturing versus Selfishness

Another area of spiritually abusive teaching is related to the concept of self. Some preachers teach any thought of self is wrong. We are told to be self-less. Any nurturing of self is condemned as selfish. Self-hatred is seen as spiritually mature.

The truth about self is God gave you yourself. Your self is all you have with which to serve God and love others. God does not want you to hate yourself. God wants you to have a healthy view of your self. The confusion arises when we try to treat self as one entity. In order to understand the theology of self in scripture, I think it is helpful to view self from three angles.

There is a sinful self which should be crucified.
There is a human self which should be disciplined.
There is an actual self which should be enjoyed.

Your sinful self is your fallen nature which needs to be "crucified with Christ". Scripture refers to it as the "old man" or sometimes "the flesh." Look how Paul differentiates between two selves in Galatians 2:20: *"I (my sinful self) have been crucified with Christ and I (my sinful self) no longer live, but Christ lives in me (my actual self). The life I (my actual self) live in the body, I (my actual self) live by faith in the Son of God, who loved me (my actual self) and gave himself for me (my actual self)"* (parentheses added). Crucified means put to death. Death means something no longer has vitality or control. What remains is the actual self filled with Christ. Think about it. When you are born again, you don't become a hollow physical body with only Christ living in it. You don't lose your actual self when you become a Christian. You are still you. But a part of you "dies" to Christ. Your sinful self is to be crucified with Christ.

Your human self, or you could say physical self, is your body and mind and personality. They must be disciplined by your new spirit empowered by the Holy Spirit. Your human self needs rest and balance, but it must be disciplined lest it cause you to sin. You were given your human self as a gift from God, and you are responsible to treat it well and maintain it. God wants you to manage yourself well and be a good steward of your human self. Disciplining your human self is your responsibility because it is inside your boundary—inside your yard.

Your actual self is the part of you which was created in the image of God. There is some debate among theologians as to what God meant when He said he created us "in His image". Perhaps it includes our physical image. Does that mean God looks like a man? Not sure about that? I think it refers to something more like our actual self. This is the part which will live on eternally. Call it what you like, but something about us is made in God's image and is good. It is also good simply because God made it. So to hate self is to hate what God has made.

When our actual self is controlled by the Spirit, we will have the ability to see other people's needs as important as well as our own. We can choose by the power of the Spirit to put their needs before our own, but that does not negate our own needs. Let me explain it this way—if we go to a restaurant and walk to the front of the buffet line, that would be selfish. But if you let someone in front of you, that is putting another's needs above your own. That is demonstrating the self-sacrificing love of God. But we are still going to wait in line because our human self needs to eat and our actual self wants to enjoy the experience! It is our responsibility to manage our own needs and our privilege to enjoy ourselves. So we don't completely deny our own needs, but we can defer them if the Spirit leads us. Otherwise we would never eat at a restaurant because we would let everyone else eat first and then not want to bother the cooks with having to feed us too! God wants our actual self to enjoy life! Enjoy *Zoe* to the Max! He wants us to enjoy the restaurant experience and at the same time, feed our human self.

Know the Truth in Your "Knower"

Pursuing truth is the key to emotional healing. But there is a difference between knowing the truth mentally and really believing the truth deep within your being. First we must learn what the truth is—that's the mental part. But once the truth is in our head, it needs to move "down" into our belief system. And finally truth needs to affect our actions. That is when truth heals us. Most of the time truth gets stuck in our heads and stops there. Like the people who know about the gospel but do not believe, there are those who have a lot of Bible in their heads, but it doesn't make it down into their beliefs. You don't really believe something until you "know it in your knower." Your "knower" is the place inside of you which is fully convinced of certain fundamental beliefs. These are the core beliefs which motivate your gut reactions. You may say you love me but I know in my "knower" Valerie loves me. I am absolutely convinced of that.

When the Bible talks about believing in God, it means "knowing in your knower". Jesus said, *"Eternal Zoe is to know you the only true God"* (John 17:3). That's not a mental "knowing," He is saying it's a "with all your heart" knowing—it is to know it in your "knower"!

All the truths I have written about to this point are all truths that need to start in your head and move to your "knower." The truth about who God really is needs to be known in your "knower." You can say you believe God is not an angry God, but if you act like He is, then what you really believe is He is angry. Truth must make the journey out of your head and into your "knower." If your mind says one thing, but your "knower" is convinced of the opposite, which do you truly believe? Your "knower" always wins out over what is in your head. You need to know in your "knower" all the truths listed above—all the truth about God and all the truth about yourself. You live out of the beliefs in your "knower," not your head.

The process of getting truth into your "knower" begins with prayer. Ask God to help you truly believe in your "knower" all that is true. Then focus on one truth at a time and begin to meditate on that. It helps to verbally repeat the truth over and over as you allow it to saturate into your "knower." Sometimes it takes a lot of prayer to remove the barriers to the truth. The lies we have believed all our lives are hard to dislodge from our "knower." Sometimes it takes the help of Christian counselors to find out what the barriers are. Next, be aware of how you respond to the next challenge against that truth. If our reflexes are not in alignment with truth, then we know we have more reprogramming to do. Once truth is in our "knower," we can move on to the second part of the healing formula.

Truth + GRACE + Time = Emotional Health

Knowing the truth in your "knower" is the first step that opens the door to healing. But emotional hurt is in a place only grace can reach. The truth heals your mind, but truth and grace are needed to heal your soul. I can know in my mind God loves me, but until I experience the feeling of Him loving me, I will not be emotionally healed.

Grace

The love of God is delivered to our souls in the form of grace. Grace is the unearned favor of God. It first brings salvation to us out of God's loving heart because of Christ's sacrifice. Out of that same benevolent heart, grace also sustains and heals us. Once we are mercifully forgiven and adopted into God's family, then, He begins the needed process of sanctification and character transformation. Grace embraces us AS WE ARE in all our immaturity and woundedness as we move toward Christ-likeness. Grace accepts us NOW and embraces us NOW in love even as we grow through cycles of victory and failure. Grace is the love of God embracing us and picking us up in our failures, weaknesses, anger, selfishness, and ignorance.

Grace Is Love, Not Justice

It's hard to understand grace because it is so far removed from justice. Justice gives us what we deserve; grace gives us what we don't deserve. I had a difficult time understanding grace in my youth because I was raised in an environment where justice was supreme. If you did well, then you would be rewarded. If you did poorly, then you would probably be punished. That is the way of justice. Grace is not like that. Grace is not about being just. Grace is not fair. Grace is about relationship and love. Grace loves us in the midst of failure and weakness. Justice punishes us, but grace embraces us, picks us up, dusts us off and encourages us to keep going. There truly is something amazing about grace.

Grace is provided by the work of Christ on the cross. Because of what Christ did, justice has been served. The punishment for all of our sins and failures has been taken by our Savior. Galatians 2:21: *"I do not set aside THE GRACE OF GOD, for if righteousness could be gained through the law, Christ died for nothing"* (emphasis added)! It was not justice that saved us—it was grace provided by Christ's death on the cross.

Emotional healing comes when we get this fact out of our heads and into our "knower". The Father is patient with this process. The Father is gracious with us. He loves us and wants us to be successful. Why? Because we are His children. He is gracious towards His children. You've got to get this in your "knower". You've got to know in your "knower" you are an adopted child of God! Not just mentally know it, but emotionally know it. You've got to experience it and feel it. Let me ask you this:

Do you FEEL like a child of God?
Do you know down in your "knower" He is your Father?

Until you feel that, you have not fully experienced grace. It is a fact you are a child of God—it is reality, but that reality needs to "soak in". You may mentally know about being adopted, but the truth of that adoption needs to be experienced in more than your mind. The grace of that adoption needs to be experienced in your inner most being. You must experience healing grace personally. How does this happen?

Three Grace Delivery Systems

<u>1. Healing Parents.</u> I believe God's ideal way for us to experience

grace is to have emotionally healthy parents who help us experience grace naturally. When we experience grace through our parents, it is much easier to believe in the grace of God. Parents have a tremendous opportunity to model grace to their children. If a child fails and experiences grace from their parents, they can more easily believe in and experience God's grace. They can think to themselves, "God accepts me in my weaknesses and failures like my parents do. God is like my dad/mom." They have experienced grace and truth together in the right balance. Truth provides the discipline to encourage change, but grace accepts us in our failures and works for change through relationship.

Unfortunately, the opposite is also true: Legalistic, unyielding or angry parents create a roadblock for their children to feel and understand grace. These children learn to be hard on themselves and unforgiving in the face of their personal failures. If you experienced that type of parenting, then you know the difficulty you have with forgiving yourself. Parents who don't understand grace produce children who don't understand grace. The children of emotionally healthy parents have a tremendous advantage because they experience grace when they fail and can more easily receive grace from God.

2. Healing Prayers. Grace can be received through the power of healing prayers. I have seen this happen in counseling sessions, small groups, and around prayer altars. When emotionally healing prayers are offered on a one-on-one basis after personal sharing, the grace of God can be experienced more deeply. The person praying is used by the Holy Spirit to bring healing grace to the wounded places. I have experienced this type of ministry from a wonderfully loving person named Pat Self. She was one of the first people I met who understood the need for and power of emotional healing prayers. She had a tremendous ministry of personal counseling and prayer out of her own wounded journey. She would conduct one-on-one counseling sessions with those who had been wounded, and then she would offer healing prayer over that person at the end of the session. These are not the theatrical "conk-on-the-forehead" type prayers, but intensely loving prayers that minister grace. It is like a personal application of truth and grace. Grace is experienced through a combination of the Holy Spirit and the loving grace expressed by the person praying. The compassion, love, and grace of the person praying allow the wounded one to hear the Father's healing words.

3. Healing People. We can all participate in providing a healing community as we model grace in our lives and grace toward others. Healing people understand how important it is to love and be loved, to know and be known, to accept and be accepted.

My pastor tells the story of a little boy who was afraid of a thunderstorm so his parents tucked him in bed and told him to pray and "trust Jesus" to be with him. When the next thunder clap occurred, the little boy went running in to his parents' room. "I'm scared!" he shouted. The parents replied, "Jesus is with you, so you don't need to fear. Now go back to your bed." The little boy went back to his room only to return a few minutes later following the next flash of lightning. The parents again prayed with him, told him Jesus was with him and encouraged him to go back to his room. This time the boy complained, "But I need a Jesus with skin on!"

Being accepted and loved by a healthy person is like experiencing first hand the grace of "Jesus with skin on." Pat Self was "Jesus with skin on" to me. She modeled grace to me more than twenty years ago as I witnessed her praying and counseling with hurting people. They were drawn to her because she was full of grace and truth. Since my emotional healing, I have become "Jesus with skin on" to others. I have been used by God as a healing person to many who have never before been embraced by loving grace or never had a "safe" person to talk to. Our Christian community needs more emotionally healthy people who can be "Jesus with skin on."

Healing people can also be experienced in small groups. Scott Marshall is my church's champion of small group relationships, and he is constantly trying to develop healthy small groups of believers so they can become healing communities. The small group I lead is such a healing community where we share the deep hurts of life and support each other as we learn truth and experience grace. Many have told me it was the first safe place they felt free to admit weaknesses and be vulnerable about the struggles they were having.

When your car needs washing, and you take it to one of those automatic car wash machines, it doesn't accomplish much cleaning to park nearby and watch other cars get cleaned. You have to drive your car into the car wash if you want it to get washed. You have to put your car in the right environment if you expect the right activity to occur. A "safe" small group is the right environment for healing. That's a group where it is "safe" to be honest without fear of judgment or gossip. Healing occurs when hurting people are accepted "where they are." Remember we were made to live in community with one another, not in isolation and independence.

If a "safe" small group like that is unavailable to you, I suggest you consult a Christian counselor in your local area. They often lead a support group or know of groups which meet together seeking to be emotionally healthy individuals. We all need at least one "safe" person in our lives who can be "Jesus with skin on" to us.

Grace Changes Your Arithmetic

How do we know we are being healed by grace? We know we are experiencing grace when we desire to forgive others and forgive ourselves rather than blame. In Robert McGee's book *Search for Significance*, the third of his four false beliefs is "The Blame Game." Blame is the desire to punish any disobedience, failure, mistakes or even incompetence in others and yourself.

Blame arithmetic goes like this:

$$A + B = P$$
Action + Blame = Punishment

If your Actions fail to meet the standards set, then Blame needs to be applied resulting in Punishment. Those who fail deserve to be punished.

Grace arithmetic is different. Grace arithmetic recognizes forgiveness is never deserved, but always available by the grace of God because of Christ. Grace arithmetic is

$$A + G = F$$
Actions + Grace = Forgiveness

It works like this: If your Actions fail, then the Grace of God needs to be applied resulting in Forgiveness and release. In this arithmetic, the grace of God is so powerful it absorbs and cancels any failure and results in forgiveness.

Grace arithmetic is radically different from blame arithmetic. The difference is found in Romans 5:8: *"But God demonstrates his own love for us in this: While we were still sinners, Christ died for us."* Christ died to pay the penalty for sinners—for people who failed. This was the greatest act of love in all eternity. Because of this action, the penalty for all sin has been paid in full. Theologically speaking, Christ was the propitiation for our sins. He was the atoning sacrifice that removed the penalty of sin, and no one needs to be punished any longer. Christ took all the punishment and was the full payment. This payment is never deserved. It is never earned. It is the gift of grace. Ephesians 2:7: *"… in order that in the coming ages he might show the **incomparable riches of his grace,** expressed in his kindness to us in Christ Jesus"* (emphasis added). The riches of His grace are without equal.

When you experience the grace of God, it changes your arithmetic. It changes A + B = P into A + G = F. The grace of God changes the desire to punish into the desire to forgive. Both begin with the same action—the same sin or failure. But the outcome is totally different.

Blame makes punishment inevitable.
Grace makes forgiveness possible.

Because of what Jesus did on the cross for you there is no need to punish other people or yourself. Christ took your punishment; therefore you do not need to punish yourself. When we fail, we stand in need of grace and resulting forgiveness. Failures don't deserve grace, but grace is always undeserved. What is deserved is punishment. That's why blame arithmetic is so prevalent.

Ask God to help you really experience grace and change your internal arithmetic. You and I need grace for our emotional and spiritual healing. But grace is not a mental experience. It is a spiritual and emotional experience. It is not only BEING released legally but FEELING released spiritually and emotionally. The journey from legalism to grace requires an experience. The change in arithmetic proves healing. But this change does not happen over night—it takes time, which is the final part of the emotional healing formula.

Truth + Grace + TIME = Emotional Health

Time

God has truth, He has grace, and He is willing to be patient and give the time that is necessary to accomplish quality healing. He has all the time in the world since He is the one who created time. He knows we need time to grow. Just like the rings on a tree are added slowly, God is willing to invest time in us to see us grow into mighty trees! Someone has said time is God's way of keeping everything from happening all at once. I like that. It takes time and experiences to apply grace and truth to our lives. It takes time for us to heal emotionally. If God moved too quickly, it would be overwhelming for us.

For example, we need time for relationships to deepen and time for activities to occur and time for conflicts to be resolved. It takes time for God to move us through these things. Time allows God to bring the necessary people into our lives in the right sequence. He has teachers and helpers who will deliver the truth and then the grace for each character lesson. Sometimes He needs to take us to a different place, churches, seminars, people, etc., so we can hear truth. Some truth builds on others. Time is necessary to build one truth on top of another.

It takes time to grieve losses. A great book on handling loss and grieving is *The Faces of Rage* by David Damico. God took six days to create the universe. He could have done it in a moment but He took the necessary time. God ordained thirty years to develop Jesus to the point He began His ministry. Jesus then took three years to complete his mission. God matured Paul for years after his conversion before he began his ministry. If God tried to teach us all the lessons we need to learn at once, we would not be able to begin to process them. 2 Peter 3:8: *"But do not forget this one thing, dear friends: With the Lord a day is like a thousand years, and a thousand years are like a day."*

From Holey to Wholly and Holy

To sum up this need for emotional health, it's as though the sinfulness and selfishness and unhealthiness of life caused holes to develop in our soul. These holes caused pain, which cries out for us to feel better. We all want to be happy. So we look for things to make us feel better. When we have a headache, we take pain medication to feel better. The same is true for us emotionally and spiritually. When we are in emotional pain, we seek medication to feel better. Some of these medications are not healthy or wholesome. We can medicate our pain with overeating, smoking, alcohol and drugs. Other sinful medications include pornography, sexual sins, idolatry, stealing, and using people. Some are not necessarily sinful in themselves, but they become idols to us such as relationships, sex, fame, success, materialism, recreation, sports, and money. We have holes.

Life and sinfulness make us holey, but God wants to make us holy and heal us wholly. He wants to move us from holey-ness to whole-ness and holi-ness. We start out holey like a dirty cloth with holes. We need to be mended in order to become whole. Then holy comes as the mended cloth gets cleaned. Sanctification begins the process of washing us, first from our sins and then from our sinfulness. As holes are REVEALED, they then can be HEALED. We must OWN what is KNOWN. That is God's way.

Emotional Healing Is Worth the Effort

My emotional healing was one of the most significant spiritual experiences of my life. I invited Christ into my life at an early age. My mother tells me I was seven. I don't really remember the actual moment but I do know I have always followed Christ. The spiritual experience I remember quite well is when I fully surrendered my life and future to Christ at the age of seventeen. But the spiritual experience closest in significance to that is my emotional healing that occurred in 1993-94.

I want to encourage you to look into this area and pursue becoming and staying an emotionally healthy person. It is a HUGE key to *Zoe* the Max! That's why I have devoted these two huge chapters to this subject. I believe it is GREATLY needed in the Christian community.

Fight for Balance

Living an emotionally balanced life is so important to learn and maintain. We need to learn when our emotional tank is running low and then go get it refilled. Our emotional health is important to maintain in order to make us the best we can be for God. If we are emotionally burned out, we don't necessarily need to go to another prayer meeting. Sometimes we need to go play golf or fiddle in our garage or watch a movie or take a nap or whatever it is that replenishes us! We are not just spiritual beings. We have an emotional part which needs to be kept healthy also. We must learn to live a life of emotional balance!

Watch for New Beach Balls

This balance is maintained as we recognize when we are experiencing a new "beach ball" eruption. Once recognized, we need to go after that "beach ball" until we let all the air out it. Recently I called my folks just to talk, and my dad answered the phone with this greeting, "How's my number one Sunshine doing?" I was surprised by that greeting because he doesn't often talk like that. But as we talked further, I felt something really warm and happy down inside, as I allowed the love of that statement to bring a new level of healing. I remembered when I was a little tot, my dad had nicknamed me "Sunshine." That was one way he expressed his love for me. He hasn't called me that in years, but I sure did like hearing it again. I like hearing I am special to him, and I like hearing I am "his number one Sunshine". That was an unexpected healing moment for me. His words were healing a part of me I didn't know was hurting. Healing words can do that.

Hurting words can have an instant impact also. They can cause pain, or uncover pain that needs healing. That's why God wants us to speak healing words to one another. Speak them as blessings. Love one another boldly. Give uninvited praise. Give unexpected compliments. Lift people up and speak healing words to them. I really try to do that. I practice random words of healing. Who knows how many hurts have been healed with those healing words?! Whom can you heal with your words? Healing words to your spouse or children or parents or friends can be powerful. Let's be part of other people's emotional healing!

Emotional healing is like peeling an onion, layer after layer. Each time you think you are peeling the last layer; you discover there is yet one more layer. The layer that was just healed by my dad's words was a surprise to me. I guess that is the way it will continue to be. Every now and then some hurt will be revealed which needs to be healed or some healing word or act will meet an unexpected need.

Remember the bump on my face? I finally went to the dermatologist and had it removed. It was quick and painless and healed nicely—flat again. Now I shave without worrying about it because it is healed. I don't have to fear cutting it any more or being careful around it any more. It is removed and healed. That is exactly what emotional healing will do for you. It will help you live more openly and freely. You will love deeper and feel more compassion for others. It will make you a better spouse, parent and friend. *Zoe* to the Max is not possible without being an emotionally healthy person. Even if you must spend a few hundred dollars in counseling or even more, it will be the best money you ever spend because it will be an investment in you and your future and family and ministry and life! You are the only instrument you have to work with, so it is good management to be the best one you can be.

Buck Stop Generation

I just got off the phone with Debbie, a friend from church. She has been trying to get her life turned around over the past few years and has recently made new strides learning about how to become a more emotionally and spiritually healthy person. She poured out the pain in her heart to me concerning a recent conflict and I talked with her about what it is like to recover from the hurts of a dysfunctional past. I listened to about twenty minutes of non-stop hurts until she finally asked me how I was able to listen to all that and to the hurts of many other people. "How do you do it, Tracy? I'm sure you have to deal with a lot of stuff of your own, and don't you just get overloaded when other people like me pour out their problems to you?" I said, "No, I have been blessed with a godly heritage from my grandparents and parents combined with my own choices to follow Christ and seek to be the healthiest person I can be. I have plenty to give because through practicing Truth + Grace + Time, I am living the blessed life God planned for all of us to live."

If you were born into a family that followed God, then you were blessed by that. If you were born into a family that was not following God, then it was harder for you. The Bible says children receive either blessings or cursings from the choices their parents make. We can choose to be the "buck-stop" generation and see a turn-around in our children's generation.

Friend, you can't change your heritage, but you CAN change

your legacy. You can be a better version of you! Don't stop until you are free inside. Free to take the risks of love. Free to love yourself and others. Free to risk failure. Free from guilt and insecurities. Free to be the real you—without masks. Free to live authentically. Free to live *Zoe* to the Max!

Chapter 17: *Zoe* Zone Part 6
Inside the Wall of Contentment

- 1 of 10—Learn to enjoy the presence of the Lord
- 2 of 10—Spend time with the Teacher and The Book
- 3 of 10—Rejoice to re-juice
- 4 of 10—Peace-ruled heart
- 5 of 10—Emotionally healthy

My Convertible

Several years ago I bought my daughter Stephanie an older VW Cabriolet convertible as her first car. I drove it to work for a couple of days and really enjoyed riding in a convertible. I've always loved driving with the windows down and feeling the fresh outdoor breeze. In fact, it irritates my family and employees because I often open the windows at the office and at home and turn on the whole-house fan and let the fresh breeze draw through the windows! I love that! So after driving this convertible, I thought I might enjoy having a convertible some day.

This past week, I saw a convertible Chrysler Sebring and stopped to write down the seller information. Valerie had been suggesting I drive a smaller car with better gas mileage than my truck. So I took the car out for a test drive and really LOVED the convertible with the automatic folding top.

I got a little sad last night at the thought the purchase might not work out. As I was praying about it this morning the Holy Spirit reminded me of the Psalm 37: 3-5, *"Trust in the Lord and do good; dwell in the land and enjoy safe pasture. Delight yourself in the Lord and he will give you the desires of your heart. Commit your way to the Lord; trust in him and he will do this."*

However, if it didn't work out I knew God would give me the contentment I needed to keep driving my truck, which is eighteen years old. Do you know what I'm talking about? I was faced with the choice between spending money on something you want or being content with what you have. God gives us contentment as a powerful *Zoe* force. He has taught me His way and His time is really the best. Do you believe that? Do you believe God's will for you is really the best way and the best time? Do you "know in your knower" God is a giving God and He has your best intentions in mind?

**The *Zoe* of Contentment Can be
Just as Enjoyable as Buying Something New!**

I have experienced that kind of supernatural contentment with what I possess. I truly am content with what I have, as long as I have the smile of God and, of course, a fresh cup of coffee! I don't have to buy that convertible to be happy. God can give me contentment and *Zoe* to the Max with what I already have. Do you know the power of that contentment?

The Mega Jackpot

Part of experiencing *Zoe* to the Max is learning to enjoy what you have now "to the max." Keeping our desires under the control of the Spirit is an important tool in maintaining our *Zoe* because if we let our desires chase after every whim, we will find ourselves in debt, in sin and in trouble!

Natural desires can grow into sin. *"Each one is tempted when, by his own evil desire, he is dragged away and enticed. Then, after desire has conceived, it gives birth to sin; and sin, when it is full-grown, gives birth to death"* (James 1:14-15). Uncontrolled desire grows to lust and full-grown sin. Contentment is the power that is available to keep our desires contained within the will of God. This powerful tool needs to be seen as a means of keeping us in the *Zoe* Zone.

One of the great teachings on contentment and the place of money in our lives is 1 Timothy 6:6-10: *"Godliness with contentment is great gain."* The Greek phrase "great gain" is *megas porismos* [meg·as, por·is·mos] which can also be translated as mega acquisition.[1] In 1 Timothy 6:5, Paul is rebuking those who use godliness as a means of financial acquisition. He contrasts this acquisition using *"godliness with contentment"* as the *"mega acquisition."* *"Godliness with contentment"* is far beyond financial. It is bigger than that. It's on a whole new level. *"Godliness with contentment"* is a **mega acquisition,** because when it is acquired it is has MEGA value!

Think of it like this—what has more value, the millionaire who is constantly distracted by his money and worried about losing it and trying to get more of it OR those who are totally content with what they have? The one who has the MORE valuable possession is the one who has learned to be happy with what they have. Lots of contentment is more valuable than lots of dollars. Do you see that? It doesn't matter how much money you have—the question is, are you happy with how much money you have? *"Godliness with contentment"* is the true mega jackpot! A mega jackpot with two components:

1. Godliness—This is the state of supremely loving God even as your character is being transformed into the divine nature of Christ-likeness, and your actions and attitudes reflect the presence of God.

2. Contentment—This is keeping an attitude of thankfulness and appreciation for your current possessions to the point that having more could **not** increase your level of happiness.

Having both of these components is the mega jackpot, because you have happiness with your God AND happiness with your possessions. That's a "mega acquisition" and worth much more than wealth alone. I am richer than the rich, because I have acquired something more valuable than mere money. I am **totally content** with the lesser amount of money I have, because I am **rich in** contentment. Alone with this richness, I am pursuing godliness as well! Therefore, I have the mega jackpot. That's *Zoe* to the Max!

Right now, as you are reading this, are you totally happy with your possessions? Or are you saying to yourself, "I just want a little more and then I'll be content." Contentment is the supernatural power to be totally happy RIGHT NOW with what you have RIGHT NOW, as you are holding this book.

Inside the Wall

Let me show you the awesome truth I found in studying what this mega jackpot is all about. The Greek word for contentment is *autarkeia* [ow·tar·ki·ah]. It is a compound word which is only used two times in the New Testament, and it means "a perfect condition of life in which no aid or support is needed."[2] Wow! Think about this. Contentment is "a perfect condition of life". How can that be? Conditions are never really perfect, so there are two possible responses to this definition. Either you can never be content or contentment is a state of mind where you are perfectly happy with your conditions. One of the secrets of *Zoe* to the Max is learning how to get in to this contented state of mind! Contentment is a condition of mind and attitude where nothing is needed because you are thankful for what you have.

As I studied the root of *autarkeia*, I discovered a real gem. The first part of the word is *autos* from which words like automobile, autopilot and automatic are derived. It simply means "himself or itself."[3] Contentment has to do with something that works by itself. The second part of the word is *arkeo* [ar·keh·o] which comes from the idea "to defend, ward off".[4] Also, Strong's Concordance shows it is "probably akin to the idea of 'raising a barrier.'"[5] Together these words gave me the picture of contentment as an automatic barrier or wall that raises up to ward off the green-eyed "want-more" monsters that try to steal our happiness.

Contentment is an automatic wall that rises up to ward off the green-eyed monsters. Inside my wall of contentment, I am living in a state of happiness with what my Father has given me. If there is something I want, I ask my Father for it according to His will and timing. I know He is a good Father and a giving Father who enjoys blessing me. I know He will give to me whatever I ask, if it is right for me and truly the best thing for me, and in the best time for me to receive it. I know God hears my prayers, and I trust His timing, therefore I will continue to be thankful for what I have now. If God chooses to give me what I have asked for, then I will also be thankful for receiving it.

Thankfulness Raises the Wall

My garage door opener raises my garage door every time I push the remote control button. Thankfulness is the remote control button that automatically raises my wall of contentment. So it could be said thankfulness is the choice to push the button. I choose to be thankful for what I have. I could choose differently. I could choose to complain. I could choose to hate what I have. I could choose to be envious for what someone else has. These are choices you and I can make. Thankfulness is the choice God wants you and me to make. He wants us to choose a habit of thankfulness. *"Give thanks in all circumstances, for this is God's will for you in Christ Jesus"* (1 Thessalonians 5:18).

Notice the verse says, *"give thanks."* There are many times when I am not "thankful," but if I start to "give" thanks, I am truly amazed at how I **become** thankful. The act of giving thanks generates the feeling of thankfulness. Thankfulness changes my attitude, increases my happiness level, and raises the wall of contentment.

Tank Full of Thankful?

What is your tank full of? Is it full of negative thoughts? Is it full of worries or fears? Is it full of complaints? God wants us to have our tank full of thankful:

*"**Always giving thanks** to God the Father **for everything**, in the name of our Lord Jesus Christ."* (Ephesians 5:20, emphasis added)

*"And **whatever you do**, whether in word or deed, do it all in the name of the Lord Jesus, **giving thanks** to God the Father through him."* (Colossians 3:17, emphasis added)

*"**Do not be anxious about anything, but in everything**, by prayer and petition, **with thanksgiving**, present your requests to God."* (Philippians 4:6, emphasis added)

*"**Devote yourselves** to prayer, being watchful and **thankful.**"* (Colossians 4:2, emphasis added)

Do you get the point?! God wants us to be full of thankfulness! Look at all the above phrases, "Always ... for everything ... whatever you do, whether in word or deed ... in everything ... with thanksgiving ... devote yourselves to being thankful." When we do this, we are **being** the kind of person that God wants us to **be**. Anyone can be thankful on occasion, but only God can create a person who is a thankful person. *Zoe* to the Max is moving from being a person who gives thanks, to becoming a thankful person. Thankfulness is a character trait that God wants to develop in His kids.

I was meditating on the character list in Ephesians 5, which includes several negative characteristics with a comment, *"...these are improper for God's holy people."* Then it lists three more negative traits that have to do with our speech and it says these *"... are out of place."* Then it gives one characteristic that is suitable and proper. What do you think that characteristic is? *"But among you there must not be even a hint of sexual immorality, or of any kind of impurity, or of greed, because these are improper for God's holy people. Nor should there be obscenity, foolish talk or coarse joking, which are out of place,* **but rather thanksgiving**" (Ephesians 5:3-4, emphasis added).

Thanksgiving is suitable and proper! Being a thankful person fits Christ-likeness. The Greek word for thanksgiving might be familiar to you if you are from a Catholic background. It is the word they use for communion. *Eucharistia* [yoo·khar·is·tee·ah], "thankfulness, the giving of thanks."[6] Thanksgiving and thankfulness are proper for God's holy people. *Eucharistia!!!!!*

Sadly, we usually have to lose something before we become thankful. Recently I was removing a face mask I wear when treating patients and inadvertently nicked the cornea of my left eye with a metal nose arch that was protruding from the mask. I decided to have my optometrist, Dr. Tonya Sylvia, look at it. She said that I had cut it "pretty bad." I had sliced almost all the way across my cornea and almost pierced my eye! That evening I kept my left eye covered with a patch and tried to carry on as normal. To my surprise, with only one eye I was not able to do many of the things I normally do. And it caused me to appreciate my left eye more than ever before. I had never thought to thank God for my left eye until then.

This habit of thankfulness keeps raising the wall of contentment, automatically allowing us to live in a state of contentment and happiness with our lives.

Contentment in Everything

The other place where the word *autarkeia* is used is in 2 Corinthians 9:8. The NIV translates it as "sufficiency," but it is the same Greek word as contentment: *"And God is able to make all grace abound to you, so that always having all sufficiency* (autarkeia—contentment) *in everything, you may have an abundance for every good deed."* Notice the word "always" and "all." God wants us to always stay in a state of happiness with what we have.

There is another Greek word in addition to *autarkeia* that means contentment. It is *autarkes* [ow·tar·kace] which means— "1 sufficient for one's self, strong enough or processing enough to need no aid or support. 2 independent of external circumstances. 3 contented with one's lot, with one's means, though the slenderest."[7] It which is used in Philippians 4:11: *"I am not saying this because I am in need, for I have learned __to be content__ whatever the circumstances"* (emphasis added). Here we see contentment is a learned characteristic. Some personalities are naturally more contented than others, but all of us can learn to be more content. It is something our teacher, the Holy Spirit, wants to teach us. If you study the context of Philippians 4, you will see Paul learned this contentment in many different states of existence. It is not just about material possessions, but also applies to learning to be content with various kinds of circumstances and conditions.

As I write this, Dr. Reeford Chaney passed away two days ago on June 25, 2005. He was the District Superintendent of the Virginia Church of the Nazarene for many years who then retired in Richmond. I knew him personally for almost thirty years as I interacted with him on denominational boards, attended church with him and was also his dentist. Over the years, he became one of my life heroes because of his great attitude. He always had an attitude of contentment and encouragement. He was not just thankful—he was a thankful person! He had hit the mega jackpot of godliness with contentment, and I admired this and want to be like him "when I grow up." In the past few years as his health declined, I witnessed his attitude did not decline. He continued to show an attitude of thankfulness and contentment even

> *This use of contentment does not imply we are to be lazy and never seek to improve our standard of living.*

with his declining abilities. He moved from walking, to using a cane, to using a walker, to riding in a wheel chair. He had learned the truth of Philippians 4:11 to be content in whatever state.

The third word for contentment in the New Testament is the root of both of the above Greek words. It is *arkeo* [ar·keh·o]. That is the root I referred to earlier which means "raising a barrier." John the Baptist used this word when he responded to a question from some newly converted soldiers in Luke 3:14, *"Then some soldiers asked him, 'And what should we do?' He replied, 'Don't extort money and don't accuse people falsely—be content with your pay.'"* This use of contentment does not imply we are to be lazy and never seek to improve our standard of living. Those of you who have worked on commission pay know you need to motivate yourself, "beat the bushes," and go after those sales. However, once you have done the best you can, God wants you to be content with that. If you feel your wages are inadequate, then of course, you should talk to your Father about that. God wants us to pray about everything! Pray for more sales! Pray for a promotion or a raise or a new job or a new career! Being content does not mean you don't have goals or thoughts about wanting an increase or a change. God wants us to give these matters to Him and then learn to be content with our present pay and circumstances. Contentment is always a "now" thing. It shows God's desire for us is that we should be happy now. If we are to experience *Zoe to the Max* we must learn to be content with our **present income**, and if we want a pay increase, we make that a matter of prayer WITH thanksgiving (Philippians 4:6). That thanksgiving keeps the wall of contentment up, which keeps us focused on being happy now. Anyone can be happy when the pay increases come in, but God wants you and me to be just as happy without one.

Money, Money, Money, Monnneeey!

If this book had audio, I would play the theme song to Donald Trump's show, "The Apprentice," "Money, Money, Monnnney." Money is not only the theme of that show, but it is the god of this world. Our relationship to money is important to our ability to find contentment and important to our relationship with God. Jesus taught us our feelings toward money are a powerful force that challenges our very love for God. If we set our heart on money, it will become our idol and our master and our god. Whatever we "treasure" shows the location of our affection (heart). We are, therefore, only to treasure God and not money.

Money is a competing idol and, therefore, our relationship to it is critical. Jesus taught this strongly in Matthew 6:19-21, 24: *"Do not store up for yourselves treasures on earth, where moth and rust destroy, and where thieves break in and steal. But store up for yourselves treasures in heaven, where moth and rust do not destroy, and where thieves do not break in and steal. For where your treasure is, there your heart will be also ... No one can serve two masters. Either he will hate the one and love the other, or he will be devoted to the one and despise the other. You cannot serve both God and Money."*

Money is so powerful! Look at what Jesus is saying:
- Money is a heart surgeon—it can change people's hearts.
- Money is a god-maker—it can make people worship.
- Money is a love magnet—it draws the affections of man's heart.
- Money is a master— it enslaves and demands obedience.
- Money is dangerous— it can cause you to even hate or despise God.

Money is like nuclear power; it is useful if properly harnessed but must be restricted and safe-guarded or it will harm you and others. Money is not a subject that can be ignored. It is a crucial issue that must be

Do I have money or does my money have me?

examined regularly, contained and monitored. The crucial issue for you and me to examine is, "Do I have money or does my money have me?" Let's look at two harmful relationships that we can have with money:

We can love money. Two Greek words used for God's love are *agape* [ag·ah·pay] and its root *agapao* [ag·ap·ah·o].[8] These words mean a total kind of love, the God-kind of affection used in the New Testament to describe God's love. 1 John 4:16: *"God is love (agape)." Agape* can also be focused on money as Jesus warned in Matthew 6:24: *"Either he will hate the one and* (agape) *love the other ..."* (parentheses added). We must not *agape* money—that is a love meant for God alone.

We can be a friend of money. The Bible warns us in Hebrews 13:5 and 1 Timothy 6:10 not to be a friend of money. The Greek word used is *philarguria* [fil·ar·goo·ree·ah].[9] This compound word is usually translated as "love of money," however, that may not be the best translation. The first part of the word is *philos* [fee·los][10] which is used 29 times in the New Testament and is always translated as "friend." The second part of the word *arguros* [ar·goo·ros][11] is translated as "silver," meaning money. So when you put them both together you come up with a "friendly with silver" or "money-friendly." I have known people who have excused their "money-friendly" attitudes by saying to themselves, "At least I don't love money." But to be a "friend of money" is what the scripture warns us about. Look at this warning: Hebrews 13:5, *"Keep your lives free from the love of money (philarguria- friendly with silver) and be content with what you have, because God has said, 'Never will I leave you; never will I forsake you'"* (parentheses added).

Because *philarguria* has been translated "love of money," many people have skipped past this verse thinking it didn't apply to them. But I contend the verse is addressing the less intense kind of "friendly feeling" with money many of us have. Being money-friendly keeps us from being content. To be money-friendly is to look to money as our resource for security as contrasted to contentment which is to look to our Father as our resource for security. Whatever amount of money or provisions He gives us is what He wants us to have for now, and He wants to teach us how to be content with that.

The "Want More" Trap

The opposite of contentment is "wanting more." To "want more" is a dangerous trap that will keep us from hitting the mega jackpot of *"godliness with contentment."* Let's look at 1 Timothy 6:7-10 and see how easily we can be trapped.

1. Money is temporary—Godliness is eternal.

1 Timothy 6:7: *"For we brought nothing into the world, and we can take nothing out of it."* See the big picture? Nothing in—nothing out = that's reality.

2. Contentment only needs food and clothing.

1 Timothy 6:8: *"But if we have food and clothing, we will be content with that."* We rationalize so many things "we need," but the minimum daily requirement is food and clothing.

3. "Get rich" thinking is a trap with MANY foolish and harmful end results.

1 Timothy 6:9: *"People who want to get rich fall into temptation and a trap and into many foolish and harmful desires ...."*

People with "get rich" motivations are into a thinking pattern that will ensnare them. Think about those bear traps that you see in the old cartoons—the ones that look like huge steel jaws. When you step in the middle of the jaws, they slam together and invariably clamp on the guy's rear end! That is the picture of a person stepping into "get rich" thinking! It's a trap that will chomp you.

The simple DESIRE to "get rich"
or
"have more" does the damage

Some people think that this doesn't apply to them because they don't want to "get rich," they just want to "have more." But let me point out the fact both the "I want to get rich" and the "I just want to have more" desires have similarities:

- Both of them reveal discontentment.
- Both of them want more than they presently have.
- Both desires are outside of God's will for us.
- Both of them keep you from experiencing *Zoe* to the Max!

God's will is for us to experience
the *Zoe* of contentment with what we have.

4. The "get rich" trap leads to ruin and destruction.

1 Timothy 6:9b: "*... that plunge men into ruin and destruction.*"

If we are driven by "get rich" and "want more", we will ruin ourselves eventually. Constant discontentment is ruinous to our health, our relationships and our happiness. That's not the way we want to end up.

5. Friendship with money breeds evil.

1 Timothy 6:10a: "*For the love of money is a root of all kinds of evil.*"

There's that translation of *philarguria* again. Remember that means "friendly with money." The root of all kinds of evil can be traced back to someone having the wrong relationship with money.

6. Friendship with money pulls us away from God.

1 Timothy 6:10b: "*Some people, eager for money, have wandered from the faith and pierced themselves with many griefs.*"

If you are Wesleyan-Armenian in your theology, that means backsliding. If you are Calvinistic in your theology, it means stumbling and loss of close fellowship with God. Either way, we know a wrong relationship with money can pull us away from closeness to God and cause much grief.

Money is a tool

The right attitude toward money is that money is a tool. It is a tool which can do much good, but it is also a dangerous tool if mishandled. Of course, money is actually amoral in itself, but if we become friends with it, the amoral becomes immoral, and the result is that evil will grow.

Does that mean it is wrong to get more money or have more money? No. If it is God's will for us to have more money, then praise God! OR if it is God's will for us to NOT have more money, then praise God! Either way, we should be able to praise God the same and learn to be content with what we have.

Eight Lessons on Proper Tool Usage

How are we to use the tool of money? There are a lot of good books about money management you can read by Ron Blue and Larry Burkett and others. The only point I want to make here is the one made at the end of this passage in 1Timothy 6. Beginning in verse 17, there are eight lessons addressed to *"those who are rich in this present world."* Most of you might eliminate yourself from the rich group, but may I remind you compared to most people on this planet right now, you are in the "rich" category. I was discussing this with my friend Fredrick. He brought up a new thought to me. He said that most of us live better than the kings of centuries past. We have electricity, air conditioning, automobiles, telephones, televisions, microwaves, refrigerators, etc. We live better than kings! I think the only question is "How rich?" Okay, maybe if "you live in a van down by the river," then you are exempt from the following verses and can skip down to verse 20. Otherwise the eight lessons apply to you to some extent:

"Command those who are rich in this present world not to be arrogant nor to put their hope in wealth, which is so uncertain, but to put their hope in God, who richly provides us with everything for

our enjoyment." (1 Timothy 6:17-19)

1. Don't think you are better than anyone else. God could take your money away anytime He wants. God has allowed you to have whatever money you possess. Don't look down on people who have less money than you.

2. Money is unreliable so look to God for your hope because He is dependable. The stock market is uncertain, health is uncertain, calamity is possible. Do not depend on money to secure you. God is your security.

3. God gives us everything we have to enjoy. Satan is the liar who says God wants us to suffer and live in poverty the rest of our lives. Instead, God wants you to experience *Zoe* to the Max and all the good things come from Him. Enjoy!

"Command them to do good, to be rich in good deeds, and to be generous and willing to share." (1 Timothy 6:18)

4. Do good with your money. Your money is given to you to meet your needs and to be shared with others.

5. Measure true richness by counting the number of good deeds you do. So, how rich are you? The next time you think of how much money you are making, try thinking about how many good deeds you are doing with it. Instead of counting how many dollars per hour you make, count how many good deeds per hour you do! That's how God counts true riches, and we should count what He counts.

6. Be generous and be willing to share your money according to how much God wants you to share. Do people call you generous? Are you willing to share or are you wanting to hoard? Maybe you have God's provision for someone else. Now that is a new thought! Maybe someone else is asking God to help them, and maybe God's will is to dispense that help through you? Want to be God's instrument?

"In this way they will lay up treasure for themselves as a firm foundation for the coming age, so that they may take hold of the life

that is truly life." (1 Timothy 6:19)

7. Use your money to lay up treasures for yourself in heaven. You have heard of currency conversion. We need to convert as much of our earthly, temporary money into eternal treasures as possible.

When I was in Jamaica for my brother-in-law Blaine's wedding, I converted some Jamaican money while I was there. When I was preparing to leave, I tried to get it converted back to US currency because it was going to be worthless to me the next day. The Jamaican money left in my pocket when I boarded the plane was suddenly worthless.

The day you step into eternity, all your earthly money will instantly be worthless. It will be like my Jamaican money in America—useless. If you don't convert your earthly money now, it will soon be worthless.

8. This conversion of earthly money has no risks of devaluation whatsoever and has a guaranteed high rate of return. I'm thinking of those stock trading web site advertisements on TV, like Charles Schwab. If you watch them closely, they have four or five sentences of small print that are impossible to read at the bottom of your screen. It basically says they make no guarantee you might not lose all your investment. They talk about risk management. When it comes to heavenly treasures, there are truly no risks and there is a guaranteed rate of return. Pretty sweet, huh?

Wealth Protection

In other words, godliness with contentment really is a mega jackpot of riches! Therefore, to protect your investments, you must screen the various desires that come up in your heart for possible threats to your riches. Contentment with godliness is true riches. Don't let the other kind of temporary riches steal your contentment now and your eternal riches later. Stay inside your wall. Outside the walls of contentment are all the desires for other things, all the "get rich" desires and the "bigger is better" thoughts and "you really need this" and "you deserve that" advertisements. Stay inside your wall and enjoy yourself! Inside is guaranteed happiness. Any questions? Duhhhhh!

Back to My Convertible

Let me tell you how the story about my convertible is unfolding. Remember I'm trying to stay behind my wall of contentment and at the same time check out the possibility of purchasing a car? So I called the seller and told him I was interested in talking to him. I asked him about a wet area I had discovered under the floor mats on the passenger's side. He said that he would check it out and call me back. After waiting for several days, I called him back to discover he had already sold it! What? "I thought you were going to call me?" I said and he replied, "I was but this other guy took it 'as is.'" I was disappointed for half a minute because he failed to call me and I had gotten my hopes up about buying the car, but then I immediately let it go because I KNOW IN MY "KNOWER" MY GOD HAS MY BEST INTEREST IN MIND! If He had wanted me to have that car I would have it! **I am content** with my old pickup truck.

Yes, my humanity got excited about the possibility of having something new, but my spirit and mind immediately brought me back to the truth about who God is. I reminded myself God is a good god and a giver of good things. That convertible was not the good God had in mind for me. I then began to thank God for my truck and that thankfulness raised my wall of contentment back up. This is a real-life example of the power of contentment. You saw how it unfolded during the time I have been writing this chapter. I would still like to have a convertible and maybe I will get one before this book is finished, but, as of now, I am content with where I am and with what I have. I have learned to be happy inside my wall of contentment. Even though there are different things I would like to have, and I get excited thinking I may get them, I have learned God's way of staying in the *Zoe* Zone behind my wall of contentment. I keep my thankfulness focused on enjoying WHAT I HAVE inside my walls and not focused on WHAT I DON'T HAVE outside my walls. That is the key of contentment: STAY INSIDE.

Catalogues of Discontentment

Years ago, I had a great employee who had one interesting habit. She would look through the catalogues that come in the mail or in newspapers, and she would often point to items and talk about how much she "needed" this or that. By the time she was done looking at all the advertisements, it seemed to me she had stirred up new desires to get things she didn't have. Do you see a connection here? They were catalogues of discontentment!

I noticed this pattern and asked her one day, "What are you looking for in that catalogue?" She said as she flipped the pages, "I am looking for something that I might **need**." I thought about that statement. Why did she need a catalogue to show her what she "needed"? Didn't she already know what she needed? I think what she was really doing was entertaining herself by looking for things that might spark an interest in her mind and then she could rationalize herself into "needing" them and then buying them.

"Thingies" Attract Monsters

We need to be careful with window-shopping and looking through catalogues of discontentment. The result is we move from contentment to discontentment. Is that a good move? Here's what happens: We begin to lose our contentment by allowing the desire for a new "thingy" to attract a green-eyed monster that breeches the wall of our contentment. This "thingy" could be anything we do not have. Shopping may show us the "thingy," or a catalogue of discontentment may show us the "thingy," or we may see the Joneses with one. Once we allow the thought of the "thingy" to remain in our minds, it is like bait that attracts a little green-eyed monster to come over the wall. Once we have allowed a security breech over our wall of contentment, the green-eyed monster grows larger and larger. Thoughts of "thingies" are like a growth hormone for the monsters. The more we think about the "thingy", the larger the green-eyed monster grows. He drives us to start looking for that "thingy" in other catalogues and shopping for it to compare prices. Soon the green-eyed monster is so large it dominates our thoughts and lives. Our contentment is gone now. It has been surrendered to the hunger of the green-eyed monster. We will now not be happy until we buy the "thingy". The monster drives us and compels us to find a way to "beg, borrow, or steal" until we get that "thingy"! At this point, it is hard to stop the power of the monster and get our contentment back. Most people buy the "thingy," and their monster is satisfied. I've heard it called Retail Therapy. The monster is satisfied by the therapy and a feeling of exhilaration gives us a "high."

Retail Therapy

Retail Therapy works! We feel better. But the problem is it is only temporary. The medication of the new purchase lasts for only a short period of time. When the excitement of the new purchase begins to wear off, we are "back to normal life," needing to find happiness with what we currently have. If we have not learned the principles of contentment, it is only a matter of time before we are bored with what we have. We start searching again for a new "buzz". We don't really understand what we are doing—it's subconscious. We start looking for a new "thingy" by either picking up another catalogue of discontentment, shopping, etc. The thoughts of new "thingies" begin to lodge in our minds. These thoughts attract new green-eyed monsters, and they begin to grow until more Retail Therapy is needed to satisfy them. The money we spend on Retail Therapy is not available for other things. When we have a true emergency, we now don't have sufficient funds because we spent it on the last "thingy". We complain and maybe even grumble against God because He has not provided enough money for our needs. So we suffer without or get into debt. More debt is more slavery. We don't have enough money, so financial friction strains our families. Some people take on a second job or more hours and then they don't have time for their families. Retail Therapy can become Retail Addiction.

Vacuuming Behind the Wall

How much better it is to learn contentment and the power of thankfulness! Thankfulness fills our hearts with positive thoughts, raising our wall of contentment. If we have needs, we pray about them. We trust our Father to provide in His way and in His time. If we have thoughts about or desires for new "thingies," we *"Pray about everything,"* as Philippians 4:6 shows us. Contentment doesn't mean we never want anything. It means we pray about everything we want and trust it to our Father. Prayer is like vacuuming your mind of "thingies". It removes the bait that attracts those green-eyed monsters. If you leave food crumbs on the floor long enough, you'll attract bugs! Vacuum those crumby thoughts up with prayer! Then you go back to thanking God for what you have, and the wall of contentment stays high.

I enjoy the peace of not having green-eyed monsters stomping around my mind. I don't need Retail Therapy because *Zoe* to the Max satisfies my heart much better! If God brings new possessions into my life, I enjoy them fully and then have something new for which to be thankful! But my mind is not focused on "thingies." My mind is on enjoying the *Zoe* to the Max of loving God and praying about everything I want and being thankful for all that I have. I experience contentment as "a perfect condition of life in which no aid or support is needed". Wow! That's *Zoe* to the Max!

Contentment in Various Circumstances

This concept of contentment goes beyond wages and material possessions to include all the circumstances of our lives. One example is our health. The Bible teaches us to be content even if God does not heal our illnesses as we ask. 2 Corinthians 12:8-9 shows us this by using the same Greek word *arkeo* [ar·keh·o], which means contentment. *"Three times I pleaded with the Lord to take it away from me. But he said to me, 'My grace is sufficient (arkeo) for you, for my power is made perfect in weakness.' Therefore I will boast all the more gladly about my weaknesses, so that Christ's power may rest on me'"* (parentheses added). I was surprised to learn this familiar passage uses the Greek word for content, *arkeo*, but translates it as "sufficient." If you reread the passage using the translation "contentment" instead of "sufficient," it says, *"My grace is contentment for you, for my power is made perfect in weakness."*

God wants us to pray about all our healing and then seek the grace to be content if healing is delayed or never comes. That is what Paul experienced, and that is the power of Christ that can rest on us as well. Behind the wall of contentment we learn to be thankful for our ABILITIES not our DISABILITIES. Isn't it true we are not usually thankful for our health until we get sick? We need to pray for healing and believe God hears our prayers and can heal us. However, if that healing is delayed or comes through medical science or never comes, we must trust God in everything and pray for the power of grace to be contentment for us.

When the Waiting Room Becomes Your Living Room

Often we are in "the waiting room" of life. We are waiting on God for the answer to some need or request. We are trying to live in contentment, but there is something we want or need that is not being fulfilled. Meanwhile we wait—like my dental patients in the waiting room. We flip through the magazines of life and wait for God to respond. Sometimes we wait so long the waiting room becomes our living room. Can you wait patiently in the waiting room? Can you be a patient—patient?

Waiting on God is an act of faith and self-control. Faith states God's will and God's timing are worth waiting for. And self-control monitors our minds to guard us from worrying or focusing too much on what we are waiting for. God wants us to trust His goodness and trust His timing and trust His heart in the waiting room of life. So we need to make ourselves comfortable in the waiting room by rearranging the furniture into more of a living room. There are a lot of scriptures to help us do this, but the passage which is my favorite is Psalm 37. It gives the whole picture of the seven things we should remember while waiting in the waiting room.

1. Don't be jealous of sinners. *"Do not fret because of evil men or be envious of those who do wrong; for like the grass they will soon wither, like green plants they will soon die away"* (Psalm 37:1). If I see a drug dealer driving a convertible, God does not want me to be envious of them. Instead, I need to pray for them. How insulting it must be to God for His children to be envious of sinners.

2. Trust in God and do the right thing. Psalm 37:3: *"Trust in the Lord and do good; dwell in the land and enjoy safe pasture."* God wants us to ask for whatever we desire and pray about whatever tempts us to be envious. Don't be envious, instead pray about it. Be one who does good things—a "do-gooder," if you will. Then enjoy *Zoe* to the Max as you *"… dwell in the land."* That is God's plan. Trust Him in the waiting room with the worry and then enjoy your life.

3. Delight in the Lord. Psalm 37:4: *"Delight yourself in the Lord."* The Hebrew word for delight means "enjoy, take pleasure and enjoyment in an object, implying desirability of the object."[12] That sounds like *Zoe* to the Max! Enjoy the Lord! God wants us to desire Him and look to Him for our enjoyment while we are in the waiting room. As we find our delightful *Zoe* in Him, we receive the benefits of His nature because:

4. God is a giving God. Psalm 37:4 continues, *"… and he will give you the desires of your heart."* God knows what our heart truly desires, and He wants to gives us those desires. While we linger in the waiting room, don't forget God promises to fulfill our desires.

My daughter Nena took up an interest in golf while attending Trevecca Nazarene University. Her roommate was on the golf team and took her out to play golf a couple of times, and she really enjoyed herself. Since moving back to Richmond, she has had the desire to play but doesn't have any clubs.

She worked for a couple of days during the summer, answering the phone for a vacationing receptionist at Guardian Christian Academy. One day she struck up an interesting conversation with a salesman offering fundraising activities for the school. After coming out of the meeting, he stopped to tell Nena that he had discovered that she was a first grade teacher at Powhatan Elementary School so he asked if she knew a particular teacher there. She did know the teacher and the ensuing conversation revealed he also knew Nena's favorite high school coach, Bruce Secrest, who happens to enjoy golf. Nena related her interest in golf as well. He then asked if she played much, to which she replied that she didn't have any clubs. "Would you like some?" he asked. "Sure," she said, wondering why he asked. "My part-time job at the golf course connects me with folks who are buying new golf clubs, and they want to sometimes give away an old set of clubs. I can get you a set if you like." "That would be great!" Nena said dumbfounded. "Will you be here next week?" he asked. "No, I'll be starting to get my room set up at my school." Then he shocked her again by saying, "I'll leave them at the front office of your school next week!" "Oh....ahh...okay." She smiled in amazement as she just tried to take in the conversation which had just transpired.

She considered that a stranger had come in on one of the two days she was there and offered to personally deliver a free set of golf clubs to her school 25 miles away! God had given her one of the desires of her heart! Wow, God is a giving God, and He loves to surprise us with blessings. If we delight ourselves in Him, take our desires to Him and next ...

<u>5. Commit the situations to the Lord.</u> The Hebrew word for commit means "to roll away." It's like playing volleyball with worry as the ball and God on the other half of the court. When worry comes over the net, volley it back. That's what I do with my worry. I toss it

back to God. God says in Psalm 37:5, 6: *"Commit your way to the Lord; trust in him and he will do this: He will make your righteousness shine like the dawn, the justice of your cause like the noonday sun."* Commit your problem to God and trust Him to help you handle it. The promise is He will even make justice come out. So, in the meantime, we need to ...

6. Wait patiently in the waiting room. Psalm 37:7: *"Be still before the Lord and wait patiently for him; do not fret when men succeed in their ways, when they carry out their wicked schemes."* God wants us to wait patiently for Him to work His perfect will in our situation. God wants us to wait patiently and not take action on our own. You see, there are two forms of waiting.

Waiting patiently

VERSUS

Waiting with anxiety, fear and frustration

Many people say, "I'm waiting on the Lord," but they are not waiting patiently—they are waiting with frustration. They are "waiting" like a fidgety toddler. Waiting patiently means we are waiting in faith, we are waiting with contentment. Waiting patiently is a form of trust. Waiting patiently is an exercise of vigilance because we move in and out of patience. For example, I earlier told you about my desire for the convertible that was not fulfilled. I was in a state of contentment before the opportunity came up. Then when it fell through, I had to get myself back in to contentment. I had to get re-contented.

My Convertible Story—Part II

A week later, my niece Melanie told me about another Sebring convertible that her husband Scott had seen for sale. He stopped and got the information and gave it to me. So I prayed about it and called the number and left a message for the owner. Here I go again! Was this going to be God's provision or another disappointment? Waiting patiently is an exercise of vigilance because circumstances may change. I put the new possibility in God's hands because we were only days away from leaving for a week long trip to Indianapolis for the quadrennial Church of the Nazarene General Assembly. If he did not call me soon, I would not have time to look at it before leaving. Days went by as I tried to wait patiently for God to move. It was in the back of my mind, but since the owner did not call, I dismissed it as not in God's plan for me.

Several days later, we arrived in Indianapolis and were attending an evening service when my cell phone vibrated from an unknown phone number. I left the service thinking it was one of my dental patients. It turned out to be the owner of the convertible! Oh man, here I go again! He wanted to know if I wanted to look at his car! "Yes, I would, but I'm here in Indianapolis!" After explaining the situation, I told him I would look at it when I returned if it was still available.

I then re-contented myself and gave it back to God. When we returned to Richmond, the car owner informed me he had sold the car! I have learned there is peace in a "closed door" also. A "closed door" is just as much guidance from God as an open door.

Psalm 37 goes on in verse 8 to say as you wait patiently on the Lord you need to …

7. Let anger and worry go—put your hope in the Lord.

Psalm 37:8: *"Refrain from anger and turn from wrath; do not fret—it leads only to evil. For evil men will be cut off, but those who hope in the Lord will inherit the land."* God doesn't want us to be angry as we wait. Anger and wrath are self-destructive emotions. Anger comes from frustration or hurt. If these emotions are not properly processed, they lead to anger and eventually express themselves in wrath. As I described earlier, emotional healing is needed for past hurts, then we are to process our new hurts as they arise. God will take care of the evil people. He doesn't want us to fret either. In Psalm 37:1, He started out by saying, *"Do not fret."* Here He says it again, *"Do not fret."* He wants us to live fret-free, in a relationship of forgiveness toward others and hope in Him.

As you look above at those seven things you should practice in the waiting room of life, you can see waiting patiently is not just being passive. There are some actions He wants us to take which result in placing our hope, our optimistic outlook in the Lord! That means we are to experience *Zoe* to the Max even in the waiting room of life. Here's the whole picture: *"Trust … do good … delight in the Lord … commit your situations to God and trust Him, wait patiently on the Lord and don't let negative emotions remain … be optimistic in the Lord!"*

My Convertible Story - Part III

The story of my desire for a convertible continues. As I have been writing this section, it is the end of August. My daughter Rebekah called me three days ago to tell me she saw ANOTHER Sebring convertible for sale! She and Nena were out together, and both saw the car and looked it over. Here we go again. Another convertible. Another possibility or another disappointment? I have learned to stay calm during these times because I am staying in a constant state of contentment with God's provision. If God wants me to have this convertible—great. If God does not want me to have it—great. I don't want it if God doesn't want it. Do you understand that? If God doesn't want you or me to have something, then there is a good reason for it. How do I know this? Because we have a good Daddy. He has our best interest in mind, and I want His plan—not my plan.

So I decided to go by and look at the car on my way to church. On the way, Valerie called me to let me know about the car also. She had received a call from Rebekah while she was in the same area and Valerie wanted to let me know that she liked it too. We met to see the car together. It was definitely pretty, with a new white paint job, and sparkly chrome wheels. The price was reasonable as well.

As I wrote down the number and got back into my burning hot pickup that needs the A/C recharged, I went through my normal prayer routine as I shifted the hard gears because it needs a new clutch too! "God if you want me to have that car, then show me." The human side of me thought God had better hurry up and show me because a lot of people were seeing the car and someone might buy it soon. The spiritual side of me countered that if God wants me to have it, I could relax because He would make sure no one else would buy it. He is able to frustrate and prevent the sale of anything that He has reserved for me. I can relax in the faith of that. Do you have that kind of faith? Do you understand how much God loves you and how powerful He is? If someone else buys it—good. That was not the one for me! If God wants me to have it—good. It will be there later.

So in my mind, I moved the situation to the side and went on to church to a meeting I was attending. After the meeting, I was scheduled to have a second meeting with my friend Russ, but he called and canceled due to some sick kids. So there I was. The question came to me. *"God, do you want me to call the car owner now?"* I felt a clear "Yes." I called and learned the owner drives a tow truck and was in the area where the car was located. We had the normal conversation about the condition of the car and the reason for sale. We met and went for a test drive. The car was in great shape and the man seemed trustworthy so when we returned, I felt I should negotiate a price, and I bought it! Praise the Lord!!!!

GOD GOT ME A CONVERTIBLE! My family was thrilled about it, and I was happy to finally have a convertible, but I must say that the happiness I felt is VERY DIM compared to *Zoe* to the Max God gives me every day! I thought to myself how pitiful it is people look to objects like a car for happiness because it is so small compared to what I find in Christ!

The neat thing to add to all this is that God got the car for me four days before my 50th birthday! What a God! He knows my desires, but He kept me in the waiting room until he had the right car ready at the right time. As I am writing this now, I have been enjoying my convertible for a week and I am praising God for His birthday present to me.

I Want to Be Like Dr. Chaney!

Thankfulness not only raises the wall of contentment, but it also makes you a more pleasant person to be around. If you never learn the habit of thankfulness, you will get increasingly crankier as you age because you will have more about which to complain. Old age sneaks in, one ailment at a time. So if you are focused on complaining about what's wrong instead of being thankful for what's right, you will have more and more things to complain about over time! Soon your world will be full of complaints as you gradually lose your health and abilities. Do you see that? Thankfulness is the antidote for complaining! You can't complain and be thankful at the same time.

My hero in this area was Dr. Reeford Chaney. He was never a complainer even into his eighties. He was always thankful for something! He had been thankful for so long it was his continual practice. He had developed the habit of thankfulness, and this brought him contentment. Even in his last year, as he would stumble around a little at his dental checkups, he would chuckle to himself about it. His son Lowell told me toward the last two weeks of his life, his dad couldn't eat very well, but he still wouldn't complain.

He had plenty to complain about, but he chose to be thankful instead. I know other people who have the habit of complaining, and they complain more and more until they're awful to be around! Which kind of person do you want to be? Start being thankful now. Stop complaining now! You choose what you will focus on and think about and talk about. Choices become habits. Habits become destiny.

I REFUSE TO COMPLAIN.

I REFUSE TO FOCUS ON WHAT I DON'T HAVE.

I CHOOSE TO BE THANKFUL, NOT CRANKFUL.

I CHOOSE TO SEEK ZOE TO THE MAX! EVERY DAY OF MY LIFE.

I CHOOSE TO HAVE AN ATTITUDE OF GRATITUDE.

I'LL FOCUS ON MY ABILITIES NOT MY DISABILITIES.

I WILL BE A SWEET OL' MAN!

I MIGHT DIE A SICK MAN, BUT I WANT TO BE A THANKFUL SICK MAN!

Chapter 18: *Zoe* Zone Part 7
Holiness

- 1 of 10—Learn to enjoy the presence of the Lord
- 2 of 10—Spend time with the Teacher and The Book
- 3 of 10—Rejoice to re-juice
- 4 of 10—Peace-ruled heart
- 5 of 10—Emotionally healthy
- 6 of 10—Inside the wall of contentment

This seventh area of the *Zoe* Zone is pretty big. In many ways it is the biggest area. In order for us to experience *Zoe* to the Max we need to be in complete unity and alignment with God. God wants to be able to relate to us on a level of intimacy I think we don't fully appreciate. He wants the kind of relationship with us He had with Adam and Eve in the Garden of Eden. It is the kind of relationship where He comes and walks with us *"in the cool of the day,"* (Genesis 3:8). That's why God called out, *"Adam, where are you?"* He was accustomed to meeting together and walking together in the evenings. Wow, that must have been awesome to walk with God like that! But then again, isn't that what God wants to do with us now? He wants to walk with us like that now. He wants to have an intimate level of relationship with us everyday.

Back to Eden

In order to have that kind of relationship, we must deal with what messed it up—sin. Sin messed up the intimacy. Sin always messes things up. Sin was the action WE took that caused the separation. But God is not fickle. He is not in a corner of heaven pouting. He wants reconciliation.

Consequently, salvation has been provided through Christ allowing reconciliation and forgiveness of sins. This salvation restores our relationship with God, yet we discover the disturbing truth after walking with God for a while, that the cause of sin remains intact, keeping us enslaved to the power of sin. That is when we need to go deeper with God and allow the process of sanctification to free us from the power of sin.

Sanctify means "to set apart from sin, purify and dedicate to God's use." Jesus prayed for this to happen to us in John 17:16-19, *"They are not of the world, even as I am not of it. **Sanctify them** by the truth; your word is truth. As you sent me into the world, I have sent them into the world. For them I sanctify myself, that **they too may be truly sanctified"** (emphasis added).

The word sanctify in Greek is *hagiazo* [hag·ee·ad·zo]: 1. to render or acknowledge, or to be venerable or hallow; 2. to separate from profane things and dedicate to God; 2a. to consecrate things to God.; 2b. to dedicate people to God; 3. to purify; 3a. to cleanse externally; 3b. to purify by expiation, free from the guilt of sin; 3c. to purify internally by renewing of the soul.[1]

Zoe to the Max requires the sanctification of our hearts and lives to God so we can live in complete harmony with Him. Sanctification is the purification of our lives from both the presence and power of sin because sin is always a choice. Romans 6 talks very plainly about the need for sin to be conquered. Verses 11-14 say, *"Count yourselves dead to sin but alive to God in Christ Jesus. Therefore **do not let sin reign in your mortal body so that you obey its evil desires. Do not offer the parts** of your body to* sin, *as instruments of wickedness, but rather **offer yourselves to God,** as those who have been brought from death to life; and offer the parts of your body to him as instruments of righteousness. For **sin shall not be your master,** because you are not under law, but under grace"* (emphasis added).

> **Sanctification is the purification of our lives from both the presence and power of sin because sin is always a choice.**

From this passage, we see clearly God wants us to be *"... dead to sin, but alive to God."* He says *"do not to allow sin to reign,"* but instead God is to reign. We are not to <u>cling</u> to sin, but <u>bring</u> our sin to God and present our bodies to be an instrument of righteousness. Look back at verse 14. Sin is NOT to be our master. That is a statement of fact against the power of sin in our lives. Then if you drop down to Romans 6:22 you see the conclusion: *"Now that you have been set free from sin and have become slaves to God, the benefit you reap leads to holiness, and the result is eternal life."* God's will is that we be set free from the dominion of sin and be a slave only to God. The fruit of this is leads to holiness and eternal *Zoe* with God!

Slave to Sin or Slave to God?

I know some theologies do not agree with what I have just stated. They claim sin is normal to the Christian walk and we are powerless to avoid it. But how does that fit with the above scriptures? If we could not avoid sinning daily, then we would be slaves to sin. Right? How can Romans 6:22, *"… you have been set free from sin"* be true if we sin daily?

Granted, many Christians are not living holy lives—the Holy Spirit is not reigning in their lives. He is resident, but not president. Where the Holy Spirit reigns, a person will be free from the power and dominion of sin. How can one continue to be a slave to sin if the HOLY Spirit is reigning?

> *He is resident, but not president.*

Being a slave to sin and holiness do not go together in scripture. That's why the Old Testament tabernacle and subsequent temple were set up the way they were. There were strict rules for cleansing for the priests to be able to stand before God. The Holy of Holies was far removed from sin. If we are continually sinning, how can we stand before God? The answer is Jesus. His sacrifice pays the price for our sinfulness and cleanses us from all unrighteousness. Now the presence and power of the Holy Spirit dwelling in us allows cleansing to continue. If we are filled with the Holy Spirit and truly living by the power of the Holy Spirit, then we will be able to walk in holiness because He is Holy and we are living in His power, not our own. Our holiness is, of course, not OURS BUT HIS. He acts in us, making us holy in our actions by His power. He is holy, and He is making us holy because He lives in us and where the Holy Spirit reigns, it must be holy. The angels in heaven declare, "Holy, holy, holy." No one would argue God is not holy, and when He sends His Holy Spirit to dwell in us and cleanse and empower us, how is it that we are not made holy by that presence?

I'm not supporting the doctrine of "positional holiness," which purports we are not actually holy, but only considered holy because of our position in Christ. This view is God only sees Christ's holiness when He looks at us. I deeply respect my brothers and sisters in

Christ who think differently in this area, but we are one family in Christ with some different perspectives about precisely what holiness means and how it works. Hopefully, we have a sufficient amount of maturity, grace and love to not tear one another down as we describe our different views.

I think God sees us as we actually are and He is doing the work of making us holy in our character, thoughts and actions. Maturity is the process of us allowing the Holy Spirit to do His work of holiness. In our immaturity, we often sin and need a lot of confession and repentance. Maturity comes as we change. When we sin, we confess and learn and improve. He forgives our sin when we confess it. His grace accepts us in our immature spiritual state, but He doesn't want us to stay immature. He wants us to grow up and change to become like Christ—sanctified, filled and controlled by the Holy Spirit. He wants to ACTUALLY transform our character as we mature into the level of Christ-likeness. The Holy Spirit can surely cleanse our hearts and break the power of sin in our lives! Obviously, WE cannot overcome sin on our own, but the Holy Spirit can. This is the glory of the Christian life. Paul says in Galatians 2:20, *"I have been crucified with Christ and I no longer live, but Christ lives in me. The life I live in the body, I live by faith in the Son of God, who loved me and gave himself for me."* Christ lives in us and His power is active in our lives to overcome sin. 1 John 3:8-10 (emphasis added), *"He who does what is sinful is of the devil, because the devil has been sinning from the beginning. The reason the Son of God appeared was* **to destroy the devil's work.** *No one who is born of God will continue to sin, because God's seed remains in him; <u>he cannot go on sinning</u>, because he has been born of God. This is how we know who the children of God are and who the children of the devil are: Anyone who does not do what is right is not a child of God; nor is anyone who does not love his brother."*

The reason the Son of God came was to destroy the power of sin and His "seed" remains in us to continue that victory. One of the ways we know we are born of God is because we see Him breaking the power of sin in our lives. Sin no longer controls us—no longer reigns over us.

Sin? Unusual but Not Extinct

On the other hand, we sometimes fail to obey and need forgiveness. As long as we are in this sin-marred body and in this sinful world, we have the opportunity to sin and sometimes we take that opportunity. We are fallible humans and susceptible to sin. We always retain the choice to sin and the possibility to give into temptation, but we do not need to be **slaves** to sin. Sin is always possible, but it is not required nor should it be our practice or habit. When I sin, I immediately confess it to God and then feel pretty stupid for allowing it to happen. Sin is always the choice to be stupid rather than follow the power and leading of the Holy Spirit. As television Pastor Ed Young, Jr., says, "When we say 'I will' we get 'His will.'" His will is we be holy, *"But just as he who called you is holy, so be holy in all you do; for it is written: "Be holy, because I am holy"* (1 Peter 1:15-16, emphasis added). God does not ask us to do something that is unattainable; otherwise many of the commands of the Bible are unattainable.

We don't have to give in to the temptation to sin. The Holy Spirit always provides an escape route from temptation. The escape route is promised by God's faithfulness. 1 Corinthians 10:13: *"No temptation has seized you except what is common to man. And God is faithful; he will not let you be tempted **beyond what you can bear**. But when you are tempted, he will also provide a way out so that you can **stand up under it"*** (emphasis added). This is God's promise that temptation does not have to overwhelm us. God is faithful—we will not have an irresistible temptation. We don't have to give into the temptation—we can "stand up under it".

I can testify sin does not reign in my life. I don't lie or steal. I'm not addicted to gossip or coveting. I don't hate anyone, and I keep my eyes from lust. I do sin OCCASIONALLY but not HABITUALLY. The power of Christ reigns in my life to overcome sin. I do not say this boastfully because it is made possible ONLY by the power of the Holy Spirit. I boast in Him and His power to make me an overcomer. When I say, "I will" I get "His will".

My Sanctification Experience

On April 23rd, 1973, I sat in a pew listening to the final words at a revival service. Would I go all the way with God? Would I "go anywhere and do anything" God called me to do? Those were the questions I faced as a seventeen-year-old that Tuesday night. Evangelist Floyd Baker issued the challenge, "If you are serious about following God and are ready to totally commit yourself to Him, I want you to stand up and come down here to this altar—with no music—I'm not even going to ask the congregation to stand. If you are serious about fully surrendering your life to God, then YOU stand up and come down here now!" That was the challenge I needed.

I struggled with Satan whispering, "Don't do it. God will make you go to Africa as a missionary, and you will never have anything." As always, Satan is a liar. I decided God was a good God and so I was willing to go anywhere, anyplace, at any time He sent me. That night the Spirit of God filled me as I fully surrendered to His sanctifying power. I remember as I drove home I stuck my head out of my '67 VW bug and shouted to the top of my lungs into the night skies, "Glory to God!"

Something radical happened in my life after that night. I sensed a new power and new desire to do God's will. I sensed a new cleanness and focus in my heart. After I attended religion classes in college the next year, I learned theologically what happened to me that night. I was cleansed and filled with the Holy Spirit.

From that point on, I have been radically committed to a lifetime of following God and growing in that relationship. I was sanctified by the Holy Spirit and set apart to God. The power of sin was broken that night, and even though sin occasionally snags me, it is not my practice, love or addiction. I am a "slave to righteousness" not a "slave to sin".

The Holy Spirit is President of my Life

I elected God as president of my life in a landslide election! He is boss of my life, and I like it that way! It's not a struggle. I don't fight Him. We must have it straight in our minds and actions that God is supreme. God is god, and we are not. He must be more than resident. He must be president of our lives. President means He is the head, the leader. I have a vote, but He has veto power. There is no power struggle in my life. I may argue with Him over specifics, but obedience has already been determined. Jesus Christ is Lord to the glory of God!

From Lord-ship to Love-ship

Holiness started out as a struggle for the presidency of my life. It was a struggle for who was lord of my life. But it then graduated from a lordship emphasis to a love emphasis. The first and great commandment is to, *"Love the Lord your God with all your heart and with all your soul and with all your mind"* (Matthew 22:37). What started out as lordship is now love-ship! Early in my experience, I followed out of obedience to His position as president of my life, but now I follow Him out of love because He is the love of my life. I don't want to do anything to hurt my relationship with God. It took me many years to move from Lord-ship to Love-ship and enjoy the difference. God wants have a father-child relationship with us—not ruler-slave.

Temptation Is an Opportunity To Show Love

Previously, I looked at temptation as a totally negative experience, but I have learned I can turn it into an opportunity to show my love for God! Pastor Hancock taught me this concept. Temptation is a chance to sin, but it is also a chance to love!

Temptation to sin in the area of lust has always been my weakest area. I've slipped into mental sin in this area over the years more times than I care to admit. Our world is filled with sexual images in every media. Sensuality rules our society. You don't have to go looking for it because it comes looking for you! But thank God for the victory the Holy Spirit has brought in my life! Every temptation is an opportunity to reinforce my love for God. Even this morning as I got up early, started my coffee and turned on the TV there was a "Girls Gone Wild" video ad. The ads themselves are pornographic. It only took a few seconds for me to recognize the temptation and hit the remote with a "God, I love you more!" affirmation. What started out as a chance to slip became a chance to demonstrate love!

Holiness Is About the Heart

The Holy Spirit gives us the power to choose what we will think about and what we will view. The battles are in the mind. Romans 8:6: *"The mind of sinful man is death, but the mind controlled by the Spirit is life and peace."* The mind that is controlled by the Spirit yields life—that word for "life" is *Zoe!* *Zoe* comes when we allow the Holy Spirit to control our minds.

If you are still struggling with slavery to sin, I challenge you to pray right now. Ask God's Holy Spirit to sanctify your heart and mind and free you from the power of, and slavery to, sin. Remember, when you say "I will" you get "His will." His will is that you allow the Holy Spirit to make you holy and mature so you can be in complete alignment and unity with Him. That way, He can bless you with *Zoe* to the Max!

Chapter 19: *Zoe* Zone Part 8
Authentic Relationships

- 1 of 10—Learn to enjoy the presence of the Lord
- 2 of 10—Spend time with the Teacher and The Book
- 3 of 10—Rejoice to re-juice
- 4 of 10—Peace-ruled heart
- 5 of 10—Emotionally healthy
- 6 of 10—Inside the wall of contentment
- 7 of 10—Holiness

Getting along with others is an important part of God's plan for a happy life. We need to love others and be loved by others. That's the way God made us. Everyone wants to be liked, accepted, respected, and appreciated by others. This is a universal need, and authentic relationships are essential to experiencing this kind of happiness and being able have *Zoe* to the Max with others.

God Cares About the Quality of Your Relationships

Much of the New Testament and much of Jesus' teaching have to do with how people relate to each other. Jesus talks about the power of forgiveness and love. Much of the content of Paul's epistles has to do with developing good relationships.

Dick Wulf has compiled a list: *THE "TOGETHERS OF SCRIPTURE" LIST* (Copyright 1995 Dick Wulf. All rights reserved.)[1] He has compiled all the scriptures where God has given instructions for how He wants us to function together. He has identified 65 "togethers" or plural commands for the church found in Scripture (Check the footnote for contact information if you want to get the whole list). He grouped the 65 into ten broad groups:

THE TOGETHERS OF RELATIONSHIP WITH GOD
THE ATTITUDINAL TOGETHERS
THE TOGETHERS THAT HOLD TOGETHER

THE TOGETHERS THAT STRENGTHEN
THE TOGETHERS THAT HEAL
THE TOGETHERS OF SPIRITUAL GROWTH
THE TOGETHERS OF INVOLVEMENT IN THE WORLD
THE TOGETHERS OF EVANGELISM
THE TOGETHERS OF BATTLE
THE TOGETHERS OF PERSEVERANCE

God wants His family to function together in authentic harmony. Remember how important it is that we love people. Love God; love people. Those are the top two priorities. Matthew 22:37-40: *"Jesus replied: 'Love the Lord your God with all your heart and with all your soul and with all your mind. This is the first and greatest commandment. And the second is like it: Love your neighbor as yourself. All the Law and the Prophets hang on these two commandments.'"* The quality of our relationships demonstrates we are Christ-followers. Christ said in John 13:35, *"By this all men will know that you are my disciples, if you love one another."*

God cares how well you get along with other people, and being happy includes learning how to have excellent, quality relationships with others. So that's why the eighth area in the *Zoe* Zone is having authentic relationships. I want to encourage you to be well read on this subject. There are many excellent books dealing with all aspects of relationship. Be a student of interpersonal relationships. For now, I would like to address seven aspects of what I think an authentic relationship looks like and then tackle some problems which contribute to less than authentic relationships.

Seven Aspects of an Authentic Relationship

In authentic relationships:

1. The "real" you feels safe enough to be "real." Authentic relationships are when the "real" you is relating to the "real" other person. Often people are insecure and afraid to be who they really are around others. They are afraid of rejection or criticism, so subconsciously they put on a different persona. It's as if they put on "masks" they think will be more acceptable. They put on different masks for different people and different situations. Authenticity is hindered because you don't see the real person—only the mask. The insecure person never feels totally accepted in the relationship because his or her real self is not revealed.

Off with the masks. God wants to heal our self-image and make us secure in ourselves so we don't need masks any more. Authentic people can have authentic relationships. Authentic people are the same wherever they go. They are simply "who they are" because God has healed them so they are satisfied with "who they are".

When we are emotionally needy, we often look for other people's approval to prop us up. We try to impress them because we need their approval, or are afraid of their disapproval. As long as we are needy, we can never be secure enough to be authentic. Remember, no one can "kick a chair out from under you" if you are not first standing on that chair. When we are secure in Christ and emotionally healed, then we don't NEED other people's approval, although we always enjoy having it. Being authentic is a place of strength. You are strong in Christ and confident in whom He has made you.

Model authenticity. Your goal is to know others and be known by others. When you are totally comfortable with yourself, then others will sense your openness and comfort and will begin to disclose themselves to you more. They may begin by throwing out little "test" statements to see how you will react. If you accept their statements without judgment, then they will try a deeper level of disclosure. Being yourself and letting others be themselves is a key to an authentic relationship.

Accept other's differences. Allow others to be different from you. It is good you are different from others and others are different from you. Different does not mean bad. Accept others as they are, not as you want them to be. It takes maturity to accept differences you don't understand or like. Love is being "real" because love is being mature. Grace is being "real" because grace is strong. People who are comfortable with themselves can be strong in Christ and can accept others as they are—not as they ought to be. Accepting others does not mean condoning their sinful behavior, but it means accepting them as God accepts them. Mature love can accept the person in spite of their behavior.

Be careful what you share. Being authentic does not mean full disclosure to everyone. There are certain private things which should only be shared with those who have proven themselves. Our fallen nature tempts us to gossip, so don't throw out your "dirty laundry" to unproven people.

Give and receive compliments and criticisms. Emotionally healthy people are able to handle both compliments and criticisms. They are able to give generous compliments and gentle criticisms. They are secure in Christ so they can see beyond any criticism. They also can graciously accept compliments without deflection. I have experienced times when I tried to show appreciation to someone who refused to accept it, even admonishing me to give my thanks to God. They deflect the compliment. This discouraged me from expressing appreciation to them again. I believe true humility accepts compliments graciously and discerns if it is necessary to gently redirect a misguided compliment.

In authentic relationships:

2. There is mutual care. Caring is not something which can be demanded, but it is the byproduct of love invested. A relationship is like a bank account. There must be deposits before there can be withdrawals. Authentic relationships require authentic deposits: deposits of time, thought, and actions. Each person needs to be 100% invested in the relationship. The 50/50 idea doesn't work because it becomes tit for tat. Each one holds back and waits on the other to respond with "their turn." The relationship becomes a game of mental scorekeeping. Mutual care means each one is 100% involved, not waiting for the other to match deposits. Deposits, however, are not guaranteed by the FSLIC. Sometimes the other person consistently does not make deposits. This can be frustrating and require some investigative questions. Sometimes relationships need an honest quality update. Asking a simple question like, "It seems we haven't gotten together much lately. Is anything wrong?" Or "The last time I shared something with you, it seemed you weren't very interested." Or "That hurt my feelings because it felt like you didn't really care about what I care about." These inquiries never threaten an authentic relationship but can serve as a wake-up call.

In authentic relationships:

3. There is respect for one another's boundaries. As I discussed previously, boundaries are very important in authentic relationships.

Boundaries are about respect—respecting what belongs to the other person and respecting the other person's feelings, preferences and responsibilities. When we run over the other person's wishes or invalidate their feelings, we are disrespecting them as a person. Quality relationships are built on mutual love and respect for one another's boundaries.

In authentic relationships:

4. There is equality. One person does not feel or act superior to the other person. If one feels superior then, by definition, the other is inferior. If one is always instructing the other, that is a teacher/student relationship and not an equal relationship. If one is always protecting or caring for the other, that is a parent/child relationship, not an equal relationship. If one is dominating the other, that is a leader/follower relationship, but not an equal relationship. Authentic relationships occur when each person treats the other as an equal.

In authentic relationships:

5. There is both giving and receiving. Reciprocity is key to an authentic relationship. This means both people are giving to each other, and both are receiving from each other. If one is emotionally needy, the relationship will not be reciprocal. One may try to give too much—which reveals co-dependence. One may try to take too much—which reveals self-centeredness. Either way, the relationship will not be healthy. Authentic relationships are balanced.

In authentic relationships:

6. There is openness and honesty about personal struggles. When you call some people on the phone, it seems you always get the answering machine greeting. "Sorry, but no one is available to take your call. Please leave a message after the beep." Often the truth is that they are NOT sorry, and there IS someone available to take my call, but they don't want to talk. In the same way, when you talk to many people and ask, "How are you doing?" it's like they respond with their pre-recorded answering machine message, "Fine." In authentic relationships, people DON'T answer with their answering machine message. They truthfully answer the question and honestly tell you how they are really doing, and it is accepted without overreacting. I often ask my almost-authentic friends "the double question." I ask sincerely, "How are you doing?" Then if I sense they have their answering machine on, I will ask it again more slowly and deliberately, "Now, how are you REALLY doing?" This gets their attention and lets them know I didn't want the pre-recorded answer, but I actually care about how they are REALLY doing.

In order for this to work, we must accept the honest answers we are given without pouncing on the person for being honest. If they are having a bad day, an appropriate response is "I'm sorry." with possible follow-up comments about how you feel when you have a bad day or when you last had a bad day. Don't try to correct them or pry into their business or instruct them or put them down for being honest. If they want to tell you more, they will. If that's all they want to say, then accept it. When I am irritated, I don't usually want to talk about the details because having to relive it just makes me MORE irritated. I appreciate my authentic friends who sense that and just reply, "I'll pray for you" or "Sorry about that."

Talk About the Elephant

In order to have and maintain authentic relationships, sometimes there must be a tough conversation. If the other person has done something that has hurt you, then you owe it to the relationship to inform them of that hurt.

My friend Wynne Lankford is the executive pastor at my church and he preaches two or three times a year and does an excellent job. He and I have an authentic relationship so when he speaks, I critique his message. He welcomes this and returns the favor when I speak. Once I remember giving him some feedback to improve a message he had just delivered. I was talking to him while we were standing around after the Saturday night service with a few friends. The next day Wynne asked if he could talk with me in private. He shared how the conversation the previous night had bothered him. Even though he knew my heart and appreciated my feedback, it had embarrassed him to receive it in the presence of other people. He asked for me to give him future feedback in private. It was a great conversation and after hearing his perspective, I apologized and agreed in the future I would give those types of critical comments in private. That conversation proved the authenticity of our relationship. Wynne had the courage to initiate a tough conversation. If he had held that hurt inside and ignored the obvious "elephant in the room" it would have hindered our relationship. Our relationship was closer after that. Of course, all confrontations are not guaranteed to turn out that well, but if a relationship cannot survive talking about elephants, then it is a rather fragile relationship and certainly not authentic—yet. We must validate one another's feelings and allow ourselves and others to be "in the process" of improving. Wynne could have rebuked me in anger, but he didn't. Instead he gently, but honestly, shared his feelings. I learned from him I must be more sensitive about delivering criticisms because sometimes my frankness can hurt my friends.

That was not the first time I hurt someone's feelings by being too frank in a public setting. My friend Stacy had the courage to share with me she felt I had embarrassed someone in my small group by using them as a lesson illustration. I was again being insensitive. Because these friends share like this with me, I not only have a more authentic relationship with Stacy and Wynne, I am more conscious of my weaknesses in this area. Sometimes talking about the elephant can move a relationship into the authentic realm as well as improve the other person. I encourage you to talk about the elephant before he steps on something or you step in something!

In authentic relationships:

7. The problem is attacked, not the person. Wynne did exactly this with me in the situation I just shared. He attacked the problem, not me personally. He accepted responsibility for his need to become more secure in receiving public criticism, but, at the same time, he was honest with his hurt. He could have blasted me, "How dare you embarrass me like that in front of everybody!" That would have been an attack directed at me personally and could have escalated the hurt into a bigger conflict.

He also didn't attack my motives. He affirmed my heart was right, but the method of communication was the problem. When an elephant is in the room, it is wise to make the elephant the problem and not the other person. We get into a lot of trouble when we assume negative motivations. That almost guarantees an angry response. If we are wrong in our evaluation, then we have just created a secondary hurt in the attempt to address the first one. No one likes to be falsely accused of having a negative motivation. How much better to assume the best!

My pastor and I have a similar agreement. When we hear about or see a situation that appears negative, we have agreed we will assume the best of each other. For example, I am in charge of our service planning committee so we meet each week to plan the components of our worship services. When I hear through the grapevine he has changed the service plan and not informed me, I try to assume the best. I assume he has a good reason for his actions, and I don't let myself come to negative conclusions. I could assume he doesn't appreciate all the work we go through in planning the services or that he is disrespecting our opinion. The same process is true when I do something he doesn't understand. We sometimes begin a tough conversation with the preface, "I'm assuming the best here, but I need you to explain this situation to me." Assuming the best of each other keeps authentic people from unnecessarily hurting each other.

"Less-than" Relationships

Most of our relationships, sadly, do not measure up to the seven characteristics of an authentic relationship. So what should we do? I believe we should do our part to try to move all our relationships closer toward authenticity. This involves a five-part recipe:

<u>1. Healing prayers.</u> God is certainly interested in us having authentic relationships, so it isn't going to bother Him for us to pray for those relationships. Remember? Love God; love people. Some people are so dysfunctional only God can help them, so praying for their healing is the right place to start.

As I wrote in the chapters on emotional health, the quality of our relationships is one of the greatest indicators of our emotional health. Emotionally unhealthy people have many relationship problems. Their emotional unhealthiness causes them to act and react in ways that keep others at a distance. That's why I placed the emotional health chapters ahead of this subject—emotionally unhealthy people CAN NOT have authentic relationships. That's because their dysfunctions work against intimacy and authenticity. If you are emotionally unhealthy, seek help and health as I recommended. If the other people are unhealthy, then pray for the Holy Spirit to open their eyes to seeing their need and softening both your heart and theirs.

2. Maintain good boundaries. We must always remember the principle of boundaries that states each person is responsible for their own feelings, attitudes, and actions. If someone does not want to have a better relationship with you, there is nothing you can do about it. After having a conversation with the person about your desires for a better relationship, you must recognize you cannot change another person. That is God's responsibility. You can only wait to see if the other person will respond and be ready to assist them.

3. Huge helpings of God's grace. When you are dealing with relationships, God's grace is needed in huge doses. If you are one who keeps score, you won't make much progress in improving your relationships. Grace is God's unearned, unmerited blessings. God is rich in grace, so if we are going to make progress in healing relationships, we need to first get our own tummy full of grace. Then we can be ready to forgive hurts and forbear with irritations.

4. Bold love-moves. If healing is going to come, it will be necessary for YOU to climb over the wall of separation FIRST. When hurt comes in a relationship, a wall of separation is built. Pastor Jerome Hancock taught us this concept in a sermon about forgiveness. There is a wall of silence and defensiveness that is built both to protect and punish. Both parties feel justified. Both parties think the other should act first. If any progress is going to be made, someone must climb the wall. You should climb the wall first. That is the Christ-way. Jesus took the initiative to love boldly. He didn't wait for others. He didn't make a 50/50 deal. He climbed over the wall for our salvation so we could be reconciled to God. If both persons are Christians, then the more mature one should prove that by climbing the wall first.

Wall Climbing 101

Climbing the wall takes forgiveness, humility and courage.

A. Forgiveness. It takes forgiveness to let go of the hurt. Of course, forgiveness does not excuse the offense or lessen the crime. It does not let the other person "off the hook," because they are still on God's hook. They will still account to God for hurting you. But forgiveness is letting them off YOUR account. It is forgiving the debt because of what Christ did for you.

Collecting the Debt

Forgiveness does not require the other person's request. Forgiveness is a gift which is given by one person to another. It is not necessary the other person know they have been forgiven. If you are waiting to hear an "I'm sorry" out of them before you forgive, then you are requiring a down payment. Keeping the wall up is a type of collection system. Refusing to climb the wall is like putting them in debtor's prison until they pay. Forgiveness is clearing the debt off your books because of Christ's example. Forgiveness is not about justice; it is about grace. Grace is not fair. Grace is generous and undeserved. Forgiveness is made possible by the forgiveness that has already been given to you by God. You know what it's like to have your huge debt cleared off God's books. Matthew 18:23-35 tells the parable of the king who forgave his servant of millions of dollars in debt. The king then expected the forgiven servant to release others of their smaller debts. When the servant refused to forgive like this, he was rebuked by the king. Matthew 18:32: *"Then the master called the servant in. 'You wicked servant,' he said, 'I canceled all that debt of yours because you begged me to. Shouldn't you have had mercy on your fellow servant just as I had on you?'"*

That is the key forgiveness question Jesus is asking you today, "Shouldn't you have mercy on your fellow servant just as I had on you?" Forgiveness is climbing the wall when you shouldn't have to climb it. It is canceling the payment plans, opening debtor's prison and simply releasing the person because Jesus released you from your debt.

Withholding forgiveness means you don't fully appreciate the forgiveness you have received from Christ. You are inflating the value of the debt owed to you. Remember in the same parable the amount owed to the king was equivalent to millions, but the debt owed to his servant was only a few dollars. That is analogous to the value of our "debt to God" versus our "debts to each other." When you and I refuse to forgive, we are "cooking the books" to inflate the debt that is owed to us by others.

<u>B. Humility.</u> True forgiveness is humbling yourself and recognizing the fact you have been forgiven much more than you are being asked to forgive. Pride causes us to inflate the amount of debt owed to us. The debt was not more than we ourselves were forgiven by

God. By not forgiving, we are devaluing Christ's death on the cross! Humility is being willing to obey Christ by climbing the wall first. Since we so greatly value our forgiveness, we are now forgiving the other person, even if it is difficult to be the initiator.

Receiving forgiveness also humbles us. When we REALLY appreciate how valuable it is to have received the great gift of forgiveness, it is extremely humbling. In my dental practice, I often give my services to the poor and disabled. I try to be careful not to embarrass them when doing this. But the fact is, when someone gives you something that you TOTALLY don't deserve, it is very humbling. I recently received a note of thanks from one of my patients who is a pastor's wife. The dental work I donated to her at no charge was greatly appreciated. She began to cry in the office and profusely thank me for helping her. It was very humbling to her to receive that gift largely because when she went into the ministry with her husband, she was very afraid to give up her dental insurance. It humbled her to receive at no cost what she had paid for in the past. This is similar to the feeling of being forgiven by God. It humbles us to receive the undeserved gift of forgiveness.

C. Courage. After you have released their debt in your own accounting books and humbled yourself and decided you need to climb the wall, the only thing that remains is the courage needed to act. It takes courage to make that phone call or have that face to face meeting. Sometimes a letter or email is easiest to "break the ice," but when using those methods you have no way of knowing how it was received or even if it was received. How do you know they didn't throw away the letter or delete the email?

Face to face is best because they can read your body language, and you can read theirs. If they have questions, they can ask them right then and get immediate answers. It's also a chance for immediate reconciliation. It's a chance for you to possibly receive forgiveness, as well as give forgiveness. The best outcome is for both parties to reconcile. But you cannot control their reactions—you can only control your responses. Your goal is to give forgiveness and seek reconciliation. If these are shunned, you must be ready to leave it at that and let time and the Holy Spirit do their work.

D. What to say? Often a blockage comes because you don't know what to say. Here are some pointers: Begin with the words "I'm sorry

...." Then take responsibility for whatever part of the conflict was your responsibility or wrong doing. This is more difficult to do when you feel you were justified in whatever you did, but you can still say "I'm sorry that we had a conflict over ___________." In saying that, you are not confessing wrong doing but you are stating your regret for your role in the conflict.

Next you need to express the kind of relationship you want to have with them. Say something like "I want us to have a better relationship. I want us to be able to put this behind us and ______." This paints a picture of how you want the relationship to be in the future. Normally, the other person, inwardly, wants a better relationship also. Unless the person is consumed with bitterness and hatred, the wall should begin to crumble.

If all goes badly because the person refuses to accept the forgiveness or reconciliation, make sure you are prepared to not let yourself get pulled down into another round of conflict. Hold your ground and express your regrets, and do not withdraw your offer of forgiveness. It's easy to say, "Fine, well I guess I just wasted my time talking to you!" That pulls you down to the other's level of behavior. Your forgiveness needs to be so genuine, even if they do not accept it, you don't withdraw that forgiveness. Ideally, you want to leave the situation without regrets for what you say or how you say it. The best way to end the conversation is to say, "I'm sorry we haven't been able to resolve this, but I want you to know I want to resolve it and have a better relationship with you." They may end with some negative, defensive statement, but don't get sucked in to retaliating. At that point, you have done your part in trying to reconcile. The rest is left to the offended person and God.

In review, the recipe for making authentic relationships begins with:

1. Healing prayers
2. Remember boundaries
3. Huge helpings of God's grace
4. Bold love-moves

And, finally, adding in
5. Adventures in authenticity.

Make some adventuresome test moves of being authentic with the other person. Gradually try being more authentic with him or her. Authenticity does not happen instantly, but is a gradual deepening which occurs over time. Be prepared for setbacks and additional conflicts. Remember conflicts reveal areas of emotional unhealthiness and character flaws. Don't give up. God wants us to always be a healing force.

Romans 12 is a great chapter on relationships. Romans 12: 17-18 say, *"Do not repay anyone evil for evil. Be careful to do what is right in the eyes of everybody. If it is possible, as far as it depends on you, live at peace with everyone."* Don't get into retribution. God wants you and me to *"do what is right in the eyes of everybody."* He wants us to be peacemakers who are doing whatever we can do to *"live at peace with everyone."* The qualifier is *"If it is possible, as far as it depends on you."* That is a great verse concerning the boundary principle. It is not possible to be at peace with someone who does not want peace. You and I are called by God to do the loving and giving and forgiving thing, but we are not responsible for another's lack of forgiveness.

There is a fine line between being a giving, loving person and an emotionally unhealthy "doormat." You may need to seek the counsel of wiser people to work through the difference when dealing with difficult people. The bottom line is to act in love. Love acts in the best interest of everyone involved. Be a peacemaker, not a judge. A judge is always seeking justice. Peacemakers are seeking solutions that bring peace, not necessarily justice. Remember we are to dispense grace not judgment.

Beware Of Rocks in Your Shoe and Leaning Trees

Remember the leaning tree that crashed down on my driveway? When we have conflict with others and say hurtful things, it may not show up right away just as that tree didn't fall right away. But the conflict may have done some damage by creating a "leaning tree." The best thing to do is immediately try to fix all the damage done. Fix fallen trees. Straighten leaning trees.

After the conflict is past, sometimes little nagging questions begin to form in your mind. We've all experienced how irritating it is to walk around with a rock in your shoe. That's the way it feels to have an unresolved question rolling around in your mind. My pastor and I use that picture with each other when we are addressing a lingering question that one of us has. One of us begins our conversation saying, "I have a rock in my shoe I want to talk to you about." It's not an accusation. We realize it is probably a misunderstanding or misinterpretation of a comment or situation. If we haven't been able to dismiss it on our own, we need to get the rock out of our shoe.

Accepting Stuckness

I can't finish this chapter without acknowledging that not every relationship will become authentic. Some people are not going to change. They are more comfortable with the way they are and they are not willing to become authentic. We need to acknowledge that reality and accept them in their "stuckness." We should not "write them off," but instead accept where they are and make the best of it. You and I need to act lovingly toward everyone—not only those who are responding, but also those who are not responding. Hopefully, one day they will improve, but we are not going to ignore them nor are we going to let them monopolize our thoughts.

Meanwhile, we will continue to grow and change and experience *Zoe* to the Max with an ever-increasing number of authentic relationships. I have found the older I get, the more people I influence with the consistency of my attitude toward everyone. If you keep sowing good seeds, you will reap more and more good harvests. If you keep being authentic with yourself and others, you may upset or disturb some folks, but you will draw more to yourself and Christ. People are longing to be authentic, but they don't see very many modeling it. They see lots of people who claim "to be right" but who are not real.

BE WHO YOU ARE,
NOT WHO PEOPLE EXPECT YOU TO BE.

You can't be authentic if you are overly worried about your public relations image. Politicians are always worried about how they may appear to their constituents. I know someone who has a constant need to explain himself to others because he is afraid others will think poorly of him. In reality, he is revealing his own insecurity and hypersensitivity towards other people's opinions. He causes more suspicions than he answers. It reminds me of the ancient saying, "Me thinks thou dost protest too much." An integrity question is raised in other people's minds.

Being perceived as authentic is much more valuable
than being perceived as right.

An authentic person is just being who he or she is—period—without excessive explanations or fears of not being perceived correctly. If we are overly conscious of our PR image we are probably not being authentic.

To sum this subject up, enjoying a network of authentic relationships is part of living in the *Zoe* Zone. We should always be working toward upgrading all our relationships to the authentic quality level. At the same time, we don't let the "less than" relationships which are not improving "rent" too much space in our heads!

- 1 of 10—Learn to enjoy the presence of the Lord
- 2 of 10—Spend time with the Teacher and the Book
- 3 of 10—Rejoice to re-juice
- 4 of 10—Peace-ruled heart
- 5 of 10—Emotionally healthy
- 6 of 10—Inside the wall of contentment
- 7 of 10—Holiness
- 8 of 10—Authentic relationships

The *Zoe* Zone requires the balance of work and rest. Some of us have the impression Christianity is slave labor. They think serving God means we must work ourselves to a state of exhaustion and then be glad about it. That's not true. God designed us to have cycles of work followed by cycles of rest. We must learn good energy management" and know our limitations in order to experience *Zoe* to the Max! We must learn when to stop and when to "cry uncle," and when to say "No". We all have limited energy and need to recognize when our fuel tank is low and needs refilling.

Some of the sermons and songs I was raised with didn't teach me this balance. I remember the words of the song "I'm going to give, give 'til there's no more to give" and "work for the night is coming." I also remember sermons which glorified the virtues of exhaustion and overwork. It seemed if we kept back any energy for ourselves, we were carnal. I remember a sermon about how we are called to be the lowest of all slaves—the ones rowing in the bottom of the ship! ... Uhhhh ... sign me up for that! Sadly, the church often glorifies workaholics as "wonderful servants of Christ." Instead, I would classify them as emotionally unhealthy and, yet, sincere people who are probably neglecting their families as well as themselves in the name of serving Christ. No doubt they are serving Christ, but NOT IN THE WAY CHRIST WANTS THEM TO SERVE.

People who are serving Christ in unhealthy ways may be living in a state of chronic weariness which can cause them to have an attitude of grumpiness or complaining. They mumble to themselves about how badly they are being treated or about how lazy and uncommitted others are. Psalm 100 says, *"Serve the Lord with gladness"*! Without the proper rest God has ordained that they have, their weariness keeps them from enjoying their service.

Instead, Jesus wants to teach us how to rest and how to work within emotionally and physically healthy limits. Matthew 11:28-30: *"Come to me, all you who are weary and burdened, and I will give you rest. Take my yoke upon you and learn from me, for I am gentle and humble in heart, and you will find rest for your souls. For my yoke is easy and my burden is light."*

I know some theologians interpret this passage as a teaching against the spiritual weariness of legalism or Judaism. That is one application, but I think Jesus was also addressing people who are living in the state of chronic weariness and the chronic state of overload. These are two states where we shouldn't live! Let's look at both of them.

The State of Chronic Weariness

The original Greek word for weary is *kopiao* [kop·ee·ah·o], which means to grow weary, tired, exhausted (with toil or burdens or grief).[1] This word emphasizes the fatigue that is felt. Jesus does not want us to exist in a state of chronic fatigue. Its root translates as "a beating or a beating of the breast with grief or sorrow."[2] Have you ever felt so fatigued you felt you had been beaten up?

Jesus teaches when you start to feel like you've been beaten up, you need to go to Him for rest and to learn how to handle that situation in a healthier way. God does not want us to live in a chronic state of weariness. The Christian's walk is not to be one weary day of getting beaten up followed by another weary day of getting beaten up. That is living in an unhealthy manner. *Zoe* is found as we live in the ways of health that God designed. In other words, you can do the right thing but in unhealthy ways.

Of course, He is not referring to normal daily weariness. Our bodies are designed with a limited supply of energy which runs out usually in twelve to sixteen hours. Jesus was addressing a condition of chronic exhaustion—the feeling of being continually worn out. I believe too many Christians live in a more or less chronic state of weariness. *Zoe* to the Max is learning to live within your limits of energy, both by increasing your energy capacity and decreasing your energy expenditures. I'll talk more about this later, but first let's look at the second group Jesus was addressing—those in the state of overload.

The State of Chronic Overload

The Greek word for burdened is *phortizo* [for·tid·zo], which means "to place a burden upon, to load." Its root is *phortos* [for·tos] which is "to weigh down with the freight of a ship."[3] That is to say, you are overwhelmed with the load you are carrying. Most translations use two words to describe the full meaning: heavy laden or heavy loaded or heavy burdens. We were not designed to carry the freight of a ship. You and I have limitations. We have a maximum freight capacity. The dump trucks and 18-wheelers we see traveling down the highway have a maximum capacity limitation displayed on the sides of the truck. It lists an empty weight and a maximum load weight. If that truck tries to carry more than its maximum load, it will do damage to itself and the roads it travels on. Not violating this load limit is why there are weigh stations along our interstate roads monitoring each truck.

God didn't tattoo our maximum load weight on our bodies. Nevertheless, we do have a maximum capacity. If we exceed that capacity, we are overloaded. Wouldn't it be funny if we had "weigh stations" that would tell us when we are taking on too much? I think our weigh stations are often our spouses or close friends. Has someone close to you ever told you you were doing too much and that you needed to slow down? Did you listen? Maybe they would get your attention better if they put on a state police uniform and wrote you a ticket for "exceeding maximum load capacity."

If you are living in a state of chronic overload, then you are not experiencing *Zoe* to the Max even though you are doing good things. If you feel like you are carrying around the freight of a ship, Jesus says to go to him for rest and learn how to lighten your load to a manageable weight. God does not want us to live in a chronic state of weariness, and we were not designed to carry the freight of a ship.

God has a remedy for weary and overburdened people. The promise is rest for those who turn to Him. The Greek word for "rest" is *anapauo* [an·ap·ow·o]: "to permit one to cease from any movement or labor in order to recover and collect his strength."[4]

Three Steps for Weary People

<u>Step one: Go to Jesus.</u> Don't have a pity party—have a Jesus party. Don't whine and complain—go to Jesus. Ask Him to give you rest and help. He is gentle and humble. He's not going to beat you up more. He will gently help you find rest and teach you how to downsize. He is humble—He is not going to "chew you out." He can relate to your weariness because He experienced physical limitations and weariness Himself.

As you study His life, you see He had times of work followed by times of rest. He had times with the crowds and time alone in prayer. He was once so tired, He slept through a storm.

<u>Step two: Receive His Rest Therapy.</u> God made your body with limitations so you need to learn to respect them and live within them. You need to have your strength regularly renewed. In the passage from Matthew 11, when the tired come to Jesus, He offers them rest. Notice He does not offer more strength to keep going. He offers rest. Rest is God's ordinary answer for those who are tired. You need to rest so your energy can be replenished the way God designed for your body to work.

Pastor Jerome Hancock, in a sermon series on the Ten Commandments, fashioned a shortened three- or four-word version of each command. For the Sabbath Day commandment he said, "Commandment number four, rest and restore." The Sabbath Day was observed as a day of rest. The root of sabbath is *shabath* [shaw·bath]: to cease, desist, rest.[5] God provided a day of weekly rest in the calendar because our bodies and emotions and minds need regular rest (for further study, see endnote [6]). The saying is true, "A week without a day of rest makes one weak." Daily physical rest was also designed by God into our daily routine by rotating the earth, creating cycles of day and night. The day was for energy expenditure and the night for rest, sleep, and restoration. Our bodies need this cycle. We need to work to exercise our bodies and keep them healthy, but if we do not sleep seven or eight hours each night, we will be chronically fatigued. In addition to that, He built rest into the yearly religious calendar. Several times throughout the year there were special festival days and weeks for community celebration for spiritual, emotional, and physical restoration. Rest is needed in all three categories: daily, weekly, and yearly. If you and I violate this pattern, we will suffer the consequence of exhaustion.

Regular rest is a part of *Zoe* to the Max! Sometimes when I don't feel well and stop to evaluate the possible causes, I find often all I need is simple rest. Sometimes a nap is the most spiritually and physically replenishing thing I can do. We must learn to recognize when we are tired and then enjoy the *Zoe* of rest that we need. We do not have unlimited energy. We need to learn how to enjoy the expenditure of our energy and when it is gone we need to enjoy the rest of replenishment.

Our strength is not only physical but is emotional and spiritual as well. Remember your three tanks. Check your levels.

<u>A. Physical:</u> How's your physical energy? Are you getting adequate physical rest? Are you practicing daily, weekly, and yearly sabbath rests?

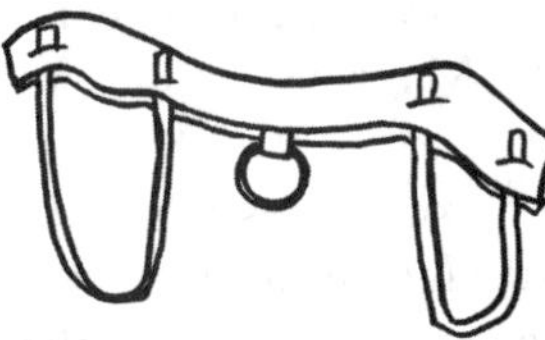

<u>B. Emotional:</u> Are you emotionally burned out? Do you need recreation or entertainment, or should you call a friend? Are you in a small group community? Remember you were made to live in community with others, not in isolation and independence.

<u>C. Spiritual:</u> How are your worship and prayer and good times with God? Remember the promise in Isaiah 40:31, *"But those who hope in the Lord will renew their strength. They will soar on wings like eagles; they will run and not grow weary, they will walk and not be faint."*

<u>Step Three: Learn and Apply Yoke Theology.</u> *"Take My yoke and learn from me,"* was the advice of Jesus. If we are trying to carry too much on our own, we need to learn to work with Jesus in His yoke. Jesus used the analogy of a yoke to teach us how to work with Him. In His days, everyone knew what a yoke was. Today many of us need some yoke lessons.

A yoke was a device that fit around the neck of a workhorse or ox. The plow or cart to be pulled was attached to the yoke. Yokes could be single or multiple and were adapted to fit the neck of the animal(s). A yoke which did not fit properly would be inefficient or injure the animal by chafing it. When Jesus said, *"My yoke is easy,"* He was referring to this idea of wearing a well-fitted yoke. The word "easy" is not the best English translation here. To us "easy" means that a task is simple and effortless. That's not the complete picture of this word. The Greek word *chrestos* [khrase·tos] means fit, fit for use, useful.[7] It doesn't mean wearing the yoke is effortless—rather that it is workable. It is useable. Jesus is saying here "My yoke is good for use. It fits well. Your yoke is wearing you out!"

We don't know if Jesus was referring to a single or double yoke in the passage. I think He most likely meant a double yoke because that reflects the relationship we have with Him described in other parts of the scriptures. He does not just strap us into a yoke and send us off to work alone, but He labors with us. 1 Corinthians 3:9 says, *"We are God's fellow workers."* "Fellow workers" is translated from the Greek word *sunergos* [soon·er·gos][8] Our English word synergistic comes from this and means two things working together. I think when you put this picture together with the Holy Spirit as our *parakletos* who "comes alongside to help," the picture of a double yoke is easily visualized.

Maggie and Major

My family and I went to Lexington, Virginia, to celebrate my daughter Rebekah's seventeenth birthday. She is interested in the Civil War Confederate general, Stonewall Jackson. His museum is located in a home he lived in while teaching at Virginia Military Institute. We toured the historic town in a carriage drawn by two veteran horses named Major and Maggie. The two were yoked together, and the guide spent quite a bit of time talking about how Maggie pulls "all the weight" while Major was just "along for the ride". As I observed them pulling together, I couldn't really see this was true. Both horses walked in lock-step, but the driver knew who was really taking the lead in responding to her instructions. Maggie was the lead horse. She was pulling harder than Major.

I thought of Jesus and his teaching about yokes. Jesus wants to teach how to yoke together with Him. He is Maggie, and we are Major. He wants us to understand He is the one who carries the

"Maggie" share of the load. He takes the lead, and we are Major who walk beside Him and are more "along for the ride".

The reason some of you are so weary is that you pull too much. You are taking too much of the load, and it's wearing you out. You need to learn to trust Jesus and allow Him to carry the heavy part. Some of you have that backwards. You are slow to pray and trust— and quick to pull and lift on your own. You and I must recognize our limitations.

Jesus said His yoke was "easy" and His load was "light". The Greek word for "light" is *elaphros* [el·af·ros]: light in weight, quick, agile.[9] He is promising to pull the "Maggie" share of the load. We must learn to walk in step with Him. Let Him do the worrying. We can be concerned and think about what we should do, but then it is His job to do the worrying. We are to trust His lead and His timing. Think about the double yoke. If you get ahead of Jesus, then you start pulling too much of the load. If you don't get alongside Jesus, you get dragged along. The question is not, "How am I going to handle this situation?" The question is, "How are Jesus and I going the handle this situation?"

But What If My Truck Won't Start?

Just as I am writing this I should be helping my daughter Nena to move from one apartment to another about ten miles away. We moved the light things last night, and today we were to move the bigger things. But when I tried to leave, my truck wouldn't start! It's done this a couple of times recently, and my mechanic has not been able to find out the cause. Previously, I had learned if I let it sit for a while, it starts up like normal, but it didn't this time.

So what do you do when a situation like that happens? I prayed and asked God to help me get it started. I opened the hood and opened up the air filter. It didn't help, but that was about all I knew to do. I then gave the situation to God.

At times like these, I remember what my college president, Dr. Mark Moore, told our student body thirty years ago.

"Do the best you can with what you have, where you are."

I've tried to live by that so I decided I would make the best of the situation. I saw a bush that needed to be trimmed, so I trimmed it and came back to try to start the truck again. No luck. Then I thought, "This truck needs vacuuming." So I did that and tried again. No luck. Then after a couple more prayer sessions with God, I called Nena and told her the situation. She was occupied with the final things that needed to be done. So then I decided to make the best of the situation and fix A CUP OF COFFEE! Yes! Then I sat down and opened my laptop and typed this. I'm not sure what will happen yet, but that is a situation which is out of my hands. There's nothing I can do other than call my friend Russ and ask to borrow his truck, but I'd rather not risk using his truck in this situation so I will wait for a while and hope that mine starts. This problem is not going to "rent space" in my head. I don't have any extra space up there anyway. I will let Jesus pull the "Maggie" share of this, and meanwhile I will do some "Major" resting and walk beside Him.

Division of Labor/Drag Therapy

When we pull too much, we get weary. On the other hand, when we don't pull our part of the load, a different type of problem results. It's "yoke confusion" on our part. When Major lags behind Maggie, the yoke starts dragging him. The dragging is actually quite uncomfortable and unproductive. I guess that's where the phrase "getting jerked around" comes from! Major is better off keeping pace with Maggie. Tracy is better off keeping pace with Jesus. There is a "division of labor" in the Kingdom of God. Jesus didn't say He would take me out of the yoke and let me ride in the carriage. He didn't say I would have to pull it all on my own. It's a division of labor. I have a part, and Jesus has a part. This is what Jesus has taught me. He said *"take my yoke upon you and learn of me."*

Sometimes when people ask us for financial assistance, we need to be careful not to "take their yoke upon" ourselves. I often have the ability to help them, but the question is more should I help them? Sometimes helping is actually NOT helping them. There are several reasons this can be true. What if God is trying to teach them something? Or would I be robbing them of experiencing a miracle? God may want to supernaturally provide in another way, and I would spoil that by intervening. Or God may want me to just offer prayer and counseling.

Helping Others Too Much

God's plan is for everyone to do his or her part and allow Him to do His part. This is the proper division of labor. John Townsend and Henry McCloud did a great job of teaching me the division of labor in Galatians 6:2-10. Verse 2: *"Carry each other's burdens, and in this way you will fulfill the law of Christ. If anyone thinks he is something when he is nothing, he deceives himself."*

Here are some lessons from that passage:

1. Help others with their heavy burdens. The Greek word for burdens is *baros* [bar-os]: burdensome, weight in reference to its pressure"[10] The idea is to help each other with the loads that are too heavy to carry alone. This fulfills the law of Christ—that we should love one another. At the same time, we are not to be boastful as though we think of ourselves as being better than the one we are helping because without God we are "nothing." We are deceiving ourselves if we think otherwise.

2. Each one should scrutinize their own business. Galatians 6:4: *"Each one should test his own actions. Then he can take pride in himself, without comparing himself to somebody else,"* The Greek word for "actions" is the word *ergon* [er-gon], which means "business, employment, that which any one is occupied."[11] The Greek for "test" is *dokimazo* [dok·im·ad·zo]: to test, examine, prove, scrutinize (to see whether a thing is genuine or not), as metals; 2. to recognize as genuine after examination, to approve, deem worthy.[12]

So it could be easily translated as "mind your own business." Each one should take care of his own business and own work. This is so each one can *"take pride in himself."* God wants me to take pride in my own accomplishments without being dependent on others. That way I won't compare myself to someone else, but will be happy with my own efforts.

3. Each one should carry his own freight. Galatians 6:5: *"for each one should carry his own load."* We each have our own "Major" share of freight to carry, but we should help others with their "heavy burdens." There is the balance. Each one has some freight. We all have problems. All of us have automobile breakdowns. All of us have bills to pay. All of us must earn a living. But, occasionally, other people have an overwhelmingly heavy load they cannot carry, and that is when we are to help. That is re-emphasized in Galatians 6:10: *"Therefore, as we have opportunity, let us do good to all people, especially to those who belong to the family of believers."* So we are to help others who have unusually heavy loads, but each one is to ordinarily mind his own business and carry his own freight.

Wisdom is needed to figure out the difference between freight and heavy burdens. In the financial realm, people often get themselves into trouble by overspending, under working, or allowing money to be their idol. God provides us with enough income to meet our needs. If we overspend, we will not have enough resources. In this case, we must learn self-control in spending. If we need more income, God will show us that. If money has become an idol in our lives, then God will sometimes discipline us by allowing our finances to fail. Sometimes God uses money to get our attention—as he has in my life (remember my 4 bucks story!). When we don't tithe, then money has become an idol in our lives. Tithing demonstrates the lordship of God over money in our lives every pay period.

If we help someone, we need to be sure we know what the situation is. Otherwise, we might be working against what God is doing, or we might be keeping them from learning a lesson in "freight management."

Workaholism

Zoe to the Max is experienced by those who have learned to enjoy both work and rest. Some people work too much. They turn work into an escape or an idol in their lives. Instead of working on their problems and improving relationships, some people just get busy doing work to try to ignore their problems. Work can also be a substitute for worship. Some people substitute workaholic religious activity for spiritual growth. I heard Bill Hybels say, "Don't let your work **FOR GOD** ruin the work **OF GOD** in you."

Workaholism can also be a substitute for proper self-esteem. Some work too much in order to "be somebody" by striving for success in business. I think of some of the Olympic athletes who desire winning to the point they would sacrifice ANYTHING to win in order to "be somebody". How sad. In Christ we are already "somebody."

A sure sign of a workaholic is one who has difficulty relaxing. Enjoying rest is hard for those who are addicted to the rush of adrenalin. Workaholics see rest as lost productivity. Adrenalin lovers see rest as time wasted between times of the real fun—work. I know this because I was a workaholic and an adrenalin lover. Enjoying rest has been something God has taught me. In the past, I saw rest as a sign of one's weakness. I considered the strong to be the ones who would press on by sheer willpower, while only the weak stopped to rest. God and my wife have taught me rest is a part of God's plan. It is not a weakness to rest. I learned to understand and accept my limitations. There is *Zoe* in both accomplishment and rest. Jesus wants to teach us to enjoy both. To rest is to admit and experience our own neediness. It is humbling to admit our bodies, minds, emotions, and spirit need refreshing and refueling, but we must learn how to nurture ourselves.

Zoe to the Max is experienced by people who have learned to get the most out of their energy cycles and then get the most out of their resting cycles. The one who learns to rest is neither lazy nor wasting time. He is restoring his body and enjoying the *Zoe* of rest. The one who is working, however, is not to be pitied. He is enjoying the *Zoe* of action and accomplishment.

I mentioned in an earlier chapter about being sick and having to cancel an entire day of my practice. During that day I analyzed myself. How is my *Zoe* doing today? I was able to compare the difference between how my body feels and how my spirit feels. I have a peace that reigns in my spirit and heart that is not affected by my sick body. The health of my body DOES affect how I feel overall. I wrote, "I was not kicking up my heels today, but inside of myself I am resting in God and content with where I am today. Even as I am writing this, my head is throbbing with sinus pain and my runny nose is irritating me, but inside myself I am rejoicing in the Lord for His blessings, and my heart is at perfect peace. I know God is with me and that He loves me."

Bait and Switch

You have heard of the sales tactic "bait and switch." This is when a salesman brings something you are interested in and then switches over to another more expensive product. I must confess I changed the original title of this chapter from "Physically Healthy" to "Physically Rested". I knew some of you would skip this chapter if you thought it was just another lecture about nutrition and exercise. I understand that. Being physically healthy is the hardest area for me to maintain. But we must be "big boys and girls" and take a serious look at our physical health. It involves the need for:

1. Proper rest
2. Good fuel
3. Proper activity

Not only do we need proper rest so we can be restored, our bodies need the right fuel to work as designed. This means good nutrition. Our bodies are like engines. Engines need the proper fuel to work well. If you put oil in your automobile's gasoline tank, it will not work right. The same is true for our bodies. If we use the wrong kinds of fuel, our bodies will not work well. We should think about what kind of fuel our body needs rather than just what tastes good. If I have a lunch that is high in carbohydrates, I will feel sluggish all afternoon. Too much of the wrong kind of fuel causes weight gain, and subsequent health problems.

Our bodies also need a certain level of activity to be healthy and to function well. Since many of us lack enough physical activity in our daily lives, we must provide it through exercise. This is the part which is hardest for me. Dentistry does not provide enough physical activity to keep my body healthy—unless I am chased out of the office by a patient! I don't like to exercise. It's boring.

My A.D.D. brain needs more stimulation than boring exercise.

My A.D.D. brain needs more stimulation than boring exercise. I have tried for several years to find a way to exercise that works for me. I tried exercise videos and gym memberships and buying a few of those exercise gadgets, but only in the last year have I found what works for me consistently. I found I need to couple exercise with something else I enjoy. I like to watch news programs, so I started walking on my treadmill at the same time as the programs play. I then mounted a shelf bracket on my treadmill so my laptop can rest on it. I discovered if I walk at a steady pace, I can think and write on my laptop at the same time! I can read a book or magazine or open my mail while I walk! I end up walking for thirty to sixty minutes while my mind is distracted by the activities I like. It sounds crazy, but it works for me. I do other little things like climb stairs rather than take the elevator and park away from the entrance so that I walk a little more. God designed for our parts to be active so if they don't, problems occur in our "engine". If you exercise:

1. **Injury is less likely.** If we are not physically fit, we are more likely to pull a muscle accidentally.

2. **Weight gain is less likely.** I don't think dieting alone works well. No one likes starving themselves. I would rather add in some extra activity and eat reasonably.

3. **Endorphins will get released.** Science tells us exercise releases into our bodies the hormones that make us feel good. If you are sitting there feeling depressed, a brisk walk in order to release those endorphins will make you feel better.

4. **Live longer and feel better while you live.** Studies show even a small amount of regular exercise makes you healthier, live longer and feel better.

When you eat the wrong kinds of fuel or too much fuel and don't keep your "engines" running regularly, you become overweight and out of shape. This almost guarantees you health problems! Does that make sense? We are stewards of our bodies and we need to be more concerned about our physical health. Obesity has become a national health threat equal to the risks of smoking tobacco. We tend to condemn smoking and excuse obesity. Is that consistent? Both choices have been shown to be medically harmful. Our church denomination teaches stewardship of the body and warns against the health risks of smoking and drinking but doesn't address obesity. I guess it's because we don't want to offend sweet, old "Brother so and so" who loves the Lord, but is out of shape and a hundred pounds overweight. We need to apply the same standards.

Many books have been written on this subject, so I summarize with only two comments about diet and exercise:

1. JUNK FOOD MAKES JUNK BODIES.
2. IF MOVEMENT IS NOT CHOSEN, PARTS WILL GET FROZEN.

If we want to enjoy *Zoe* to the Max we have got to factor in our physical bodies. That is what we live in, right? That is what we are going to be living in for as long as we are here on earth. Doesn't it make sense to do some maintenance now? We need to maintain ourselves spiritually, emotionally, and physically. All must be functioning well in order for us to experience maximum *Zoe*.

Chapter 21: *Zoe* Zone Part 10
Sweet Spot Ministry

- •1 of 10 - Learn to enjoy the presence of the Lord
- •2 of 10 - Spend time with the Teacher and The Book
- •3 of 10 - Rejoice to re-juice
- •4 of 10 - Peace-ruled heart
- •5 of 10 - Emotionally healthy
- •6 of 10 - Inside the wall of contentment
- •7 of 10 - Holiness
- •8 of 10 - Authentic relationships
- •9 of 10 - Physically rested

The tenth area of the *Zoe* Zone is to find and follow your life's calling. Preacher Andy Stanley uses the analogy of a golf driving iron to teach an important principle in finding your ministry. I don't know much about golf, but I'm told there is an area on the head of a golf club that is the ideal area to hit the ball. Somehow the physics of the metal and the swing and the ball can all line up if you connect with the head at the right spot. Golfers tell me you can feel it when you hit the ball in the "sweet spot."

Each one of us is like that driver. God created us for a purpose. Our purpose is to minister to others with the gifts and abilities we have been given. These gifts were not given to us for selfish consumption; we were designed to have a function in the Kingdom of God. *"Each one should use whatever gift he has received **to serve others,** faithfully administering God's grace in its various forms"* (1 Peter 4:10, emphasis added). When you and I are ministering to others in exactly the right ways, we will be most effective and "it will feel right". That's our "sweet spot ministry".

Specific Design for Specific Function

God's universe is full of specially designed creatures. Every species functions a little differently by design. I'm thinking about birds right now as I listen to them sing this morning. The woodpeckers are designed with a beak and head that were made to pound into wood invaded by insects. The geese are designed to fly and swim. The eagles fish and hunt. The sparrows flutter around and scratch. Each of these birds flies, but each has a slightly different design for a slightly different purpose.

God has created you differently from others. He did that with a specific ministry and function in mind. *"For we are God's workmanship, created in Christ Jesus **to do good works,** which God prepared in advance for us to do"* (Ephesians 2:10, emphasis added). These good works are done in different ways according to our differing gifts. *"There are **different kinds of gifts,** but the same Spirit. There are **different** kinds of service, but the same Lord. There are **different** kinds of working, but the same God works all of them in all men"* (1 Corinthians 12:4-6, emphasis added). We have different gifts to serve in different ways.

Along with these gifts are personality differences, differences in culture, location, experience, and skill. When put all together in endless combinations, we are really quite unique. God has a unique ministry sweet spot to match your uniqueness. He made you to be unique and knows exactly your unique sweet spot.

> *God has a unique ministry sweet spot to match your uniqueness.*

Our job is to follow Him in the discovery of that sweet spot. It would be handy if God would provide us with an instruction manual, but it is the glory of God to help us discover how. It's like hunting Easter eggs. Your parents want you to experience the fun of discovery. Self-discovery is part of the adventures of walking with God. We don't know exactly how things will unfold, but we know God will help us on the journey.

Do you know your sweet spot? If I were to ask you to list your spiritual gifts, would you be able to list them? There are tests available to discover your spiritual gift. There are also many books on this subject. Your gifts are going to complement your natural abilities. For example, a salesman will usually have a people-gift, like encouragement or evangelism. An introverted person may have the gift of mercy, service, or administration. A person who enjoys studying may have the gift of teaching or wisdom.

Start doing something! Begin by volunteering for anything which sounds like something you can do. If you know what your main gift is, then find a ministry that utilizes that gift. As you begin to get involved, God will guide you from there. It's hard to steer a parked car! As you minister in what you know, the unknown will open to you. Some doors will never open for those who do nothing.

Move Around

Once you start volunteering, you will begin to discover some things about yourself. The pursuits which are the most natural to you are probably your gifts. Let the ministry leader know you are trying to discover where you should be involved and that you are not sure if that is your gifted area, but you want to try it. That way you can more easily make a ministry shift, if you find something for which you are better suited. Sometimes people get "stuck" in a ministry out of obligation or out of fear of disappointing someone. That's giving in to false guilt and the fear of man. You should be involved in ministry because you are serving God and others out of love.

I began my ministry as a college volunteer in the children's bus ministry at First Church of the Nazarene in Nashville, Tennessee. I was an assistant to the bus captain and eventually became a bus captain for a new route. I discovered I hated "knocking doors" to invite kids to ride my bus to church, but I did it out of obligation. What I enjoyed was making friends with the kids and loving them. That was the beginning of discovering my gift of encouragement. Then I was asked to teach the Bible lesson and started to discover I had a teaching gift. That's the way discovery happens. After a few years, I discovered I enjoyed adult ministry more than children's. I started teaching a young couple's class. I used my gift of teaching and encouragement to my target group of adults rather than children.

Use It or Lose It

I found, as I use my gifts, God gives me additional gifts. This process continued until God had entrusted me with a number of gifts. I don't say that boastfully but as a matter of fact. God gives gifts as HE chooses, and He gives more to those who are already using the ones they have. This is found in Matthew 25:14-29 where Jesus is teaching about the principles of ministry. Let me pull those principles out for you:

"Again, it will be like a man going on a journey, who called his

servants and entrusted his property to them." (Matthew 25:14)

1. God entrusts us with His gifts.
The talents belonged to the owner and were entrusted to the servants. Whatever gifts we have are RECEIVED GIFTS. You and I cannot take credit for having the gifts. We can only choose to invest them or withhold them.

"To one he gave five talents of money, to another two talents, and to another one talent, each according to his ability. Then he went on his journey." (Matthew 25:15)

2. Different numbers of gifts are given according to one's ability.
God gives the ability to match the gifts. I have often been rebuked by some who have tried to get me to "focus on one area and do it right". That sounds good, but it would be sinful for me to do that. I have been given many different gifts which have me involved in many different ministries. It's challenging to handle, but it is what God has called me to do.

"The man who had received the five talents went at once and put his money to work and gained five more. So also, the one with the two talents gained two more." (Matthew 25:16-17)

3. God wants us to put our abilities to work and be productive.
Notice the one who was given five talents "went at once." Don't wait around for the perfect opportunity. Do something now!

"But the man who had received the one talent went off, dug a hole in the ground and hid his master's money." (Matthew 25:18)

4. The one-talent person buried his.
Bad move. He did not put his talent to work as the others did, but instead he hid it.

"After a long time the master of those servants returned and settled accounts with them. The man who had received the five talents brought the other five. 'Master,' he said, 'you entrusted me with five talents. See, I have gained five more.' His master replied, 'Well done, good and faithful servant! You have been faithful with a few things; I will put you in charge of many things. Come and share your master's happiness! The man with the two talents also came. 'Master,' he

said, 'you entrusted me with two talents; see, I have gained two more.' His master replied, 'Well done, good and faithful servant! You have been faithful with a few things; I will put you in charge of many things. Come and share your master's happiness!'" (Matthew 25:19-23)

5. God will evaluate our performance.

Each of us will be evaluated by God for our performance. Romans 14:12 says it this way, *"So then, each of us will give an account of himself to God."*

6. Proportionate rewards for efforts

The five-talent person and the two-talent person were each given the same commendation: *"Well done, good and faithful servant!"* They were each rewarded with the same reward, *"I will put you in charge of many things. Come and share your master's happiness!"* The Master was happy with them both because they invested His talents and were productive. God wants you and me to do the same. He has entrusted us with certain valuable abilities and resources. He wants us to be productive.

"Then the man who had received the one talent came. 'Master,' he said, 'I knew that you are a hard man, harvesting where you have not sown and gathering where you have not scattered seed. So I was afraid and went out and hid your talent in the ground. See, here is what belongs to you.'" (Matthew 25:24-25).

7. Blame and fear cause inaction.

First of all, the one-talent person blames the Master. He calls him a "hard man". He indicts him for expecting too much. The servant blames his behavior on the Master. Today people are still blaming God for their lack of involvement. They excuse themselves by saying, "If I were more talented, I would get more involved." My answer is, "No, you wouldn't." I know people who are multi-talented and are doing little or nothing for God's Kingdom, and I know one-talent people who are doing the same. Don't blame God for not giving you the right kind of package. Use what you have.

The one-talent person said that he was afraid and his fear motivated him to hide. Many people are afraid to get involved. They are afraid of failure or afraid of being exposed as an untalented person.

They are afraid of being humiliated or afraid of commitment. Those reasons are all about self. At the time of accounting, the one-talent person returned the talent to his Master. We want to give him credit for at least not losing it! But that is not how the Master viewed his inaction.

"His master replied, 'You wicked, lazy servant! So you knew that I harvest where I have not sown and gather where I have not scattered seed? Well then, you should have put my money on deposit with the bankers, so that when I returned I would have received it back with interest." (Matthew 25:26-27)

<u>8. Strong rebukes for the uninvolved.</u>

God's evaluation was clear, *"You wicked, lazy servant!"* Wow! How many of you want to hear that as your report card? Not me. Then He declared the servant knew that productivity was expected. The reason the master expected to reap where he had not sown is he expected his servants to sow seeds and reap a harvest for him.

I don't want to hear God say to me, *"You should have."* I am asking God now, "Show me what I should do." Whatever He wants me to do is what I am going to do. He told me to write this book and that is why I have been writing for the past year. It wasn't my idea; it was God's. I admit I have totally enjoyed the experience, but my prayer is always, "God show me what You want me to do."

<u>9. God expects productivity.</u>

He expected His talents to be returned WITH INTEREST. That means God expects us to be productive with our time, talents and treasures so we have something to show for our time here on Earth.

"Take the talent from him and give it to the one who has the ten talents." For everyone who has will be given more, and he will have an abundance. Whoever does not have, even what he has will be taken from him." (Matthew 25:28-29)

<u>10. Talents are taken away from the lazy and given to the diligent.</u> An abundance of talents are part of God's reward for the productive.

It's a scary thought, but I believe I have seen the lazy lose their gifts. Talents can be given and taken away. If you and I are faithful and productive with our talents, we will be given more. This has certainly been proven true in my life. People have commented, "You certainly have a lot of talents." All through my life, I have prayed fervently God would make me one hundred-fold fruitful in my ministry for Him (Mark 4:8). The parable in Mark 4 teaches some soil is thirty-fold fruitful, some sixty-fold fruitful and some one hundred-fold fruitful. I want to be the one hundred-fold soil! I believe God has done

> *I have tried to use my talents to the fullest extent I can and still maintain balance in my life.*

that. I have been willing to do whatever He has asked of me. I have tried to use my talents to the fullest extent I can and still maintain balance in my life. I am not a workaholic, and I do not neglect my family, but I am consistently at a maximum level of ministry involvement. I am as close to the edge of over involvement as I can be and still be healthy and balanced. Because of this productivity, God has periodically given me more talents. I haven't always been able to do all that I can now do.

I remember when God led me to ask Pastor Hancock if I could begin to help him with sermon research eleven years ago. We started meeting weekly when he would tell me what sermon topics were on his mind. I started researching illustrations that might go with his sermon ideas. Then I offered Bible references and suggested sermon outlines. As time has passed, we have worked together each week on the sermons. We forecast preliminary sermon titles a year in advance. Soon Pastor Hancock learned God could work through me to give some of the message points. As the years have gone on, we have become a great team. This has freed up a lot of time for him to focus on other leadership issues. I love to do research and write sermons. He takes them and modifies them, improves them, adds illustrations and then uses his awesome gift of communication to deliver the message. We are a great team! I love to research and find good things which should be said—that's my sweet spot. He loves to communicate in a passionate, captivating and compelling way—that's his sweet spot. My gifts of teaching, encouragement and wisdom are linked up with his gifts of exhortation and communication. He has shared with me sermon research was always the hardest component of sermon preparation for him. God knew that, so He teamed us together. This has become one of my primary ministries and a way I have been able to impact our whole church over the past several years. This is an example of utilizing the diversity of gifts in the Body of Christ. As we have studied other great churches, we have found other pastors have a similar team approach. This is one way the Body of Christ works together to be more productive.

I also remember very distinctly when God told me He was going to give me the gift of preaching. This was years ago, and it did not come to pass immediately, but in the last ten years I have been improving in my ability to preach as God has been opening the door of opportunity for me. I now preach at our church a couple of times a year and other churches as God opens the door.

Last year, God told me to write this book. I protested, "But I'm not a writer!" He didn't say anything back to me, but He may be giving me that ability even though in school English and writing were my weakest subjects! I had to retake college English Composition 101! I have poor grammar and don't know a single thing about writing a book—but by faith, I believe you will be holding this book one day! You're reading a new work of God in my life because I honestly don't know much of anything about how to do this. For example, I don't know how long this book is going to be. I don't know how to organize my thoughts into a book. I don't know how it is going to be published. I don't know when I'm going to be done. I'm just writing as God leads. In the same way, as you are faithful in using your abilities, God may decide to give you more!

Do Something—Anything—Even If It's Wrong!

The lazy servant would have been far better off if he had just done something—anything! Inaction is the worst choice! If you aren't using your gifts because of some fear or insecurity, my advice to you is to try something! Far better to risk failure than to risk the rebuke and disappointment of the Master! God doesn't condemn people who attempt and fail; it is inaction that is unacceptable. Die with failures, but don't die with unused potential! Unused potential is the saddest of all outcomes. I know so many stories of people whose potential is trapped inside of them. It may be due to their self-centeredness or their emotional unhealthiness, or just plain laziness.

Sweet Spot Indicators

How do you know when you have found your sweet spot? I think it involves the intersection of several factors. One is a ministry which challenges you and engages your passion. I believe God has given us a passion for a certain ministry area. This passion differs depending on your gifts. For example, if you have the gift of encouragement, you love to see people encouraged. If you have the gift of service, you love to help behind the scenes. If you have the gift of leadership, you love to be out in front and make your voice heard. Whatever you are passionate about will help locate your sweet spot. The other factor is your enjoyment of the ministry. This does not mean it is always easy, but it is fulfilling—satisfying, if you will. Another intersecting factor is the impact your involvement is having. If you are gifted in that area, your work will make a difference. Do others notice you are good at your ministry? Do you see the value of what you are doing? Does it fit your personality and gifts? The place where all these factors intersect is where your sweet spot is. It may take you several years to find it, but keep being faithful and keep looking.

Delegate and Focus

It is important for us to mentor others in ministry. We may find as we do this, they may be God's person to take the lead in that ministry. Consider changing and focusing on something else. I have discovered as I train others, they may rise to become more passionate about the ministry than I am. That's when I know to make room for them and step back to a more supportive role. This allows me to switch my energies to other areas where God may be leading me. If I don't delegate, I can't focus on finding or staying in my sweet spot, and it keeps others from finding their sweet spot. I have held many positions and served in many places of ministry over the years. As our church has grown, full-time staff has taken over what were my ministries one at a time. They were not easy to let go of because I am passionate about each, but God was focusing me toward my sweet spot. I remind myself God is in control and I am working for the success of His Church. I am not dependent for fulfillment on a position or place—only a person—God! I am His, and He is in charge of guiding me to do what He wants. So then I release ministry to others and refocus on what is next. To sum it up:

RELAX ... RELEASE ... AND REFOCUS

Three Pointers about Ministry

<u>1. You are called by God so be consistent and dependable.</u> No matter how good you are, or how much you promise, if you aren't dependable, you will never reach your potential. If people can't depend on you, you will have a reputation for talking the talk, but not walking the walk. Ministry is a serious assignment FOR GOD, so take it seriously. You are called by God to do this ministry, so you should be just as, or even more, committed to this than your career because this is about your worship and vocation in God. This is your calling from God to minister for God. Full-time paid staff should not be more dependable or committed than you. You are "full-time" on God's payroll.

My church is unusual in that our church staff is comprised of both paid and volunteer ministers. I am on my church's staff in charge of service planning, but I do it as a volunteer. I take the responsibility just as seriously as my paid colleagues. We are a team. We are serving God and His Church according to God's direction. He wants them to be paid by the church. He wants me to be self-supporting. I don't work for money; I work for God.

I see too many volunteers who are slackers. They may or may not show up depending on whether some other more interesting opportunity presents itself! Would they act like that about their jobs? We need to take our calling and ministry assignments seriously and be consistent and dependable.

<u>2. Your spiritual maturity will be your greatest impact.</u> What you are is more important than what you do. People may be impressed with your skills, but they will be impacted by your character and spiritual maturity. It's what you ARE that makes the most impact. Your sweet spot in ministry is the place of maximum impact of your gifts, but your character exceeds that in importance. I say it like this, "What you are speaks so loud I can't hear a word you say."

<u>3. Serve with gladness!</u> Psalm 100: 2: *"Serve the Lord with gladness!"* If you are really serving the Lord, you should do it with a glad attitude. God wants us to enjoy our service for Him! *Zoe* to the Max is finding your sweet spot and serving with passion, power and gladness! If God is good, then serving God should be good! Right? Don't gripe and complain about how others are not serving like they should. You just keep your focus on God and thank Him for the privilege of serving. Your attitude will become contagious as others see their own negativity in the light of your "positivity"!

"Do everything WITHOUT COMPLAINING or arguing, so that you may become blameless and pure, children of God without fault in a crooked and depraved generation, in which you shine like stars in the universe as you hold out the word of (Zoe) life" (Philippians 2:14-16, emphasis added). Don't be a complaining servant of the Lord. Serve the Lord with gladness! This will make you shine like a star in the universe serving the Lord without complaining, holding out the word of *Zoe* to others.

Nothing reflects on God's goodness better than happy servants. God wants glad-service, not sad-service. He doesn't want "ought-to, got-to" motivation. God wants happy servants. That's why the scripture says *"God loves a cheerful giver."* Those who serve in the name of Jesus with guilt-driven, sad-service, or because they "gotta," or "oughta" are not fully pleasing to the Lord. They don't seem to understand the WAY they serve the Lord does not PLEASE the Lord.

Pleasing the Lord can be seen in our attitude as we serve. Ephesians 5:10-20 talks about this. It says in verse 10, *"find out what pleases the Lord."* This involves walking in the light and living in love and serving with a thankful attitude. Ephesians 5:17-20: *"Therefore do not be foolish, but understand what the Lord's will is. Do not get drunk on wine, which leads to debauchery. Instead, be filled with the Spirit. Speak to one another with psalms, hymns and spiritual songs. Sing and make music in your heart to the Lord, always giving thanks to God the Father for everything, in the name of our Lord Jesus Christ."* That sounds like happy service, doesn't it? A *Zoe* to the Max life is serving out of the overflow of love, not out of guilt or compulsion. Obligation-motivated service is slavery. A judgmental attitude condemns, but a grace-filled heart sings praises and gives thanks to the Lord for the privilege of serving! Find your sweet spot and serve with a sweet attitude!

Chapter 22: Step into the Zone

There you have it! Ten out of ten areas working well in your life puts you in the center of the *Zoe* Zone. Examine those ten areas, honestly looking for where you could move up. Let's take a quiz. Look down through the list below and grade yourself. A for excellent, C for "okay, but could improve" or F for not doing very well in that area.

The *Zoe* Zone Self-evaluation				
Grade				**The Zone Area Questions**
A	**C**	**F**		
			1	Actively seeking and enjoying the presence of the Lord moment by moment
			2	Finding & applying a daily Zoe Word
			3	Rejoicing to re-juice
			4	A peace-ruled heart
			5	Emotionally healthy
			6	Living inside the wall of contentment
			7	Holiness of heart and life
			8	Developing authentic relationships
			9	Physically rested, healthy & exercising
			10	Found, and doing sweet spot ministry

Which area needs improvement the most? *Zoe* is experienced to the maximum when all ten areas are working well together. Jesus wants you and me to experience *Zoe* to the Max as we *"live and move and having our being"* in Him and live by His principles. Each area is like a piston in a ten-cylinder motor. It takes intention to keep each cylinder firing and fully functioning. It is my lifelong goal to stay in the *Zoe* Zone and enjoy my life as much as God wants me to. I am regularly monitoring myself and tuning up which ever area may be lagging so I am really enjoying myself "to the max." In fact, I am pausing right now as I type this sentence to ask myself the question I ask myself dozens of times every day, "Am I enjoying myself as much as God wants me to right now?" I realize I am not. I was letting the thought of how to get this chapter started weigh me down and wasn't really trusting God and enjoying myself to the max—so I stop and pray out my worry and stress as I breathe in His Spirit, and receive His joy and power. I thank Him for His presence and wait for Him to speak peace to my heart. Tapping into and getting reconnected with God's joy is my strengthener. *Zoe* to the Max!

ZOE IS GOD'S WILL AND MY WILL, AS WELL

God has MUCH more available to you EVERY MOMENT of EVERY day if you will remember to tap into it. We can step into "moments of heaven" before we get to heaven. Step out of our situation and step into heaven. That's our privilege. *Zoe* to the Max is not automatic. It's a conscious choice to either step into the *Zoe* Zone or stay where we are. Those who choose to step into The Zone will experience *Zoe* to the Max and receive more blessings, but those who don't will be dependent on whatever the current circumstances deliver.

Seize and Squeeze

Even tonight, the Holy Spirit reminded me as I was participating in my church's Easter musical drama, "Tracy, relax and enjoy this." There was no reason why I couldn't seize the moment and squeeze the *Zoe* out of it. Seize and squeeze! It is amazing to me how fast I can seize and squeeze the *Zoe* out of a moment. I can be sitting at my office and talking to a patient or preparing to do a procedure when the Holy Spirit reminds me I am not enjoying myself at that moment AS MUCH AS I COULD.

If I find myself dreading an upcoming event, I seize and squeeze by praying about it and asking God to help me enjoy it and enjoy Him before and during the time. It's amazing how I begin to relax and enjoy the "now" of my life. You have the option of enjoying nearly every event of every day. If you feel yourself bored or worrying, that is when you need to do a *Zoe* attitude transformation. Stop and focus on changing your attitude until you are peaceful and hopeful about the coming event.

I was asked to sing at a local church leadership retreat, and although I wanted to do it to help my pastor friend and wanted to support the church, I still was dreading it somewhat and was annoyed that it was interrupting my plans. When I realized how I was feeling, I decided to have a *Zoe* attitude transformation about it. I chose to enjoy myself and look forward to the event as a great opportunity to minister. I envisioned how the group was going to appreciate my ministry. I told myself I was going to have fun and I was going to enjoy myself. It was amazing to me to note how differently I felt after that. I completely stopped all the negative feelings and began to live *Zoe* to the Max!

In May I was asked to be the commencement speaker for Southside Baptist Christian School. I had never done that before and realized the importance to the high school graduates and their families. I wondered if I was going to be adequate. Several times I found myself anxious, but each time anxiety came in, I chased it out with *Zoe*! Seize and squeeze! I gave my fears to God and trusted Him to give me the right words and believed that if He called me to do it, I was going to do a good job and that it was going to be an enjoyable experience. Our faith is so powerful! It can turn a dread into anticipation! You can do this! Seize and squeeze!

Nike!

The bad situations and circumstances we face should not control us. God has designed for us to be overcomers. Revelation 3:21 says this: *"To him who overcomes, I will give the right to sit with me on my throne, just as I overcame and sat down with my Father on his throne."* The word "overcomes" is the Greek word *nikao* [nik·ah·o] which comes from the word *nike*. Sound familiar? It means "to conquer, to carry off the victory, to come off victorious."[1]

Nike! God means for you and me to be *nike* (victorious) in this life! So step into the *Zoe* Zone! Don't surrender your happiness to the bad circumstances. God is greater than them all! His will is that we be *nike* over every obstacle and situation. *Zoe* is our inheritance. Receive it!

Nike!

SECTION THREE

Living in the Zoe Zone

Chapter 23: Living in the Zone

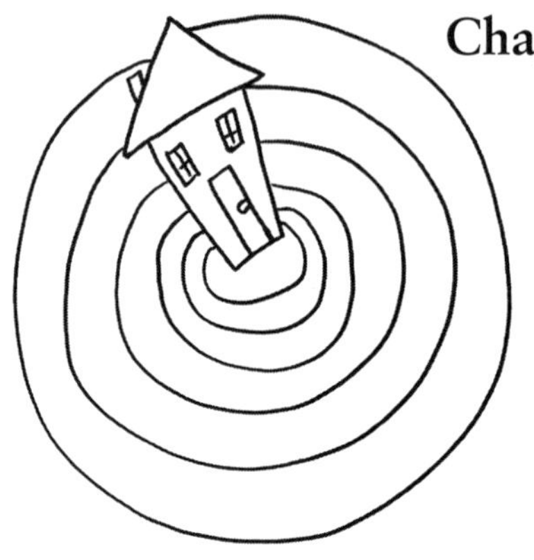

How do we live practically in the *Zoe* Zone in the midst of the problems of life? How do we overcome the everyday obstacles?

Achieving success in ten out of ten areas allows us to enter the *Zoe* Zone, but living in the *Zoe* Zone requires the "hands on" help of the Holy Spirit. The Holy Spirit is our *Parakletos* [par·ak·lay·tos], as we learned earlier. He is the "one summoned, called to one's side, especially called to one's aid." He is there to "help" us experience *Zoe* to the Max throughout our daily lives. It doesn't matter what I need or even if I don't know what I need. I can connect with my *Parakletos* and ask for immediate help. When I don't even know what I need, He does!

Romans 8:26-27 gives us the assurance we can take our prayers and weakness and neediness to Him. *"In the same way, the **Spirit helps us in our weakness…"*** (emphasis added). When we feel weak and exhausted, we are not alone! We have *Parakletos*—our Helper—who is waiting to assist us even when we don't know what to do or what to ask. *"…We do not know what we ought to pray for, but the Spirit himself intercedes for us with groans that words cannot express. And he who searches our hearts knows the mind of the Spirit, because the Spirit intercedes for the saints in accordance with God's will"* (Romans 8:26-27). God's will is to allow His Spirit to lead us into a program of total transformation of our character and attitude into that of Christ.

Living in the *Zoe* Metamorphs Us.

Living in the *Zoe* Zone is learning to value and enjoy this continuing work of character transformation into the likeness of Christ. We are *"transformed into his likeness with ever-increasing glory, which comes from the Lord, who is the Spirit"* (2 Corinthians 3:18). What does it mean to be transformed? The Greek word for "transformed" is *metamorphoo* [met·am·or·fo·o].[1] I immediately think of the English word *morph* and Clark Kent's transformation into Superman after entering a phone booth. *Metamorphoo* is used only three other times in the New Testament. Here the *metamorphoo* is into "his likeness." So we aren't just recharged in attitude, mind and energy, but we are changed in character. We come out as more like Jesus than Superman. That's the awesome thing about being a Christ-follower. We are actually metamorphed into His likeness!

Metamorphoo is used twice when referring to Jesus on the mountain of transfiguration. He was supernaturally metamorphed there. Matthew 17:1-2: *"After six days Jesus took with him Peter, James and John the brother of James, and led them up a high mountain by themselves. There he was (metamorphoo) transfigured before them. His face shone like the sun, and his clothes became as white as the light"* (parentheses added). *Metamorphoo* changes the appearance. I believe when we have truly met with God, we should emerge visibly changed. Our countenance should change, and our attitude should be transformed. People should be able to notice if we have been in the presence of God!

The other place the word *metamorphoo* is used is Romans 12:2: *"Do not conform any longer to the pattern of this world, but be transformed (metamorphoo) by the renewing of your mind"* (parentheses added). When we are metamorphed by the Spirit, our minds are metamorphed because we begin to think differently. Our worry is metamorphed to trust. Our confusion is metamorphed to the clarity of God's will *"...Then you will be able to test and approve what God's will is—his good, pleasing and perfect will."*

Metamorphed with Ever-increasing Glory

This metamorphosis is *"with ever-increasing glory"* (2 Corinthians 3:18). Each day and week we can be morphed into ever-increasing degrees of glory! So as we grow older there is good news—we CAN grow better! We can experience ever-increasing levels of glory, and it never has to get old. We should never stop growing! Let me ask you—how many levels of glory do you think you have experienced? How many do you think there are? Instead of increasing, sadly some are ceasing or even decreasing. This is an unnecessary waste of opportunity. Won't it be sad when we stand before God in all of His glory and SEE all of what we could have experienced?

When we get to heaven, a lot of people will be kicking themselves when they SEE all they missed out on! Please don't be that person! Experience all of God you possibly can NOW. Explore all of God you can NOW.

This book was written because God wants to get this message to you—THERE IS A LOT MORE OF HIM LEFT TO EXPLORE! So let's become lifelong explorers!

Metamorphed into an Explorer

Living in the Zone makes us into explorers who are exploring the glory of Christ. How many believers have stopped searching and exploring Christ? Many have gone to Sunday school and heard a bazillion messages. Some of us have even taken Bible courses in college and attended seminars, and we think we have pretty much heard it all. This is sad but true. Many of our pastors have even stopped exploring God and have been camping on their past experiences and preaching out of their back pockets full of lint. This has given many seasoned Christians the false impression of camping as the goal. No. The goal is not to walk until you arrive at the camp and then stop. I'm here to tell you that *Zoe* to the Max is only experienced by explorers! Explorers are those who are digging until they discover some new perspective or new insight. Those who get lulled into the "camping mentality" start lying back and become spiritual couch potatoes!

Explore the Unsearchable Territory

God the Father, Son, and Spirit and His character and Word are like a vast territory open for exploration. It is a mystical territory—full of hidden treasures, mysteries, and surprising joys. God is so vast and complex we do not have the time, if we spent our whole lives, to fully search Him out or fully know Him! He is unsearchable and impossible to fathom! That does not mean He is hiding from us—it means He is THAT BIG. Ephesians 3:8: *"...preach to the Gentiles the unsearchable riches of Christ."* The word unsearchable is the Greek word *anexichniastos* [an·ex·ikh·nee·as·tos]. This is a compound word literally meaning "cannot be traced out, cannot track the footprints."[2] This word is used only twice in the entire Bible, and both times it describes the untraceable vastness of God's nature. He "cannot be searched out, cannot be comprehended."

The exciting thing about His un-trace-able-ness, is we will ALWAYS be discovering new things about Him, so it will ALWAYS BE NEW AND EXCITING to walk with Him. No matter how many new things I discover in my exploration, I will always be finding new things! It reminds me of going on Easter egg hunts when I was a child. It was so exciting to run and look around every tree and rock to find a new egg or piece of candy! Eureka! I found a new one .... and another new one! In the same way, I find new discoveries and new glimpses of the glory of God! Hallelujah! Can you see me standing and shouting?! Well, I am!

Not only is He beyond being traced out, but the adjective *unsearchable* is attached to the phrase "riches of Christ." The word *riches* when used by Paul in his writings almost always refers to "the abundance of goods," not the abundance of money. So "the riches of Christ" is the abundance of who He is—a vast wealth of discoveries! The nature of Christ is rich with new things to learn and experience! His vastness cannot be measured or counted. Even if we could follow Him for our entire life and read the writings of others who are following Him, there is so much of Him we could never exhaust the "rich" supply of all He is!

Explore the Immeasurable Dimensions

Check out Ephesians 3:17-19: "*And I pray that you... may have power, together with all the saints, to GRASP HOW WIDE and LONG and HIGH and DEEP is the love of Christ...*"(emphasis added). He's talking about measurements here, and he describes four dimensions. What He's saying is we can't trace out His width or length. We can't measure how high it is, or how deep in the opposite direction! Do you see how vast the love of Christ is? And love is just one attribute! Have you fully grasped all the dimensions of the love of Christ? Then why would you stop exploring?

Measuring God's character and nature is like measuring the universe. Scientists can only guess how big the universe really is. No matter what type of technology they use to look into deep space, they cannot "see" the end of it. How unsearchable is God! That means no matter how hard you and I seek to understand Him, or how many years we walk with Him, or how intense our pursuit of Him, there will always be new, unexplored areas! Wow!

Why, then, do we yawn like we've figured God out? Is it not

because we have surrounded ourselves with campers who haven't searched out any more than we have? I've observed, as we keep on growing in God, eventually we will surpass those whom we previously looked to for challenge. I've also found it helpful to look outside of my local church and outside of my denomination to find mentors and teachers who challenge me. The Body of Christ is huge, and we shouldn't stay locked up in our denominational corrals. We should explore the resources God has for us in other parts of His Body. Reading books (like this one, hopefully) is a great way to stretch your horizon and be challenged to a new area of exploration.

When I first tried kayaking, I didn't know anyone who kayaked; so I went to the store where I bought my kayaks and tried to learn a few things. The clerk gave me a book showing many rivers where kayakers have already explored. The author has canoed rivers where I have never been. He chronicled every stretch of the rivers and described what could be seen and how the water flows. He was an explorer who challenged me in his explorations. Now I want to go there myself and experience what he did.

That's how we grow spiritually. We should go to where the knowledgeable people meet—church. Learn from them all you can, and they will help connect you with others who know more. Also books, radio, CDs, and conferences will help challenge you further. Some of my mentors have been Ed Young Jr., Dallas Willard, Henry Cloud, John Townsend, Bill Hybels, John Ortberg, Lee Strobel, Brian Newman, Rob Bell, John Maxwell, and Andy Stanley. But there are limits to how far anyone else can take you. I have found the best "nuggets" are those *Parakletos* teaches me as I dig into God myself. Others can help point me in a new direction, but the *Parakletos* helps me find the new "eggs." I don't depend on my pastor or anyone else to "feed me." The mature Christian learns to feed himself with the *Parakletos* as the ultimate master teacher. You can learn this as well. That's part of what I want you to get from this book. Find new ways to feed yourself and challenge yourself to look for more than you have found.

Explore the Unsurpassable Knowledge

Ephesians 3:19 goes on to say: "*... and to know this love that SURPASSES KNOWLEDGE*" (emphasis added). The word translated "know" is *ginosko* [ghin·oce·ko], which, as we discussed earlier, means far more than intellectual knowledge. It means experientially knowing or having personal experience with. So when Paul prayed for us to "know" this love, he desired for us to "personally experience" this love. And this experience is so vast it "surpasses knowledge." It surpasses our ability to experience it, in all of its untraceable nature. That is where exploring comes in. Why do you and I think we have personally experienced all of the multi-dimensional love of Christ since it surpasses knowledge? Why are we camping when we should be exploring?

Then the passage climaxes with our goal: *"--that you may be filled TO THE MEASURE OF ALL THE FULLNESS OF GOD"* (Ephesians 3:19, emphasis added). Have you been filled with all the fullness of God? Do you even know what the fullness of God is? Then why are you camping?! Explore the fullness of God!

Explore the Mystery

God is complex. Colossians 2:2-3 gives us this new perspective on this exploration. Not only is it vast in measurement, but it is complex in understanding. Paul said to the Colossian Christians: *"My purpose is that they may be encouraged in heart and united in love, so that they may have the **full riches of complete understanding**, in order that they may **know the mystery of God**, namely, Christ, in whom are **hidden all the treasures of wisdom and knowledge"** (emphasis added). This exploration takes a lot of understanding. We can be rich in our understanding of God! Wow! Then he further teaches about personally experiencing "the mystery" of God. God is a mystery. The word translated "mystery" here is *musterion* [moos·tay·ree·on] –"a hidden or secret thing, not obvious to the understanding."[3] There are things about God which are not easily understood and can be found only by investigators and explorers!

Unsearchable Territory! Immeasurable Dimensions! Unsurpassed Experiences! And Unsolved Mysteries! So with all this in mind, why do we live like—act like—we have finished with growing? Why are we satisfied with where we are? There is so much more out there to discover! Experience the thrill of discovery! Get your hiking shoes on and get exploring!

Chapter 24: Made Fresh Daily

Living in the *Zoe* Zone requires a daily rejuvenation because our relationship with Christ is not a stagnant relationship to be maintained until we die. Love must be refreshed daily.

Let's unwrap this truth beginning in 2 Corinthians 4:16: *"Therefore we do not lose heart. Though outwardly we are wasting away, yet inwardly we are being renewed day by day."* God doesn't want us to lose heart or become discouraged. Even if our physical body is breaking down or getting older, our inner person is be made new continuously. The verb tense of "being renewed" indicates it is a continual process—day by day.

Daily doesn't mean renewal will automatically happen because 24 hours pass. So many believers think because the sun rises on a new day, they will automatically grow in Christ or their chronological age causes spiritual maturity. I know many Christians who have been believers for thirty or forty years, but their spiritual maturity does not match their chronological age. Time does not cause growth; it only makes us older. Our spiritual maturity is related to the PERSONAL MOTIVATION we have to grow. God is ready. The Word of God is always available. The missing link is always our own personal motivation to seek God for renewal day by day. Growth is a personal choice we can make each day.

Each day is a new opportunity to be renewed. What does it mean to be renewed? There are two Greek words for renewal. The first word is the one used in the above scripture which is *anakainoo* [an·an·neh·o·o]: 1. to cause to grow up, new, to make new; 1a. new strength and vigor is given to one; 1b. to be changed into a new kind of life as opposed to the former corrupt state.[1] It is a compound word with the prefix *ana* [an·ah], meaning–again.[2] And kainos [kahee·nos], which means "to be made new in quality, the fresh, unworn."[3] So putting the compound word together creates the idea of being refreshed in quality again. It is the freshening up of our relationship in quality each day.

Ask yourself this question: "Is my relationship fresh today?" You've seen those advertisements about bread—"Made fresh daily." In fact, I just thought of the connection between Jesus as the bread of *Zoe* and this idea of baked fresh daily. Are we eating of the fresh bread of *Zoe* each day, or is it stale from last Sunday? Our goal is to eat fresh *Zoe* bread "made daily." We need fresh words from the Lord each day. Fresh grace and fresh mercy daily. Fresh love for Christ and fresh love FROM Christ. Fresh zeal for walking in joy and peace. Fresh enthusiasm for serving Christ and others! That's *Zoe* to the Max!

Brand Spankin' New

Anakainoo is used one other time in Colossians 3:10: *"and have put on the new self, which is being renewed in knowledge in the image of its Creator."* Here we see a whole bunch of goodies! First, there is the idea of putting on the "new" self. The Greek word for "new" is *neos* [neh·os] which means "recently born, young, youthful, new."[4] God has a recently born self to replace our old self. It is a "brand new" self. It is a new creation. 2 Corinthians 5:17: *"Therefore, if anyone is in Christ, he is a new creation; the old has gone, the new has come!"* I often teach new Christians to repeat that verse to themselves over and over. *"The old has gone, the new has come."* God wants to change our old for His brand spankin' new.

The new self is *"being renewed."* This verb tense again affirms the process is "made fresh daily, and this freshness is *"in knowledge in the image of its Creator."* The Greek word for "knowledge" is *epignosis* [ep·ig·no·sis], which means "more than an intellectual knowledge." It is an experiential knowledge—a knowledge based in personal experience.[5] So God wants us to have a fresh personal experience with Christ.

This new personal experience is to be "put on." The Greek word translated "put on" is *enduo* [en·doo·o], which gives the picture "to sink into (clothing), put on, clothe one's self."[6] The new self is like sinking into brand spankin' new clothes! We love to put on new clothes, right? Every day we can put on the new clothes of Christ! We can be clothed in the fresh, new clothes of experiencing Him in a new way, each day.

So if you put it all together, we are to put on the new clothes of our Christ-self, which is being made fresh daily, in our personal experience of being transformed into the image of Christ, our Creator. Wow! You can chew on that for quite a while!

The Fountain of Youth

There is one other Greek word translated as "renewed." It is used only one time in the New Testament—in Ephesians 4:22-24: "*...put off your old self, which is being corrupted by its deceitful desires; to be made new in the attitude of your minds; and to put on the new self, created to be like God in true righteousness and holiness.*"

Notice the similarity with the Colossians 3:10 passage: changing clothes by putting off the old self and sinking into the new clothes of Christ. The additional insight indicates the old self is in the state of "being" corrupted by deceitful desires—it is still under the corrupting influence of deceitful desires. This is opposed to the new self, which is "being" created fresh daily in the image of Christ. The goal of the new self is to "*...be like God in true righteousness and holiness.*" I have really enjoyed meditating on that phrase for weeks.

I want you to especially note the phrase *"to be made new"* as used above. It is the Greek word *ananeoo* [an·an·neh·o·o]: to renew (in the mind).[7] It is a compound similar to *anakainoo* used above in Colossians 3:10 and 2 Corinthians 4:16. The first part of the word is the same *ana*, but its root is different—*neos* [neh·os], which means "recently born, young, youthful, new."[8] In this compound word it means to, again, be made brand new. This accentuates the quality of newness in age rather than freshness.

Put both verses together—we are to put off our old self and be made brand new again in the attitude of our minds and put on the new clothes of our brand new self created to be like God! Newness in terms of quality and newness in terms of youth—we get both! We can be renewed in freshness and renewed in youth. We truly have the Fountain of Youth in Christ!

Notice also the phrase "attitude of your minds." God wants to refresh our attitudes daily with a new level of transformation into the image of God. God is in the business of attitude renewal. He wants to refresh the way we are looking at our world. A new attitude of seeing things from God's perspective in true holiness and righteousness is what He gives us. It is not corrupted by the attitudes of our old self with its deceitful desires. As Johannes Behm says, "free from the old being and free for the new."[9]

Each day is an opportunity to be made new again. Following Christ must NEVER get old. If it does, then we know we need to be rejuvenated because fresh Bread of *Zoe* is available daily. Like the Manna, it has to be gathered daily or it will stink; and too many Christians have stinky, stale attitudes. This is not just a figure of speech—we can be actually renewed in our relationship and attitudes and character. Christians are to be "made fresh daily." And as each year compounds, we find, like the sunrise, we begin small and become increasingly bright and apparent until we are awesome, bold, and powerful—*"Created to be like God in true righteousness and holiness"* (Ephesians 4:24)! Jesus said, *"A city that is set on a hill cannot be hid"* (Matthew 5:14). So let your light shine brightly, as you reflect the ever-fresh image of God

Drunk with the Spirit

This need for continual newness can also be demonstrated with the analogy of drinking alcohol. Ephesians 5:18-20: *"Do not get drunk on wine, which leads to debauchery. Instead, be filled with the Spirit. Speak to one another with psalms, hymns and spiritual songs. Sing and make music in your heart to the Lord, always giving thanks to God the Father for everything, in the name of our Lord Jesus Christ."* The comparison is made between being under the influence of alcohol and being under the influence of the Spirit. The Greek phrase "be filled" is *pleroo* [play·ro·o]: 1. to make full, to fill up; i.e., to fill to the full; 1a. to cause to abound, to furnish or supply liberally. To render full, i.e. to complete, to fill to the top: so that nothing shall be wanting to full measure, fill to the brim.[10] We need to drink of the Spirit until we are completely inebriated with the Spirit. We are to be filled with the Spirit until we are full-filled. In other words, filled until we feel fulfilled. I know that we can't always go on feelings, but I believe God gave us feelings for a reason—He wants us to feel them!

When you start living *Zoe* to the Max, some people will ridicule you like many on the day of Pentecost ridiculed the 120 newly-filled believers who came from the Upper Room. The spectators saw the joy and the *Zoe* of those who were freshly filled with the Holy Spirit. The only explanation was they must be drunk. Acts 2:12-16: *"Amazed and perplexed, they asked one another, 'What does this mean?' Some, however, made fun of them and said, 'They have had too much wine.' Then Peter stood up with the Eleven, raised his voice and addressed the crowd: 'Fellow Jews and all of you who live in Jerusalem, let me explain this to you; listen carefully to what I say. These men are not drunk, as you suppose. It's only nine in the morning! No, this is what was spoken by the prophet Joel'"*(emphasis added). The 120 were so filled with joy and *Zoe* they appeared to be drunk. When was the last time you were so filled with the joy of the Lord and *Zoe* to the Max someone thought you must be drunk? If you have never experienced that kind of joy and amount of *Zoe*, then you need to know it is available!

When I was in dental school, there were many hours of classes and many hours of labs. These lab rooms looked like science classrooms with about fifteen students in a room. We really got to know those students well because we spent a lot of time together from late at night to early morning. The students saw me under all kinds of situations and pressures. I totally depended on God to make it through the 30 to 40 credit hours per semester we were required to take. Mornings were critically important for me because I would spend time with God and memorize scripture as I walked down several blocks of sidewalk of downtown Richmond after parking. The ten-minute walk was time for me to get myself pumped up on *Zoe* and the joy of the Lord. I would review the scriptures I was memorizing, which became my *Zoe* Words throughout the day.

I would arrive at school freshly filled with God and the joy and power of His Word. The atmosphere I entered was quite heavy and depressed. I would often come down the hall humming or whistling, and I suppose the contrast was quite striking.

> *...my lab partners would ask me, "What are you high on this morning?"*

My classmates would comment from time to time about my happiness and perkiness. I remember a couple of times when one of my lab partners would ask me, "What are you high on this morning?" Over those couple of years, I had the opportunity to share my faith with several. They would then jokingly say, "Here comes Spaur high on God," or something less flattering.

We can all experience this kind of *Zoe* and make others curious. Psalm 23:5 says: *"...my cup overflows."* We can live in the overflow.

Most of us live with a partially filled cup. God wants our cup to overflow with His Spirit everyday!

Not Automatic

You don't get drunk with wine until you drink enough of it. You don't stay drunk unless you KEEP drinking it. So we must drink of the Spirit until we are drunk with Him. *Zoe* is not automatic. We must deliberately get a fresh daily filling until we are inebriated.

Chapter 25: Coffee

My daughter Rebekah and I were kayaking down the James River one Saturday morning. As I paused for a sip of coffee, she jokingly said, "Dad, why don't you write a chapter in your book about coffee?" She and I are both great coffee lovers. In fact, one of my other daughters Stephanie works at Starbucks (which I call prefer to call SPAURBucks), and, yes, I own shares of Starbucks stock. I even preached a sermon called "Caffeinated Dads!"

Hang with me for a moment as I tout the blessings of coffee:

• God blessed us by creating more than 25 species of the tropical evergreen shrub known as Coffea.

• He blessed these Coffea shrubs with the ability to produce a cherry fruit which later became known as the coffee bean.

• In the first century, He blessed some Ethiopian goats with the curiosity to eat those coffee beans.

• The wise Ethiopian goat herder named Kaldi observed his goats jumping around and acting quite lively after eating those coffee beans.

• Kaldi then tried the coffee bean himself and found it to be quite invigorating and energizing. He made a hot beverage from the beans and shared it with the nearby Catholic monks.

• The monks found it kept them alert during prayers and meditation, so they shipped the beans to distant monasteries across Europe until, finally, the Pope blessed coffee declaring it "a truly Christian beverage."

• Then God blessed the French to create the greatest coffee bean roasting method known to man and produce French Roast coffee!

• Besides all these blessings, a recent study cited the health benefits of coffee as helpful in preventing type 2 diabetes![1]

Can you tell I like coffee? Seriously now, coffee is one example of the many good things God has given us to enjoy in this life. Living in the *Zoe* Zone is learning to explore and fully appreciate all the great foods and beverages with which God has blessed us. Think of the food or dessert you enjoy the most. God gave these for your enjoyment! He created good things for your pleasure.

The Bible tells us Jesus enjoyed providing a great breakfast for His disciples. *"When they landed, they saw a fire of burning coals there with fish on it, and some bread* (the original fish & chips meal!). *Jesus said to them, 'Bring some of the fish you have just caught. Come and have breakfast.' None of the disciples dared ask him, 'Who are you?' They knew it was the Lord. Jesus came, took the bread and gave it to them, and did the same with the fish"* (John 21:9-13, parenthesis added).

God wants us to enjoy the life He has given us. If you are a parent, you know how much fun it is to see your child enjoy eating an ice cream cone or something good you have provided. God is the same. *"A man can do nothing better than to eat and drink and find satisfaction in his work. This too, I see, **is from the hand of God,** for without him, who can eat or find enjoyment?"* (Ecclesiastes 2:24-25, emphasis added).

Zoe to the Max includes being thankful for and enjoying all the good food God has given us because He gave it to us to enjoy! Good food is *"from the hand of God."* So when you eat breakfast, lunch, and dinner, enjoy and give thanks to God for the simple pleasure of eating. Eating nourishes our bodies and gives us pleasure as well. I've noticed when some people "give thanks" in prayer before a meal they say, *"Bless this food to the nourishment of our bodies and our bodies to Your service."* Do we eat only because we must have nourishment so we can keep serving God? What about thanking him for HOW GOOD it's going to taste? God gave us taste and enjoyable foods to take pleasure in as a part of the *Zoe* of this life.

What about Hedonism?

Some would call enjoying these pleasures hedonism. No, Hedonism is seeking unrestrained physical pleasure without regard for God or others. The Giver of all good things does warn us of making a god out of pleasure. The Bible calls this unrestrained, flesh-controlled condition the sinful nature. God's remedy for the sinful nature is to be "crucified" with Christ. *"Those who belong to Christ Jesus have crucified the sinful nature with its passions and desires. Since we live by the Spirit, let us keep in step with the Spirit"* (Galatians 5:24-25).

God wants our sinful nature (old self) to be crucified with Christ, and our human (natural) self to be set apart (sanctified) as an instrument of righteousness. Romans 6:6-14: *"For we know that our old self was crucified with him so that the body of sin might be **done away with**, that we should no longer be slaves to sin—because anyone who has died has been freed from sin. Now if we died with Christ, we believe that we will also live with him. For we know that since Christ was raised from the dead, he cannot die again; death no longer has mastery over him. The death he died, he died to sin once for all; but the life he lives, he lives to God. **In the same way**, count yourselves dead to sin but alive to God in Christ Jesus. Therefore do not let sin reign in your mortal body so that you obey its evil desires.*

*Do not offer the parts of your body to sin, as instruments of wickedness, but rather **offer yourselves to God**, as those who have been brought from death to life; and offer the parts of your body to him **as instruments of righteousness**. For sin shall not be your master, because you are not under law, but under grace"* (emphasis added).

The Theology of Self

Our actual self, sanctified by the Spirit, is to be enjoyed! Our bodies are not evil in themselves; they are "instruments"—used for evil or good. I think that a wrong understanding of the theology of self can keep us from fully enjoying our sanctified self.

**Don't let a faulty understanding of theology rob you
of fully enjoying God-given pleasures!**

God is the one who made our physical bodies and the pleasures we enjoy. Satan and sin came in and messed up Paradise. Let's not forget God made us to live in the Garden of Eden!

God is the One who gave us
eyes to see beauty,
ears to hear music,
noses to smell coffee,
taste to enjoy food,
skin to enjoy touch,
sex to enjoy the love of our spouse.
Every good thing came from God!

Why then would we NOT allow ourselves to fully enjoy the pleasures God has given us? Instead we need to awaken our senses to appreciate all the blessings God has provided for us. The abuse of these pleasures is hedonism, but proper enjoyment of them is God's gift to us.

We should exuberantly enjoy the good gift of these pleasures while maintaining control over our desires. Our desires should not control us, but we should control them and enjoy them. God designed for our "spirit man" to control our "physical man." Those who don't have God in their lives are under the control of the desires of the "physical man." Believers, however, can enjoy the pleasures of the body, mind, and spirit in addition to the blessings of God.

That's what makes fasting so useful and powerful. We can periodically exercise the muscles of the Spirit over the desires of the body. God's plan is to have the spirit of man would rule over his body. Fasting reminds the body "who's boss."

Don't let the fear of being hedonistic rob you of fully enjoying the gifts of God. Pleasures are our inheritance! Don't let Satan or others "decaffeinate" your life! Enjoy the good "coffee" God has given you. Enjoy living in the zone of *Zoe* to the Max! Enjoy your meals! Taste the delicious things! Smell the coffee! Enjoy the sunrise! Listen to great music! Visit fun places! Enjoy the feeling of wind and rain and sunshine! Have great sex! Enjoy being with friends! Do fun things! Love the life you live.

Chapter 26: *Zoe* Party

Heaven is a continuous party. No one there is biting his/her fingernails wondering if God's team is going to win. Living *Zoe* to the Max is learning to join the heavenly party in your mind because we have read the back of the book, and as my pastor says, "Our team wins!"

We have so much to party about. We are following the Winner, and He has recruited us to be on His team; therefore, we will win also. This is the day the Lord has made, and God wants us to rejoice and be glad about it! This needs to be our mindset. We don't have to wait for eternity to begin the celebration—we can start now! Romans 12:11: *"Never be lacking in zeal, but keep your spiritual fervor, serving the Lord."* God wants us to be excited; we are to serve the Lord with gladness and enjoy the ride! Disneyland has a song saying, "This is the happiest place on earth." I don't think so. The happiest place on earth should be inside of you.

Jesus said in John 8:31-36: *"To the Jews who had believed him, Jesus said, 'If you hold to my teaching, you are really my disciples. Then you will know the truth, and <u>the truth will set you free</u>'"* (emphasis added).

"They answered him, 'We are Abraham's descendants and have never been slaves of anyone. How can you say that we shall be set free?' Jesus replied, 'I tell you the truth, <u>everyone who sins is a slave to sin.</u> Now a slave has no permanent place in the family, but a son belongs to it forever. So if the Son sets you free, <u>you will be free indeed</u>'" (emphasis added).

We are free in Christ to party! I love the song "I am Free" by Third Day. Its lyrics rejoice, "I am free to run, I am free to dance. I am free to live for You. I am free." We are free to love and be loved. Free from worry, fear, anxiety, and boredom.

Look at 2 Corinthians 3:17: *"Now the Lord is the Spirit, and where the Spirit of the Lord is, there is freedom."* Is the Spirit of the Lord in you? Then there is freedom! Galatians 5:1 says: *"It is for freedom that Christ has set us free. Stand firm, then, and do not let yourselves be burdened again by a yoke of slavery.*" The "yoke of slavery" was the burden of religious requirements. Because Christ has already fulfilled the religious requirements of the Old Testament law, He wants us to be free and to enjoy our freedom!

Zoe Talk

Freedom needs to be in our attitude and our talk. *Zoe* is incorporated into the way you and I talk to ourselves and others. Your self-talk needs to be *Zoe*-producing as you speak the will of God into your life. *Zoe* self-talk is learning to say the truth of God to yourself. I need to say to myself what God says about me. I often say to myself, "Enjoy yourself now." God says this in Psalm 118:24: *"This is the day that the Lord has made! Let us rejoice and BE GLAD IN IT."* To be glad IN it includes IN every moment inside of the day. I think most Christians are not being glad enough. God wants us to be glad in the day He has made and experience *Zoe* to the Max now.

I often remind myself of the *Zoe* Word God has given me for the day and say it to myself frequently through the day. Other times I just praise God or thank God for His blessings, or I might pray and worship Him. Ephesians 5:19: *"Sing and make music in your heart to the Lord."* We are to sing in our hearts and be thankful in our attitudes. That's *Zoe* Talk. Verse 20 says: *"**always giving thanks to God the Father for everything**, in the name of our Lord Jesus Christ"* (emphasis added). *Zoe* talk is thankful talk.

After you have been doing this for a while, you will stock-pile in your mind a number of *Zoe*-producing verses. This is what it means when the scripture says, *"Let the Word of Christ dwell in you RICH-LY ..."* (Colossians 3:16). We are to be rich in the Word of God, swimming in His *Zoe*-producing words! Our very words should be done in the name of Jesus. Whatever we do, *"whether in word or deed, do it all in the name of the Lord Jesus, giving thanks to God the Father through him"* (Colossians 3:17).

We can talk *Zoe* talk because we have *Zoe* power for whatever we need in life. 2 Peter 1:3-4: *"His divine power has given us everything we need for [Zoe] life and godliness through our knowledge of him who called us by his own glory and goodness.*

Through these he has given us his very great and precious promises, so that through them you may participate in the divine nature and escape the corruption in the world caused by evil desires" (emphasis added).

He gives us the power to have *Zoe* in everything. It is His divine power giving us, *"everything we need for Zoe."* What a powerful promise! No matter what our circumstances, God can grant us the power to really *Zoe*! But this power is not just given to us like a gift is given. It is granted to us like an opportunity is presented. The Greek word translated "given" in this passage is *doreomai* [do·reh·om·ahee]. It means "to present or bestow."[1] The Greek synonym not used is *didomi* [did·o·mee], which simply means "to give."[2] In other words, we are **granted the opportunity** to join the *Zoe* party! The opportunity is presented to us. We must choose to join the party and choose to take the opportunity presented to us. It is the opportunity to claim the promise of *Zoe* for *"everything we need... ."* We can talk the *Zoe* talk and walk the *Zoe* walk!

The power of *Zoe* is experienced *"...through the knowledge of Him."* Remember, "knowledge" is translated from the Greek word *epignosis*, which means a "personal, experiential knowledge." Experiencing Jesus is the key to everything we need to *Zoe*. And out of this He gives His *"...very great and precious promises,"* which lead us to *"...participate in the divine nature!"* Woo who! We get to share in God's nature! We have the opportunity to experience who He is and participate in His very nature. God wants a *Zoe* party going on in our heads as we experience *Zoe* to the Max and talk the *Zoe* talk and walk the *Zoe* walk.

Zoe is a witness

What happens when a lost person sees you and me living in a *Zoe* party? They know something unusual is going on! All of my employees at my office are Christians, but, occasionally as God leads, I take on temporary employees. These people will inevitably comment about the wonderful atmosphere in the office. What they are feeling is *Zoe* in action and love in action and brotherly kindness in action. At first, they falsely think it is because, "Tracy is such a wonderful boss." I thank them for the compliment but point them to our source of *Zoe* and love. It's always good to be reminded—*Zoe* is noticed.

My patients notice it too. Some read my printed testimony posted in the waiting room. Others notice the contemporary Christian music on the radio and I often sing along with it. Others notice the joy of our attitudes or the kindness of our demeanor. I have had patients tell me they have come back to a close relationship with Christ because of their exposure to my practice environment. That is the way it should be. *Zoe* is a powerful witness in this negative and self-centered world. One of the best ways for you to be a more effective witness is to live *Zoe* to the Max! People want to be happy, and we have a corner on the happy market! *Zoe* to the Max! Woo who!

Chapter 27: Failure

Living in the *Zoe* Zone does not eliminate failure from our lives. Stress and unexpected problems still come our way and test our responses. One of my patients lost her front tooth at a Mexican restaurant the other day. While she was having dinner with a friend, they were dipping chips in the guacamole when she realized her front tooth was missing! "Where's my tooth?" she said in shock, as she quickly scanned around the table and floor. "Ahhhh, I think this might be it!" her friend mumbled as he spit some hard thing out of a mouthful of guacamole. "I thought something was kind of hard in that last dip!" How horrible! Her tooth had dropped into the guacamole, and her friend had scooped it up in his last dip. Yuck. I'd say there's nothing worse than scooping up some-one's tooth in your guacamole!

Accidents can suddenly throw us into a storm of stress. Unexpected problems test our responses. Sometimes we don't respond very well. Sometimes we "lose it" when our tooth falls in the guacamole dip. Our responses can range from inappropriate all the way to down-right sinful. When we fall short of our expectations and know that we have failed, we must go into recovery mode. Failure humbles us as we "replay" the tapes of the incident in our minds to see what went wrong.

Do a "Post-game" Analysis

A losing football team usually analyzes the videotapes of the game to see what went wrong. In the same way, after I have experi-enced a failure, I do a "post game" analysis of the situation and my responses. I think about how I reacted to the situation to determine how I can learn from it and improve. If I reacted less than best, I can usually trace it back to the fact I wasn't "on top of my *Zoe* game." When I am zooming with *Zoe*, I can handle most situations pretty well. On the other hand, if I "lose it" and have a melt-down, then I need to do some radioactive cleanup.

Nuclear Melt-Downs

The storms of life push us beyond our normal limits, and we can fail to respond properly. Those poor responses can involve our attitude, our actions, our words, or all three. Personally, my most common poor/sinful response is to blame and be judgmental. Instead of asking, "WHAT went wrong?" I usually ask, "WHO caused this?"

Our failures reveal areas needing improvement. These areas become our new character goals. We should not run from character flaws but run toward them. We are not to live by excuses, denial, rationalizing behavior, or blaming others. Christ-followers are children of light who walk in Truth. We don't run from the light—we run to the light. Our goal is not to avoid discovery of flaws but to identify and fix them.

WE SHOULD TURN FAILURES INTO GOALS!

In my dental practice, I often hear a patient say to me after one of my hygienists has cleaned his or her teeth, "You better not find anything, Doc," or they joke, "You don't need to look because there's nothing wrong." It's amazing to me the number of people who want to live in denial and pretend there's nothing wrong. If there is something wrong with your teeth, don't you want to know so you can get it fixed before it gets worse? I do. And if it is important in the dental world, how much more important is it in the spiritual world?

"Being" Goals

I want to continue to improve in my character and responses. I don't want to be the least I can be; I want to be the best kind of person I can be.

MY GOAL IS TO BE CHRIST-LIKE IN CHARACTER,
ATTITUDE, AND ACTIONS.

I want my wife to say I was the best husband I could be. I want my kids to say I was the best dad I could be. But most of all, I want God to say, "Well done." Isn't that what you want also?

We need goals of "being" and goals of "doing." "Being" goals have to do with what kind of person we want to become. "Doing" goals have to do with our actions and what we want to accomplish. We should desire to be all God wants us to be and to accomplish all God wants us to do.

"BEING" GOALS
SHOULD ALWAYS HAVE PRECEDENCE OVER
"DOING" GOALS.

I was walking across a field behind our church on a beautiful spring afternoon when I noticed a little yellow flower out in the middle of the field. It was as small as your pinky fingernail, but it was so bright and colorful. I thought to myself, "What a shame for that flower to go unnoticed out here in the middle of nowhere." Then the Holy Spirit said to me, "I'm enjoying it, and you just enjoyed it." He went on to remind me the beauty of our character is like that. Even though others may never see it, God sees; and His enjoyment of me is the "audience of one" I must value the most. *Zoe* to the Max is learning to fully enjoying our inner life of "being." My greatest joys may be shared by only God and me.

One of my favorite verses I referred to earlier applies here. Acts 17:28: *"For in him we live and move and have our being."* I have "my being" in God. He and I together constitute my being. Therefore, I have "being" goals that God and I share. My overall "being" goal is found in Ephesians 4:13-15: *"... become mature, attaining to the whole measure of the fullness of Christ. Then we will no longer be infants, tossed back and forth by the waves, and blown here and there ...instead... in all things grow up into him who is the Head, that is, Christ."*

Our maturity as a Christ-follower should be progressively increasing and our character improving. As we do honest "post-game" analysis and then improve weak areas, our times of melt-down will become less frequent and less destructive.

Re-booting After a Melt-down

Once you have done your "post-game" analysis on your failure and identified where you need to improve, then it is time to reboot. Here are the steps of rebooting and realigning.

<u>**Step #1 Repent.**</u> Repent means to confess whatever sinfulness there has been. Repentance encompasses a decision to change.

Change is by God's power, yet activated by our decision. We must decide we want to change and admit God alone has the power to change us. Repentance is a change of mind toward our failures. We repent when we decide we truly want to change and engage with God's power to see the change happen.

Step #2 Repair. What needs to be done to repair the situation? This often means reconciliation with those who have been offended by the melt-down. The question is not WHO was at fault? The question is WHAT can we do to repair the damage? Someone has to be willing to initiate the repair. That someone ought to be you. If you are a passionate follower of Christ, then prove it by being the first to act. Romans 15:1-3: *"We who are strong ought to bear with the failings of the weak and not to please ourselves. Each of us should please his neighbor for his good, to build him up. For even Christ did not please himself... ."* It takes humility and strength to start the repair and reconciliation, but that is the character of Christ.

Step #3 Resolve to Realign. Learn from the incident and make the inner resolve to improve. If your weakness was exposed, then target the area for improvement. Resolve to make something good come out of the situation. Realign yourself to walk on the higher road and become a better person because of it. Forgive those involved and don't make a monument to the incident.

Move on—Don't Build Monuments

Some personalities have trouble moving on from failure. Instead they tend to keep talking about it and keep thinking about it. It's as if they build monuments to their failures. They replay the "tape in their heads" over and over again. The failure becomes a monument in their lives. They make it more significant than it needs to be.

If you are unwilling or unable to forgive yourself, let it go and move on; otherwise, it shows you have some unhealthiness. Here are some possibilities:

An overactive conscience—It makes you feel too much guilt. You may be too sensitive to failure. You must accept the fact God is not mad at you. He wants to forgive you and help you improve and move on.

Too hard on yourself—You may be harder on yourself than God is. *"Let us then approach the throne of grace with confidence, so that we may receive mercy and find grace to help us in our time of need"*

(Hebrews 4:16). He wants you to come boldly to Him to receive mercy and grace when you need them. I find many do not understand the grace of God and instead operate out of a sense of justice. This requires them to punish themselves as an act of penance. When they have punished themselves sufficiently, they feel they have earned the right to ask for forgiveness. This is mistaken theology and is not how God wants us to treat ourselves. A great book to go further into this issue is *Receiving Love* by Dr. Joseph Biuso and Dr. Brian Newman.

Take failure personally—Some people don't just experience failure; they take it on as an identity. Instead of experiencing a failure, they ARE a failure. It confirms their inner belief—they are defective. This is called "shame-based" identity. It is very destructive and often requires Christian counseling to dig out its roots. Having a failure does not mean YOU ARE a failure. It's not what happens "to you" that damages you; it's what happens "in you" that can do the most damage. Life is unpredictable, and the statement of Jesus is true: *"In this world you will have trouble"*(John 16:33).

How you deal with failure is often more important than the failure itself. You cannot experience *Zoe* to the Max if you are concentrating on building monuments to your failures. Dr. John Maxwell has a great book on this called *Failing Forward*, which I highly recommend.

Encouragement

Pray for encouragement from the Holy Spirit. I cannot tell you how many times I have prayed for and received encouragement from the Holy Spirit. Encouragement is promised in 2 Thessalonians 2:16-17: *"May our Lord Jesus Christ himself and God our Father, who loved us and by his grace gave us eternal encouragement and good hope, encourage your hearts and strengthen you in every good deed and word."* You haven't fully processed your failure until you have been encouraged by the Holy Spirit. His encouragement completes the full cycle.

Temptation - Obedience

Remember temptation is not sin. Temptation presents the option to either sin or to show love to God. If we fail the test and sin, we need to ask God to forgive us and then forgive ourselves and move on. When we resist the temptation, we demonstrate our love for God.

When we sin, we demonstrate our need to grow in love. Jesus talked about this in John 14:15&23: *"If you love me, you will obey...if you do not love, you will not obey."* God doesn't make up rules just to trip us up. They are the guard rails of life. They are principles of how to live *Zoe* to the Max! They show us how to stay close to God.

The kingdom of God is about keeping a close relationship with God, not just about resisting temptation. Romans 14:17-18: *"For the kingdom of God is not a matter of eating and drinking, but of righteousness, peace and joy in the Holy Spirit, because anyone who serves Christ in this way is pleasing to God and approved by men."*

1. Righteousness—Righteousness is living in a way to maintain a right relationship with God. Righteousness is not "a matter of eating and drinking." Paul is referring to the controversy in the early church concerning eating food that had been offered to idols. Righteousness was not gained from abstaining from certain foods. Righteousness was about pleasing God from the heart.

2. Peace—Peace comes when Christ is president, not just resident. God wants us to know a peaceful heart and be at peace with others. Live **IN** peace and be **AT** peace with God, ourselves, and others.

3. Joy in the Holy Spirit—This is *Zoe* to the Max! The Kingdom of God is about having joy! It's about being happy in God and enjoying life as much as God wants us to—that's the Kingdom of God! Happy children are a good reflection on their Father.

When we concentrate on these three: Being in right relationship with God (righteousness), being right with others (peace), and enjoying the journey (joy in the Holy Spirit), then we will stay in the *Zoe* Zone. Failure is an event, not an identity. Focus on *Zoe* to the Max—your failure rate will go down drastically, but it will never be eliminated. When failure happens, just admit it, forgive yourself, repair the damage, learn what you can, and move on. Don't make a monument out of anything but God!

Chapter 28:
Zoe–Zapping Thoughts

One of the necessary skills to stay in the *Zoe* Zone is to learn to control your thoughts and attitudes. Faulty thinking patterns lead to faulty conclusions. When I was a freshman in college, for a period of a couple of months, I formed the dumbest notion. Because I felt my breath tasted bad to me after I brushed my teeth, I concluded my brushing may be upsetting the eco-system in my mouth. I then theorized brushing my teeth was upsetting the natural bacterial balance in my mouth, thus causing bad breath. My conclusion was I would have fresher breath by not brushing my teeth so the natural flora could live in harmony. Now how STUPID was that! My conclusion was based on wrong reasoning. Wrong thinking produces bad ideas. And bad ideas produce bad results.

Your thoughts have a powerful influence on the level of *Zoe* you experience—what you allow yourself to think about will either help you or hinder you. When the Bible says, *"Love the Lord your God with all your...mind..."* it includes loving Him, and pleasing Him in the way you think and with the attitudes you choose. Some thinking habits are what I call *Zoe* Magnets; they attract *Zoe*. Other thinking habits are what I call *Zoe*-Zappers; they zap your *Zoe* just like one of those bug-zapping mosquito lights. Let's look at some *Zoe*-Zapping patterns of thinking:

1. Letting the "Whatever" Take Over

One bad habit is to allow the small irregularities of life to distract us from enjoying the rest. This pattern is to focus on the "less-than-ideal" things and allow them to keep us from enjoying life as much as we could. People let the "whatever" take over their attention. They are often distracted by whatever is not ideal. It may be the temperature of the room or a piece of lint or a piece of trash on the floor. They are "bugged" by things other people don't seem to care about much. Instead of enjoying themselves, the "less-than-perfect" environment sidetracks their attention.

The problem with this kind of thinking pattern is there are so many "whatevers" in the world! Therefore, life becomes a series of interruptions as we stop and try to fix them all. Don't let your *Zoe* be hijacked by the "whatevers." Learn to live with imperfection. It is everywhere, and if you don't learn to accept it, you will be controlled by it. God wants you focus your attention on the important things, not the imperfect things.

2. "Right after I get this done."

"Right after I get past this event, then I will…" This pattern puts a pause on *Zoe* until after a certain event. People with this *Zoe*-Zapping pattern excuse their state of unhappiness by blaming it on an event. God wants us to enjoy *Zoe* right now…not later, right now… as you are reading this sentence. No event should control the ability of God to give you *Zoe* right now. You must learn the "right now" habit. My friend Russ told me, "I can get distracted by life so I can't really live life." You and I need to enjoy God right now, enjoy life right now, relax right now, and find *Zoe* right now.

3. "I'll enjoy myself after work."

This pattern postpones *Zoe* to a leisure time. You and I need to learn to enjoy ourselves WHILE we work. The "right now" habit is the habit of continually reminding ourselves to enjoy *Zoe* to the Max in the present. God wants us to learn to enjoy our work, not wish our lives away. This type of *Zoe* Zapper will eat your lunch! Why should we "wish away" part of our lives? Why don't we take the challenge of "seizing the moment"? Grab that moment. Grab the time you were getting ready to wish away.

I find myself falling into this pattern at the end of the day when I'm seeing my last patient or am a little weary or bored. Once I recognize I'm not enjoying myself, I decide to slow down and find something to enjoy. I can enjoy the fact this is my last patient. I tell myself to "seize the moment" and not waste the time or wish it away. I turn on my "enjoyment finder" and try to appreciate the fact I am helping someone and they are valuable to God. As I do these things, I find I can turn myself around and really enjoy the time. Then, once I'm finished, I can enjoy the fact I'm done! Do you see what I'm talking about? Enjoyment is a choice God has given us. Don't wish your time away. God has made it possible for us to enjoy all of our lives, all of the time.

4. "The Weather Stinks."

The weather is a common *Zoe* Zapper if people allow it to determine their happiness. This attitude has always been one of my pet peeves, so let me get on my soapbox and preach! I resent the weathermen who tell me it is going to be a "dreary day" or "a nasty day." I want them to just report the weather, and I will decide how it's going to affect me.

It seems some people surrender entire chunks of their lives over to "bad weather." They complain if it is rainy or even cloudy. They concede their happiness to the clouds. But think about this: How many "clear days" are there in a year? I found a website showing the number of clear days in 2004 for the Richmond, Virginia, area. Check out the chart.

Do you see how the clouds stole every month except January and December! But then it's too cold to enjoy them anyway. June was a disaster—only one good day! You couldn't even get a full good week out of July, and the remaining months had only one nice week out of four. What a terrible year—cloudy 73% of the time!

Number of Clear Days:	
January	15 days
February	9 days
March	6 days
April	6 days
May	9 days
June	1 days
July	5 days
August	9 days
September	6 days
October	8 days
November	10 days
December	15 days

Furthermore, if you let temperature be a *Zoe* Zapper in your life, it would even narrow your good days further. What temperature is too cold or too hot for you? Look below and see how many months you might surrender to temperature in 2004.

If you only like the 70's and complain when it is cooler or warmer, it limits you to 5 months a year to enjoy; but if you subtract the cloudy days from those, it reduces your enjoyable days only 30 "good" days a year. Then if you knock out five of those days when

Average Temperature	
January	33.3
February	38.7
March	50.0
April	59
May	73
June	74.6
July	78.6
August	75.6
September	71.6
October	60.1
November	52.6
December	42.3

the temperature was in the 90's, it leaves you with only 25 "good" days a year. You are surrendering 93% of your life to weather!

It all comes down to two choices: Either change your attitude or change your location. If weather affects your happiness so much, than move! Why spend the rest of your life suffering with "bad" weather? Move to somewhere more to your liking. Unfortunately, the problem would still follow you there to some extent because it is an attitudinal problem. Even in the warmer southern states, people still complain about the temperature.

For most of us, changing location is not a reasonable option, so the best decision is to change your attitude. You can expand your attitude of enjoyment and stop complaining. You can learn to find enjoyment in all types of weather. On cold days you can find enjoyment in the warmth of your house or coat or car heater. You can enjoy the fresh snow or the beautiful ice-covered trees. I love the sparkly sun shining on the whiteness of everything. I have learned to appreciate the cozy feeling of rain—restful and relaxing.

Expand your definition of "good weather." Dr. John Maxwell taught me "when you can't change your circumstances, you can always change your attitude toward your circumstances." I know some people who have such a bad attitude even on their "good" weather days they say something like, "You better enjoy it because it's not going to last long." Or they say, "It's about time we had a decent day." And as soon as the weather changes, they say, "I knew it wouldn't last long!"

Don't' be like that! Be the opposite! The weather is ALWAYS good—JUST DIFFERENT KINDS OF GOOD. No doubt, we have our favorite kinds of weather, but don't let weather shrink your world of appreciation. Learn to expand your world of climate appreciation to good and great. Even in the "bad" weather, learn to turn on your "enjoyment finder."

<u>**5. "I hate my job."**</u>

Job hating is another *Zoe*-Zapping mindset. A recent Harris poll showed 41% of employees are dissatisfied with their jobs. Dissatisfaction can have legitimate roots, but I think it is mostly attitudinal. I know in my own profession there are many practitioners who hate dentistry. Such discontent probably exists in most fields. The problem is in our attitude. Many people have a strong "hate finder" inside their heads. They have DEVELOPED a propensity to hate many things. It's an attitudinal choice.

I observed this in dental school. We were required to spend time in each specialty of dentistry as a part of our rotations. I observed some of my classmates' attitudes caused them to hate one rotation after another, until they had narrowed their world of dentistry to only a few procedures.

The Power of Your Attitude

As you can see, most of these *Zoe*-zapping thinking patterns are really attitudes. God has given us the power of choosing about what we will think and talk. Choices become habits; habits become attitudes. One important attitudinal skill is to learn how to find enjoyment in every task you do. You've got to learn enjoying something or hating something is largely a choice of your attitude. My friend Tim Spivey says, "When things go wrong, don't go with them." That's a good thinking pattern. I have proven this to myself time and time again. I have been in the middle of something I was NOT enjoying and even hated, when I decided I would change my attitude and try to enjoy it. To my amazement it draws *Zoe* like a magnet! I can do this almost anytime I choose, and so can you. God has given you a tremendously powerful ability—to choose your attitude towards life. You can choose to enjoy yourself more or complain more. You can turn on your "enjoyment finder" or your "hate finder." The choice is yours. Your ability to enjoy *Zoe* to the Max depends on learning to do this. Enjoying life itself is a choice of focus and attitude. If you hate your life, it is largely because you have chosen to hate it. If you love your life, it is largely because you have chosen to love it.

Experiencing grace has much to do with our enjoyment of *Zoe* to the Max, our understanding of God, and our ability to get along well with others. Grace is God's unearned favor to us. Through grace we receive all the good things we don't deserve. Grace is God's love in action as He blesses us out of His benevolent heart. The opposite of grace is legalism. Legalism dispenses justice based on performance. Legalism gives only what is deserved—nothing more.

In the past, I was deficient in my understanding and experience of grace. I was much more comfortable with justice than grace. I understood obedience and disobedience both had consequences. If I lived right, I would be blessed; if I lived wrong, I would be punished. But the concept of grace was difficult for me to receive. As I shared earlier, a huge part of my emotional healing was embracing and experiencing the reality of the grace of God. I experienced the reality— God was too good to me, for no good reason, no merit of my own. It was all about His generous love because God is about grace. Legalism is about earning things and deserving things.

Self-generated Justification

Because I had been diligent in doing what I was told to do, I developed an inward sense of self-justification. I reasoned since I was obeying God, I was receiving His blessing. An inward sense of entitlement developed. God was simply doing "the right thing" in blessing me because I was following His rules. This caused me to become a legalistic person with self-generated justification. I was legalistic toward myself and others. I didn't see myself as being self-righteous, but as being obedient. I reasoned, if others would be obedient, they too would be blessed. If others failed, the consequences were their own fault. I had relegated grace only to God's act of providing salvation. After saving me, by His grace, it was up to me to be obedient.

This legalistic system of belief had to be reworked in my life as I learned the truth about God's grace. Jesus was full of grace AND truth (John 1:14), but I was only acquainted with His truth side.

Grace is about God giving and about our receiving His gift. We must grow in this understanding and experience of grace. We must learn to live in grace and act in grace towards ourselves and others.

A Ridiculous Employer

Jesus taught a parable I think illustrates our propensity to be legalistic rather than gracious.

Matthew 20:1-16: *"For the kingdom of heaven is like a landowner who went out early in the morning to hire men to work in his vineyard. He agreed to pay them a denarius for the day and sent them into his vineyard."*

The agreement was just. The landowner would pay one denarius for twelve hours of work. It was the fair and going wage for a day's labor. The work day commonly began at 6 o'clock. The spiritual analogy is those who have been believers the longest are the ones who begin early in the morning and are promised fair compensation for serving God—the landowner. They are grateful for this arrangement, and all begins well.

Then at 9 o'clock other people are hired.

Matthew 20:3-5: *"About the third hour he went out and saw others standing in the marketplace doing nothing. He told them, 'You also go and work in my vineyard, and I will pay you whatever is right.' So they went."*

Notice it was the landowner who went out and hired more workers. They did not approach him; he took the initiative to hire them. His financial arrangement with them was unclear. The only agreement was a promise to "pay you whatever is right." The spiritual application is those who come to Christ later in life must trust God to do "whatever is right." They can never "catch up" with the "early believers" in terms of living their whole lives for God.

Then the landowner goes out at noon and hires even more workers:

Matthew 20:5b: *"He went out again about the sixth hour and the ninth hour and did the same thing."*

He hires a noon crew and an afternoon crew. My assumption is they are told the same as the 9 o'clock crew and would be paid "whatever is right." These new crew members are just glad to be able to at least get in a half day of work. The early morning crew was probably assuming:

- 9 AM workers would earn ¾ of a day's wage.
- 12 PM workers would get a ½ day's wage.
- 3 PM crew would get ¼.

The spiritual analogy is God invites people to enter into His Kingdom even if they waste some or most of their lives away from Him. God sees them idle without purpose. He wants to help them. God is a good and compassionate God. He is also just and can be trusted to treat everyone right at the end of the day.

Then the landowner does the seemingly ridiculous. He goes out at 5 o'clock in the afternoon and hires some workers at the last hour of the day!

Matthew 20:6-7: *"About the eleventh hour he went out and found still others standing around. He asked them, 'Why have you been standing here all day long doing nothing?' "'Because no one has hired us,' they answered. "He said to them, 'You also go and work in my vineyard.'"*

Ridiculous Hiring Practices

Why would He bother with these last-minute folk? They couldn't be much help to the work. It shows us how generous our God is! He cares about us to an extreme extent. No doubt, the 6 o'clock folks were really scratching their heads at what the landowner was doing. These late-day workers were probably not going to make much. How could they feed their families on one hour's wage?

At 6 o'clock the whistle blew, the work was over, and it was pay time. Notice the order of who was paid first and how much they got.

Matthew 20:8-9: *"When evening came, the owner of the vineyard said to his foreman, 'Call the workers and pay them their wages,* **beginning with the last ones hired** *and going on to the first. The workers who were hired about the eleventh hour came and each received a denarius"* (emphasis added).

Ridiculous Wage Scale

Unbelievable! He paid a whole day's wage for only one hour! Twelve times more than they earned! How ridiculously generous is our God! How good and gracious is He to pay them a full day's wage for only a partial day's work! That's grace! They didn't deserve so much goodness!

This demonstrates the grace of our God. He gives full salvation even to the late-comers. You may have wasted most of your life away from God, but He is gracious and gives you full benefits and full inheritance in the Kingdom of Heaven! You have experienced the unearned favor of God!

All of the rest of the crews probably rejoiced in astonishment at what was given to the last crew! They probably thought, "Man, do we have a generous, high-paying boss! There's no telling how much we are going to make!" The unfathomable fact is the 9 o'clock, 3 o'clock, and 12 o'clock crews all received one denarius wage! The 3 o'clock crew was astonished because they were paid a full day's wage for only three hours of work. The 12 o'clock crew received a full day's wage for only a half day's work. They were all happy. But I imagine the 9 o'clock crew may have felt a little more resentful because they were getting the same wage for nine hours of work the others got for fewer hours. "We worked a lot longer and harder than they did."

The last to get paid was the 6 o'clock crew. They had worked a full twelve hours. Let's see what they were paid.

Matthew 20:10-12: *"So when those came who were hired first, they expected to receive more. But each one of them also received a denarius. When they received it, they began to grumble against the landowner. 'These men who were hired last worked only one hour,' they said, 'and you have made them equal to us who have borne the burden of the work and the heat of the day.'"*

Labor Grievance Filed

What!? Only one denarius? What a rip-off! They began to grumble against the landowner they previously praised as fair, compassionate, and even generous. The landowner was TOO good to the other workers. He was too generous; he was too gracious. Everyone else was praising the gracious and generous landowner except the 6 o'clock crew. They were grumbling and complaining because they felt they deserved more than all the other crews, especially the last crew. They probably expected to get paid three or four denarii, at least!

What a picture of legalism! The 6 AM crew was jealous of the landowner's gracious gift to the 5 PM crew. Mind you now, the 6 o'clock crew received EXACTLY what had been promised. The landowner's generosity took nothing away from them. But they still had a sense of unfairness. They grumbled. Legalistic Christians tend to grumble a lot and compare themselves with others. Legalist Christians want justice, not grace. The landowner answered their grumbling complaints with this:

Matthew 20:13-16: *"But he answered one of them, 'Friend, I am not being unfair to you. Didn't you agree to work for a denarius? Take your pay and go. I want to give the man who was hired last the same as I gave you. Don't I have the right to do what I want with my own money? Or are you envious because I am generous?' So the last will be first, and the first will be last."*

God's grace is not about being fair. It is about showing equal love. Legalism wants everyone to be treated the same. Grace wants everyone to be treated WELL. The landowner was interested in meeting ALL the needs of ALL the crews. He cared about the 3 o'clock and 5 o'clock crews just as much as the 6 o'clock crew. God loves each one of us equally, regardless of when we entered His family.

Grievance Dismissed

The landowner tells the grumbling 6 o'clock crew to "take your pay and go." Ungrateful, grumbling people displease God. He doesn't want them hanging around complaining. Instead He wants them to appreciate what they have and stop being envious of the undeserved good He does for others. Those who have walked with Jesus for a long time need to pay special attention to this parable. God is going to bring many people into His family, and He is going to be very generous to them, giving them full benefits. Those of us who have been part of the family for a long time will be tempted to treat these late-comers as second-class "step children." We will tend to be envious of all the good God does for them and grumble against Him. We might think to ourselves, "Who are you to have a valid opinion? I have been at this church for years! I know better than you." Remember God treats everyone equally well. He doesn't have second-class members in His family.

If we have a heart of grace, we will rejoice with the "late-comers." We will be glad for the "death-bed" and "fox-hole" and "jail house" conversions. We will want everyone to experience the great grace of our generous God.

Grace versus Legalism

In the end, too many of us resent the person who spends most of his or her life in sin and self-centeredness but, at the end of life, receives the full gift of salvation. This one will be in the same heaven as those who "served God" their entire lives. It's not fair, we conclude. Or think of a mass-murderer, rapist, child molester, or whoever you think is the worst of sinners. If such a one comes to God on his or her "death bed" at the end of his or her evil life, why should he or she receive the same grace as we? This is where the "rubber meets the road." Should any of them be forgiven and receive the same gift of grace as you and I? Should any be allowed into heaven after all the resulting sin and harm?

Grace says, "Yes!"

Legalism says, "No."

Grace is generous to the undeserving. Legalism wants them to justly suffer for their sins. Legalistic people would probably approve the concept of two or more levels of heaven—one for them, and a lesser level for the second-class "late-comers." Legalism wants people to earn their standing and receive exactly what they deserve. Grace wants God to be generous to all, regardless of seniority.

> *Legalism wants people to earn their standing and receive exactly what they deserve. Grace wants God to be generous to all, regardless of seniority.*

We should listen to the statement of the landowner to the jealous ones, *"Don't I have the right to do what I want with my own money? Or are you envious because I am generous?"* God can be as generous as He wants to be! He is God. If we are envious of His generosity, then we are trying to control God.

There are many legalistic groups. I just heard last week about a Christian radio network who decided to kick the well-respected "Turning Point" broadcast by Dr. David Jeremiah off its network because Dr. Jeremiah's church plays contemporary Christian music at its radio rallies and worship services! Even though none of the music is played on the actual radio broadcast, the fact Dr. Jeremiah's church has a different music style preference from the radio network is grounds for removal? A legalistic mindset tends to be more and more exclusive and becomes more and more controlling and demanding. It's scary and almost cultish. Such an organization proclaims the attitude, "If you don't do it exactly the way we do, then you are worldly, and we will exclude you." It reminds me of the church with a huge sign outside of its building reading "Jesus only." A storm came through and blew off the first three letters so it read "us only."

Grace is much more open and generous with differences. It could be seen as even irrational and lavish. Think about the landowner—he went out and hired new workers at three and five o'clock. That doesn't make much sense. Then he "wasted his money" on those people who did not carry their share of the work. What a waste! What kind of a businessman is He? You see, grace doesn't make much sense. Grace isn't fair because grace is about a love going all the way to Calvary for undeserving sinners like you and me.

Ridiculous Grace

The tendency to become more legalistic increases with time. The longer we are in the church, the easier it is to forget about the radical gift of grace we received. I've seen this from time to time as I have worked with new believers. At first, they are overwhelmed by the generous gift of grace they received. But as time passes and they grow and become stronger, they seem to become less and less accepting of newer people's failures. They gradually take on more characteristics of legalism and less of grace. They reason to themselves, "I did it, so why can't they?" First, notice the word *reason*. Whenever we start to explain grace with reason, we will gravitate toward becoming legalistic. Grace doesn't make rational sense because it is not motivated by justice and rewards and punishments. Grace is motivated by love, a love *"rich in mercy and not willing that any should perish."*

Zoe to the Max is learning to live in the glory of this grace. Living in legalism steals the joy of celebrating the generosity of our gracious God. Legalism is performance-based. It celebrates good performance and punishes bad performance. Grace celebrates love. The issue is love. God's love came down to us and was received by us; now it is to be passed on by us to the world. We are to live *Zoe* to the Max as we celebrate the grace of God for us and others. Legalism gives itself a pat on the back for its own performance. Grace gives

God a standing ovation because it has little to do with us and all to do with our generous God!

Judgmental-ism

Pronouncing judgment on others is the natural outcome of living by performance. Legalism leads us naturally to become a more judgmental person by claiming, "I'm not being any harder on them than I am on myself." However, being judgmental is wrong for both you and others.

God has not called us to be judges. He does not want us to enforce the rules. Our job is not to judge. Certainly, we can warn others in love and humility, but we need to understand most people must learn "the hard way." A judgmental person will be harsh on the one who fails, saying, "I told you so." A grace-filled person embraces the one who fails, saying, "God wants to help you succeed."

Forgiveness or Justice

Grace forgives and cleans the slate. Justice judges and keeps records of the debt. If you and I are going to live in grace, we must forgive others. If we don't forgive them, we are choosing to side with the legalists. Legalists would rather have repayment than to forgive the debt completely. Legalists demand justice. They want an apology. They consider unforgiveness as just and fair. Grace, in their minds, is unjust—too good, too easy. But grace cannot co-exist with unforgiveness. They are on opposite poles. Forgiveness is the language of grace. Unforgiveness is the language of legalism.

Remember in the parable the folks working the entire day were mad because of the "injustice" of the landowner to pay the same wage to those who worked fewer hours. God is not seeking to get sinners back for their sins and make them pay. Jesus died on the cross—so they would not have to pay. Jesus has already paid the price for your sins and mine and the person who owes you. He took their punishment, too. No sinner needs to repay his debt because Christ has already paid the debt. Therefore, you and I do not need to collect on the debts owed to us because God has released us; and He, in turn, wants us to release our debtors and clean the slate. If you have a problem with forgiveness, you also have a problem with grace; and you also have a problem with God. Unforgiveness is a *Zoe* Zapper. Don't let it zap you.

Chapter 30: Worry

One of the major *Zoe* Zappers is worry! Many Christians miss enjoying their *Zoe* because of a mind clouded with worry. Worry comes from having an undisciplined mind. An undisciplined mind is allowed to focus on "what if's," which leads to worry and doubt. This is the topic of the book of Philippians. Paul tells us about the disciplined mind in Philippians 4:7 —the mind guarded by the peace of God because of right thoughts and right prayers—frees us from worry.

What is worry? Our English word "worry" comes from an Anglo-Saxon word meaning "to strangle"; worry certainly does strangle people physically, emotionally, and spiritually. The Greek word translated as "worry" or to "be anxious" is *merimnao* [mer·im·nah·o].[1] This comes from the root word merizo [mer·id·zo] - to divide, to separate into parts, cut into pieces.[2]

Worry comes when the thoughts of our mind divide us and pull us in different directions and "split us" into pieces. Thoughts in the mind create feelings in the heart. If the mind is divided, the heart will feel anxiety. That's why James 1:8 says: *"He is a double-minded man, unstable in all he does."* The undisciplined mind is allowed to meditate on problems. This meditation weighs down the heart with negative feelings, creating a vicious circle of worry and depression.

I took my kayaks to the ocean on vacation this summer for the first time. The big challenge was to get them launched against the incoming, crashing waves. We finally realized the nose of the kayak needed to be guided over the first couple of waves until we could get paddling enough to steer it. After we got out in the ocean a short distance, the waves turned to gentle rolls, and it was an easy ride. After my friend Victor and I had been out for about a half hour, we decided it was time to head back. I started to look for an opening among the people on the beach for me to land. I had previously knocked one little girl for a loop the first time I landed because a wave caused me to lose control as I beached the kayak.

As I was paddling along and spying out for the best spot to land, I didn't notice behind me had developed a large breaking wave! For a split second I had to decide if I was going to ride this one in or turn into it and ride over it. I hesitated too long because before I could fully turn my kayak, I got caught slightly side ways and flipped over. So I had to hold on to my kayak and swim in. One split second of indecision did me in! When our minds are divided and undisciplined, some parts tell us not to fret, but other parts doubt. We end up getting dumped.

Some of our negative thoughts were implanted deep within us years ago and now lurk in our subconscious minds. These subconscious doubts and fears formed our inward beliefs and now subconsciously interject themselves into our minds.

We must understand this fact:
WRONG THINKING CAUSES WRONG FEELINGS.

Wrong thoughts or wrong attitudes toward people, circumstances, and things create worry. Notice in Philippians chapter 4 Paul has no worry about people (vv. 1–5), circumstances (vv. 10–13), or the material things of life (vv. 14–19). Of course, Paul had developed the "single mind" of chapter one and gained victory over circumstances; he had the "submissive mind" of chapter two and overcame troublesome people; and he had the "spiritual mind" of chapter three and triumphed over physical circumstances. The result was the "disciplined mind" of chapter four. His mind and heart were at peace and could not be disturbed by people, circumstances, or things.[3]

Thinking Inside The Boxes

I recommend you organize your worries and put them in one of three imaginary boxes. If the event has already happened, then put it in the "past box." Everything in the "past box" needs to be processed and forgiven, then closed. Closing the "past box" means you discipline your mind not to dwell on thoughts related to events in that box.

If the event has not yet happened, then it is to be put in the "future box." Everything in the "future box" is to be prayed about with thanksgiving. Then ask God for help in preparing for the event as much as you are able. Finally, close the box, trust God with the outcome, and thank Him in advance for how He is going to help you.

If the worry is about a present event, put it in the "present box." The "present box" is the only box you can leave open; the others need to remain closed. We are to ask God to help us deal with the "present box" items now. God is the God of now. He will be with you now. He will help you now. Opening the "future box" causes worry. Opening the "past box" causes regret. Both boxes should stay closed.

Philippians 4:6-7 is very clear about this: *"Do not be anxious about anything, but in everything, by prayer and petition, with thanksgiving, present your requests to God. And the peace of God, which transcends all understanding, will guard your hearts and your minds in Christ Jesus"* (emphasis added). God does not want you and me to worry about anything.

God's Remedy for Worry

God does not want you to be anxious about ANYTHING! But His remedy is to …

P-R-A-Y

W-I-T-H

T-H-A-N-K-S-G-I-V-I-N-G.

As I said in the chapter entitled "Peace Ruled Heart," pray with a "thank you" note attached. *Zoe* to the Max requires worry to the mini. You can't say you trust God if you worry because the worry shows you aren't trusting. Worry and trust cannot coexist.

The pace of life can be a *Zoe Zapper* when we try to do too much, too fast. Unfortunately, I am very susceptible to both conditions! I tend to take on too much and then try to do it in too little time. I'm like a pickup truck trying to carry the load of a dump truck, and then driving 70 mph on a curvy road posted 45 mph. I ignore my "maximum load capacity" and my "maximum safe speed."

When we ignore maximum load limits, we usually strain or break something. When we ignore our maximum safe speed limit, we become stressed out or run off the road of life. For each one of us, God has a healthy pace of life. It's like the maximum safe speed for our vehicles, carrying our loads, on the type of road we travel.

We don't like to admit it, but we do have time and physical limitations. I often have trouble stopping myself from the compulsion to finish a task even when I have run out of time. For example, right now as I am writing this, I should stop and get ready for work. It takes me a certain amount of time to shave, shower, get dressed, pack up, and drive to work. All this takes me 40 minutes, if everything goes perfectly. With this in mind, I somehow think I can defy Murphy's Law by leaving myself the minimum 40 minutes. When I do this, I don't take into account that "stuff happens." Some task inevitably takes a little longer than normal, or I forget about something. I am stressed from rushing around blaming my lateness on the school bus, or the phone call, or "whatever." I'm trying to improve in this area by learning to accept my limitations and slow down the pace of my life. I'm trying to have the self-control to stop myself from pushing my limits. I must stop deceiving myself in to thinking I can "create more time." Time is fixed and limited. That's why I need to stop NOW and finish this later... bye!

Set the Pace

Zoe to the Max comes from learning what our limits are and respecting them. Enjoying the pace of life requires us to plan wisely and leave time to handle the unexpected. The pace of our life is something over which we like to complain as if we were victims of some uncontrollable force like the "Wicked Witch of the West" in the *Wizard of Oz*. She peers at us through her crystal ball and sends her little mean monkeys to swoop down on us. "It's the monkey's fault," we rationalize. The truth is...

THE PACE OF OUR LIFE IS SET BY
THE COMBINATION OF
THE MANY SMALL DECISIONS <u>WE</u> MAKE.

Some of you may argue with this premise because of the things in your life over which you have no control. This can be true to a certain extent, but I contend we put too many things in the "uncontrollable" box. Let's think about it together. I want you to think about your activities and put them into one of two mental boxes:

Controllable Things	Uncontrollable Things

A controllable thing is an activity like watching television. You have control over which programs you watch and how much time you spend watching them. No one forces you to watch it—it's a controllable activity. I know a person who tells me often how busy her life is and she doesn't have time to do things. Yet I know through overhearing casual conversations she's been watching various TV shows. There's nothing wrong with watching TV, except it is a "controllable" activity. IT IS HER CHOICE and it affects the pace of her life.

If the pace of our life doesn't allow for enough time to rest, then we should look in our "controllable" box for the solution. When we make the choice to watch TV rather than get needed rest, we are choosing to be tired. In geometry I learned if A=B and B=C, then

A=C. So rather than playing the victim saying, "I'm so tired because my life is so busy," we more correctly should say, "I stayed up too late watching TV last night." Take responsibility; A=C.

Our victim tendencies compel us to label as many things "uncontrollable" as possible. Then we don't have to take responsibility for them. But when I choose to do "one more thing," I can't blame my lateness on the guy who was driving "so slow." I AM the one who chose to not give myself enough time. I am the one who added "one more, quick little thing." I am the one who creates the pace of my life.

Managing the Uncontrollable Box

Uncontrollable things are activities or situations created by others or required by life itself. An example is one's employment. You are required to have employment to live. You may not have control over the pace of activity at your employment because you were hired with certain expectations. However, you do have some options to manage these "uncontrollable" situations and slow the pace.

- You can try to think of time-saving changes to slow the pace of your work routine.
- You can meet with your boss and ask for suggestions to slow your pace. Sometimes things will improve after you share your limits.
- If things don't change, you can ask for a transfer in job assignments, or you can change jobs.

A job should not be a death sentence. This is your one life, so slow down BEFORE you break something! We must recognize 90% of the situations we deal with in life are actually controllable. There are really only a few truly uncontrollable things in life such as sickness, crime, accidents, car breakdowns, taxes, weather, parenting events, birthdays, anniversaries, etc. Controllable things are everything else!

Management Techniques

We can manage the uncontrollable. I was talking earlier about the leaning tree falling on my driveway. I could not control what happened TO me, but I could control what happened IN me. Things beyond my ability to control are NOT beyond my ability to manage.

IF YOU CAN'T CONTROL IT, YOU CAN MANAGE IT.

1. You can manage with your attitude. Dr. John Maxwell taught me, "You can't choose your problems, but you can choose your attitude toward your problems." You can choose your response toward the uncontrollable—that is how you manage the uncontrollable. "When things go wrong, don't go with them." You can choose to praise the Lord. You can choose to be thankful. YOU are the one who chooses how powerful your problem will be. YOU are the one who chooses how much of your life and happiness you will surrender to your problems. You can manage your attitude.

2. You can manage by setting up boundaries. You can set up a boundary to protect yourself from an uncontrollable person. For example, if someone is "controlling" your life by calling you too often, you can set up a boundary by screening your calls. You can return a call later. Too often we act like victims, when we simply must be willing to set boundaries. It is our responsibility to set boundaries and protect ourselves. Don't surrender to the victim mindset. Ask others for help building up your "boundary muscles." So...

Change the changeable.
Manage the manageable.
Adapt to the difficult.
Accept the inevitable.

3. Build margins into your life. Several books have been written about the importance of building "margins" of time into your life. "Margins" are buffer-zones of extra time built in before and after demanding events in our lives. Margins allow for possible problems and time to rest after draining events. I am personally trying to improve in this area. I tend to over-schedule, over-estimate my abilities, and plan no margins. You and I need to plan in margins.

Slow Down!

If your life is like the National Car Rental slogan, "Faster than the speed of life," then maybe you need to listen to the advice of John Ortberg, who urges us to ruthlessly "get rid of hurry." When I was a teenage driver and my dad rode with me, he would often say, "Choke 'er down, boy!" When I realize now I am rushing, I consciously try to "choke 'er down" and escape to the *Zoe* Zone. I remind myself, "Hey, man, slow down. You are too tense. Enjoy this moment. This is it. This is your life. Enjoy it." Feeling tense will not get you there any faster, so relax and enjoy the moment. Don't let your pace of life zap your *Zoe*!

Chapter 32:
The Power of Imagination

With *Zoe* Zappers limited and managed, we need to learn to engage the power of our imagination. When I go into the *Zoe* Zone, I often close my eyes and imagine the presence of God. I imagine my Helper (*Parakletos*) being right there with me. He is not "way up there." He has told us in John 14:23 He will come to us. I imagine Him being right beside me.

Don't be afraid to use your imagination. God gave us this ability for our good. Since the spirit world is beyond our ability to see, we can use our imagination as a faith tool. Our imagination can envision the presence of the Holy Spirit with us. It can aide us in prayer and experiencing *Zoe* to the Max! I often imagine God coming to me as my Daddy-Father to His dearly loved child. I breathe Him in. I exhale worry, anxiety, boredom, and fear. I quote my *Zoe* Word for the day, or I say some other scripture , prayer , praise, or thanksgiving. When I can't feel His presence, I imagine His presence. I know by faith He is there. I know He will never leave me, so when I don't feel Him, I close my eyes and invite Him to come close. I engage my imagination to aide my faith experience. This exercise combining faith and imagination strengthens me.

Here's an imagination exercise. Imagine the place you love to vacation. For me it is the beach or an Appalachian mountain top. Wherever your place is, close your eyes and remember how it feels to be there. Imagine breathing in the cool breeze and the restful and peaceful feeling of that environment. You are using your imagination to change the way you feel. Your circumstances didn't change. You didn't actually go there, but you were able to remember the feelings in your imagination. In the same way, you can engage your imagination to aide your faith and experience the *Zoe* God has for you. God has given us the power of imagination so use it!

Sometimes when I am tense, I use my imagination to remember what if feels like to be "Zooming in *Zoe* Zone," and by faith, I get myself back there. Once I am there, I am reminded of how enjoyable it is to live *Zoe* to the Max. I breathe in His presence and let Him wash away all my anxieties. With the tenseness gone, I return to whatever I was doing with a new sense of peace. The state of enjoyment of *Zoe* is what I want to keep coming back to throughout the day. The more I stay there, the better the *Zoe* experience I have. Even as I am writing this right now, I am experiencing *Zoe* as I write and rewrite these sentences. I am in a full sense of enjoyment right now. There's nothing else I would rather be doing right now, and there's nothing else I would enjoy any better than this. I am truly the happiest man in the world, and I want everyone to experience this. *Zoe* to the Max is truly an awesome way to live!

Chapter 33: *Zoe* Strategies

To consistently live in the *Zoe* Zone requires strategies to overcome the various obstacles life throws at you. Here are some of the practical tips I have learned in maintaining daily *Zoe* to the Max.

The *Zoe* Question

It's important for you to develop the habit of monitoring your *Zoe*, moment by moment. I have developed the habit of asking myself the question, "Am I enjoying myself as much as I possibly can right now?" If the answer to the question is "No," then I check myself in a number of areas listed below. It's like checking the gauges on the instrument panel of my inner life.

<u>Fuel check</u>—I check my three tanks. Am I physically tired? Am I emotionally spent? Am I spiritually dry?

<u>Speed check</u>—Is the pace of my life healthy? Do I need to slow down and "soak it up?"

<u>Praise and thankful check</u>—Is my tank full of thankful? Do I need to do a fresh inventory of thankfulness?

<u>Heart check</u>—Is my heart at rest, or am I striving? Is peace ruling my heart right now?

<u>Worry check</u>—Am I anxious about anything? Have I prayed about all my anxious thoughts with thankfulness?

<u>Attitude check</u>—Is my attitude right? Do I need an attitude adjustment?

<u>Coffee check</u>—Do I just need a cup of coffee! Do I need to take a break and do something refreshing?

This checking of my gauges is now habitual, intuitive, and automatic. I know within ten seconds what I need to do. Often I need to adjust the way I'm thinking about the problem I am facing. Here are some of the strategies I have developed to help me change my mental attitude.

Zoe Attitude Strategies

Romans 12:2 says: *"…be transformed by the renewing of your mind."* To renew our mind means to change the way we think so it lines up with God's way of thinking. In other words, God's Word—His *Logos*—renews our minds so we can think in the right patterns, recognize false thinking patterns, and change them to God's way of thinking.

"Adopt That Plan" Strategy

When your assumptions about an event are not coming to pass, it often leads to anger or frustration. For example, you are driving down the road, and a slow-moving vehicle gets in front of you. Frustration boils. Our plans are getting messed up! At that moment you have two choices. You can boil with anger because your plans have been hijacked, or you can change your plans to adapt to the situation. I call this the "Adopt That Plan Strategy." Adopt the situation and own it as your new plan based on the new circumstances. Instead of steaming about the changes and being angry, you relax and adopt this as YOUR new plan.

While going to Food Lion recently and turning down one of the parking lot rows, I noticed the driver behind me was quite agitated and animated. She quickly accelerated past me. I looked over to see her mouth was wide open as she angrily yelled at the passenger in her SUV. I smiled at the message on her vanity plates—RELAX! Ha! She needed to read her own license plate.

"Adopt That Plan" strategy means, accepting the new circumstances as your new plan.

In the example of the slow vehicle, you would decide to adopt this new plan and take a leisurely drive and enjoy the scenery. So you slow down to enjoy the journey more. You're no longer in a hurry. Meditate on your *Zoe* Word, fellowship with God in your *mone*, listen to music, start a conversation with someone in the car, call a friend on the cell phone, or just look around for something to enjoy. You've adopted this as your new plan. The car in front of you is not blocking you or frustrating you any longer—this is YOUR new plan to slow down and enjoy the journey.

We all have plans, either conscious or subconscious. We have presumptions in our mind as to how things should proceed. As long as things go as presumed, we enjoy ourselves; but when circumstances change, we often "lose it." Some people allow the change in circumstances to completely take control of their happiness. I see many people fight their circumstances instead of accepting their circumstances. They are livid with anger about the people and things and situations blocking their preconceived notions. This reaction holds their *Zoe* hostage. Why waste half the day complaining about the new circumstances with an agitated demeanor which is unpleasant to be around? How much better it is to enjoy *Zoe* to the Max in the midst of changing circumstances!

"Nip That Dread" Strategy

When I face an event like meeting a difficult person or attending an awkward event, I use the "Nip That Dread" strategy. These dreaded events have the power to zap the *Zoe* right out of us for hours, days, or even weeks! We can sit and sulk about how bad it's going to be, OR we can implement the "Nip That Dread" Strategy.

"Nip That Dread" strategy is to refuse to dread
an upcoming event until the event itself begins.

It is refusing to surrender the time before the event to the power of dread. One recent Friday night as I was falling asleep, I felt the fog of dread roll over me as I thought of an event scheduled for the next day. Then I employed the "Nip That Dread" strategy and refused to allow the event to rob me of the enjoyment of my sleep and the enjoyment of every minute up to the dreaded event. I focused myself completely on enjoying myself just as if the dreaded event was never going to happen. I used my imagination to think of how happy I would feel if the dreaded event was canceled. Then I hold on to the good feeling until the very last moment before the unpleasant event. Think about it.

The "time before" the event does not have to be surrendered to dread. It is your choice to lived it in dread or live it in *Zoe*. Too many people allow dreaded events to take over huge chunks of time saying, "Oh great! The whole day is ruined." They haven't learned that...

**When you change the way you think,
you begin to change the way you feel.**

You can refuse to allow a dreaded situation to steal any more *Zoe* from you than is necessary.

The "Waiting Vacation" Strategy

Waiting is difficult for most of us. Some personalities can handle waiting better than others. I see it all the time in the waiting room of my dental office. Some folks spend their time fidgeting and looking all around. They stand up, stare out of the window, sit down, only to stand up again and look over at my receptionist as if she can shorten their wait. They are totally dominated by the wait and trapped in a time warp until their name is called and they can be set free! (By the way, this behavior really aggravates my receptionist, but don't tell her I said so.)

Once you realize you are tense about waiting, it's time to take a "Waiting Vacation." This happens when you use the power of your imagination to relax yourself and envision taking a vacation while you wait. Part of the reason you feel relaxed on a vacation is you have told yourself, "I am on vacation" and to "relax and enjoy it." Vacation is mostly a state of mind. You can be there most anytime you tell yourself to be there.

My receptionist Ginger enjoys vacation starting weeks in advance. She has fun just thinking about it. Then there are other people I know who complain because of all the stuff they have to do to get ready for their vacation. They grumble about loading up the car and then complain about the traffic on the way. You get the picture? Some time later on, they finally give themselves permission to relax and enjoy themselves. Before the vacation comes to an end, they tell themselves to stop enjoying the relaxation because the vacation is almost over!

I want you to realize much of the enjoyment of a vacation is when you **give yourself permission** to relax and enjoy it. You can "copy and paste" permission to enjoy yourself into most any time and place you choose.

Just now as I am writing this section, I am waiting for my daughter Nena to call about joining me kayaking on the James River today. Instead of putting my life "on hold" and being anxious about when she is going to call, I've decided to enjoy myself and have a "Waiting Vacation" and get another cup of coffee!

"Soak It Up" Strategy

I've found I don't always fully enjoy and absorb the good times. For example, sometimes I don't fully enjoy the preparation steps leading up to a recreational activity. The "Soak it Up" Strategy is to…

**Stop yourself mentally, seize the moment,
look for "the roses," and smell them.**

You've heard the old song, "You've gotta stop and smell the roses." That's what the "Soak It Up" strategy is. I tell myself to enjoy the smell of the fresh breeze, the sound of the birds singing, the presence of my wife or children, the passing of recreational time. I've found I don't always take in all of the good, of the good times. I have to remind myself to slow down and soak up the good.

My friend Nancy told me about how her granddaughter Alyssa once found some rocks in the driveway and was delighted with how beautiful they were. Alyssa thought they were like precious jewels and she should give them away as presents, to which Nancy said, "Okay, let's go wrap them up." Nancy said to me, "That's how God wants us to live. He wants us to stop and see the wonder of the little things. Some parents would have fussed at their children for playing in the gravel, but I think we can learn from the wonder of a child."

Zoe is all around us, but we need to "Soak It Up" like a puddle of water on the kitchen counter is soaked up by a dry sponge. That's what we need to do. Soak up all the *Zoe* around you like a sponge!

My "hurry-up" tendency works against my enjoyment of life. If I set my mind on the goal of arriving at a destination, I tend to not be satisfied until I get there. The "Soak It Up" strategy requires me to recalibrate my goal. My goal is no longer to "get there" but to soak up all the *Zoe* I can find around me on my journey. Enjoy the journey, not just the destination. So many people are like little kids in the back seat of the car of life asking, "Are we there yet?" They are anxious to arrive so they can start enjoying themselves. Listen, much of life is about the ride. If you don't enjoy the process of "getting there," you are wasting a good portion of your life. Learn to "enjoy the ride."

"Soak It Up" is learning to absorb *Zoe* wherever we are. If we take our kitchen sponge and wipe quickly through the puddle of water, we'll end up splashing the water instead of absorbing it. Too often we speed down the "counter top of life," crash through the puddles of *Zoe*, and end up splashing it away from us instead of absorbing it. Jesus came so you and I might have *Zoe* and have it to the Max. I think that we miss much of the *Zoe* available to us because we are moving too fast. Remember to soak up the puddles of *Zoe* wherever you are.

Look for the puddles of *Zoe* all around you. Turn on your "enjoyment finder" and look for the good. Develop the habit of finding enjoyment rather than complaining or dreading. Making lemonade out of the lemons in life is not just a different way of looking at things—it is God's plan for us! When God says, "In everything give thanks," He means it! He means to find the good—look for flowers, ignore the weeds.

Recently my dermatologist determined some irregular looking spots on my arms should be frozen because they could become pre-cancerous. So there I was in the front room of the office waiting for the procedure to begin. I could choose to be anxious and frustrated, or I could turn on my "enjoyment finder." I discovered I could appreciate the doctor removing these pre-cancerous lesions. I could appreciate my health, and this was a good time to get this procedure done. I ended up enjoying myself! Turn your "enjoyment finder" and soak up the *Zoe*!

"I'm Havin' a Great Time" Strategy

This is a strategy the Lord taught me based on Colossians 3:17: *"And whatever you do, whether in word or deed, do it all in the name of the Lord Jesus, giving thanks to God the Father through him."* I make a positive statement to myself reminding me to maximize Zoe in the name of the Lord Jesus. I tell myself, "I'm havin' a great time." This confession reminds me to maximize my appreciation of whatever I'm doing. God has taught me the power to enjoy and the power to hate an activity are opposite sides of the same coin. When I decide to hate what I'm doing, I hate it more. When I decide to enjoy what I'm doing, I enjoy it more. When I decide to ENJOY what I'm HATING, I hate it less and enjoy it more. It's amazing to me the power God has given us through the choices we make and attitudes we take on.

As I sat in my sunroom writing this section, I stopped and told myself, "I'm having a great morning." As I did this, I suddenly heard a bird singing. He had been singing, but I had not been listening. I started appreciating the scenery God has provided in my backyard. I took note of the colors, the air, the temperature, and the coffee! What a great morning! Thank God! *Zoe* to the Max! I AM having a great morning!

But what about...

Now for my melancholy personality type readers, I acknowledge there are times when I do not and cannot enjoy what is going on around me. There are some awful situations and painful times in life. That is acknowledged. No one likes those situations, but we try to get through them as best we can. My point: We shouldn't make the bad times bigger than they have to be. Contain the damage. It's your choice how much of your life you are going to surrender to the bad times.

Here in the South, we have this annoying plant called kudzu. I understand it was brought over here from Asia because it is a fast-growing, ground-covering plant to prevent erosion. The problem is it is so fast-growing it takes over everything. In many regions it has gotten out of control and smothered all other vegetation, including tall trees. Some people let their problems and bad times grow over and take over their whole world like kudzu. Don't magnify the bad—magnify the good!

"Relax! Enjoy *Zoe* to the Max!"

When I listen to my phone messages, the pre-recorded operator says, "to save this message press 3." I can press 1 later and listen to the message over and over again. I want you to press 3 and save the following phrase in your mind and then listen to it over and over again: "Relax! Enjoy *Zoe* to the Max." This phrase is a combination of two things Jesus said. "Relax!"—Matthew 11:28-29: *"Come to me, all you who are weary and burdened, and I will give you rest. Take my yoke upon you and learn from me."* "Relax!" sums up the verse. Stop pulling so hard on the yoke. Jesus is saying, *"Come to me... rest... take my yoke... learn."* Then *"Zoe* to the Max" is, of course, from John 10:10: *"I have come that you might have Zoe and have it to the Max."*

Matthew 11:28,29 + John 10:10 ="Relax! Enjoy *Zoe* to the Max"

I've developed the habit of repeating this phrase to myself periodically throughout the day: "Relax! Enjoy *Zoe* to the Max!" It reminds me to let the *Zoe* in and push the other stuff out. It reminds me to pray and praise and stop my "yoke confusion." When I feel anxious, or if I am running late somewhere or behind in my schedule, I say the words of my Savior, "Relax! Enjoy *Zoe* to the Max!."

When I say this, I feel my body responding to God's Word. My stomach muscles loosen, and I take in a fresh breath of air. I sometimes lean back in my chair and breathe in the Holy Spirit and breathe out everything else. I feel His peace wash over me. What I am doing is confessing my faith in God to enable me to experience *Zoe* to the Max! I think this is what it means to rejoice in the day and be glad IN it.

SECTION FOUR

Staying in the Zoe Zone

Chapter 34:
The University of Adversity

Imagine the following scenario—I am approaching a university registrar seeking to enroll in the "U of A's" academic program:

Registrar: Come in, Mr. Spaur. Welcome to U of A. How may I help you?

Me: Yes, I saw your advertisement about how the U of A builds excellent character.

Registrar: That's right! Our goal is improving and proving excellence in character.

Me: Well, that's what I want. I want to improve my character, so sign me up!

Registrar: Ah, you've been enrolled for a long time.

Me: What?

Registrar: You've been enrolled for several years and have taken a number of classes.

Me: I have?

Registrar: (pulls out my transcript) Yes, you have taken a lot of classes, but you haven't passed very many of them.

Me: What do you mean? I'm a good student!

Registrar: Not in these classes. I see here you complained a lot about the classes, did not listen to the instructions you were given, and failed many of the final exams.

Me: What? I don't remember any of that!

Registrar: You have taken several classes over and over again. Here's one class entitled "Learning to Get Along Well with Others." You've taken that class over 200 times and still haven't passed it.

Me: (embarrassed) Well, I admit I'm not too good with relationships. Nobody can seem to get along with me! I don't know what's wrong with people!

Registrar: Sir, you need to read your textbook and pay attention in class.

Me: But I'm not in a class.

Registrar: Yes, you are.

Me: What kind of university is this anyway if you don't even know when you're in class!

Registrar: (looks down and points at the transcript) Mr. Spaur, you are currently taking, "How to Be Content in Spite of Your Lousy Finances."

Me: I am? Well, good, because I am currently dealing with a lot of adversity in that area!

Registrar: That's why we're called the University of Adversity.

Me: Is that what U of A stands for? I don't want any adversity!

Registrar: But, Sir, you said you wanted to improve your character—you wanted excellent character.

Me: I do. But what does that have to do with adversity?

Registrar: Mr. Spaur, you cannot develop character in a vacuum. Character is proved when you have adversity. Adversity gives you the opportunity to develop character here at the University of Adversity.

Me: What kind of a university is this? We don't even have textbooks.

Registrar: This book is your textbook. It's called the Bible.

Me: I don't have time to read that ....

Registrar: Then, Sir, I'm afraid with your attitude you are never going to pass and improve your character. It's all part of the curriculum leading up to the CLC certification.

Me: What is a CLC certification?

Registrar: It stands for Christ-like Character. Christ had the greatest character of any man who ever lived. Don't you want to have outstanding character?

Me: Yes, but can't I just get a quicker, easier degree?

Registrar: Yes, we offer other associate degrees ... let's see, you can settle for the popular "Immature, Baby Character," or there is "The Professional Complainer" associate's degree and "The Arrested Development" associate's degree.

Me: None of those sound very good. Isn't there an easier way to develop character? Can't I just take some classes online?

Registrar: There's no such thing as easy character, Sir. Easy character is an oxymoron—it's really the same as no character. The University of Adversity is the only way to improve and prove excellence in character. You need to decide if you want easy character or excellent character.

How to Improve Your Character

Easy character or excellent character—the choice is ours. We're all enrolled in The University of Adversity, but are we passing our classes? Some of you started a new class this past week. Some of you will start a new class next week. Some of you may feel like you're a full-time student! You see, adversity always reveals your level of maturity. Adversity will prove the quality of your character, AND it will give you an opportunity to improve the quality of your character.

The quality of your character can't hide from adversity. Adversity will expose your character for exactly what it is, especially relationship adversity. I thought I was a "saved and sanctified Christian" until I got married. Then I thought I was at least "saved" until I had teenagers! Now I'm not sure about either!

Let me clarify something. Adversity does not cause character improvement. I know people who have been through all sorts of adversity, but their moral fiber hasn't improved at all. Adversity is an opportunity to grow.

How to Pass Your Class in the University of Adversity

Growing begins when you recognize The University of Adversity is in session, and it's time to either grow or gripe. You choose which you will do. Are you going to gripe your way through or grow your way through? People who "gripe their way through" are not pleasant to be around, and they fail the class. People who "grow their way through" are a lot more pleasant to be around during the class; and by improving their character, they pass their exam.

Let me ask you a question: Are you the best version of YOU there can be? Or is this "it" for you? The Christian music band *Switchfoot* has a song asking this question: "This is your life; are you who you want to be?" Is God done with your character, or have you just settled for what you are? This is your life. This is it. Connect the dots and pass your classes.

Some people excuse their immature character by saying, "Oh, this is just the way I am!" And there's a Greek word for that— "Baloney!" **You are the person who you are because you have CHOSEN to be who you are!**

The Bible is very clear about who God wants you to be. Romans

8:29 says: God has *"...predestined (us) to be conformed to the likeness of his Son, that he might be the firstborn among many brothers."* God wants you and me to have the character of Jesus, not an excuser, a "professional complainer," or a victim. People should be able to look at you and see the likeness of Jesus.

So once you decide to grow and pass your class in the University of Adversity you need to...

1. You have a great teacher. Your teacher is the Holy Spirit. Jesus told us this in John 14:26: *"But the Counselor (remember Parakletos), the Holy Spirit, whom the Father will send in my name, will teach you all things and will remind you of everything I have said to you"* (parentheses added). Ask your teacher for the study guide for this character lesson. You ask Him to improve your character through this adversity.

2. Look to the Book. The Bible is your guidebook for life. It is your textbook for every class. Let's look at James 1:2-4 and study it one phrase at a time. James 1:2: *"Consider it pure joy, my brothers, whenever you face trials of many kinds."*

Pure joy? Are we masochists? Are we supposed to enjoy pain? NO. It doesn't say we have to FEEL joy; it says we are to CONSIDER IT joy. The Greek word translated, "Consider it' is not just a passive thought. It carries the idea of a chief or a ruler who pronounces a verdict. The Greek word is *hegeomai* [hayg·eh·om·ahee]: 1. to lead, to rule, command, to have authority over: 2. to consider, deem, account, think.[1] It "denotes a belief resting not on one's inner feeling or sentiment, but on the due consideration of external grounds, and the weighing and comparing of facts."[2] This means it is not about feeling joy—it is about taking authority over the adversity and commanding it to be pure joy like a ruler commands his subject to obey.

3. Value character more than comfort. Who would you rather have in your life...someone who values comfort more than character? Or character over comfort? A person of character is far more pleasant to be around than a person who values only his or her own comfort. We "count it all joy" because Christ-like character is our highest value; and it runs counter culture to American society, which values comfort over character.

I referred earlier to a visit to my dermatologist about a suspicious spot on my left arm. The treatment was spraying it with short bursts of freezing liquid nitrogen. I couldn't really feel it and was glad she was getting rid of it and other abnormal looking spots. How much better it is to remove pre-cancerous lesions before they become cancerous later! Some character flaws are pre-cancerous and need to be dealt with before they cause problems later.

James 1:3: says: *"because you know that the testing of your faith develops perseverance."* Perseverance is a Christ-like characteristic that is key to developing other Christ-like characteristics. Perseverance is highly valuable. Some people say, "Don't pray for patience because you will get more problems!" They have the wrong perspective. Problems are needed to develop our end goal of Christ-like character. Problems help us develop perseverance, and perseverance is the important key to maturity in Christ and completeness of character. We see in James 1:4: *"Perseverance must finish its work so that you may be mature and complete, not lacking anything."* Perseverance develops Christ-like character, but you and I must ALLOW perseverance to do its work. We must learn to …

4. <u>Cooperate with perseverance rather than complain.</u>

These are our choices: cooperate or complain. When we cooperate with perseverance, we become more mature and complete, not lacking anything. The Greek word for "mature" is *teleios* [tel·i·os]: brought to its end, finished, complete, full grown, adult, of full age, mature.[3]

Maturity is like a ripe red apple. It is full-grown. It is *teleios*. But an unripened apple is not *teleios*. It needs more time. God wants us to be *teleios*, mature. If you bite into a ripe apple, it has a crisp, sweet, delicious taste. If you bite into an unripened apple, it's more sour tasting. When our character is not mature, then the world gets a sour taste of what being a Christian is.

The Greek word for "mature" is *holokleros* [hol·ok·lay·ros]: complete in all its parts, in no part wanting or unsound, complete, entire, whole, without blemish or defect, complete in all respects, consummate.[4] A *holokleros* apple is whole, complete, and sound. A rotten apple is not *holokleros*. God wants us to be whole and holy.

God is the ultimate "fix-it" man. He can take anything broken and make it whole. He can take junk and make something good, something useful—something beautiful out of it! He is the King of Restoration. He can complete the incompleteness in our lives.

When we cooperate with perseverance, God uses it to make us like a ripe (*teleios*), whole (*holokleros*) apple—mature and complete, lacking nothing!

Five Sources of Adversity

Some folks blame every adversity on either God or Satan. Usually, if the situation resolves into good, they praise God. If not what they want, they blame Satan. Their theology is too simplistic. I think adversity can come from five sources.

1. Self We bring a lot of adversity on ourselves by doing stupid things or making bad choices. They can be fairly innocent actions like being disorganized or being chronically late. Sinful actions can allow negativity into our lives. When God says something is sinful, He's trying to keep us from negative consequences. When you break God's laws, you are really breaking yourself.

The Bible teaches *"You reap what you sow."* When you sow seeds of lying, then you reap a harvest of people who don't trust you. If you sow seeds of meanness, you will reap a harvest of people paying you back. If you sow a lot of sinful and selfish seeds, don't blame God when the harvest comes in!

If you decide to eat too much candy and drink too many sodas, you're going to get cavities! It's not God, it's not the devil—it's you. I asked four-year-old Jeremy who was recently in my office, "Jeremy, what kind of food causes cavities?" He said, "Eating all that chicken and stuff!" He didn't have it quite right. Some of us don't understand quite right either, and we can bring on our own adversity.

Pastor Jerome Hancock, says, "Learn from the mistakes of others because you don't have time enough to make them all yourself." God's way is to learn wisdom from others. The Bible is—wisdom from God about the best way to live! God didn't design your head to be pounded against a tree. Woodpeckers' brains were designed to withstand continuous impact, but yours wasn't. So stop pounding your head against the same old trees. Learn to stop putting yourself through needless adversity.

2. Life Accidents, bad health, mechanical breakdowns, and job losses all happen to Christians, too. We don't live in an insolated cocoon from the adversities of life. Ecclesiastes 9:11: *"...time and chance happen to them all."* Stuff happens. When Hurricane Isabel came through central Virginia, a tree hit my house. When it happened, I didn't take it personally. I didn't think God was punishing me. I don't think it was God or Satan; I think it was Isabel because *"Time and chance happen to us all."* My advice to you is this: Stop asking "why" questions. We drive ourselves crazy asking "why" questions because often times we can't figure things out. This world is not heaven. This is a fallen world messed up by sin, Satan, and selfishness. Sooner or later, life gives you and me adversity. Your body is breaking down right now: disease, cholesterol, free radicals, ultraviolet radiation, triglycerides—they're all ganging up on you!

And no matter how many vitamins you take, how nutritious a diet you eat, how much you exercise, and how much plastic surgery you have, sooner or later you are going to lose! You're fighting a losing battle! But I've got good news for you.

A. This is not your final destination. One day your entire body is going to get an extreme makeover by God himself! The old song goes, "This world not my home. I'm just a passin' through."

B. God can make glad come out of bad. If life gives you lemons, GOD has a great lemonade recipe in Romans 8:28: *"And we know that in all things* (including the good the bad and the ugly!) *God works for the good of those who love him, who have been called according to his purpose"* (parentheses added). This is the great advantage we have as Christians. This is our hope! God can bring good out of bad, no matter what the adversity.

<u>**3. God**</u> God can enroll us in The University of Adversity. Adversity is often a test drive of our faith. In the Bible there are many examples of this in the lives of people like Joseph and Daniel. God brings adversity to test us and improve our character.

<u>**4. Others**</u> Other people can put us into adversity—sometimes good people, sometimes evil people. Often times testing can come from our own family and friends. God gives other people free will to make choices, and sometimes THEIR choices cause US adversity. Some will take advantage of your generosity or kindness. Sometimes even members of your own family will shun you. This is called persecution. 2 Timothy 3:12: *"Everyone who wants to live a godly life in Christ Jesus will be persecuted."*

Abdul Rahman made world headlines as an Afghan Christian who converted from Islam and was on trial to be executed for simply converting to Christianity. He's one of over 200 million believers who live in countries where they are persecuted for their faith. So if you get snubbed at work or by a family member, don't claim martyrdom. Deal with it. It's part of the package.

<u>5. Satan</u> Sometimes our adversity comes from Satan attacking our confidence in God. But to hear some Christians talk, their lives are one big battle, surviving one attack after another. They are binding evil spirits and rebuking demons left and right. I think Satan gets a lot more credit than he deserves. While it is true Satan's attacks are real, having witnessed them firsthand, I think to be

> *To be devil-focused means we are taking our focus away from God.*

"demon-focused" is a *Zoe* Zapper and is not God's plan for us. Scripture tells us: *"…Your enemy the devil prowls around like a roaring lion looking for someone to devour. Resist him, standing firm in the faith, because you know that your brothers throughout the world are undergoing the same kind of sufferings"* (1 Peter 5:8-9).

I think we need to recognize when Satan attacks, resist him, and get back to enjoying *Zoe* to the Max. To be devil-focused means we are taking our focus away from God. Let's keep our eyes on the winner. Focus on *"The King of Kings and Lord of Lords"* and remember: *"The God of peace will soon crush Satan under your feet"* (Romans 16:20).

I like Neil Anderson's approach to spiritual warfare. His "Freedom in Christ" teachings are based on walking in victory and living in truth. I recommend his book *Victory over Darkness*. He emphasizes believing and living the truth will keep Satan from staying because he is "the father of lies." Satan cannot remain where there are truth and light. If our focus is on walking in the truth

> *…believing and living the truth will keep Satan from staying because he is "the father of lies."*

and living in the light, then Satan has no permission to stay and will leave us for "softer targets." I have taken my small group through Anderson's *Steps to Freedom in Christ* and recommend the curriculum. The booklet lists ten steps through an inventory of your past and present activities, looking for possible satanic footholds. Each step ends with a confession of truth and renunciation of the possible lies you may have knowingly, or unknowingly, embraced. He helps scan the disk of your life for possible viruses found in past hurtful activities and relationships, ending with a prayer of release and forgiveness. I like to think of it as a "just in case" measure because *"...the truth will set you free"* (John 8:32).

Every attack of Satan is also an opportunity to glorify God! It's an opportunity to show God how much you love Him and turn the tables on Satan! What he designs for pulling us away from God, we can turn around as an opportunity to draw closer to Him!

Don't Ask "Why?" Ask "What?"

In the University of Adversity, it is best to not ask "why?" questions but ask "what?" questions. When we try to figure out why things are happening, we can get frustrated. It is much better to ask "what?" questions. Questions like, "WHAT can I learn? WHAT can change in me? WHAT do I need to do?" Or ask "how" questions like, "How can God use this situation? How can I grow through this adversity?" It really doesn't matter from where the adversity comes—our God is able to make glad out of bad. God's lemonade recipe works for lemons from any tree. So the best thing to do is work your adversity. Use The University of Adversity to your benefit. Pass your class and upgrade your character. The Verizon telephone company has a great slogan: Make progress every day. I like that. Turn every proving session into an improving session!

Stuck in the Muck

The alternative to growing is griping. When we gripe, we don't make much progress toward maturity. When we fight perseverance instead of cooperate with it, we don't get to mature our character and become complete, lacking nothing. We stay stuck in the muck of static and stagnant character.

I was raised in the country on a small farm in Louisa County, Virginia. We had a dozen or so chickens with a rooster or two. They did the morning crowing like you see portrayed on movies and TV. We also had a large garden, some pigs and even a pony for a while. The farm animal we had the longest time was a milk cow named Elsie (apologies to my good friend Elsie Koolhaus). Elsie was our milking cow. My chore was to milk Elsie every evening. The worst thing about milking was when "nature called" on Elsie. She would plop out a pile of fresh pies, and I don't mean chocolate pies either! There's nothing like the smell of freshly made cow pies to clean out your sinuses!

In the wintertime, Elsie would spend a lot of time in the barn making pies. Day after day of pie making during the winter months would create a pit of manure about four feet wide, twelve feet long, and a foot deep. I remember one time I decided, for some reason, to walk around the posterior end of Elsie, and suddenly my shoes sank deep into the manure pit until I was literally "stuck in the muck." There is no feeling quite like getting stuck in a foot of slimy cow manure. There was no easy way out—falling backward was not good, and falling forward was not good. With no one there to help me, I had no choice but to crawl out on my hands and knees.

When it comes to character development, some of you are stuck in the muck of your stagnant character. If some of you would be honest with yourself, you would have to admit your attitude stinks. And the way you treat other people stinks. Your character is stuck in the muck. The good news is when you're stuck in the muck of who you are, you don't have to fall on your hands and knees and crawl out. I'm glad to report to you God is standing ready to reach down a helping hand and do a vertical rescue. He's good at getting people unstuck from their own muck. Psalm 121:1-3: *"I lift up my eyes to the hills— where does my help come from? My help comes from the Lord, the Maker of heaven and earth. He will not let your foot slip."*

Chapter 35:
"The Perfect Storm"

Even with The University of Adversity in mind as a reality of life, some days are so bad nothing seems to make sense. There are a few days when "everything" goes wrong at the same time. Like the movie *"The Perfect Storm,"* sometimes bad circumstances, poor health, frayed emotions, and evil people seem to gang up on us.

This past week I had one of those "Perfect Storm" days. Every evening, Valerie and I were involved in a Neighborhood Bible Club, one of twenty clubs our church sponsored all over the county as our version of Vacation Bible School. My dental practice schedule was extremely packed after returning from family vacation. My cell phone had drowned in the ocean waters, and the replacement phone was not coming in until Friday. Then the electrical power went off momentarily at my main office and damaged the computer at the front desk. My receptionist Ginger was flustered—the charts were stacking up, and Ginger's work was backing up. I thought reinstalling the software on Wednesday would work, but it didn't. The charts kept stacking up. I gave the whole situation to God and focused on my work. Later, I received a difficult phone call from my oral surgeon about one of my teenaged patients who had a rare gum disease likely to cause loss of a number of his teeth. Then another patient called to let me know she was not pleased with the color of a crown I had recently delivered, which meant I would have to make it all over again. Oh, did I mention my thumb got jammed at the beach?

Thursday I installed new dental software on my laptop and used my backup data to get Ginger back to work again! Praise the Lord. But I still couldn't check my email or do my online banking. It took Ginger all day to update the laptop computer with all the information from the previous days. Meanwhile, one of my "strange" dental families came in with their seven children, causing a lot of stress with kids running loose and coming in and out of the waiting room. I walked past Ginger's desk in the midst of this and mumbled to her,

"You are now witnessing the grace of God working in my life!" Later, I had to inform the parent of my young patient about the rare gum disease. After several other phone calls, I was very behind schedule and had to work through lunch to catch up. By the time our Neighborhood Bible Club ended, Valerie and I were really tired and hungry. We pulled into a gas station to fill up on the way home, and guess what? The van wouldn't start! "What next?" I thought, "This is too much, Lord." It was "The Perfect Storm." Did we have jumper cables in the back? No, of course not! We had jumper cables in EVERY OTHER vehicle, but not in the van! It was a very bad day. I shook my head and thought to myself, "I am not feeling *Zoe* to the Max right now! Lord, I need your help." I didn't have my cell phone to call for help; fortunately, however Valerie had hers. She called my daughter Rebekah, who was nearby. Rebekah didn't have jumper cables in her car either! By then I was in a "whatever!" attitude. We walked across the road to an auto supply store and bought TWO sets of jumper cables, one for each vehicle. Fortunately, the van started right up, and we made it home and flopped in bed, dead tired.

We have all had "Perfect Storm" days. In retrospect, my actions were pretty well self-controlled, and I was glad for the character God has developed in me to give "grace under fire." I had nothing of which to be ashamed, but I definitely did NOT enjoy myself most of the day and did NOT feel like saying, "I'm the happiest man in the world."

Even during "Perfect Storms," however, we don't have to "lose it" and throw a temper tantrum. Graceful endurance is the minimum expectation for a mature Christ follower. Sometimes the power of God is most evident when we don't "lose it" in the midst of bad days. We are certainly not masochists, who enjoy

> *Graceful endurance is the minimum expectation for a mature Christ follower.*

bad days or are emotionally disconnected from reality. The Bible says there will be days when, *"We are hard pressed on every side, but not crushed; perplexed, but not in despair; persecuted, but not abandoned; struck down, but not destroyed"* (2 Corinthians 4:8-9).

When a bad day threatens to overwhelm you, the power of the Spirit can help you stabilize yourself. Try to calm yourself and realize God knows where you are and knows all about your situation. Getting flustered really doesn't help anything. Right now, as I write this section, I am sitting on the steps of my office, locked out of my daughter Rebekah's car—the only transportation option I have to get home. I have just been traumatized three times by her car's alarm system, which goes off every time I unlock it with my key. I reminded her to disarm the alarm, but she forgot. It is 8 o'clock in the evening, and I am sitting here waiting for her to arrive to "push the clicky button" and disarm the alarm system. I have two choices: Focus on being upset at her and the inconvenience, or accept the situation and make the best of it. I decided to sit down and make the best of it by doing some writing. After all, Rebekah is more important than this inconvenience. I'm not sure what "good" will come out of this, but I will just sit here and sip on God's lemonade (Romans 8:28) while I wait.

Chapter 36: Entering the Fog Zone

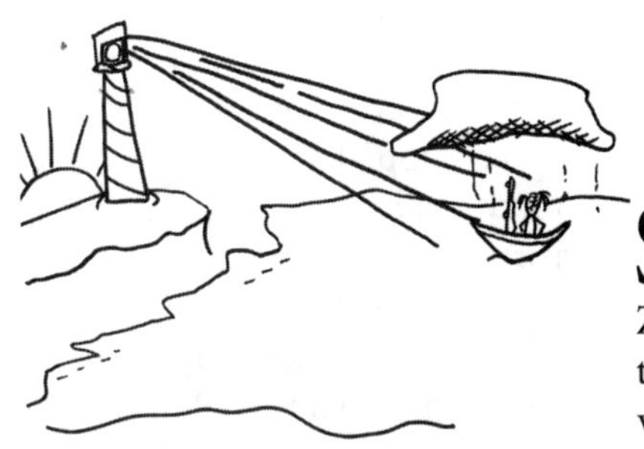

Sometimes it's not the bad things that knock you out of the *Zoe* Zone. Sometimes it's the good things. It can be a good project like writing this book. I have found myself jumping into writing, morning after morning, and inadvertently allowing this to be a substitute for really pursuing intimacy with God. Or it can be something less spiritual and more stupid keeping me up too late. Then I have trouble getting up and connecting well with God the next morning. A couple days of not putting in the "fuel" of intimacy with God will, naturally, cause my passion level to lower. Then I miss the "sweetness level" and, instead, feel the weariness or boredom start creeping in like a fog. Rather than staying in the *Zoe* Zone, I find myself in the "Fog Zone." When I realize this, I begin to readjust my priorities and renew intimacy. Sometimes, however, the fog doesn't lift immediately; I wish it did. I wish I could just say, "Lord, I'm back," and immediately see the Son rise and burn away the fog, but it doesn't work like that.

Building back the "sweetness level" begins with repentance. I tell the Holy Spirit I am sorry for pushing Him aside and making other things a priority above Him. I return to pursuing Him with my whole heart and open up His Word. I've found it takes three elements to build back the "sweetness":

<u>1. Prayer</u>—Seek God with your whole, hungry heart until you know you are reconnected. Sometimes journaling helps me here.

<u>2. Word</u>—Dig and search until you find the "Manna" from God's Word you need to lift your spirit.

<u>3. Persistence</u>—Sometimes you've got to do the above for a while before you sense a breakthrough to the "sweetness" level. *Zoe* to the Max is a romance. It's a love affair between you and God. Because you have decided to get back close with God doesn't mean He must "snap to attention." There are times when God deliberately withholds the "sweetness" level because He is disciplining me. He is

showing me what life would be like without intimacy with Him.

Many Christians settle for a more or less mechanical relationship with God. They read a devotional reading. They pray a little prayer and go about their daily routine. They go to church as usual, but the touch of "sweetness" is not there. They've slipped into the "Fog Zone" of religion. Instead of talking about what God is teaching them, they talk about the weather or sports or whatever. It's easier. It's more manageable because it doesn't take much heart. Religious fog is easier than the *Zoe* Zone because religion only takes only a few obligatory actions—not the heart. Religious fog doesn't need a new "word from the Lord" or bubbling joy. People in the "Fog Zone" look to the church service to make them feel better because they have lost their own passion for the "sweetness level." They find themselves looking to old habits for excitement. They look to TV or the movies, sports or a "good" book, work or new possessions, or whatever. Living in religious fog makes them susceptible to stumbling into temptation and worldliness.

Don't stay in the "Fog Zone!" Get back in the "*Zoe* Zone!"

Chapter 37: Tsunami of Hope

Hope. Hope is the result of staying in the *Zoe* Zone. Sometimes when I meet with God in my *mone*, I become overwhelmed with a fresh wave of hope! Here's an example from my journal entry: "Thank you for your joy and peace and the overflowing hope. That's what I'm feeling is hope! Just the optimistic feeling this is going to be a great day, I can't stop smiling. Tears are rolling down my cheeks, as the God of hope is overflowing me with hope by the power of the Holy Spirit!" Wow! That's the way I want to live!

Zoe to the Max involves being hit by an occasional tsunami of hope. Tsunami means "a long high wave caused by a disturbance."[1]

What is the disturbance causing a tsunami of hope to overwhelm us? The Greek word for "hope" is *elpis* [el·pece], and its primary root means "to anticipate, usually with pleasure, the expectation of good."[2] I sum it up with the word *optimism*. Hope is the optimistic outlook because of expected good. It is the positive anticipation that God is going to make a difference and He will make good things come our way in the future.

We've learned *Zoe* to the Max requires dealing with our PAST and then fully enjoying our PRESENT. Now we add in hope which covers our FUTURE! Hope is one of the lasting virtues listed in 1 Corinthians 13:13: *"And now these three remain: faith, hope and love. But the greatest of these is love."* Other things will fade, but these three will remain:

Faith—believing God

Hope—expecting good from God

Love—loving God and others

Consider faith and love are both listed as a fruit of the Spirit in Galatians 5:22-23, but hope is not listed. Interesting! It is a lasting virtue, but not a fruit of the Spirit. Why? I think it is because hope is the RESULT of living the *Zoe*-kind of life God intends. His Spirit ruling in you changes your attitude to a hopeful attitude and changes your outlook to a hopeful outlook. Hope elevates the altitude of your attitude! It changes the way you see things. You begin to see things from God's perspective.

Whenever I take a plane flight, I am always amazed at how my perspective changes as the plane climbs in altitude. The cars and mansions, previously so impressive, become very tiny as we begin to see an entire county in one view. Those small people cannot be seen any more. Did they shrink? No—we now have a higher perspective. That's what *Zoe* does for us. It gives us the higher perspective of hope.

God of Hope

The most fabulous verse I have found about hope is Romans 15:13. I want to break it down, phrase by phrase, so I can show you all the good stuff. It begins by stating God is the *"God of hope... ."* He is the God OF optimism; it is part of His nature. If you are looking for optimism—look no further; you have found the author of optimism! *Zoe* to the Max includes being filled with an optimistic attitude because we are filled with and transformed by the God of optimism! This God of optimism wants to fill us because we don't always have a lot of hope naturally. He wants to fill us with hope. He is a giving God!

But that's not all—let's look further and see what else the God of hope has in store for us. Romans 15:13: *"The God of hope fill you with ALL JOY..."* (emphasis added). Wow! The God of optimism wants to fill you and me with ALL JOY. That's a lot of joy—in quantity and quality. It's not most joy or a lot of joy but ALL joy!

But there's still more! Verse 13 continues: *"The God of hope fill you with all joy AND PEACE ..."* (emphasis added). Think of it! We not only get filled with ALL joy but also filled with ALL peace! Peace of heart and mind. All kinds of peace! No wonder the result is *Zoe* to the Max! Why don't we see having a daily time with the God of optimism is so critical to experiencing joy and peace? Our problem is we want to do a twenty-second NASCAR type pit stop with God. No wonder we experience *Zoe* to the Mini because that's about all the time we give to our pit-stop/drive-through/snack-time with God.

The key to receiving the joy and peace is found in the next

phrase: *"...as you trust in Him..."* (Romans 15:13). Trust is what pleases God (Hebrews 11:6), so He is not going to just dump joy and peace on us automatically when we wake up. He wants to see some trust. Trust (same Greek word as faith) in the Bible is always a belief demonstrated by an action. Faith is not just the confidence or belief something is true. Faith always requires an action demonstrating our confidence. For example, when the Bible says our salvation comes through faith in Christ, it means more than just intellectual agreement that Jesus is the Son of God. It is demonstrated through the actions of inviting Christ to be our personal Savior, followed by actions showing a willingness to follow Christ as a lifestyle. Therefore, when we are trusting God to fill us with joy and peace, there must be an action demonstrating that trust. In this case, trust is demonstrated by the act of meeting together with God in our *mone* and also trusting the God of optimism to fill us with all joy and all peace. Sometimes I will literally open my arms wide toward the heavens like a satellite receiver and thank God for filling me with joy and peace. I keep my "satellite" in the receiving mode as an act of trust until I sense the infilling of God.

All of this is the "disturbance" creating the tsunami at the end of Romans 15:13: *"...SO THAT you may overflow with hope..."* (emphasis added). The result of the God of optimism filling us with all joy and all peace as we trust in Him is a tsunami of optimism! Hallelujah! The joy and peace triggered by the underwater earthquake of trust, creates a tsunami of hope overwhelming us. What a generous God! He fills us with so much hope it engulfs us! God wants us to experience so much hope until it gushes out of us and blesses others. And this is when witnessing is the natural overflow of hope.

Hope Causes Curiosity

*"...Always be prepared to give an answer to everyone who asks you to give the **reason for the hope** that you have"* (1 Peter 3:15, *emphasis added).* The hope, the optimism we have, is evident to others and makes them curious. The optimistic way in which we live and react and talk is apparent to other people around us. When they comment on our optimism, we have the opportunity to witness for God. That's why we are *"to be ready to give an answer,"* because hope is a rare commodity in this negative world. Jesus said, *"You are the light of the world. A city on a hill cannot be hidden"* (Matthew 5:14).

Optimism shines out like a spotlight and cannot be hidden!

My dental patients will often comment on my cheerfulness or they hear me singing or humming. It gives me an opportunity to share my source of optimism and *Zoe*. Even the tellers at my bank notice the hope. One of them told me the other day, "I love the way you're always in a cheerful mood." I remember a few weeks ago on a Friday she said, "I see you're happy because it's a Friday." "Oh, yes," I said, "I'm happy for every day, not just Fridays. Do you realize if you're only happy on the weekends, you're missing 70% of your life?" If you want to be a witness for God, seek to overflow with hope, live *Zoe* to the Max, and people WILL notice.

Not only does hope give us opportunities to witness, but hope brings us joy. Romans 12:12: *"Be joyful in hope... ."* Apparently, not only does joy bring hope, but hope is another source of joy. What a wonderful mystery!

Hope also keeps us from being disappointed. Romans 5:5: *"...hope does not disappoint us... ."* When we get disappointing news, we can remind ourselves of our hope and ward off the disappointment. Remember: "When things go wrong, don't go with it." When things get disappointing, don't go with it. Even with disappointing news, hope can still anticipate the good showing up later, even if later means heaven.

It is God's will that we anticipate the future with pleasure and have an expectation of good, all made possible by the last phrase of Romans 15:13: *"...by the power of the Holy Spirit."* It is only by the supernatural power of God we can experience this tsunami of hope! We are the most optimistic of all people because we are filled with the God of optimism—the God of hope!

Zoe Hope

The top of my head about came off when I found this next verse because it links together *Zoe* and hope. 1 Peter 1:3: *"Praise be to the God and Father of our Lord Jesus Christ! In his great mercy he has given us new birth into a living [Zoe] hope through the resurrection of Jesus Christ from the dead"* (parentheses added).

Zoe: Enjoying the life you are living now
Hope: Anticipating good things will happen

Hope is awesome, but "*Zoe* hope" is exponentially awesome! *Zoe* hope is optimism alive with vitality both now and forever! When you have *Zoe* hope, you have an energetic, positive, and optimistic outlook. You don't dread the future because you know you have *Zoe* now and optimism for *Zoe* in the future! You can expect good things will happen because you have living optimism! No wonder each one of us can say, "I'm the happiest person in the world!"

But there's more in 1 Peter 1:3:

1. This Zoe hope comes out of "His great mercy." It is not out of what we deserve or what we can earn. God gives us *Zoe* hope out of His mercy—out of the benevolence in His heart. Since it comes from His GREAT mercy, it is available for everyone, AND there is plenty of it. It is not reserved for the wise, the rich, and the religious. *Zoe* hope is for average people like you and me!

2. It has been "given" to us as a result of our new birth. We are born into this *Zoe* hope—born again. We were...

Misshaped by earth
Shaped by birth
Reshaped by New Birth

This reshaping is a continuing process beginning with our New Birth and gives us an opportunity to experience *Zoe* hope for the rest of our lives!

3. This Zoe hope is "through the resurrection of Jesus Christ from the dead." It comes out of supernatural resurrection power. Jesus was dead—no life in Him. It was all over. But resurrection power changed all that! It is the power to bring *Zoe* out of death— hope out of hopelessness.

—No matter how "dead" you may feel,

—No matter how dead your circumstances may be,

—No matter how hopeless your life may seem,

Resurrection power can change the situation! It can bring *Zoe* hope from the dead! Resurrection power is more powerful than any force, including death. Thus, the headlines read: No matter what your circumstances are, you can receive New Birth into a vital, *Zoe* hope through resurrection power because of God's great mercy! Wow! I'm ready for anything! Woo who!

Hope "Now and Later"

1 Peter 1:4 takes us on into eternity. We have *Zoe* now and *Zoe* hope for a never-ending future, *"...an inheritance that can never perish, spoil or fade—kept in heaven for you."* When I was a kid, there was a candy named "Now and Later." It had a taffy-like consistency to last a long time. *Zoe* hope is like that. It will be good now, and it will be good later all the way into eternity! When the Bible talks about hope, it is primarily in reference to our hope of eternal life and ultimate deliverance by God. Jesus said in John 17:3: *"This is eternal zoe, that they may know me...and Jesus Christ."* Knowing Jesus produces *Zoe*. Zoe comes from knowing—experiential knowledge of God and Jesus beginning now. Since we have a "Now and Later" hope, we are getting to know Him now, AND we anticipate knowing and living with Him in heaven throughout all eternity.

Until then, *"Surely goodness and love will follow me all the days of my life, and I will dwell in the house of the Lord forever"* (Psalm 23:6). We are assured goodness and love will follow us ALL the days of our life! What cause for hope and optimism! We need to be looking behind us for the goodness and love following us. The promise is it will continue as long as we live. What a source of optimism we have in God! We are living eternal *Zoe* now!

Remote Broadcast of the Eternal Party

We tend to divide this future from the present, but that's because the reality of time is our only frame of reference. We are stuck in a "time warp" now, but God is not. He has been enjoying a party with His family for eons. When we are born into His family, we get to join the party. Jesus gave us a window into this eternal party in Luke 15 when he told the three stories of the lost sheep, the lost coin, and the lost son. After the lost were found, there was a party: *"I tell you that in the same way there will be more **rejoicing in heaven** over one sinner who repents than over ninety-nine righteous persons who do not need to repent"* (Luke 15:7, emphasis added).

*"In the same way, I tell you, there is **rejoicing in the presence of the angels of God** over one sinner who repents"* (Luke 15:10, emphasis added).

"'Bring the fattened calf and kill it. Let's have a feast and celebrate. For this son of mine was dead and is alive again; he was lost

and is found.' So they began to celebrate" (Luke 15:23-24, emphasis added).

We join the eternal celebration party when we are found by God. The eternal party is being broadcast live from heaven, and we can begin enjoying it now; soon, however we will get un-stuck from this time warp and join it "live"! Soon we will be "there." *"Now we see but a poor reflection as in a mirror; then we shall see face to face. Now I know in part; then I shall know fully, even as I am fully known"* (1 Corinthians 13:12).

We experience the party through a mirror for now, but later it will be face to face. We experience only parts of the party now, but later on, we will fully experience Him! Soon we will be released from our time warp, put away the mirrors, and join it "live". 1 Corinthians 13:13 continues: *"And now these three remain: faith, hope and love. But the greatest of these is love."* Hope will endure eternally as the "live party." We will continue to trust (faith) and continue to be optimistic (hope) and continue to love throughout all of eternity!!!!

You and I will be blessed now and later if we will believe all the *Zoe* to the Max Jesus has provided for us now before we see it with our eyes later. Jesus told doubting Thomas in John 20:29: *"...Because you have seen me, you have believed; blessed are those who have not seen and yet have believed."* He was talking to you and me there, too. We are part of the blessed group who has not seen, yet we can believe! I think heaven is going to be one huge surprise for us as we realize all we could have experienced—"If we had only known." I believe God will reply, "I told you, but you wouldn't believe."

"I Coulda' had a V8!"

I don't know if you remember the V8 vegetable juice TV commercials showing the guy slapping his forehead with the open palm of his hand exclaiming, "I coulda had a V8!" I think heaven will begin with one huge forehead-slapping session, and you and I saying, "We coulda' had *Zoe* to the Max!"

Blessed are you who are reading this book right now and believing the words Christ said, *"I have come that you might have Zoe and have it to the Max."* Will you join me and many others who are committed to pursuing *Zoe* to the Max for the rest of our lives? Jesus said, *"Blessed are those who have not seen and yet have believed"*

(John 20:29)! Blessed are you who believe *Zoe* to the Max is for you beginning now and continuing in ever-increasing degrees of glory as you are renewed day by day, until one day we give up mirrors and get magnifiers! Hallelujah!

"...Now I know in part; then I shall know fully, even as I am fully known" (1 Corinthians 13:12). One day we get full knowledge and full experience of the partial enjoyment of God we have already been experiencing! This partial experience will be fully revealed and enjoyed throughout all of eternity!

But let me ask you, "How partial is that partial experience?" I don't think He meant only 1 or 2%. I studied the Greek word for "part" used in 1 Corinthians 13:12 and found that it is doesn't mean a small part. It is translated as "portion or divided part."[3] It's the same word that the "prodigal son" used when he asked for his portion of his father's inheritance saying, *"'Father, give me my share of the estate.' So he divided his property between them"* (Luke 15:12). His riches were divided "between them." It was a sizable portion because Luke 15:13 says he: *"squandered his wealth in wild living."* (emphasis added). How much wealthier is our Heavenly Father than the prodigal's father? So how much larger might be the "portion or part" of our knowing? The "partial" experience of God that is available to us is HUGE!

I believe that when Jesus said, "*Zoe* to the Max," He meant it to be a sizable portion, a sizable share of *Zoe* that we can experience NOW and, even more, throughout all of eternity! Don't you want to experience ALL the *Zoe* that Jesus meant for you to experience?

I am finishing writing this book on Easter Sunday, and I am reminded that the God who brings life out of death offers us a *Zoe* hope! Our hope is nothing less than the fullest measure possible! Make it your aim...right now...to experience all the *Zoe* that you can for the rest of your life!

Zoe—beyond the norm, superabundant surplus,
exceeding the usual!

Zoe to the Max!

Endnotes

Introduction

[1] Strong, J. (1996). *The exhaustive concordance of the Bible: Showing every word of the text of the common English version of the canonical books and every occurrence of each word in regular order.* (electronic ed.) (G5456). Ontario: Woodside Bible Fellowship.

Chapter 1

[1] Strong, J. (1996). *The exhaustive concordance of the Bible: Showing every word of the text of the common English version of the canonical books and every occurrence of each word in regular order.* (electronic ed.) (G2222). Ontario: Woodside Bible Fellowship.
[2] Zodhiates, S. (2000, c1992, c1993). *The complete word study dictionary: New Testament* (electronic ed.) (G2222). Chattanooga, TN: AMG Publishers.

Chapter 3

[1] Strong, J. (1996). *The exhaustive concordance of the Bible: Showing every word of the text of the common English version of the canonical books, and every occurrence of each word in regular order.* (electronic ed.) (G4053). Ontario: Woodside Bible Fellowship.
[2] Strong, J. (1996). *The exhaustive concordance of the Bible: Showing every word of the text of the common English version of the canonical books, and every occurrence of each word in regular order.* (electronic ed.) (G5463). Ontario: Woodside Bible Fellowship.
[3] Strong, J. (1996). *The exhaustive concordance of the Bible: Showing every word of the text of the common English version of the canonical books, and every occurrence of each word in regular order.* (electronic ed.) (G3107). Ontario: Woodside Bible Fellowship
[4] Strong, J. (1996). *The exhaustive concordance of the Bible: Showing every word of the text of the common English version of the canonical books, and every occurrence of each word in regular order.* (electronic ed.) (G21). Ontario: Woodside Bible Fellowship

Chapter 4

[1] Strong, J. (1996). *The exhaustive concordance of the Bible: Showing every word of the text of the common English version of the canonical books, and every occurrence of each word in regular order.* (electronic ed.) (G4077). Ontario: Woodside Bible Fellowship.
[2] Strong, J. (1996). *The exhaustive concordance of the Bible: Showing every word of the text of the common English version of the canonical books, and every occurrence of each word in regular order.* (electronic ed.) (G242). Ontario: Woodside Bible Fellowship.
[3] Ibid (G4215).

Chapter 7

[1] Strong, J. (1996). *The exhaustive concordance of the Bible: Showing every word of the text of the common English version of the canonical books, and every occurrence of each word in regular order.* (electronic ed.) (G2322). Ontario: Woodside Bible Fellowship.

Chapter 8

[1] Strong, J. (1996). *The exhaustive concordance of the Bible: Showing every word of the text of the common English version of the canonical books, and every occurrence of each word in regular order.* (electronic ed.) (G4735). Ontario: Woodside Bible Fellowship.

[2] Strong, J. (1996). *The exhaustive concordance of the Bible: Showing every word of the text of the common English version of the canonical books, and every occurrence of each word in regular order.* (electronic ed.) (G1238). Ontario: Woodside Bible Fellowship.

Chapter 11

[1] Strong, J. (1996). *The exhaustive concordance of the Bible: Showing every word of the text of the common English version of the canonical books, and every occurrence of each word in regular order.* (electronic ed.) (G3737). Ontario: Woodside Bible Fellowship.

[2] *Theological dictionary of the New Testament.* 1964-c1976. Vols. 5-9 edited by Gerhard Friedrich. Vol. 10 compiled by Ronald Pitkin. (G. Kittel, G. W. Bromiley & G. Friedrich, Ed.) (electronic ed.) (Vol. 4, Page 579). Grand Rapids, MI: Eerdmans.

[3] Kittel, G., Friedrich, G., & Bromiley, G. W. (1995, c1985). *Theological dictionary of the New Testament.* Translation of: Theologisches Worterbuch zum Neuen Testament. (Page 582). Grand Rapids, Mich.: W.B. Eerdmans.

[4] Strong, J. (1996). *The exhaustive concordance of the Bible: Showing every word of the text of the common English version of the canonical books, and every occurrence of each word in regular order.* (electronic ed.) (G3306). Ontario: Woodside Bible Fellowship.

[5] Strong, J. (1996). *The exhaustive concordance of the Bible: Showing every word of the text of the common English version of the canonical books, and every occurrence of each word in regular order.* (electronic ed.) (G3614). Ontario: Woodside Bible Fellowship.

[6] Strong, J. (1996). *The exhaustive concordance of the Bible: Showing every word of the text of the common English version of the canonical books, and every occurrence of each word in regular order.* (electronic ed.) (G5117). Ontario: Woodside Bible Fellowship.

[7] Strong, J. (1996). *The exhaustive concordance of the Bible: Showing every word of the text of the common English version of the canonical books, and every occurrence of each word in regular order.* (electronic ed.) (H5643). Ontario: Woodside Bible Fellowship.

[8] Strong, J. (1996). *The exhaustive concordance of the Bible: Showing every word of the test of the common English version of the canonical books, and every occurrence of each word in regular order.* (electronic ed.) (G1172). Ontario: Woodside Bible Fellowship.

[9] Strong, J. (1996). *The exhaustive concordance of the Bible: Showing every word of

the text of the common English version of the canonical books, and every occurrence of each word in regular order. (electronic ed.) (G1173). Ontario: Woodside Bible Fellowship.

[10] Strong, J. (1996). *The exhaustive concordance of the Bible: Showing every word of the text of the common English version of the canonical books, and every occurrence of each word in regular order.* (electronic ed.) (G5315). Ontario: Woodside Bible Fellowship.

[11] Strong, J. (1996). *The exhaustive concordance of the Bible: Showing every word of the text of the common English version of the canonical books, and every occurrence of each word in regular order.* (electronic ed.) (G26). Ontario: Woodside Bible Fellowship.

[12] Strong, J. (1996). *The exhaustive concordance of the Bible: Showing every word of the test of the common English version of the canonical books, and every occurrence of each word in regular order.* (electronic ed.) (G2795). Ontario: Woodside Bible Fellowship.

[13] Strong, J. (1996). *The exhaustive concordance of the Bible: Showing every word of the test of the common English version of the canonical books, and every occurrence of each word in regular order.* (electronic ed.) (G1097). Ontario: Woodside Bible Fellowship

Chapter 12

[1] Strong, J. (1996). *The exhaustive concordance of the Bible: Showing every word of the text of the common English version of the canonical books, and every occurrence of each word in regular order.* (electronic ed.) (G4487). Ontario: Woodside Bible Fellowship.

[2] Strong, J. (1996). *The exhaustive concordance of the Bible: Showing every word of the text of the common English version of the canonical books, and every occurrence of each word in regular order.* (electronic ed.) (G3875). Ontario: Woodside Bible Fellowship.

[3] *Theological Dictionary of the New Testament.* 1964-c1976. Vols. 5-9 edited by Gerhard Friedrich. Vol. 10 compiled by Ronald Pitkin. (G. Kittel, G. W. Bromiley & G. Friedrich, Ed.) (electronic ed.) (Vol. 5, Page 800-802). Grand Rapids, MI: Eerdmans.

[4] Strong, J. (1996). *The exhaustive concordance of the Bible: Showing every word of the text of the common English version of the canonical books, and every occurrence of each word in regular order.* (electronic ed.) (G4851). Ontario: Woodside Bible Fellowship.

[5] Kittel, G., Friedrich, G., & Bromiley, G. W. (1995, c1985). *Theological Dictionary of the New Testament.* Translation of: Theologisches Worterbuch zum Neuen Testament. (Page 1255). Grand Rapids, Mich. W.B. Eerdmans.

Chapter 13

[1] Harris, R. L., Harris, R. L., Archer, G. L., & Waltke, B. K. (1999, c1980). *Theological Wordbook of the Old Testament* (electronic ed.) (Page 159). Chicago: Moody Press.

[2] Swanson, J. (1997). *Dictionary of Biblical Languages with Semantic Domains: Hebrew* (Old Testament) (electronic ed.) (HGK1635). Oak Harbor: Logos Research Systems, Inc.

[3] Harris, R. L., Harris, R. L., Archer, G. L., & Waltke, B. K. (1999, c1980). *Theological Wordbook of the Old Testament* (electronic ed.) (Page 879). Chicago: Moody Press.

[4] Strong, J. (1996). *The exhaustive concordance of the Bible: Showing every word of the text of the common English version of the canonical books, and every occurrence of each word in regular order.* (electronic ed.) (H8055). Ontario: Woodside Bible Fellowship.

[5] Strong, J. (1996). *The exhaustive concordance of the Bible: Showing every word of the text of the common English version of the canonical books, and every occurrence of each word in regular order.* (electronic ed.) (G5463). Ontario: Woodside Bible Fellowship.

[6] Strong, J. (1996). *The exhaustive concordance of the Bible: Showing every word of the text of the common English version of the canonical books, and every occurrence of each word in regular order.* (electronic ed.) (H5273). Ontario: Woodside Bible Fellowship.

Chapter 14

[1] Kittel, G., Friedrich, G., & Bromiley, G. W. (1995, c1985). *Theological dictionary of the New Testament.* Translation of: Theologisches Worterbuch zum Neuen Testament. (Page 207). Grand Rapids, Mich: W.B. Eerdmans.

[2] Strong, J. (1996). *The exhaustive concordance of the Bible: Showing every word of the text of the common English version of the canonical books, and every occurrence of each word in regular order.* (electronic ed.) (G1515). Ontario: Woodside Bible Fellowship.

[3] Ibid (G5432).

[4] Osbeck, K. W. (1990). *Amazing grace: 366 inspiring hymn stories for daily devotions.* Includes indexes. Grand Rapids, Mich.: Kregel Publications.

Chapter 16

[1] Swanson, J. (1997). *Dictionary of Biblical Languages with Semantic Domains: Hebrew* (Old Testament) (electronic ed.) (HGK3711). Oak Harbor: Logos Research Systems, Inc.

[2] From *Living Free in Christ* by Dr. Neil Anderson, Freedom in Christ Ministries, 491 E. Lambert Road, La Habra, California, 90631

Chapter 17

[1] Strong, J. (1996). *The exhaustive concordance of the Bible: Showing every word of the text of the common English version of the canonical books, and every occurrence of each word in regular order.* (electronic ed.) (G4200). Ontario: Woodside Bible Fellowship.

[2] Strong, J. (1996). *The exhaustive concordance of the Bible: Showing every word of the text of the common English version of the canonical books, and every occurrence of each word in regular order.* (electronic ed.) (G841). Ontario: Woodside Bible Fellowship.

[3] Strong, J. (1996). *The exhaustive concordance of the Bible: Showing every word of the text of the common English version of the canonical books, and every occurrence of each word in regular order.* (electronic ed.) (G846). Ontario: Woodside Bible Fellowship.

4 Strong, J. (1996). *The exhaustive concordance of the Bible: Showing every word of the text of the common English version of the canonical books, and every occurrence of each word in regular order.* (electronic ed.) (G714). Ontario: Woodside Bible Fellowship.

5 Strong, J. (1996). *The exhaustive concordance of the Bible: Showing every word of the text of the common English version of the canonical books, and every occurrence of each word in regular order.* (electronic ed.) (G714). Ontario: Woodside Bible Fellowship.

6 Strong, J. (1996). *The exhaustive concordance of the Bible: Showing every word of the text of the common English version of the canonical books, and every occurrence of each word in regular order.* (electronic ed.) (G2169). Ontario: Woodside Bible Fellowship.

7 Strong, J. (1996). *The exhaustive concordance of the Bible: Showing every word of the text of the common English version of the canonical books, and every occurrence of each word in regular order.* (electronic ed.) (G842). Ontario: Woodside Bible Fellowship.

8 Strong, J. (1996). *The exhaustive concordance of the Bible: Showing every word of the text of the common English version of the canonical books, and every occurrence of each word in regular order.* (electronic ed.) (G25, G26). Ontario: Woodside Bible Fellowship.

9 Strong, J. (1996). *The exhaustive concordance of the Bible: Showing every word of the text of the common English version of the canonical books, and every occurrence of each word in regular order.* (electronic ed.) (G5365). Ontario: Woodside Bible Fellowship.

10 Strong, J. (1996). *The exhaustive concordance of the Bible: Showing every word of the text of the common English version of the canonical books, and every occurrence of each word in regular order.* (electronic ed.) (G5384). Ontario: Woodside Bible Fellowship.

11 Strong, J. (1996). *The exhaustive concordance of the Bible: Showing every word of the text of the common English version of the canonical books, and every occurrence of each word in regular order.* (electronic ed.) (G696). Ontario: Woodside Bible Fellowship.

12 Swanson, J. (1997). *Dictionary of Biblical Languages with Semantic Domains : Hebrew* (Old Testament) (electronic ed.) (HGK6695). Oak Harbor: Logos Research Systems, Inc.

Chapter 18

1 Strong, J. (1996). *The exhaustive concordance of the Bible: Showing every word of the text of the common English version of the canonical books, and every occurrence of each word in regular order.* (electronic ed.) (G37). Ontario: Woodside Bible Fellowship.

Chapter 20

1 Strong, J. (1996). *The exhaustive concordance of the Bible: Showing every word of the text of the common English version of the canonical books, and every occurrence of each word in regular order.* (electronic ed.) (G2872). Ontario: Woodside Bible Fellowship.

2 Strong, J. (1996). *The exhaustive concordance of the Bible: Showing every word of*

the text of the common English version of the canonical books, and every occurrence of each word in regular order. (electronic ed.) (G2873). Ontario: Woodside Bible Fellowship.

[3] Strong, J. (1996). *The exhaustive concordance of the Bible: Showing every word of the text of the common English version of the canonical books, and every occurrence of each word in regular order.* (electronic ed.) (G5414). Ontario: Woodside Bible Fellowship.

[4] Strong, J. (1996). *The exhaustive concordance of the Bible: Showing every word of the text of the common English version of the canonical books, and every occurrence of each word in regular order.* (electronic ed.) (G373). Ontario: Woodside Bible Fellowship.

[5] Strong, J. (1996). *The exhaustive concordance of the Bible: Showing every word of the text of the common English version of the canonical books, and every occurrence of each word in regular order.* (electronic ed.) (H7673). Ontario: Woodside Bible Fellowship.

[6] *My thoughts about The Sabbath Day:* In the New Testament, the spiritual significance of the Sabbath Day was fulfilled in Christ's work on the cross, so we now live in a continual "Sabbath Day rest", because Christ has done the work of Salvation. The Sabbath Day was one of many spiritual rituals in the Old Testament (Temple sacrifices, circumcision, culinary rules, etc.). They were symbolic of Christ and fulfilled in Him—they foreshadowed things to come. This is discovered when you put together a study of Hebrews 10:1, Galatians 3:24-25, Colossians 2:16-17, Hebrews 4:1-10, Galatians 4:9-11, and Romans 14:4-6.

[7] Strong, J. (1996). *The exhaustive concordance of the Bible: Showing every word of the text of the common English version of the canonical books, and every occurrence of each word in regular order.* (electronic ed.) (G5543). Ontario: Woodside Bible Fellowship.

[8] Strong, J. (1996). *The exhaustive concordance of the Bible: Showing every word of the text of the common English version of the canonical books, and every occurrence of each word in regular order.* (electronic ed.) (G4904). Ontario: Woodside Bible Fellowship.

[9] Strong, J. (1996). *The exhaustive concordance of the Bible: Showing every word of the text of the common English version of the canonical books, and every occurrence of each word in regular order.* (electronic ed.) (G1645). Ontario: Woodside Bible Fellowship.

[10] Zodhiates, S. (2000, c1992, c1993). *The complete word study dictionary : New Testament* (electronic ed.) (G922). Chattanooga, TN: AMG Publishers.

[11] Strong, J. (1996). *The exhaustive concordance of the Bible: Showing every word of the text of the common English version of the canonical books, and every occurrence of each word in regular order.* (electronic ed.) (G2041). Ontario: Woodside Bible Fellowship.

[12] Strong, J. (1996). *The exhaustive concordance of the Bible: Showing every word of the text of the common English version of the canonical books, and every occurrence of each word in regular order.* (electronic ed.) (G1381). Ontario: Woodside Bible Fellowship.

Chapter 22

[1] Strong, J. (1996). *The exhaustive concordance of the Bible: Showing every word of the text of the common English version of the canonical books, and every occur-*

rence of each word in regular order. (electronic ed.) (G3528). Ontario: Woodside Bible Fellowship.

Chapter 23

[1] Strong, J. (1996). *The exhaustive concordance of the Bible: Showing every word of the text of the common English version of the canonical books, and every occurrence of each word in regular order.* (electronic ed.) (G3339). Ontario: Woodside Bible Fellowship.

[2] Strong, J. (1996). *The exhaustive concordance of the Bible: Showing every word of the text of the common English version of the canonical books, and every occurrence of each word in regular order.* (electronic ed.) (G421, G2487). Ontario: Woodside Bible Fellowship.

[3] Strong, J. (1996). *The exhaustive concordance of the Bible: Showing every word of the text of the common English version of the canonical books, and every occurrence of each word in regular order.* (electronic ed.) (G3466). Ontario: Woodside Bible Fellowship.

Chapter 24

[1] Strong, J. (1996). *The exhaustive concordance of the Bible: Showing every word of the text of the common English version of the canonical books, and every occurrence of each word in regular order.* (electronic ed.) (G341). Ontario: Woodside Bible Fellowship.

[2] Strong, J. (1996). *The exhaustive concordance of the Bible: Showing every word of the text of the common English version of the canonical books, and every occurrence of each word in regular order.* (electronic ed.) (G303). Ontario: Woodside Bible Fellowship.

[3] Strong, J. (1996). *The exhaustive concordance of the Bible: Showing every word of the text of the common English version of the canonical books, and every occurrence of each word in regular order.* (electronic ed.) (G5852). Ontario: Woodside Bible Fellowship.

[4] Strong, J. (1996). *The exhaustive concordance of the Bible: Showing every word of the text of the common English version of the canonical books, and every occurrence of each word in regular order.* (electronic ed.) (G3501). Ontario: Woodside Bible Fellowship.

[5] Kittel, G., Friedrich, G., & Bromiley, G. W. (1995, c1985). *Theological dictionary of the New Testament.* Translation of: Theologisches Worterbuch zum Neuen Testament. (119). Grand Rapids, Mich.: W.B. Eerdmans.

[6] Strong, J. (1996). *The exhaustive concordance of the Bible: Showing every word of the text of the common English version of the canonical books, and every occurrence of each word in regular order.* (electronic ed.) (G1746). Ontario: Woodside Bible Fellowship.

[7] Strong, J. (1996). *The exhaustive concordance of the Bible: Showing every word of the text of the common English version of the canonical books, and every occurrence of each word in regular order.* (electronic ed.) (G365). Ontario: Woodside Bible Fellowship.

[8] Strong, J. (1996). *The exhaustive concordance of the Bible: Showing every word of the text of the common English version of the canonical books, and every occurrence of each word in regular order.* (electronic ed.) (G3501). Ontario: Woodside Bible Fellowship.

[9] *Theological dictionary of the New Testament.* 1964-c1976. Vols. 5-9 edited by

Gerhard Friedrich. Vol. 10 compiled by Ronald Pitkin. (G. Kittel, G. W. Bromiley &
G. Friedrich, Ed.) (electronic ed.) (Vol. 4, Page 900). Grand Rapids, MI: Eerdmans.
[10] Strong, J. (1996). *The exhaustive concordance of the Bible: Showing every word of
the text of the common English version of the canonical books, and every occurrence
of each word in regular order.* (electronic ed.) (G4137). Ontario: Woodside Bible
Fellowship.

Chapter 25

[1] *Coffee Consumption and Risk of Type 2 Diabetes Mellitus*
An 11-Year Prospective Study of 28,812 Postmenopausal Women
By Mark A. Pereira, PhD; Emily D. Parker, MPH; Aaron R. Folsom, MD, Archives
of Internal Medicine. 2006;166:1311-1316.

Chapter 26

[1] Strong, J. (1996). *The exhaustive concordance of the Bible: Showing every word of
the text of the common English version of the canonical books, and every occurrence
of each word in regular order.* (electronic ed.) (G1433). Ontario: Woodside Bible
Fellowship.
[2] Strong, J. (1996). *The exhaustive concordance of the Bible: Showing every word of
the text of the common English version of the canonical books, and every occurrence
of each word in regular order.* (electronic ed.) (G1325). Ontario: Woodside Bible
Fellowship.

Chapter 30

[1] Strong, J. (1996). *The exhaustive concordance of the Bible: Showing every word of
the text of the common English version of the canonical books, and every occurrence
of each word in regular order.* (electronic ed.) (G3309). Ontario: Woodside Bible
Fellowship.
[2] Strong, J. (1996). *The exhaustive concordance of the Bible: Showing every word of
the text of the common English version of the canonical books, and every occurrence
of each word in regular order.* (electronic ed.) (G3307). Ontario: Woodside Bible
Fellowship.
[3] Wiersbe, W. W. (1997, c1992). *Wiersbe's expository outlines on the New
Testament* (Page 569). Wheaton, Ill.: Victor Books.

Chapter 34

[1] Strong, J. (1996). *The exhaustive concordance of the Bible: Showing every word of
the text of the common English version of the canonical books, and every occurrence
of each word in regular order.* (electronic ed.) (G2233). Ontario: Woodside Bible
Fellowship.
[2] Strong, J. (1996). *The exhaustive concordance of the Bible: Showing every word of
the text of the common English version of the canonical books, and every occurrence
of each word in regular order.* (electronic ed.) (G5837). Ontario: Woodside Bible
Fellowship.
[3] Strong, J. (1996). *The exhaustive concordance of the Bible: Showing every word of
the text of the common English version of the canonical books, and every occurrence

of each word in regular order. (electronic ed.) (G5046). Ontario: Woodside Bible Fellowship.

[4] Strong, J. (1996). *The exhaustive concordance of the Bible: Showing every word of the text of the common English version of the canonical books, and every occurrence of each word in regular order.* (electronic ed.) (G3648). Ontario: Woodside Bible Fellowship.

Chapter 37

[1] *Oxford Dictionary, Tenth Edition*

[2] Strong, J. (1996). *The exhaustive concordance of the Bible: Showing every word of the text of the common English version of the canonical books, and every occurrence of each word in regular order.* (electronic ed.) (G1680). Ontario: Woodside Bible Fellowship.

[3] Strong, J. (1996). *The exhaustive concordance of the Bible: Showing every word of the text of the common English version of the canonical books, and every occurrence of each word in regular order.* (electronic ed.) (G3313). Ontario: Woodside Bible Fellowship.

Appendix A— Complete List of *Zoe* Verses

Below are the 134 times the word *"zoe"* is found in the New Testament. My study found that in 123 of the verses *zoe* is used to mean "the vital, divine, enjoyable life." The remaining 11 times (Luke 1:75, 12:15, 16:25, Acts 5:20, 8:33, Romans 8:38, 11:15, 1 Corinthians 3:22, 15:19, Hebrews 7:3, James 4:14), it is used to mean simply "life" as opposed to death.

Englishman's Concordance complete list of Strong's Greek word #2222

Matthew 7:14	...and narrow is the way, which leadeth unto **life,**	and few there be that find it. ...
Matthew 18:8	...it is better for thee to enter into **life**	halt or maimed, rather than having two ...
Matthew 18:9	...it is better for thee to enter into **life**	with one eye, rather than having two ...
Matthew 19:16	...shall I do, that I may have eternal **life**	?And he said unto him, Why ...
Matthew 19:17	...is, God: but if thou wilt enter into **life,**	keep the commandments. He saith unto ...
Matthew 19:29	...receive an hundredfold, and shall inherit everlasting **life.**	But many that are first shall ...
Matthew 25:46	...into everlasting punishment: but the righteous into **life**	eternal. And it came ...
Mark 9:43	...it is better for thee to enter into **life**	maimed, than having two hands to go ...
Mark 9:45	...is better for thee to enter halt into **life,**	than having two feet to be cast ...
Mark 10:17	...shall I do that I may inherit eternal **life**	?And Jesus said unto him, Why ...
Mark 10:30	...persecutions; and in the world to come eternal **life.**	But many that are first shall ...
Luke 1:75	...righteousness before him, all the days of our **life.**	And thou, child, shalt be called ...
Luke 10:25	...Master, what shall I do to inherit eternal **life**	? He said unto him, What is ...
Luke 12:15	...heed, and beware of covetousness: for a man's **life**	consisteth not in the abundance of the ...
Luke 16:25	...Abraham said, Son, remember that thou in thy **Lifetime**	receivedst thy good things, and likewise Lazarus ...
Luke 18:18	...Master, what shall I do to inherit eternal **life**	?And Jesus said unto him, Why ...
Luke 18:30	...present time, and in the world to come **life**	everlasting. Then he took unto him
John 1:4	...made that was made. In him was **life;**	and the life was the light of ...
	...was made. In him was life; and **the life**	was the light of men. And ...
John 3:15	...in him should not perish, but have eternal **life.**	For God so loved the world, ...
John 3:16	...in him should not perish, but have everlasting **life.**	For God sent not his Son ...
John 3:36	...He that believeth on the Son hath everlasting **life:**	and he that believeth not the Son ..
	...that believeth not the Son shall not see **life;**	but the wrath of God abideth on ...
John 4:14	...a well of water springing up into everlasting **life.**	The woman saith unto him, Sir, ...
John 4:36	...that reapeth receiveth wages, and gathereth fruit unto **life**	eternal: that both he that soweth...
John 5:24	...believeth on him that sent me, hath everlasting **life,**	and shall not come into condemnation; but ...
	...into condemnation; but is passed from death unto **life.**	Verily, verily, I say unto you, ...

John 5:26	...shall live. For as the Father hath **life** in himself; so hath he given to ...
	...hath he given to the Son to have **life** in himself; And hath given him ...
John 5:29	...they that have done good, unto the resurrection **of life;** and they that have done evil, unto ...
John 5:39	...for in them ye think ye have eternal **life:** and they are they which testify of ..
John 5:40	...not come to me, that ye might have **life.** I receive not honor from men....
John 6:27	...but for that meat which endureth unto everlasting **life,** which the Son of man shall give ...
John 6:33	...he which cometh down from heaven, and giveth **life** unto the world. Then said they ...
John 6:35	...Jesus said unto them, I am the bread **of life:** he that cometh to me shall ...
John 6:40	...Son, and believeth on him, may have everlasting **life:** and I will raise him up at ...
John 6:47	...you, He that believeth on me hath everlasting **life.** I am that bread of life....
John 6:48	...hath everlasting life.I am that bread **of life.** Your fathers did eat manna in ...
John 6:51	...is my flesh, which I will give for **the life** of the world. The Jews...
John 6:53	...man, and drink his blood, ye have no **life** in you. Whoso eateth my flesh, ...
John 6:54	...my flesh, and drinketh my blood, hath eternal **life;** and I will raise him up at ...
John 6:63	...unto you, they are spirit, and they are **life.** But there are some of you ...
John 6:68	...we go? Thou hast the words of eternal **life.** And we believe and are sure ...
John 8:12	...walk in darkness, but shall have the light **of life** . The Pharisees therefore said unto him, ...
John 10:10	...destroy: I am come that they might have **life,** and that they might have it more ...
John 10:28	...me: And I give unto them eternal **life;** and they shall never perish, neither shall ...
John 11:25	...said unto her, I am the resurrection, and **the life:** he that believeth in me, though he ...
John 12:25	...life in this world shall keep it unto **life** eternal. If any man serve me, ...
John 12:50	...And I know that his commandment is **life** everlasting: whatsoever I speak therefore, even as ...
John 14:6	...him, I am the way, the truth, and **the life:** no man cometh unto the Father, but ...
John 17:2	...over all flesh, that he should give eternal **life** to as many as thou hast given ...
John 17:3	...thou hast given him. And this is **life** eternal, that they might know thee the ...
John 20:31	...of God; and that believing ye might have **life** through his name. After ...
Acts 2:28	...Thou hast made known to me the ways **of life;** thou shalt make me full of joy ...
Acts 3:15	...unto you; And killed the Prince **of life,** whom God hath raised from the dead; ...
Acts 5:20	...to the people all the words of this **life.** And when they heard that, they ...
Acts 8:33	...and who shall declare his generation? for his **life** is taken from the earth. And ...
Acts 11:18	...God also to the Gentiles granted repentance unto **life.** Now they which were scattered abroad ...
Acts 13:46	...and judge yourselves unworthy of everlasting **life,** lo, we turn to the Gentiles....
Acts 13:48	...and as many as were ordained to eternal **life** believed. And the word of the ...
Acts 17:25	...needed any thing, seeing he giveth to all **life,** and breath, and all things; And ...
Romans 2:7	...seek for glory and honor and immortality, eternal **life** :But unto them that are contentious,
Romans 5:10	...being reconciled, we shall be saved by his **life.** And not only so, but we ...
Romans 5:17	...of the gift of righteousness shall reign in **life** by one, Jesus Christ.) Therefore as
Romans 5:18	...free gift came upon all men unto justification **of life.** For as by one man's disobedi- ence ...
Romans 5:21	...grace reign through righteousness unto eternal **life** by Jesus Christ our Lord. ...
Romans 6:4	...even so we also should walk in newness **of life.** For if we have been planted ...

Romans 6:22	...your fruit unto holiness, and the end everlasting **life.** For the wages of sin is ...
Romans 6:23	...death; but the gift of God is eternal **life** through Jesus Christ our Lord. ...
Romans 7:10	...And the commandment, which was ordained to **life,** I found to be unto death....
Romans 8:2	...Spirit. For the law of the Spirit **of life** in Christ Jesus hath made me free ...
Romans 8:6	...is death; but to be spiritually minded is **life** and peace. Because the carnal ...
Romans 8:10	...dead because of sin; but the Spirit is **life** because of righteousness. But if
Romans 8:38	...For I am persuaded, that neither death, nor **life,** nor angels, nor principalities, nor powers, nor ...
Romans 11:15	...what shall the receiving of them be, but **life** from the dead? For if the ...
1 Corinthians 3:22	...or Apollos, or Cephas, or the world, or **life,** or death, or things present, or things ...
1 Corinthians 15:19	...in Christ are perished. If in this **life** only we have hope in Christ, we ...
2 Corinthians 2:16	...unto death; and to the other the savor **of life** unto life. And who is sufficient for
	...to the other the savor of life unto **life.** And who is sufficient for these things?...
2 Corinthians 4:10	...body the dying of the Lord Jesus, that **the life** also of Jesus might be made manifest ...
2 Corinthians 4:11	...alway delivered unto death for Jesus' sake, that **the life** also of Jesus might be made manifest ...
2 Corinthians 4:12	...So then death worketh in us, but **life** in you. We having the same ...
2 Corinthians 5:4	...upon, that mortality might be swallowed up of **life.** Now he that hath wrought us ...
Galatians 6:8	...to the Spirit shall of the Spirit reap **life** everlasting. And let us not be ...
Ephesians 4:18	Having the understanding darkened, being alienated **From the life** of God through the ignorance that is ...
Philippians 1:20	...magnified in my body, whether it be by **life,** or by death. For to me ...
Philippians 2:16	...in the world; Holding forth the word **of life;** that I may rejoice in the day ...
Philippians 4:3	...my fellowlabourers, whose names are in the book **of life.** Rejoice in the Lord alway: and ...
Colossians 3:3	...earth. For ye are dead, and your **life** is hid with Christ in God....
Colossians 3:4	...in God. When Christ, who is our **life,** shall appear, then shall ye also appear ...
1 Timothy 1:16	...them which should hereafter believe on him to **life** everlasting. Now unto the King eternal, ...
1 Timothy 4:8	...godliness is profitable unto all things, having promise **of the life** that now is, and of that....
1 Timothy 6:12	...good fight of faith, lay hold on eternal **life,** whereunto thou art also called, and hast ...
1 Timothy 6:19	...come, that they may lay hold on eternal **life.** O Timothy, keep that which is ...
2 Timothy 1:1	...the will of God, according to the promise **of life** which is in Christ Jesus,To ...
2 Timothy 1:10	...Christ, who hath abolished death, and hath brought **life** and immortality to light through the gospel:...
Titus 1:2	...after godliness; In hope of eternal **life,** which God, that cannot lie, promised before ...
Titus 3:7	...made heirs according to the hope of eternal **life.** This is a faithful saying, and ...
Hebrews 7:3	..., having neither beginning of days, nor end **of life;** but made like unto the Son of ...
Hebrews 7:16	...commandment, but after the power of an endless **life.** For he testifieth, Thou art a ...
James 1:12	...he is tried, he shall receive the crown **of life,** which the Lord hath promised to them ...
James 4:14	...be on the morrow. For what is your **life** ? It is even a vapour, that appeareth

1 Peter 3:7	...and as being heirs together of the grace **of life;** that your prayers be not hindered. ...
1 Peter 3:10	...a blessing. For he that will love **life,** and see good days, let him refrain
2 Peter 1:3	...given unto us all things that pertain unto **life** and godliness, through the knowledge of him ...
1 John 1:1	...and our hands have handled, of the Word **of life** ;(For the life was manifested, and
1 John 1:2	...handled, of the Word of life;(For **the life** was manifested, and we have seen it, ...
	...bear witness, and shew unto you that eternal **life,** which was with the Father, and ...
1 John 2:25	...promise that he hath promised us, even eternal **life.** These things have I written unto ...
1 John 3:14	...know that we have passed from death unto **life,** because we love the brethren. He that ...
1 John 3:15	...and ye know that no murderer hath eternal **life** abiding in him. Hereby perceive we
1 John 5:11	...record, that God hath given to us eternal **life,** and this life is in his Son....
	...hath given to us eternal life, and this **life** is in his Son. He that ...
1 John 5:12	...Son. He that hath the Son hath **life;** and he that hath not the Son ...
	...hath not the Son of God hath not **life.** These things have I written unto ...
1 John 5:13	...that ye may know that ye have eternal **life,** and that ye may believe on the ...
1 John 5:16	...he shall ask, and he shall give him **life** for them that sin not unto death. ...
1 John 5:20	...Christ. This is the true God, and eternal **life.** Little children, keep yourselves from idols. ...
Jude 21	...mercy of our Lord Jesus Christ unto eternal **life.** And of some have compassion, making ...
Revelation 2:7	...will I give to eat of the tree **of life,** which is in the midst of the ...
Revelation 2:10	...death, and I will give thee a crown **life.** He that hath an ear, let ...
Revelation 3:5	...blot out his name out of the book **of life,** but I will confess his name before ...
Revelation 11:11	...after three days and an half the Spirit **of life** from God entered into them, and they ...
Revelation 13:8	...whose names are not written in the book **of life** of the Lamb slain from the foundation ...
Revelation 17:8	...whose names were not written in the book **of life** from the foundation of the world, when ...
Revelation 20:12	...another book was opened, which is the book **of life:** and the dead were judged out...
Revelation 20:15	...whosoever was not found written in the book **of life** was cast into the lake of fire. ...
Revelation 21:6	...is athirst of the fountain of the water **of life** freely. He that overcometh shall inherit ...
Revelation 21:27	...they which are written in the Lamb's book **of life.** And he shewed me ...
Revelation 22:1	...he shewed me a pure river of water **of life,** clear as crystal, proceeding out of the ...
Revelation 22:2	...side of the river, was there the tree **of life,** which bare twelve manner of fruits, and ...
Revelation 22:14	...that they may have right to the tree **of life,** and may enter in through the gates ...
Revelation 22:17	...And whosoever will, let him take the water **of life** freely. For I testify unto every ...
Revelation 22:19	...take away his part out of the book **of life,** and out of the holy city, and ...

ABOUT THE AUTHOR

D r. E. Tracy Spaur is a dentist, teaching pastor, lay counselor, and retreat speaker. He volunteers as part of the leadership team of Southside Nazarene Church, a growing 1,500-strong ministry in Chesterfield, Virginia.

He practices dentistry in Powhatan, Virginia, making his home there with Valerie his wife of 30 years. Their three daughters are Nena, a first grade teacher at Powhatan Elementary School; Stephanie, a student in the School of Art Education at Virginia Commonwealth University, Richmond, Virginia, and Rebekah, student at Trevecca Nazarene University, Nashville, Tennessee.

In 2003, the Virginia District Church of the Nazarene honored Dr. Spaur by naming an annual award in recognition of outstanding volunteer service the "Tracy Spaur Lay Servant of the Year."